Marketing:

Origins, Concepts, Environment

Marketing:

Origins, Concepts, Environment

Ray Wright

Business Press
Thomson Learning™

Australia • Canada • Denmark • Japan • Mexico • New Zealand
Philippines • Puerto Rico • Singapore • South Africa • Spain
United Kingdom • United States

Marketing: Origins, Concepts, Environment

Copyright © 1999 Thomson Learning

Business Press is a division of Thomson Learning. The Thomson Learning logo is a registered trademark used herein under license.

For more information, contact Business Press, Berkshire House, 168–173 High Holborn, London, WC1V 7AA or visit us on the World Wide Web at http://www.itbp.com

British Library Cataloguing-in-Publication Data
A catalogue record for this book is available from the British Library

ISBN 1-86152-526-5

First edition published 1999 by Thomson Learning

Typeset by Saxon Graphics Ltd, Derby
Printed in the UK by TJ International, Padstow, Cornwall

Contents

Preface

Marketing has never been more relevant to markets both at the national and the international level. State controlled organizations, monopolies, cartels, government protection and subsidies are all on the decline as politicians insist that the most productive way to manage an economy is through a free competitive market where demand and the allocations of products and services should be governed by consumer choice. No area seems safe from some form of customer participation and say in which products and services should be produced, which levels of quality should be offered and which prices should be charged. This includes all organizations from manufacturing, retail, leisure and financial, to education, health, charities and the professions such as law, banking and accountancy. The overriding theme is the same, the most important consideration for success in any organization must be ultimate customer satisfaction. If this is not achieved then the organization will not succeed and deserves either to have a change of management or to go out of business.

Benefits for students studying marketing

In very simple terms marketing is all about offering value for money and concern for the end-user whether this be on the sale of a chocolate bar, a pension, a hip operation or the law involved on the sale of a house. Every organization needs some form of marketing expertise and it must permeate every nook and crevice of the organization. One function, one department, one employee can impair or even destroy this tender relationship between organization and user by an inappropriate word or action.

This means that every organization should have some form of marketing presence whether this be in a formal or informal way. Whatever the job – accountant, solicitor, buyer, administrator, charity worker, doctor, banker, engineer, manager, researcher, lecturer, salesperson and so on – some form of knowledge of, and skill in, marketing will be an invaluable asset for the student to offer the prospective employee. This is as well as the ever-growing numbers of jobs that already exist in marketing and marketing related areas such as sales, product design and development, advertising, sales promotions and marketing research. A potential employee, having studied marketing, whatever the chosen career, can offer real added value and so must enhance their career prospects as well as enjoying the academic stimulation of studying such a wide-ranging and stimulating subject.

About the book

The book is divided into ten chapters covering in simple form the ideas that underpin the discipline of marketing. It moves from a history and introduction to the origins and basic concepts of marketing and then on to the tools and techniques used by marketing practitioners. The book takes a systematic approach to the subject building on the concepts as it moves through from the simple to the more complex. Theory is combined with the more practical, diagrams are given and models used where appropriate, and real life examples are shown to highlight particular points that are being made. Each chapter has a series of ten questions at the end, based on that particular chapter, which can be used as assignment titles, tutorial tasks or seminar discussion vehicles. Each chapter also has a case study which can be used in a similar way.

Of course any book is out of date as soon as it is written, because marketing is a live dynamic business subject that is changing and developing continuously, ideas and practices change and some concepts move out of fashion and others move back in. However as long as these limitations are recognized it is felt that the underlying structures articulated in this book are sound and if understood by the student can be adapted and developed to modern practices, theories and ideas.

I

Introduction to marketing origins, concepts and the environment

AIMS AND OBJECTIVES

By the end of the chapter the student should:

I have a basic understanding of the meaning of the term 'marketing';

2 appreciate the underlying concepts and be able to give definitions;

3 be able to outline the relationships between marketing research, the marketing mix and eventual customer satisfaction;

4 be able to identify all the factors that make up both the internal and external environment of an organization and appreciate how both interact and continuously change.

Introduction

What is marketing?

There is a lot of confusion about the meaning of the term 'marketing'. In asking an assorted group of people it can often seem to mean different things, even amongst those who work in a 'marketing' department or have some form of marketing role within the organization.

We can begin by coming up with some form of definition which will then be explained in more detail as we move through the chapter.

The following statements could all be said to describe the role of marketing:

- marketing is putting the customer first;
- marketing is putting the customer at the very centre of all the activities the company undertakes;
- the customer is 'king';
- marketing is understanding the needs and wants of clearly identified groups of people and producing products and services, at a profit, to satisfy these needs;
- marketing is matching the resources of the company to the needs of the market;
- marketing is an exchange process; satisfying customer wants in return for some form of payment.

As you can see there are many possible definitions and all are correct as far as they go. The overriding factor for all these definitions is that concern for the customer is of paramount importance to the well-being of the organization and so must be at the very centre of all its activities. As we move through the book this simple concept – concern for the customer – must be continuously remembered.

Misconceptions

Many students when first coming to marketing have preconceived ideas about its meaning and often suggest that marketing is either advertising, public relations, sponsorship, selling, competitions, price discounts, packaging, merchandising, direct mail, distribution, branding and so on. It is true that marketing *includes* all these factors but it is crucial to understand that each of these elements plays only a small part and marketing is much more of a total concept approach to products and markets.

In marketing, concern for the customer has to be at the very heart of all the activities the organization undertakes.

The development of marketing

'Marketing' as an intuitive method of trading has been with us for thousands of years. It is as old as time itself and to many successful practitioners over the ages it just happened naturally or was passed down within families. Concern for the customer and an understanding of their needs was seen as the best way to sell one's self, one's product or one's service, whatever that product or service might be. It was 'common sense'.

THE CUSTOMER FORGOTTEN

However there seem to be certain trading circumstances which enabled companies to forget the simple 'common sense' view on the importance of the customer. These trading circumstances include:

- holding a monopoly position in products and/or markets;
- the demand for products or services being greater than the supply;
- little competition;
- restrictive information available, to prevent the customer shopping around;
- protected markets.

All of these factors contribute to a position where a company can become inward-looking and forget or ignore who it is that finally purchases the product or the service.

THE CHANGING ENVIRONMENT

However a constantly changing, increasingly competitive global business environment now means there are very few of the protected market circumstances, identified above, within which a company may operate. The opening up of world markets have produced greater competition both at home and abroad, new technology leading to mass production has created surplus products and mass communication now offers almost unlimited information on availability and price to an increasingly sophisticated market. Governments are breaking up monopolies and introducing more pro-consumer legislation concerned with making the customer the ultimate decider on what will and will not be produced. It is almost impossible in today's environment for the customer to be ignored by any organization.

 The protected business environment where the consumer can be ignored is no longer sustainable.

THE NEW PROFESSIONALISM

Because of the market changes identified above some companies found trading increasingly difficult, revenue and profits began to fall and many organizations went out of business. Others appreciated the need to take on a more professional management approach to competitive and open markets. This new 'professionalism' included adopting the business discipline of marketing that seemed to hold many of the answers.

WHY COMPANIES HAVE ADOPTED MARKETING

Although the basic concept of customer concern seems to be obvious, many managers appear to have problems either in understanding how this relates to their business or in putting the process into practice. This is often more so the case as a company grows and the decision makers become more and more detached from the needs and wants of the end-user.

An example of this might be a small sole trader business, such as a restaurant. The owner opens up, fully aware of the need to attract customers. The owner is pleasant, obliging, open when the customer requires, reactive to complaints, offering good value and pleasant surroundings and the business thrives. But what happens as the company grows? Untrained staff are taken on, the boss becomes complacent and inward looking and is more concerned about functional matters than the welfare of the customer. The customer begins to be taken for granted and service and value decline. Eventually competition moves in and customers move away.

Many large organizations, especially in the public sector, are classic examples of businesses that have forgotten (or perhaps never knew) who the customer was, forgotten why they were in business and what the corporate objectives were. It is as if they have existed for the benefit of the management and staff who work within them. People become a nuisance – engendering the 'this would be a good job if it wasn't for all those customers who keep coming through the front door and disturbing my routine' syndrome.

Without competition less companies would adopt marketing.

It seems to be an unfortunate fact that many organizations do not act pro-actively and come to marketing willingly. Where there is a stable environment and little or no competition there is a tendency for managers to offer levels of quality and service that suit the company rather than the customer. Producers become complacent believing that the customer will always be there and so there is little or no pressure on the company to offer ever improving products and services.

However these circumstances change as more efficient businesses enter the market offering better value forcing backward looking companies to either adopt a more customer focused approach or lose sales.

The historical background to marketing

'The producer is king'

So what is marketing and why have some companies adopted the concept willingly whilst others have been forced into submission? To understand the process it is important to begin with a simple historical overview of the development of marketing in the UK since the Second World War (1945).

Marketing comes late to the UK

Marketing as an essential activity came late to British business. The USA, always further advanced in marketplace disciplines than other Western economies, had 'discovered' marketing soon after the First World War. Unbridled capitalism, the search for the 'American dream', the encouragement of free enterprise and most important of all an economy that encouraged free and open competition lead to a realization by the budding entrepreneur that if, and in many cases only if, they gave their customer the products and services they demanded, the customer would purchase – and if satisfied would come back time and time again. Otherwise the customer would go elsewhere to achieve satisfaction.

SHORTAGES, QUEUEING AND RATIONING

In the period after the Second World War there was a shortage of all types of products, especially consumer products. Industry had been geared up to producing for the war effort and after the war had finished there was a period of time before the manufacturers could switch back into producing peace time goods. This meant that rationing for certain types of products (introduced at the outbreak of war) continued until 1956. Even after rationing finished it was quite usual to have to queue for some products, because of shortages, and for the most part the British public did this uncomplainingly.

FULL PRICE

At this time the customer also had to pay the manufacturer's full recommended price wherever the product was purchased. By law the producer could insist that this happened and if a retailer refused to comply supply could be restricted or withdrawn from the offending outlet. The producer could also choose who would sell their products and who would not. If a retailer did not come up to the manufacturer's specification they would not be offered a dealer account.

CAPTIVE MARKETS AND GOVERNMENT PROTECTION

As the country moved into the 1950s British industry gradually tooled up to manufacturing in a peace time economy and consumer products became more abundant. But the UK still had a captive market in the British Empire and many of the products produced went abroad. Government-imposed controls also prevented the import of certain products from abroad that might threaten indigenous industries. However, the public, gradually being exposed to consumer product possibilities, clamoured for more: but the demand could not be fulfilled. Products were still rationed, but this time not through official Government channels but by price and by manufacturer and retailer rationing.

WAITING LISTS

In the late 1950s and into the early 1960s if the retailer wanted to purchase washing machines or TVs it was not unusual for the buyer to be told that not only was there a three months waiting list but also the full order would not be fulfilled. Likewise, when the customer went into the outlet to purchase the washing machine or fridge from the retailer, they would be told that they could purchase, but only if they were prepared to wait three months, pay in advance, and pay the full manufacturer's retail price. (Retail price maintenance, RPM, the Government act that allowed the producer to dictate the price a product was sold at, was only finally abandoned in 1964.)

AFTER SALES SERVICE – MINIMAL

Customer after sales service was minimal; it was as if the manufacturer or the retailer really felt that their obligation to the customer ended as soon as the customer walked out of the door. To take back a product that had some kind of fault was to elicit an almost universal response that the customer must have 'misused the product', or the product was 'used in an unacceptable way', or 'what more was expected at the price offered'. If taken in for repair, it was not unusual for the customer to be expected to wait months for the return of the repaired item.

ALL EXTRAS CHARGED FOR

Every extra could be, and was, charged for. If a new motor car was purchased 'extras' to be paid for would include the spare wheel, the jack, seat covers, number plates, the radio, colour if other than black, and delivery from the manufacturer to the showroom. You would also have had to wait for delivery. This was on top of paying the full manufacturer's retail price.

Demand exceeds supply

Despite the restrictions and demands identified above, the customer was still prepared to wait and to pay high prices with little complaint as they knew no better. Demand exceeded supply (although gradually the situation was changing), people were hungry for any form of consumer product and the manufacturer or supplier of the service was in the superior power position in the relationship with the customer. This powerful position allowed producers to concentrate their efforts on producing more and more products knowing that almost anything they could produce they would sell.

 In the relationship between producer and consumer taking place in the market circumstances described above it was the producer that had all the power.

'It was the producer that was king'

Your own experiences should inform you that the marketplace of the 1990s and into the new millennium bears little resemblance to the historical picture described above. So what was it that caused the change from the position described here for the 1950s and 1960s to the one we experience at the present time?

Changing customers and markets

'The consumer is king'

The changing markets

Gradually and imperceptibly markets began to develop and change. During the 1950s, the 1960s and into the 1970s UK companies lost their captive markets abroad forcing them to look more toward the home market. Import controls and other trade barriers began to be eased and competition entered the home market from all around the world. Italy, France and especially Germany began exporting products into the UK. Japan, once a standing joke as the producer of cheap imitative products, began exporting better and better products at increasingly competitive prices (in little over a decade they destroyed the once great British motorcycle industry and moved into the motor car business where they now dominate). Products began flooding in from Hong Kong, Taiwan and Singapore as well as from the USA and Germany.

COMPETITION ENCOURAGED

It was recognized by leading economists and politicians in the UK that competition had to be encouraged and industry protection abolished if businesses were to become more efficient, more productive and so more able to compete on equal terms in world markets.

It was also argued that Retail Price Maintenance (RPM) eliminated competition, kept prices artificially high while taking off price protection stimulated competition, forcing prices down and leading to more demand and eventually more employment. So in 1964 RPM was abolished for all but two types of products (at the time of writing, pharmaceutical companies can still insist on fixing retail prices, but the 'netbook agreement' that fixed the price on books has now come to an end).

NEW TECHNOLOGY

Intense home and world competition, the loss of captive markets abroad, the ending of RPM and the removal of subsidies and trade and tariff barriers meant that companies had to be continually looking towards price and costs reductions if they were to survive in the marketplace. This encouraged the greater use of new technology and the questioning of exisiting methods of manufacturing. Any company not aware of what was happening, that could not adapt and change to an industrial and commercial world – that was itself changing at a faster and faster rate – would go out of business.

ECONOMIES OF SCALE, MASS PRODUCTION AND MASS CONSUMPTION

To compete in this unprotected price and profit environment an organization had to invest in new capital to manufacture more efficiently and at a lower cost. As more products were sold 'economies of scale' were gained allowing further cost savings, lower prices and even more products sold. This continuous process lead to the 'mass production' of products and, because of lower and lower prices, to more and more of the population able to purchase, it also led to 'mass consumption' (Figure 1.1).

THE MOVEMENT FROM LOCAL TO NATIONAL AND INTERNATIONAL MARKETS

Over this period there was also movement from local to national and international markets. As companies grew, products once produced and sold within the same town or county were now being offered for sale on a national and international level. Distribution became easier with improvements in all forms of transport. The Japanese could produce products and ship them halfway around the world and still undercut home markets on price.

MASS COMMUNICATIONS

Huge technological advances in methods of communications meant that messages could be sent to all corners of the world instantaneously. The world was truly becoming a 'global village'.

MARKET ECONOMY VERSUS A PLANNED ECONOMY

With the collapse of communism at the beginning of the 1990s, and with it the arguments for a planned economy, there is a political will abroad that seems determined to balance the relationship between the private and state sector opening up as much of the state system to free enterprise as possible; and it seems that no sector of business is now safe from the rigours of competition.

PRIVATIZATION AND THE DISCIPLINE OF THE MARKETPLACE

The privatization of state utilities and services has taken place at an ever-increasing rate both in the UK and across the world (British Airways, British Telecom, steel, electricity, gas, water, coal, etc.) in an attempt to expose them to the demands and the disciplines of the marketplace. In education, in health and in the civil service there has been the development of clearly identified business units all with clear mandates to manage identified resources in some form of competitive market environment.

Management and workers alike, working in state services that have been protected in the past from full accountability, are having to face an uncertain

---

Figure 1.1

Mass production ⟶ Mass communications ⟶ Mass consumption

future where they are having to justify to their customer the service they are offering. They are having to learn new skills, to learn about customer care, to try to understand this discipline called 'marketing'.

FREE MARKETS

Markets, both at national and international level, are now more open and more accessible than at any other time in history and the process continues apace. At both a national and international level the reduction in all forms of trade barriers (e.g. The European Union legislation, the General Agreement on Trade and Tariff (GATT) www.wto.org) allows for the free flow of goods and services from country to country with as little restriction as possible. In theory, and increasingly in practice, competitors are able to enter and leave markets at will dependent only on their ability to compete on equal terms.

The changing customer

MORE INFORMED AND MORE EDUCATED

The customer too has changed from the customer who bought goods in the 1950s and 1960s. The customer in the 1990s is more aware of what is going on in the international marketplace. Inexpensive mass communications have enabled them to be more informed, more educated and more discerning about the availability and value of a whole mass of products. (For example 24 hour TV and with digitalization a possible choice of 3000–4000 more channels, as well as the use of ever more sophisticated information technology and multi-media options make product information readily available.)

AFFLUENCE AND CHOICE. The continuous increase in the standard of living and the rise in the availability of credit for most people has meant more disposal income to spend on products and services. Products that 'fit' individual needs are insisted upon, complete choice is sought and if a company is unable to supply the exact product demanded customers know that somebody else will.

LITTLE LOYALTY. Customers will display little or no loyalty to a company moving from product to product as their mood fits. They are highly fashion conscious, buying habits change at an ever-increasing pace and any company not anticipating future directions will find their customer has moved on to purchase from more forward thinking companies. Customers are not prepared to queue for products and will shop around for the best available value.

THE RISE OF 'CONSUMERISM'

We have also seen the rise of 'consumerism' with more and more legislation being introduced to protect the buyer from the overtures of the seller and to encourage the free and unfettered inter-play of market forces. There are pressure groups, magazines, radio and TV programmes all offering advice and protection to the consumer. The customer taking back a product for repair will know 'their rights' and will even quote from the Trade Description Act, the Consumer Protection Act, the Sale of Goods Act, the Consumer Credit Act or the Unfair Contracts Terms Act (Office of Fair Trading, www.oft.gov.uk). A new product will be demanded if the present one is not of 'merchandisable quality' and consumers will not be prepared to wait months for a repair or a replacement.

The market has moved dramatically from *caveat emptor* (let the buyer beware) to *caveat vendor* (let the seller beware). The more enlightened companies have pre-empted legislation and introduced their own 'codes of practice' in their dealings with the public. The more tardy will have to change or there is no doubt that unwelcome events will eventually overtake their business activities.

Supply outstrips demand

In general terms the opening up of reciprocal trade has led to world markets awash with consumer products and services. In most cases supply now outstrips demand causing the balance of power to shift from producer to consumer. If the product or service offered does not match the benefits demanded by the target customer, at the price considered to be appropriate, the customer will have little or no hesitation in going elsewhere.

In the past it was the producer that was king, now it is the customer. 'The consumer is king'

It is the customer who must be central to the thinking of an organization, and any company that fails to understand this will inevitably pay the price in terms of falling sales, loss of business and closure or takeover.

Marketing as a 'matching' process

Marketing is a natural development from the opening up of the world economy system because it places the concerns of the customer at the very heart of the company's business. It does this in a coordinated manner so that it matches all the resources of the company to the needs of the customer in the most effective, efficient and economic way.

If customers' needs are to be satisfied then these needs must be identified. This involves talking to customers and consumers and listening to their demands.

The above point should be self-evident but present and historical empirical evidence shows how often this critical process is ignored, forgotten or submerged in bureaucratic procedures by companies, resulting in lost sales and eventual bankruptcies as customers go elsewhere to gain satisfaction.

LISTEN TO THE CUSTOMER

The marketing process really begins with *talking* and *listening* to present and potential customers in an attempt to identify their ever-changing needs and wants. This is not an easy process, as we shall see later on. Human behaviour can be changeable and unpredictable. People will often say one thing but mean another and some 'wants' seem to reside below the level of the consciousness and so cannot be overtly articulated. Because buying habits are changing at an ever-increasing rate it is essential that this 'talking to the customer' is continuous and iterative and that this process is recognized and formalized within the company.

IDENTIFY THE CUSTOMER

If the organization is to be able to talk and understand their customers' present and future wishes and desires they must be first identified. It may be that a company has different groups of customers for different products, or different customers expecting different benefits from the same product, or it may be that the customers are at different levels of understanding.

Some companies will have little problem with end-customer contact because the nature of their business enables them to easily identify and talk to the people buying their products (e.g. those who sell directly to the customer such as retailers and hoteliers). Others will have more of a problem (those who sell indirectly to the customer such as producers and manufacturers or whose customers are in an overseas market). Improved communication techniques now make it much easier for most companies to identify and develop a dialogue with the customer and this will be discussed in more detail as we move through the book.

CUSTOMER IMPORTANCE IGNORED

It is surprising how the simple concept of knowing and understanding the importance of the customer is often either forgotten or given a low priority by many companies despite having 'sophisticated' marketing departments. In many cases this could be because it isn't *really* believed or really understood by all the employees. A director will articulate the concept but put short-term profit considerations first. A front-line employee will be able to repeat the mantra of customer care but interact with the customer in an automatic people-weary manner (a question of paying 'lip service' to a fashionable idea understood in the head but not believed in the heart).

ORGANIZE RESOURCES TO MATCH IDENTIFIED DEMAND

Once the exisiting or potential target market has been identified and the 'wants' that need to be satisfied are discovered then the company's resources can be organized to meet these clearly identified demands. The company should interact with the customer as the product is being developed: market testing, honing, shaping and refining back and forth, continuously talking until satisfaction has been achieved. In theory the end result should be a product or service that has been produced in consultation with the customer and so will be purchased willingly, almost making selling superfluous.

MARKETING AS A BENEFIT EXCHANGE PROCESS

Another way to look at marketing is as an exchange process where the producer offers product and service benefits to satisfy identified customer needs in the marketplace and in return receives some form of benefit back. This is usually money, but it could be other benefits such as the barter of products or services for other goods and services, for example a lawyer trading with a plumber or a company trading tractors in return for oil. Similarly a charity might offer some form of guilt reduction, or feel-good benefit in return for voluntary assistance (Figure 1.2).

With a little imagination we can see that marketing oneself to others can be seen in the same exchange process way. The employer will advertise for staff offering benefits (salary) in return for satisfying certain needs. The potential employee should then tailor the application with benefits that satisfy these needs. If both parties are satisfied the exchange of benefits (the job of work in return for an agreed wage) can take place (Figure 1.2).

Marketing and competition

The company must recognize that there will be other organizations competing in the same market, all going through the same process. In many cases it is the company that gets in first with a product or service that will be successful. The competition is fiercer in some industries (financial services and groceries) than in others (pharmaceutical goods and compact discs) and the organization must be aware of their competitive environment.

This leads us to understand that there is the need for a company to anticipate future demand and future trends before the others if competitive advantage is to be achieved.

There are many examples of company success arising from anticipating future consumer needs before others (the Sony Walkman; Mars ice cream; Direct Line car insurance; Tetra-Pak long-life milk and soft drinks packaging; Amazon Books

---

| **Figure 1.2** | *Marketing as an exchange process* |

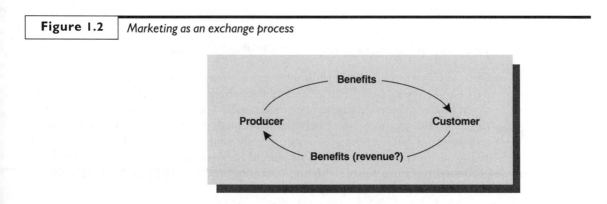

on the Internet) and just as many examples of failure caused by staying with an existing product when warning signs were indicating consumer boredom and the wish for product improvement or a new product (IBM main frame computers; 'kick-start' motor bikes; TV rental; Typewriters). The pro-active marketing organization will develop a culture and an information system that is able to allow for this need to anticipate future trends and demands before customer boredom drives them to look elsewhere.

A definition of marketing

A working definition of marketing can now be put together. There are many acceptable definitions of marketing and there is no such thing as one correct version. In its simplest form it could be expressed as a concern for the needs of the customer above all other considerations.

However if we take into account the factors identified throughout this chapter we can arrive at a more informative and all embracing definition.

Anticipating, identifying, satisfying, customers needs and wants.

However, this definition on its own is not enough. Any fool can satisfy customers wants. All that has to be done is to manufacture a TV costing £100 and sell it for £50. The customer will be happy but the company will lose money and soon go out of business. So it seems we need to add 'at a profit' to our definition.

Anticipating, identifying, satisfying, customers needs and wants *at a profit*.

This is fine as applied to the public liability company or the private commercial firm. But there are organizations (not-for-profit, NFP) that have corporate objectives other than a return on investment (ROI) or making a profit. Charities, schools, public utilities, the health service, welfare organizations, museums, the Boy Scouts, the Girl Guides (www.charity-commission.gov.uk), all of which may have objectives other than profit making. It is argued that marketing can be just as relevant in all these areas. This must lead us to a definition that expresses the return to the organization in terms other than profit and the following, used by The Chartered Institute of Marketing (www.cim.co.uk), is chosen.

Marketing is:
A management process that is involved in identifying, anticipating, satisfying customers needs and wants through the efficient and effective use of the company's resources (Figure 1.3).

Product, market, market and society driven approach

Of course, in reality, not all organizations adopt the rigorous customer-centred marketing approach to business argued for in this chapter. The reason for this is

| **Figure 1.3** | *The concept of marketing* |

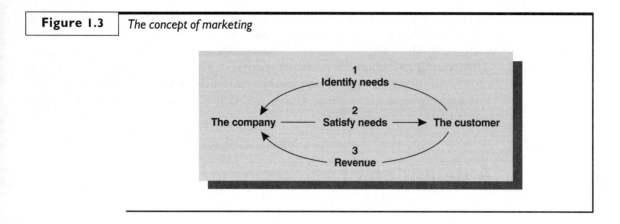

that different product and market conditions exist for different companies and these differing circumstances will affect the attitude and approach taken by the company to its customers. If there is little competition and high levels of demand for the product, then the attitude to the customer will be different than if there is intense competition and low levels of demand. It could be argued that this should not be the case, but empirical evidence informs us otherwise.

It is important to realize that as the market circumstances change then the attitude to the customer taken by the organization must also change otherwise the customer will become dissatisfied and shop elsewhere.

The three main approaches to the market, product driven, market driven, and market *and* society driven, will each be considered in turn

Product driven

Where demand is greater than supply and organizations can sell all they produce they tend to concentrate on producing the product or services and can be said to be 'product driven'. They produce products or services under the belief that they know what it is the consumer wants, what will sell, what is 'good for' their customers. They show little concern for customer research (in some cases not even knowing who it is who actually purchases their products) and will adapt and develop products to their own specification.

These companies begin the exchange process by thinking 'product'. This can be a successful approach in business where the company has a monopoly, a patent on a product, some sought-after unique skill or where there is no competition. Equally, it can be a disaster if none of these situations exist, or if tastes and fashions change (Figure1.4).

Many of the old nationalized utilities, for example telecommunications, gas, electricity, water, could have been seen as examples of 'product driven' companies (they would argue that they are striving to change this).

Figure 1.4	*Product driven*

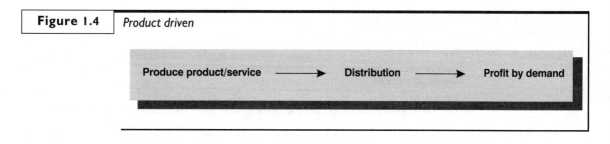

Market driven

Where supply is greater than demand and competition is rife, the organization has no choice but to concentrate its effort on the needs of the customer and can be said to be 'market driven'. It is argued that this business approach is the inevitable result of the liberal market economy philosophy espoused by the wealthiest industrial nations and discussed earlier in the chapter.

Marketing can be said to exist where all the marketing resources of the organization are integrated in such a way as to seek continuous customer satisfaction (Figure 1.5). Possible examples of market driven companies are legion and will include: Coca-Cola, Procter & Gamble, Kodak, McDonald's, Tesco, Wal-Mart etc.

Market and society driven

However, many argue that most sophisticated of all the market approaches is where a company adopts the market driven approach identified above *whilst also having a care for wider social and environmental issues in both the short and long term.*

So the organization that is concerned with 'green issues' (both in its immediate and its wider environment) in terms of the affect it is having on the ecology, or on the community in both the short and long term, and demonstrates this in how it goes about its business, and is market driven, will be seen by marketeers to be in the most sophisticated stage of marketing (Figure 1.6).

It can be argued that organizations adopt an ethical and moral approach to the way they undertake their business so as to attract favourable publicity and to be seen to be a caring corporate citizen in the hope of consequently selling more products. On the other hand many argue that this view distorts the very real

Figure 1.5	*Market driven*

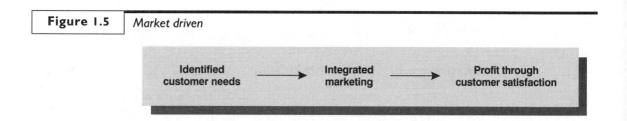

| **Figure 1.6** | *Market and society driven* |

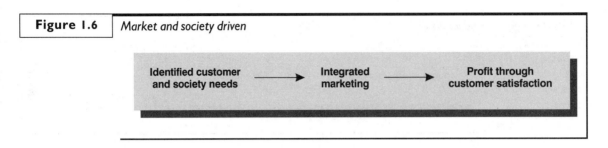

concerns that many major companies now have about the effect their operations have on the environment. Examples of organizations that could be said to be marketing driven and are socially aware include:

- The Body Shop; with its promise never to use cosmetic products that have been tested on live animals or products that have in some way helped to damage the environment in their manufacture.
- The Co-operative Bank; with the promise never to invest the customer's money in any country that has a repressive or dictatorial government.

Changing market circumstances dictate approach

It might be argued that all the above approaches exist (in some form or other) at the same time or, as is much more likely, organizations have been forced to move from being product driven to being market driven as changing market circumstances become more customer orientated.

It can also be argued that public and customer concern for environmental issues such as the destruction of the rainforests, damage to the ozone layer, projects that decimate the countryside, dumping disused oil rigs in the North Sea, the use of factory farming methods, etc. will eventually force all, or most, companies to adopt the market and society driven approach.

Marketing as a philosophy and a management function

The concept of marketing can be viewed both as a corporate philosophy and as a management function of the organization and it is important to distinguish between the two.

Marketing as a corporate philosophy

Marketing seen as a corporate philosophy places the needs and concerns of the customer at the very centre of *every* activity the company undertakes. This concern should permeate every department from administration, secretarial and reception through to distribution, production, finance, research and development (R&D) and, of course, sales and marketing. It should become part of the company culture understood and *believed* by all from the managing director down to the car park attendant and it should find expression in the company mission statement (the mission statement is a set of corporate aims spelling out the sort of company it intends to be). It may be idealistic to believe this can happen in all companies but there is no doubt that it has been achieved by a few and is sought after by the many.

Marketing as a management function

Marketing is also a function within the organization in common with finance, production, human resource management, administration, etc. As a company function it is concerned with integrating the marketing effort and focusing it on the needs of the market.

Where marketing sits within the organizational structure may be an indication of the role that marketing plays within that organization. However it should be said that there are some companies that have a marketing manager and marketing department that are not truly marketing driven. Conversely, there are companies that seem to have no formal marketing department and no designated marketing manager but are in fact still marketing driven. In fact there are those that argue that marketing should not reside in any one department but should be the responsibility of all within the organization.

At its simplest it could be said that marketing is a philosophy of the mind (and of the heart) that puts genuine concern for the customer before all other considerations; this should then translate into company policies and processes. If marketing is to succeed it must become an integral part of the organization's overall corporate strategic thinking and it should not be seen as just an *ad hoc* tool to be used intermittently when circumstances dictate.

The marketing environment

It was argued above that marketing is putting concern for the customers' needs and wants at the very heart of the organization's operations. To try to understand how this might happen in practice, the many factors that are involved in the whole marketing process must first be identified and examined. This task is undertaken using the general heading of the 'marketing environment'.

A company will produce products and services on a farm, in a factory, in a warehouse, a restaurant, a department store, a shop, an office and so on. There are many internal resources that will be used in the process and ideally these should all be utilized so that the final product or service offering is such that the customer, whoever that might be, will want to purchase and at a price that allows a reasonable profit. If this happens then the organization might be considered to be successful. If the customer refuses to purchase, for whatever the reason, then the company will go out of business.

However it is not enough to only consider the internal resources of the organization and imagine that if these are coordinated effectively then sales success is guaranteed. No organization will undertake its business in a vacuum, that is protected and in isolation from what is happening in the outside world. This is especially true of the organization that operates on a global scale selling its products in markets as diverse as Turkey, Taiwan or Tanzania.

So, as well as utilizing its internal resources, the successful company must also identify and try to understand the many external forces that may affect its marketing process. Only if both these internal and external forces are identified and taken into account when developing products and services can marketing be said to be taking place.

Internal environmental factors are those areas within the control of the marketing manager such as market research, product portfolio development, pricing, distribution channel choice, promotions, etc. External factors such as the competition, pressure group activity, political and legal considerations and economic developments are largely outside of the control of the marketing manager.

Having said that both internal and external factors must be taken into account when developing products and services for ease of understanding it will be useful to look at the factors to be examined under these two separate headings beginning with the internal factors.

Internal environmental factors

The marketing process begins with customer identification and then the discovery of needs and wants so that relevant products and services can be produced. This causes the marketing oriented organization to have some method of facilitating the collection of market research and this is where internal factor identification can begin.

MARKET RESEARCH

The process of constantly talking with the customer so as to identify needs and wants is known in marketing terms as market research. All marketing companies should have some form of marketing research capability. This could be within the company or be by the use of an outside research agency.

IDENTIFY AND TALK TO THE CUSTOMER. To be able to talk to the customer he or she must first be identified. This may seem obvious but it is surprising how many companies are uncertain who actually buys their products. Even if the customer is known, it is not unusual for interactive dialogue to be non-existent or, if it takes place at all, for the content to be ignored. There should be a two-way communication process that should take place continuously, questions asked, feedback obtained, back and forth so that product benefits can be developed that exactly match those demanded. Because markets are constantly changing, the research must never stop. What may be the product or service benefit in demand today may change by tomorrow.

How volatile, dynamic and competitive a particular market is will vary from market to market and from product to product so the level and intensity of the research will also have to vary to take this into account. What will not alter is the overriding need to try to know and understand each and every customer and each and every customer demand.

 The first rule of marketing: know your customer and communicate continuously. This process is called market research.

A MARKETING MODEL

To help understand the marketing process and the areas of importance that need to be considered it would be helpful at this stage to introduce the concept of a 'marketing model' which it is hoped will simplify and reinforce learning. This model will be used and developed throughout this chapter (and at different times as we move through the book) to identify both internal and external environmental factors that need consideration.

The marketing model will show, in very simple terms, the stages in the marketing process and the environment within which this takes place.

We can now begin to develop the marketing model by introducing the concept of market research discussed above.

THE MARKETING 'MIX'

The concept of the marketing 'mix' can now be introduced into the marketing model. The marketing mix consists of all the tools and techniques that the organization has at its disposal so as to meet the clearly identified needs (through market research) of the target customer. It is called a 'mix' because different customers may demand different combinations of the marketing mix elements which will be described below.

The marketing mix 'tools and techniques' can be identified for ease of understanding under the headings of: Product; Price; Place; Promotion. They are also known collectively as the '4 Ps'.

Figure 1.7 | *Marketing model stage 1*

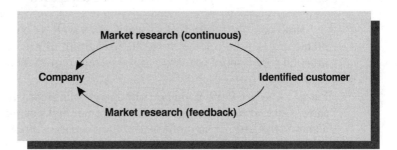

The 4 Ps is a universally known acronym used to described the very many controllable factors that can be manipulated and shaped by the marketing manager so as to eventually supply a product or service offering that will (hopefully) match exactly the customer needs. The marketing mix is at the very centre of marketing and examination and discussion about the elements involved and how the marketing team should integrate the various ingredients to achieve the best possible results for the company, in both the short and long term, will take up the majority of the space in this book.

We will begin here to identify and outline the many factors that are conveniently categorized under the heading of the marketing 'mix' or the 4 Ps beginning with the P for product/service. (The term 'product' will be used throughout the book to mean both products and services although the term 'service' will be used intermittently.)

PRODUCT/SERVICE.   Having identified, through the use of market research, the benefits the customer requires, the company can now develop and produce the exact product/service to match these desired benefits. The customer should be consulted at all stages of the development process so that the final product offering matches exactly the specification required.

Product/service variations.   There are very many different product/service benefit combinations and variations that could be offered for sale, according to the identified demand. For example, depending on the customer, the product/service demanded could be of high value or low value perfume, that is to be worn on special occasions or for everyday use; it could be a small, medium, or a large size; it could be packaged in one material rather than another (plastic or glass); it could be branded (Clinique) or own label (Boots). Another example could be a comprehensive health insurance package covering every possible contingency from cosmetic surgery through to a heart operation or it could be part coverage insuring only against time off from work.

In order to develop and shape the product to meet the consumer wants identified, the marketing personnel can manipulate the contents, the packaging, the brand name, the quality, the service offered, and so on. The end result should be a product/service offering that will match exactly those benefits demanded by the customer.

The product/service must be developed and shaped by working with the customer, talking and obtaining feedback, so as to meet clearly identified customer needs. Hopefully it will then be purchased.

However, as was indicated earlier, as well as the product the marketing manager has other elements in the marketing mix under his or her control that must be coordinated to match the customer requirements.

PRICE.   The price the company will charge will greatly affect the eventual level of sales. Get the price wrong and the customer will not purchase or sales might be achieved but little or no profit made. The price is an integral part of the product and will perform many tasks in bringing about eventual purchase. The most important of these tasks is to match the value and benefit expectations of the customer. Too high a price in relation to perceived product benefits and the customer will believe they are not getting value for money and will buy from the competition. Too low a price and the customer will think the product inferior and, again, reject it.

Price variations.   There are many alternative price variations that can be used in conjunction with the development of the product and the final price chosen must match the customer's perception of value for money. A perfume company, for example, might produce a whole range of products for different customers and different occasions all at different prices. This will be a high price for a high value product for use on special occasions, for example perfume at £75, or a low price for an economy product, for example, everyday perfume at £3.50. There are many other variations on price which we will return to later on in Chapter 7. It should never be forgotten that price is the only factor in the marketing mix that produces revenue, and hopefully profit (the other elements are all costs). A product wrongly priced will communicate unacceptable messages about the product to the potential customer, for example an up-market perfume priced at £3.50 would not be regarded as an 'up-market' perfume by customers.

It must never be forgotten that although the price of a product must reflect overall costs it is also a crucial element in the marketing mix and its use with the product must take this into account.

PLACE.   The use of the 'place' in the marketing mix is shorthand for two important areas and it is imperative that they are not confused. These can be identified as the channel of distribution and the physical distribution of the product.

Channel of distribution.   Having decided, in conjunction with the prospective customer (using market research), on the exact product offering demanded and the price they expect to pay, the issue of where, and how, the customer may wish to purchase must now be agreed. Again the channel through which purchase is agreed must match the type of product demanded and the price being charged.

Channel variations.   As with the product and price elements there are many alternative ways of making a product available to the customer. This might be directly from the manufacturer/producer or indirectly through some form of middleman or intermediary (wholesaler or retailer). Avon and Estee Lauder are examples of companies selling the same products (cosmetics) but using different distribution channels. Avon sells direct, the 'Avon Lady' calling at the customer's home, whilst Estee Lauder market through an indirect channel, for example Debenham's departmental stores.

As with price, if the wrong channel for purchase is selected then the wrong product image will be projected and the desired positioning will be destroyed, for example an up-market perfume priced at £75 for sale through a grocery supermarket is just as badly placed as an economy perfume priced at £3.50 for sale in Harrods. Also if it is in the wrong place or not available when demanded then a lost sale will be the result.

Physical distribution.　Physical distribution concerns the very many different methods that might be used in the physical movement of product from the manufacturer to the end user.

Physical distribution variations.　The variations available will include road, rail, air, water, pipeline, cable, radio waves, etc. Also covered are such things as centralized or decentralized warehousing, lease, rental or ownership of vehicles and the use of information technology in inventory management. This has been an area where many organizations have been able to gain outstanding cost savings over the last 20 years through more effective and efficient methods.

Where the product is made available for purchase must conform to customer image perceptions, be readily obtainable, and available there when it is needed.

PROMOTION.　Having developed, and positioned, the 'right' product at the 'right' price and made it available at the 'right' place the customer now needs to be informed. This takes place through the the the use of promotion, the fourth P.

Promotion variations.　As with the product, price and place, there are many methods available to help communicate, inform and persuade (promote) the customer to purchase the product.

These include such techniques as: TV, newspaper or magazine advertising; competitions and free give-aways; publicity; exhibitions; sports and pop concert sponsorship; face-to-face and telephone selling; etc. The right combination of promotional techniques must be chosen to compliment the other elements in the marketing mix, for example a high value perfume would be advertised in *Hello* magazine rather than in the *Viz* comic, while an economy perfume manufactured for the mass market would be advertised on a programme with mass appeal, for example 'Coronation Street', rather than one with a specialized and limited appeal, for example 'Gardener's World'.

It must be understood that different promotional techniques have their strengths and weaknesses in communicating messages and persuading customers to purchase. Choosing the wrong method can destroy the whole marketing effort.

THE MARKETING MIX COMPLETED

So we see that the internal *controllable* resources the marketing manager must integrate so as to achieve customer satisfaction are the products, the price, the place (channel and physical distribution) and promotion (communication and persuasion). This gives the acronym the 4 Ps or the *marketing mix*. To be successful the company must 'mix' the correct elements of product, price, place and promotion to meet the clearly identified needs of its target market. If it gets the mix right, the customer will purchase, if it gets it wrong then the customer will not.

The completed marketing mix can now be added to our marketing model (Figure 1.8).

Of course in practice the process is more complex and more complicated than demonstrated by the simple model and we will be examining the process in more detail as we move through the following chapters.

| **Figure 1.8** | *Marketing model stage 2* |

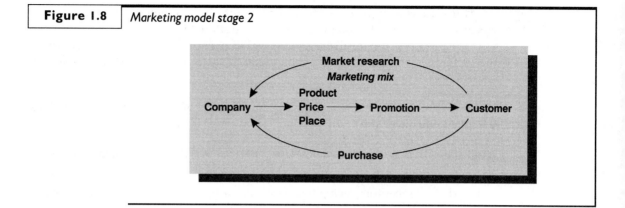

THE FIFTH AND SIXTH PS

Having identified the the marketing mix as the '4 Ps' it is worth mentioning that many marketing writers and practitioners feel that this is too limiting and want to develop the marketing mix acronym to include more areas of concern. It is intended in this book to stay within the concept of just 4 Ps but students might consider adding fifth and sixth Ps: those of 'profit' and 'people' if they found that this was of use in the learning process.

PROFIT. In the rest of the book financial implications and the need to make a profit are included under the P for price. However the reason why this might be shown separately under its own heading is that too often marketing students (and often marketing practitioners) are accused of financial illiteracy or naivety, ignoring the demands and constraints of profit and costs when making decisions about products and markets. It must be remembered at all times that every marketing decision will have some form of cost/profit/revenue implication and this *must* be included in the decision-making process.

It cannot therefore be overstressed that if knowledge of marketing is to be comprehensive it must include knowledge of all relevant financial matters and ramifications. This concept is implicit whenever the P for price is used.

PEOPLE AND INTERNAL MARKETING. Similarly, some marketers want to include a category in the marketing mix specifically for 'people'. The success of a business is more dependent on the attitudes, commitment and skills of the whole workforce than any other factor. Without a customer focused culture, energy spent on developing the marketing mix will be weakened and an organization can only ever be second best. Internal marketing is concerned with the development of this type of rigorous approach to internal resource development. By adopting this approach every employee is encouraged to continuously examine their output in terms of increasing optimum performance and in doing so add value to both the internal process and the ultimate customer product/service offering.

This is especially the case where the benefit offering includes a large element of service, for example companies such as McDonald's, Asda, Granada, and/or where the whole company itself is perceived as part of the product and any one of the employees could impair the good name of the company by an off-handed or unprofessional approach.

In this textbook people are seen as an essential part of the P for product and this is implicit whenever the term 'product' or 'service' is used.

WHERE SHOULD THE MARKETING FUNCTION SIT WITHIN THE ORGANIZATION?

It was discussed earlier how marketing can be both a philosophy and a function within the organization. As a philosophy, marketing and the belief in the pivotal role of the customer, should permeate every activity of the business. As a function it needs to be seen in relationship to the other functions that go to make up the organizational structure.

Other functions within an organization are typically finance, production, human resources, R&D, sales, distribution, administration, etc. Where marketing is positioned in the organizational structure should indicate the importance that the company gives to the marketing function. (On the other hand it should be noted that the position of marketing in the structure offers no certainty that marketing principles are being implemented.)

It would seem to be self-evident that if marketing – satisfying customer needs – is central to the success of the company, then marketing must play a central role in the running of the company. In the past, although less so nowadays, difficulties often arose because of the conflict on areas of importance between the various departments. Production might argue that it is most cost productive to produce widgets with three wheels, finance that it is prudent to spend only x amount on advertising and distribution that it is impossible to deliver on a Saturday morning.

Conversely sales and marketing people might argue that the customer wants four wheels on the widget, deliveries on Saturday and that sales forecasts have shown that more sales can be achieved by spending xy on advertising. Often, in these sorts of circumstances, conflict was resolved by political compromise rather than concern for customer satisfaction.

The more forward looking organizations gradually realized that marketing had to play more of a coordinating function within the structure if it were to have any meaning and if it were to radically affect the culture and make it more marketing orientated.

In a truly marketing orientated company customer demands should be the driving force behind the activity of every department. To see that this happens marketing should sit at the centre organizing, coordinating and working with the other company functions.

In an ideal world this should be the role that marketing performs for the organization. Of course there must always be a trade-off between the demands of the customer and the limitation on company resources, but no product and market decisions should be taken without first attempting to see through the eyes of the customer, that is from the outside looking in, and not solely from the corporate needs or the individual needs of each competing department.

In the model developed below marketing has a coordinating role and sits at the centre where it supplies marketing input into other company functions such as production, finance, human resources and distribution. However, at the very heart of the organization's activities must be concern for the customer expressed by our definition of marketing. The model illustrated in Figure 1.9 reflects these relationships.

ORGANIZATIONAL STRUCTURES

So a company must develop some way of organizing its resources so as to meet the challenges, identified earlier, of developing products for an ever-changing environment. Formal organizational charts (in theory) give an indication of the way that the company develops structures, allocates responsibilities and implement systems. Figure 1.10 illustrates a simple example of a company that could be said to be sales driven, while Figure 1.11 shows one that could be said to be marketing driven.

In the example of the sales driven company, marketing is nowhere to be seen. Whereas the marketing driven company has marketing at boardroom level and sales, distribution and R&D under the control of this function.

However, it should be understood that the existence of a formal organizational chart is no sure indication of how the company is run. Some companies without the existence of a formal marketing department may, in practice, be more marketing oriented than those without this formal acknowledgement. Ideally

| **Figure 1.9** | *Marketing at the heart of the company* |

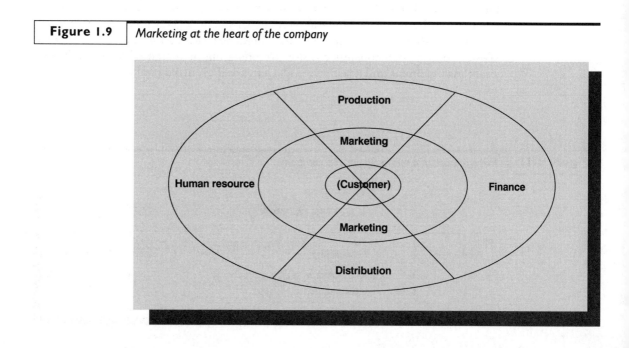

| **Figure 1.10** | *The structure of a sales driven company* |

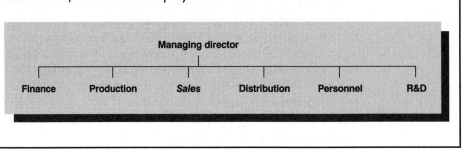

everybody within the organization, no matter what role they perform, would ulti-mately be marketing and customer driven, and if this were the case marketing as an identified separate discipline could become superfluous.

External environmental factors

It must be understood that the marketing effort does not take place in a vacuum and there are very many external factors that have to be considered. Unlike the 'internal' marketing mix factors, which can be identified as 'controllable', these 'external' factors are in the outside world and are largely 'uncontrollable'.

However all organizations have to be aware of what is happening in both the immediate and the wider environment if they are to function successfully. For a company to be unaware how incipient government legislation will affect their industry, or that demographic changes might lead to a shortage of a particular labour skill, or that consumer tastes are changing, is a sign of poor and inade-quate management and a recipe for lost sales and eventual bankruptcy.

| **Figure 1.11** | *The structure of a marketing driven company* |

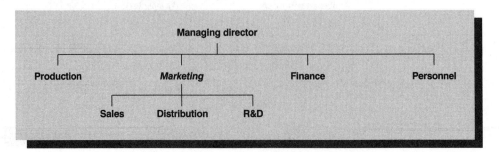

It is imperative that there is a continuous stream of up-to-date information coming into the organization, so that decisions can be made to take advantage of opportunities or defend against possible threats in both the immediate and wider environment.

Identified below are just a few examples of the many areas in the external environment that the organization must monitor. The information required could be on a national or/and international basis depending on the scope of the company's activities. It will prove useful to break down the external environment into two areas:

- the immediate environment;
- the wider environment.

It should be understood that this distinction in the external environment is artificial and is used only for ease of understanding. We will begin by looking at the 'immediate' environment.

THE IMMEDIATE ENVIRONMENT

The immediate environment (sometimes known as the micro-environment) are those external areas that the personnel within the company will probably interact with on a day-to-day basis in the normal course of business. The factors in the immediate environment include:

- Suppliers;
- Publics;
- Intermediaries (or middleman);
- Competition;
- Customers/Markets.

These factors are known by the acronym SPICC. Elements to be considered in each of these areas can be now be outlined, beginning with customers and markets.

CUSTOMERS AND MARKETS. As identified earlier, the organization must have continuous information about its customers. Who they are? When do they purchase? Why do they purchase? Where do they purchase? What do they purchase? How do they purchase? The management will also need to know the size of the market, whether it is growing or declining as well as patterns of future demand.

SUPPLIERS AND INTERMEDIARIES. Likewise the organization must monitor and control suppliers and intermediaries (sometimes known as 'middlemen'), both essential elements in the company value chain (Figure 1.12), to see that their contribution does not detract from ultimate customer satisfaction. If, for example, a company manufactures vacuum cleaners it would need to purchase raw materials such as steel, plastics, nuts and bolts, electrical components, etc. from suppliers and, after manufacture, would then sell through intermediaries, for example wholesalers or retailers such as Newey & Eyre, Currys or Comet.

| Figure 1.12 | *The value chain* |

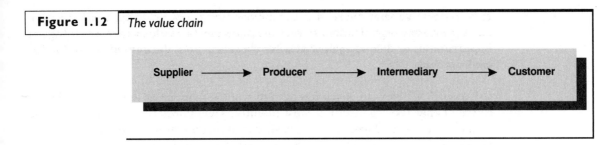

Supplier ⟶ Producer ⟶ Intermediary ⟶ Customer

A company will lose competitive advantage on its final product offering if it does not purchase quality raw materials and component parts from its suppliers, at the right price, within the time frame set by an ever more demanding industry. Likewise the intermediary represents the company and its products in dealings with the customer and must match required standards.

The value chain consists of all the organizations that are involved in getting the product from the raw material stage through to customer purchase and after sales service.

COMPETITION.   The company must have an understanding of the competitive nature of its industry. This will include all competitors in the same immediate market or which might be in the same market in the future.

Questions that need answers will include: Who are the major players and what market share do they have? Who is growing and who is declining? What are their strengths and weaknesses compared with ours? Where is the competition coming from? What marketing mix offerings do they have and what might they be developing? How do their products compare with ours? It is important to understand that no business is now safe from competition on both a national and international level and with the development and opening up of world markets competition will become increasingly intense.

PUBLIC.   Pressure groups (e.g. environmentalists), the media, local government (e.g. planning office), and the local community are categorized under the public environment. There are always local interests that must not be ignored. This might be the local community concerned about redevelopment or a local government department involved in a planning application or a pressure group concerned with environmental issues.

There are many examples of problems caused by difficulties with the public environment. This has included pollution issues such as chemical spillage into local waterways (ICI); animal welfare, the use of animals in cosmetic research (Body Shop); environmental damage, the use of scarce and unique peat-lands for fertiliser (Fisons); planning blight, building incongruously in sensitive areas (Mcdonald's); health impairment, selling products liable to cause health problems (Imperial Tobacco).

We can now add the immediate environment to the marketing model developed earlier (Figure 1.13).

| **Figure 1.13** | *Marketing model stage 3* |

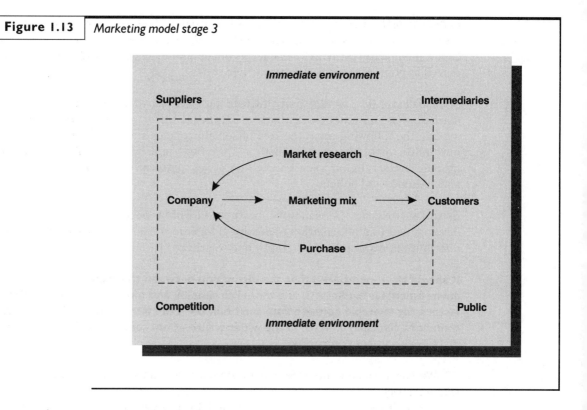

THE WIDER ENVIRONMENT

The wider environment (sometimes known as the macro-environment) will include those factors that may have a greater or lesser effect on the company's business activities in the short, medium or longer term.

Below are just a few of the main areas that companies should consider, but there are many more and the importance of particular factors will depend on the type of organization, the products produced, and the scope of the activity. An organization must be aware of developments in the wider environment subsumed for ease of understanding under the following (arbitrary) four categories:

- Political/legal,
- Economic/demographic,
- Social/cultural,
- Technical/physical.

This gives the acronym PEST which can be used as a memory aid to describe the macro-environment. Each factor is now briefly discussed.

POLITICAL/LEGAL. This will include factors such as anticipating a change of government, new legislation in a relevant area both at national and international level, the ending of trade barriers, the formation of cartels and trading groups, unrest, uprisings and war.

ECONOMIC/DEMOGRAPHIC.   This will include factors such as interest rates, exchange rates, inflation levels, employment levels, wage rates, gross national product, per capita income, investment levels, levels of economic activity, trade union activity, as well as population movements and age shifts.

SOCIAL/CULTURAL.   Social and cultural factors are of particular interest to marketers as movements can have a significant affect on the market. This will include the following area: the role of social agencies such as the family, school, university, work; changes in customs, practices and buying habits; education, literacy levels; religion, race, ethnic minorities; patterns of work, leisure pursuits and attitudes and beliefs.

TECHNICAL/PHYSICAL.   Continuous information will be needed on new technology development (e.g information technology) logistic considerations, infrastructure, distribution, geography, topography and weather.

It should be remembered that the distinction between the immediate and wider environments is artificial (it is a model to simplify and aid understanding). Some factors, for example competition, can be in both the immediate and wider environments. Similarly a factor in the wider environment today may be in the immediate environment tomorrow.

We can now add the wider environment to complete the marketing model (Figure 1.14).

Through the use of the marketing model the organization's marketing environment has been identified. Marketing activity is concerned with the relationship between the internal environment, the 4 Ps and the external, the immediate and the wider environments, through the use of market research. Successful marketing is matching all of the companies internal resources (the marketing mix) to the demands of the external environment (immediate and wider environment).

Another definition of marketing is that of a 'matching process'. Matching and coordinating effectively and efficiently the organization's internal resources to the ever-changing demands of the external environment.

International marketing

It is not intended to write at any length in this book on the international aspect of marketing and interested students should consult a textbook related specifically to this area. However, whilst looking at the internal and external environment, the following points could be made.

International marketing is self-evidently marketing at an international level. This might be an organization that markets its products to one other country, for example from the UK (as its home-base) to France, or an organization that sells in more than one other country, for example France, Germany, Italy, USA, China, Brazil, etc. Or it might be an organization that sets up its operation and produces its products in that foreign country either for home use or for export, for example Nissan in the UK, Mcdonald's in Russia, Ford in Spain or BP in the USA.

Figure 1.14	*Marketing model stage 4*

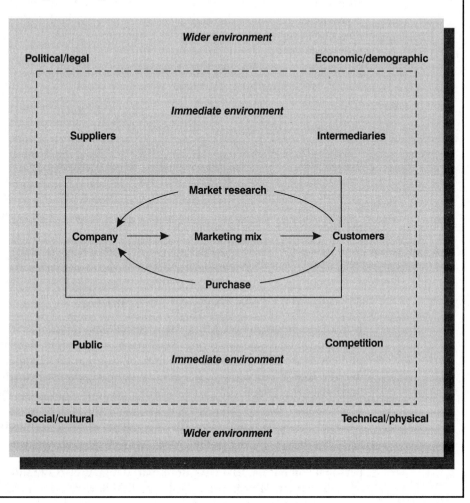

What should be understood is that there are many extra problems involved when marketing products outside of the home market. These differences will make any international marketing exercise that much more difficult and that much riskier. These 'differences' will also affect the marketing mix that will eventually be offered to the market.

DIFFERENCES WITHIN INTERNATIONAL MARKETS

Information is crucial when selling abroad and this can be very difficult to obtain. In some countries statistical information, if available, can often be suspect either in the way it has been collected or in the manner of its presentation. Information is needed because markets in different countries can be so very different from one another. At the wider environmental (PEST) level, governments, political systems, laws, barriers to entry, commission payments might all be totally different to the home market (you might want to think about marketing products to the Middle East or to China). Similarly other PEST factors identified earlier, for example GDP, literacy levels, cultural differences, infrastructure, could all take on an added dimension when selling to the other side of the world.

At the immediate environmental level, customer, competition, suppliers, intermediaries all become that much more difficult to handle when the geographical distances are vast, knowledge of markets and customers is sketchy or unknown, and information is difficult to come by. Internally products might have to be adapted to meet the different demands of different markets. Cars manufactured for the Japanese market will need more stringent emission controls than those manufactured for the UK market; Amstrad must have all manner of adaptations to allow for different voltages, language or interface between products; a pint of bitter and a packet of pork scratchings, a favourite in the local pub, cannot be sold in Muslim Pakistan.

Conversely a few companies are able to market more or less the same product almost anywhere in the world, for example Coca-Cola; McDonald's, Kodak.

Marketing and the changing environment

It needs to be emphasised that the external environment is forever changing and changing at an exponential rate. Marketing is not a rigid, fixed management discipline it must change as the demands of the market change. There is always a danger that a company may become complacent with an initially successful marketing approach only to discover, too late, that customer demands have changed and this has not been recognized by the company.

IBM is a perfect example of this type of organization. For more than two decades they dominated the mainframe computer market on a global scale only to discover in the early 1980s that their customers were demanding smaller, tailor-made, personal computers. IBM were unprepared and Apple Computers stole a large part of their market. After horrendous losses IBM have re-discovered marketing and the overall concern for *ever-changing* customer needs and are back on course.

STABLE AND DYNAMIC ENVIRONMENTS

The environment is in a constant state of change, but there are periods when the pace of change taking place is more or less placid and more or less rapid and turbulent. When this change is less rapid the environment can be said to be 'stable'. When the change is more rapid the environment is 'dynamic'. The pace can vary from market to market and the marketer must be aware of the rate of change taking place in every market where his or her company has a presence (Figure 1.15). In modern markets this pace of change is increasingly rapid.

CONSERVATIVE AND PROGRESSIVE PRODUCTS

How the pace of change will affect an organization will depend to a lesser or greater extent on the type of industry it operates in and the sorts of products/

| **Figure 1.15** | *Environmental change* |

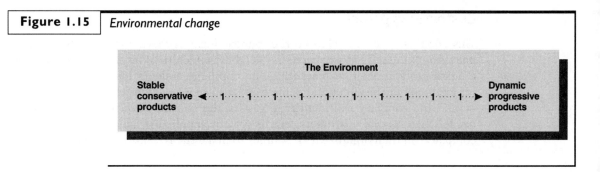

services it produces. If the products produced are less affected by change then they can be called *conservative* products/services. These tend to be low-tech products such as bread, sugar, salt. If the products are more affected then they can be known as *progressive* products/services. These tend to be high-tech products in areas such as, computers, communications, electronics.

So a company's position on the stable/dynamic environmental axis (Figure 1.15), will depend on both the pace of change in the environment and the pace of change in the particular industry.

A company with 'progressive' products working in a 'dynamic' environment must have highly sophisticated market research systems to consistently and continuously monitor the immediate and wider environment. They must also have low, flat, flexible structures to be able to react quickly to changing needs in the marketplace.

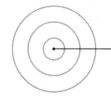

Customer, resource, technology approaches

Throughout this chapter the reader has been dogmatically exhorted to follow a very clear process of customer need identification and then develop products to meet these needs. In theory it seems simple to identify the market and then come back and make the product to match the needs of that market (the process developed earlier with the use of the marketing model). However, in practice, the process is always much 'messier' and more complex.

Unless a company had unlimited resources, and/or is starting from scratch, it will already have existing finite resources, capital equipment, people skills, and so on, which it will be unable to change in any significant way. This leads us to identify three different approaches to the marketing concept:

1. customer approach;
2. resource approach;
3. technology approach.

Customer approach

This could be considered to be the 'purest' form of marketing and the form of marketing taught by most academics and best understood by most students. With a customer approach to marketing the company collects information (market research) about the needs and wants from customers and markets. From this information the company will identify a 'gap' in the market for products or services, needed by potential customers, but as yet not supplied by any organization. The company will then organize its resources to make the required product.

Resource approach

However it might be considered unrealistic to think that companies that are conscious of the marketing process are able to come back and manufacture any product to fit an identified customer need. Most companies already have resources, capital equipment, people, production processes, etc. that they have to work with and to re-equip in these areas to meet any identified demand would be far to prohibitive in terms of costs, time and skills. To identify a need for a new type of motor car and then to think about manufacturing it is unrealistic if the factory is geared up to produce speed-boats.

A resource approach to marketing is similar to a customer approach to marketing in that the firm will need to talk to customers so as to identify possible unfulfilled needs. However this approach looks for gaps in the market that can be satisfied by utilizing its *existing* resources. It should, of course, be imaginative and flexible in how it might use and develop the existing resources to be able to do this.

An example might be of a company that had manufactured aluminium products for use in the building of ships. As shipbuilding was coming to an end, research could have taken place to look for gaps in the market for products that could be produced with existing skills and equipment. The gap might be in a similar market or in a totally new one and the possible product could be a variation on a theme or in a completely new area.

Technology approach

Some companies have a reputation for continuously introducing innovative new products and making use of new technological advances with very little, if any, market research. They tend to spend more money on technological research and development than other companies and they often have a commitment to be first to the market with the very latest new technological products or product feature (Sony, Philips, 3M).

Strictly speaking it might be argued, in the extreme, that this approach is an example of a product driven company. However there are some products for which we know there will be a demand if ever they can be produced. The 6-inch thick TV that can be hung on the wall like a picture; the computer that can perform all functions at the sound of the voice; the motor car that can run farther on less petrol; the milk carton that can be opened easily; reduced time in waiting for a surgical operation; are all examples of products and services that we know are wanted if only the technology can be developed to produce them. We do not need to undertake extensive market research to prove that this is so.

TECHNOLOGICAL 'PUSH' AND CUSTOMER 'PULL'

The level at which either technological innovation (technological push) or customer demand (customer pull) will dictate the type of product or service offered to the market will vary according to both products and markets and will tend to meet each other at differing points along a flexible axis (Figures 1.16 and 1.17).

Customer, resource and technological approach are all theoretical forms of marketing. However the practical world does not so easily fall into fixed compartments. Organizations will utilize a combination of one, two or three methods depending on their structure and the products and markets with which they are involved. So a company is, to a lesser or greater degree, more likely to be partly customer and partly resource driven rather than totally one or the other.

Likewise there seems always to be a trade-off between the forces of 'technological push' and 'customer pull'. So a company wanting to take advantage of this might, on the one hand allow its R&D department to indulge in some 'blue sky research' (allowing the scientist total freedom to research any area that he or she might wish) but, on the other hand, always be conscious of its commercial application.

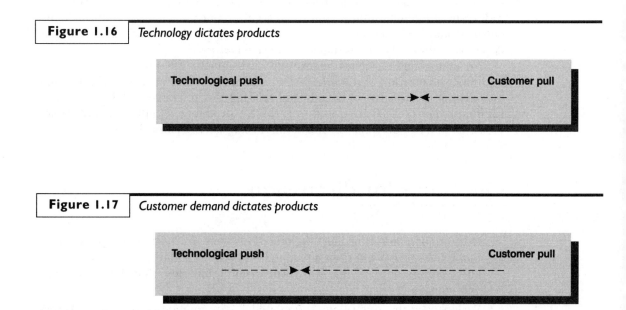

| **Figure 1.16** | *Technology dictates products* |

Technological push — Customer pull

| **Figure 1.17** | *Customer demand dictates products* |

Technological push — Customer pull

Summary

This chapter began by introducing the basic concepts and definitions behind the discipline known as marketing. Its history and development since the Second World War were discussed and reasons given why organizations now need to adopt a customer centred approach to markets.

The marketing environment was examined by breaking it down into the internal and external. It was shown that marketing research and the marketing mix: the product, the price, the place, the promotion, or the 4 Ps, are the basic tools and techniques that the marketer can control so as to make available to the customer the desired product and service offerings. The idea of two further Ps, profit and people, where introduced as a possible variation.

It was recognized that the marketing effort takes place in an ever-changing external environment and this was identified in terms of the immediate and the wider environment: the immediate environment was shown to consist of suppliers, public, intermediaries, competition and customers/markets (SPICC) factors; the wider environment includes political/legal, economic/demographic, social/cultural and technical/physical (PEST) elements. A marketing model was developed showing both internal and external factors.

An understanding of the marketing environment was brought together by outlining the position that marketing should occupy within the organization and introducing the concept of change and relating this to stable and dynamic environments and conservative and progressive products. Finally technological, customer and resource approaches to marketing were discussed.

Questions for discussion

1. How might marketing help organizations that are having to operate in a market that is moving from a planned economy to a market economy? Use as an example one of the East European countries that have rejected communism.

2. We looked at the use of a marketing model. Why are models used by marketers and how valuable do you think that they are? Give examples how the marketing model could be used with different companies.

3. What sort of information might be needed from the immediate and wider environments by companies in the following three industries:
   1. footwear;
   2. frozen food;
   3. computer systems?

   Would it make any difference if they where thinking of moving into international markets?

4. The marketing mix was identified in simple terms as the 4 Ps: product, price, place and promotion. What are the elements that might be included under these headings?

5. What input should marketing have into other areas of the organization such as production, personnel, administration, finance and so on? What difficulties might you foresee in attempting to make a company more marketing orientated?

6. Social responsibility should be the concern of all producers. How might this affect the producer of refrigerators, tumble dryers, microwave ovens and personal pension schemes?

7. Good marketing management decisions are impossible without the right sort of information. What sort of information do you think is needed?

8. World markets are in a state of ever-increasing change. How do you account for this? How must it be managed by the marketing manager?

9. Competition is now a fact of life for all organizations. What information must a company acquire to maintain a competitive advantage? Where could it get this information?

10. How might political decisions affect the success or otherwise of an organization? Would it make a difference if it were in the public rather than the private sector?

Case study

Harry Ramsden's is the world's most famous fish and chip shop and its name is known all over the world. The company was founded 60 years ago in Guisley, Leeds, and still runs the original fish and chip shop where it started. Food can either be taken away to eat or it can be consumed on the premises. When it was first opened it was advertised as the biggest fish and chip shop in the world with seating for over 300 people. It made the proud boast that better value could not be had at any other fish and chip shop in the British Isles. Such was its reputation that tourists from both the UK and from other parts of the world would make a special detour to Leeds to view and take photographs of the building and to sample its food offerings. A large portion of fried chips, a fresh piece of cod cooked in golden brown batter, a portion of mushy peas, a large pickled gherkin or pickled onion, a roll and butter, all washed down with a large mug of steaming hot tea, soft drink, or beer, was seen as the attraction.

Surprisingly, it was not unusual whilst eating in the restaurant, to find oneself seated next to tourists from as far away as Japan, the USA, France or Germany all eating, and enjoying, what had come to be seen as a traditional English meal.

However, despite the success of Harry Ramsden, many commentators had argued that the traditional fish and chip shop would gradually decline and eventually go out of business as the consumer demanded a more sophisticated menu from which to choose. Holidays abroad had given the traditional consumer a taste for more varied and exotic foods not catered for by the humble 'fish 'n' chips'.

More and more restaurants and take away food bars were opened across the whole of the country at an ever-increasing rate, they sprang up in high streets, in villages and in out-of-town shopping sites, taking advantage of this overwhelming consumer demand for new and more interesting ways to eat out or buy pre-cooked take-away meals. American, Chinese, Indian, Japanese, Italian, Taiwanese, Mexican, Turkish – the list of choices available seemed endless.

On top of this demand for varied eating opportunities came the added desire for more healthy types of food. Many health conscious consumers now wanted food that would not make them fat, give them high blood pressure or cause them to have a heart attack. Out went fatty, greasy, high in cholesterol fast foods, supplanted by vegetarian, low in polyunsaturates, nut- and fruit-rich health foods. The fish and chip shop could not survive.

But Harry Ramsden's has proved the Jeremiahs and doubting Thomas's wrong, by not only surviving but actually increasing its empire. It was launched on the Stock Exchange in the 1980s and is now a publicly quoted company. Since 1988 it has opened fourteen new restaurants. Eleven of these are in the UK (including one at Heathrow airport) with others in Dublin, Hong Kong and Melbourne. The company owns only one of these outlets (the original one in Leeds) the rest being joint ventures or franchises (the one in Dublin is a joint venture with Jackie Charlton, the ex-footballer).

The Harry Ramsden brand name has become so well-known that it now also packages frozen fish and chips which it sells through supermarkets. Its turnover for the six months to March 1995 was £1.5 million with a profit of £130,000. Three more restaurants opened in 1996, in Bournemouth, Cardiff and Belfast. Further openings are planned throughout Europe, the Middle East, the Far East and Australia.

The surprising aspect of the whole case history is how a company that sells such an old fashioned, parochial, quintessentially English food product like fish and chips cannot only expand throughout the UK, despite changing eating attitudes and practices, but market the whole concept around the world.

Case study questions

1. Harry Ramsden's is looking to expand its fish and chip business to both the Middle and Far East. What internal and external environmental factors must it take into account before undertaking this strategy?

2. Why do you think that the company has been so successful considering the seeming limitations on the product it markets? Do you think it will be the same type of customer who will want to purchase this product around the world or will this vary from country to country?

3. What part do you think that marketing has had to play in the development of so many different types of restaurants? If you where going to open a restaurant what marketing information might you need?

Further reading

Frain. J. (1999) *Introduction to Marketing*, International Thompson Business Press, London.

Jefkins, F. (1996) *Modern Marketing*, Pitman, London.

Kotler. P. (1998) *Principles of Marketing*, Prentice Hall, London.

Lancaster, G. and Massingham, L. (1997) *The Essentials of Marketing*, McGraw-Hill, Maidenhead.

Paliwoda S.J. (1986) *International Marketing*, Heinemann, London.

References

Ray Wright Website: www.raynetmarketing.com

Chartered Institute of Marketing: www.cim.co.uk

Marketing Week: www.marketingweek.co.uk

Office of Fair Trading: www.oft.gov.uk

Competition Commission (formerly Monopolies and Mergers Commission): www.mme.gov.uk

The Charities Commission: www.charity-commission.gov.uk

Procter & Gamble: www. pg.com

2

Information systems and marketing research

AIMS AND OBJECTIVES

By the end of the chapter the student should:

1 be aware of the importance of information about the marketing environment as a critical aid in the management decision-making process;

2 be able to identify both informal and formal organizational information collecting processes including knowlege on the uses of the Marketing Information System (MkIS);

3 describe and evaluate the different advantages and disadvantages of both primary and secondary research as well as the methods that both would employ;

4 be able to demonstrate an ability in questionnaire design and an appreciation of why different methods might be used in its construction.

Introduction

The importance of information

In the preceding chapter we examined the organization and its environment breaking down and identifying all the areas, both internal and external, that will have an influence on the running of the business. The affect that any one element might have on the company will vary from firm to firm and industry to industry, dependent on the many complex changeable factors identified earlier. Marketing practitioners, if they are to be successful, must make it a central part of their work to try to understand these complex changes by attaining a comprehensive knowledge of every aspect of their industry. They should also develop skills so that they are able to use this knowledge in a practical way to obtain long-term competitive advantage for their company.

The whole management process has to begin with the collection of information so that sound decisions can be made about the future strategic direction of the company. Without a continuous supply of good, up-to-date, relevant data on customers, markets and competitor movements, any attempt to forecast and plan for the future will be confounded.

It is true that some decisions have to be made without total access to all of the facts, but very often action is taken based on inadequate, or wrong information, leading to disastrous end results when, with a little more effort and planning, this could have been avoided.

Information is power

All politicians recognize the importance of having control of the dissemination of information. To be able to decide what should and should not be known and to be able to control the flow of this information has been at the heart of political power for centuries. The democratic process itself depends on the population having access to the right information so that both sides of the argument can be weighed and votes cast accordingly. Similarly, the organization that has the ability to gather the most realistic and up-to-date information on a continuous basis and then to use this advantage wisely is likely to be the one that has the most success.

Information and competitive advantage

Likewise, the most successful working person is likely to be the one who is the most knowledgeable and has the most information about the industry that they have chosen as a career. When we meet somebody that truly seems to know the business they are working in and can readily supply information requested, the results are impressive. The plumber, in business for himself, who can talk with confidence about the latest products and how a particularly difficult job might be carried out; the retail clothing saleswoman who can talk knowledgeably about current and future fashions; and the manager whom everybody goes to talk to when seemingly unobtainable information is needed, stand out like beacons in the night.

Such is its power, that if the marketing manager has more current information about present and future customer needs than anybody else, if she knows the opposition as well as her own company, and if she is able to use this information in a professional manner, her company will hold an unbeatable advantage.

The information gathering process

The information gathering process can be formal, informal or a mixture of the two and it will vary between organizations, depending on size, wealth, style and the industry itself. It will also depend on the operating climate. The more turbulent the environment and the more progressive the product the greater will be the need for a stream of relevant up-to-date information.

Informal research

Much information gathering is done on an informal basis and tends not to be seen as marketing research, but its value cannot be over-estimated. It was argued above that the successful person is the knowledgeable person who has an inquisitive and an enquiring mind, always asking questions about customers and markets, competition and products, and storing the data in their long-term memory for later use. The wise manager is the one who generates this sort of culture, encouraging employees to seek out and report back any relevant information that might have an influence on, and be beneficial to the running of the business.

Formal

As well as informal information gathering most companies will have some form of formal information gathering system and this can be identified under the heading of a Marketing Information System (MkIS).

The Marketing Information System (MkIS)

Eventually the information gathering process will need to be placed on a more formal footing. With the advent and development of information technology any organization, whatever its size and financial situation, can now afford to have access to information technology data storage and analysis equipment and services either by purchase or alternatively through leasing or rental. If the latter options are chosen there is usually an option to buy in on either a continuous or *ad hoc* basis.

For marketing to function properly it needs constant information about all the areas in the internal and external environment identified earlier. This will cover such things as size, depth and trends of markets, customers changing buying habits, competitor movements and relevant PEST factors.

The formal information gathering process, the MkIS can be broken down into the following four areas.

1. internal information;
2. marketing intelligence gathering;
3. marketing research;
4. information storage and analysis.

We will look at each area in turn.

INTERNAL INFORMATION

A company will have a whole range of internal quantitative and qualitative performance indicators within its many functions and this information is essential to the marketing manager in the performance of his or her job. It can be surprising how often this source of information is not utilized as effectively as it should be. There are examples of marketing managers seemingly unaware that certain markets are declining and that others are increasing, or uncertain about the financial contribution of one product over another and there can be no excuse for not having this information at hand.

TYPES OF INFORMATION OBTAINED INTERNALLY. The financial department can supply figures on sales and costs and profitabilities across the whole product portfolio, as well as figures on cash flow and accounts receivable and accounts payable. Production can supply figures on optimum production runs, stock positions and future needs.

Indispensable to the system are the salesforce reports coming into the company. The salesperson is in the unique position of being the eyes and the ears of the company out in the marketplace. The information that they can collect on customers, suppliers, competition, etc. must be given the recognition it deserves (this is the major reason why the salesperson's report should never be used as a method of policing and control). All employee contribution to the information gathering process should be encouraged by the use of some form of recognition and reward system.

INFORMATION COORDINATION. The marketing department will need to set up a system for collecting and analysing reports from all these different areas. Yearly and monthly trends can be monitored so as to identify how the markets are performing and how they might perform in the future. Sales and pricing can be compared with the competition and comparisons made between the different outlets and distribution channels. Qualitative observations and suggestions should also be encouraged and rewarded if this is thought to be necessary.

CONSULTATION. Companies wishing to set up an internal report system should interview the various managers to ascertain their information needs. This can then be converted into a formal system of internal reporting. Like the laying down of any system, it is essential that it is monitored and controlled to make certain that it is working and that there is a flow of the right information to the marketing department. Of course the flow should not just be one way, marketing information should be available through a well thought out communication system to which every department should have access.

The value of internal information cannot be over-emphasized and it should be formalized, monitored and controlled.

MARKETING INTELLIGENCE SYSTEM

It was stated earlier that for an individual or a company to be a success, information about the relevant industry must be collected in a systematic way. It was argued that the superior performer will know more about markets than any other participant. The marketing intelligence system is that part of the MkIS where the environment is monitored *continuously* for any information that might have some bearing, present or future, on the company's marketing performance.

INTELLIGENCE UNIT. The size of the intelligence unit collecting information is relatively unimportant and will depend on the size of the company. It may be a whole department or just one person working part time. What is more important is the motivating thrust. There should be an almost obsessional need to unearth and classify any snippet of information, no matter how small, that will relate to the company's particular industry and can be used, either immediately or stored for future use. As well as those who work directly in the intelligence unit, all staff will need to be motivated and trained in intelligence gathering techniques so that it becomes an essential part of the company culture.

In the larger firm, whole departments will spend all of their time scouring magazines, newspapers, the trade press, the world wide web and other relevant sources pulling out any article that might supply a vital insight into the workings of the business, and so help improve performance. Working in this way a database of information about the industry can be built which can then be used to analyse and forecast movements in the immediate and wider environment.

EXTERNAL INFORMATION GATHERING AGENCIES. There exist commercial companies willing to offer a specific intelligence gathering service for most industries and businesses. This might be in the form of an article collection service or a continuous research programme that looks at customers and competitive activity in a particular industry.

MARKETING RESEARCH

The difference between marketing research and intelligence gathering is one of degree and should not give the reader cause to insist that a method should be in one category rather than another. The difference between marketing research and intelligence gathering is that marketing research is taken on for a *special* purpose and intelligence gathering is something that goes on all of the time.

So marketing research will be adopted if information is needed for a new product launch, or a new advertising campaign, or if particular product sales were falling, or if a company were thinking of expanding into another country.

MARKETING RESEARCH AND MARKET RESEARCH. It is worth explaining the formal difference between 'marketing' research and 'market' research. Marketing research covers the collection of information across the whole of the marketing spectrum and will include all the following areas: market research; customer behaviour research; advertising research; sales promotion research; sales research; distribution research; location research; channel research; pricing and cost research; product research; packaging research; competitor research supplier/intermediary/agent research; PEST research. In fact anything to do with marketing.

Market research on the other hand is research that looks at the markets and the customers in those markets and so is a *part* of marketing research. All marketing research at times tends to be called market research even by advertising agency personnel and this should not cause any problems as long as there is an awareness of the academic differences.

INFORMATION, STORAGE AND ANALYSIS

Information from all the sources identified above needs to be classified stored, analysed and, where necessary, cross-referenced. In the past this task would have been undertaken manually (probably through the use of a carded classification system) but now even the smallest of companies can have access to more sophisticated information technology methods.

Information technology (IT) and the use of computers enable large amounts of information to be stored in an information database, retrieved in moments, cross-informational comparisons made, and statistical and computer models used to examine and test the scientific validity of research undertaken or assumptions formulated. Networking and the Internet allows this to be done on a national and international scale.

DATABASE MARKETING. The increasing number of uses for IT has led to the development of 'database marketing'. The amount of data now available has allowed organizations to build huge computer databases on their existing and potential customers, full of detailed information which can then be used to accurately market products directly and personally to all customers (usually using direct mail). A whole range of customer characteristics can be entered into the database and then cross-referenced so that an individual profile can be developed enabling the company to offer customized products and services that exactly match the needs of the individual customer. One industry which exploits this activity to the full is the financial services industry.

RELATIONSHIP MARKETING. The enhanced capability offered by database marketing also enables the producer to develop an ever closer relationship with existing or past customers on a *long-term continuous* basis. Research has shown that it is much more expensive to gain new customers than it is to hold on to the existing ones. So manufacturers such as Heinz and Ford are now writing directly to customers (often by-passing the intermediary) with information about new and existing products, sending free magazines and offering opportunities to be involved in some form of sales promotion. The concept underpinning this form of 'relationship' marketing is the hope that a customer can be won and held for life.

We can see in the model illustrated in Figure 2.1 that the MkIS consists of the four areas identified above all working in conjunction with each other bringing information in from the environment, storing and analysing it and making it available in usable form to allow marketing management decisions to be made.

The marketing research process

We will now look in more detail specifically at the marketing research process. As identified above marketing research is research that is undertaken for a special purpose and the following factors need to be considered when using it to gather information.

Clear marketing research objectives

The beginning of the marketing research process, and arguably the most important, is to identify what information is needed. This may sound simple but often this first part in the process is the most difficult, frequently characterized by confusion and ambiguity. If the real problem is not identified at the very

| **Figure 2.1** | *The Marketing Information System* |

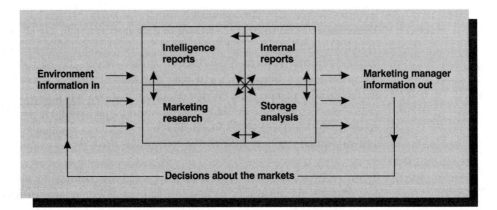

beginning, the whole process will be distorted. So the problem holder should seek, in discussion with others, to be crystal clear about the market research objectives. This will probably mean knowing the answers that are wanted before the research programme begins.

The marketing researcher, whether working for his or her own organization or for an outside agency, must develop skills in getting to the heart of the problem. This will involve talking to the client, going away and analysing the information, and then returning with a 'brief' that sets out the client's needs as the researcher understands them. This process will be repeated, back and forth if necessary, until no one is in any doubt about the purpose of the marketing research.

The budget

All marketing projects will include some form of financial cost. Marketing research is no different and so a budget will have to be decided upon. There are many ways to decide the amount to spend on the marketing research budget, including the following:

- as a percentage of sales;
- as a percentage of profit;
- based on the industry norm;
- what the company can afford;
- dependent on the objectives set and the task to be performed.

It could be argued that the best method for obtaining the budget should be by objective and task, but in practice it is probably more likely to be set according to what the company can afford.

CHOICES APPLY TO OTHER BUDGET FORMS

The choices, identified above, that have to be made in deciding the amount to allow for the research budget will also apply to other types of marketing budgets including research and development, new product development, advertising, sales promotion, publicity, etc.

Secondary and primary research

There are two distinct types of research: secondary research and primary research and the marketing practitioner will probably use a combination of both. We will look at each in turn, beginning with secondary research

SECONDARY RESEARCH (DESK RESEARCH)

The collection of information can be costly and time consuming especially if it involves calling in outside agencies. Therefore it is important to appreciate that there is a great deal of information that can be collected without the marketer ever leaving the office desk (hence it sometimes being called 'desk research').

Secondary research concerns information that has already been collected by others and is available from many sources and in a variety of forms as long as the marketer knows where to look. A number of sources of secondary research will now be considered.

INTERNAL SOURCES.   The first place to go for information will be within the company. As identified above there might well be a MkIS and it is here that the first approach should be made.

EXTERNAL SOURCES.   There are many organizations outside the company that exist to collect and collate data. These include governments, international agencies, trade and private agency sources.

Government agencies.   There are many government agencies that collect information on both a continuous and an *ad hoc* basis. The government needs information in order to develop policies that accord with future needs. Information needed will include such things as demographic trends, work patterns, the health of the population, leisure pursuits and marriage and divorce rates. It will also include trade and industry information such as imports and exports, industrial sector output and price and income movements. Some of this information is available free of charge; for some a fee will be payable.

Government sources which can be seen on the Government Information website, www.open.gov.uk, includes the following areas:

- The Office of National Statistics: www.ons.gov.uk   This was created in 1996 by the merger of the Central Statistical Office and the Office of Population Censuses and Surveys. It conducts the 10 year national census as well as a multitude of surveys on social trends, industries and businesses.
- Department of Trade and Industry: www.dti.gov.uk   The DTI will supply information and offer help in all areas of business for small, medium and large companies.
- The UK National Digital Archive of Datasets: www.ndad.ulcc.ac.uk   NDAD offers archived digital data from UK government departments and agencies.

International agencies.   The Department of Trade and Industry (DTI): www.dti.gov.uk and the many agencies attached to the United Nations will supply information at an international level on request. Web sites will include the following:

- United Nations web-sites: www.un.org
- World Bank: www.worldbank.org
- International Monetary Fund: www.imf.org

Trade agencies and professional institutions.   In addition to government statistics identified above there are statistics that are issued by trade associations and these are available on request (usually at a price). These cover most industries including the building industry, tourism, electrical and domestic appliances, the shoe industry and so on. The following bodies can provide a range of valuable information:

- The *Market Research Society* (www.marketresearch.org.uk) and the *European Society for Opinion and Market Research* (www.esomar.nl/index) are examples of market research industry bodies.

- The *Institute of Grocery Distribution Digest* contains a whole assortment of information on retailing in general, and supermarkets in particular.

- *Companies reports and accounts* are an obvious source of useful marketing data and are available on request.

- The *Chartered Institute of Marketing* (www.cim.co.uk); The *Institute of Practitioners in Advertising* (www.ipa.co.uk); *Institute of Public Relations* (www.ipr.org.uk); *Outdoor Advertising Association; Incorporated Society of British Advertisers* (www.isba.org.uk); *The Direct Marketing Association* (www.dma.org.uk) are all examples of professional bodies able to supply various forms of information.

Private agencies. There are also many independent research publishers of which the following are just a small selection:

- *Audit Bureau of Circulation* (ABC): www.abc.org.uk founded in 1931 as a non-profit making organization by the ISBA providing media user international standard verification.

- *Taylor Nelson AGB*: agb.mediatel.co.uk the largest market research company in the UK.

- *Mintel Information Service*: (www.mintel.co.uk) provide a paper clipping service on marketing articles as well as reports on many areas of industry.

- *Nielsen Retail Audit*: www.nielsen.com amongst other services provide a monthly product retail sales index.

- *The British Market Research Board (BMRB) Target Group Index*: www.bmrb.burb.co.uk identifies specific target groups of consumers and their buying habits, their newspaper and magazine readership, their TV viewing habits and the extent to which they see or hear other media. It covers most industries from pharmaceutical, toiletries, drink, confectionery and tobacco to clothing, shopping, leisure, holidays, financial services and consumer durables.

- *Hemington Scott Publishing*: www.hemscott.co.uk offers financial information on many UK companies.

- *Profit Impact of Marketing Strategies* (PIMS): www.pims-europe.com provides information on strategy development.

There are a number of statistical publications that provide information about industries and individual companies including the following:

- *Kompass*: www.kompass.com provides a directory of industries and companies by geographical location, name and address, and the relevant activity.

- *Dun and Bradstreet*: www.dunandbrad.co.uk looks at the promotion industry and provides a directory of newspapers, magazines, etc. with readership figures, prices for size of advertisement, etc. They also publish *Who Owns Whom (UK)* which gives details of parent companies, associated companies and subsidiary companies.

■ The National Readership Survey (NRS): www.nrs.co.uk offers readership data on over 245 publications.

■ Hoover's Company Information: www.pathfinder.com offers a wealth of company information around the world.

There are also services provided through the TV and computer screen by companies such as the following:

■ *Prestel* can be seen on domestic TV by the use of an adapter obtained when buying in on the scheme.

■ Free but limited services are provided by *Ceefax* and *Oracle*.

■ Last but not least we must not leave out the the *Internet* offering seemingly infinite information from around the world at the press of a computer key.

Consumer panels.   Consumer panels run by some of the agencies identified above consist of members of the public who weekly take note of their household purchases by product, brand and price paid. Trends can be developed and the results then sold to interested parties.

TV ratings panel.   As with the above panels, selected households have a monitor fixed to their TV set and linked to the agency computer. Each member of the household has a number on a shared hand control which they key in when watching a programme. This is how TV viewing figures are generated.

WHERE TO LOOK.   Secondary research gathering is a skill that needs to be developed. There are data available on any industry from fish farming through to hat making. All that is required to discover the desired information is persistence, and the knowledge that the information exists somewhere. The starting point will be the college, university or municipal/business library (books, CDs and the Internet) where an obliging librarian should direct the reader in the right direction. Some information is free while other information has to be paid for.

Advantages of secondary research.   The major advantages of secondary research are:

■ the cost – it is so much cheaper than primary research;

■ the speed – the information is available immediately;

■ the scope – it may offer extensive, in-depth information you could not afford to collect yourself.

Disadvantages of secondary research.   The disadvantages are:

■ it could be outdated;

■ it may not be strictly relevant;

■ its validity may be questionable.

PRIMARY RESEARCH

Existing research has been identified here as secondary research, but there will be many occasions when the information needed does not exist or, if it does, it is not specialized enough. When this is the case a company will need to undertake its own research. This is known as primary research.

Primary research is new research undertaken by an organization to help solve a problem that existing information cannot solve. It should never be undertaken lightly because of the high cost involved. Primary research can be broken down into three basic types:

1. experimentation;
2. observation;
3. surveys.

EXPERIMENTATION RESEARCH. With this type of research the researcher attempts to isolate the variable that needs to be tested from all other variables. Selected potential or existing consumers in the product target market are then used to test out the value of a particular assumption. The most common form of experimenta-tional primary research is the taste-test run in church halls, hotels and the homes of the public up and down the country.

This type of test is regularly used by the fast moving consumer goods (FMCG) industry for many purposes. These include the effect that packaging and branding has on customer perception of quality, the demanded amount of particular ingre-dients in the product – salt, sugar, colouring, etc. – as well as factors such as the 'crunchiness' or the firmness of the bite.

Control and experimental groups. A scientific approach is often adopted with one group being the 'control' (given the standard product) and the other group being the 'experimental' (given the amended product). The differences are then recorded. The most impressive observation to come from this kind of test is how many people have difficulty in distinguishing one product from another when blindfolded (e.g. crisps, baked beans, coke, chocolate) showing the great value of packaging and branding. Procter and Gamble, Pepsi-Cola and Nestlé are just a few of the companies which have used this type of primary research.

OBSERVATION. Observational research is attractive because it is low in cost and can be carried out by 'humans' or 'machines'. In simple terms it involves observing some phenomena and counting and recording so as to identify differ-ences and similarities. Mechanical electronic methods are used to count the number of cars that use a particular highway, turnstiles at a football match will count the numbers of supporters going in and the retail trade has developed EPOS (electronic point-of-sale) which will identify all the products by name and price and, linked to the customer loyalty card, will provide purchasing infor-mation on that customer. Video cameras have been used to study how people approach and select items off display units whilst shopping in supermarkets, and an electronic eye can register consumer patterns of movement around a particular display area. How and where products are displayed in grocery super-stores will have been decided with the help of this type of research.

SURVEYS. The use of the survey is probably the method of marketing research most recognized by the professional and the lay-person alike. The image of a person in the high street, holding a clipboard and stopping passers-by is ubiquitous. However, there are many different forms of survey that are used, depending on circumstances. A survey can be carried out by:

- post;
- telephone;
- person-to-person interviewing.

The above methods might be used singularly or in a combination of one or more methods. Each method will have advantages and disadvantages depending on the market research objectives and resources, time, and cost constraints. Increasingly, TV is used in conjunction with the telephone for a simple phone-in response. Interactive information technology networks (so called 'super-highways') also promise exciting new methods for collecting primary information. These three methods will now be examined in more detail.

Postal surveys.   With a postal survey, a questionnaire is constructed and posted out to selected households or organizations. In some cases the potential respondent has been informed (usually by telephone) and an agreement to fill it in is confirmed; in other cases the survey is sent out speculatively.

The national census (ONS) is a particular form of survey. It comes out every 10 years and is the only survey questionnaire that imposes a legal obligation on the recipient to fill in. It seeks demographic information on such things as the number, age, names and ethnic origins of household members. This information is available on request.

Advantages of postal surveys are as follows:

- It is a relatively inexpensive method and can be used to cover a wide geographical area for the cost of a postage stamp. There are research agencies that offer a research service almost anywhere in the world.

- With the increasing use of the information database and modern methods of customer targeting, the questionnaire can be posted with pinpoint accuracy. There are research companies that specialize in this form of *data-base marketing* and lists of names and addresses can be purchased or rented that will reflect the required target respondent.

Disadvantages of postal research can be as follows:

- Response rates tend to be poor and returns can often be less than 1 per cent depending on the information required. This can be improved with very tight targeting and/or the use of an incentive.

- The questionnaire must be very simple with clear directions to guide the respondent otherwise confusion will very quickly set in. This will restrict the type and the amount of information that can be requested.

- There could be uncertainty about the identity of the respondent and there is no opportunity for clarity and feedback.

More and more companies are beginning to use direct mail for research as the importance of building a solid database becomes more apparent.

The growth in the popularity of direct mail has lead to a poor image and complaints about the unsolicited letter or 'junk mail'. However it is argued that this poor image is overstated as research has shown that over 70 per cent of recipients welcome much of what comes through the post and 50 per cent of direct mail seems to be read.

The telephone and telemarketing.   Over the last decade there has a major increase in the use of telemarketing, both as a means of selling, and of collecting market research. Over 95 per cent of the population now own or rent a telephone so the marketer has potential access to the majority of the population.

The advantages of telemarketing to the marketer include the following factors.

- Like postal research the telephone is widely used because of its relative low cost, and high target accuracy.
- It is quicker than postal surveying and is highly successful for gleaning simple, limited, straight forward information.
- In some cases people not prepared to grant a personal interview will talk on the telephone.

However, there are disadvantages, as the following list indicates.

- Similar to postal surveys, the telephone cannot be used for the more in-depth research. The maximum time respondents are prepared to talk on the telephone is about five minutes so questions must be uncomplicated and limited.
- Respondents may also give the answer that first comes to mind in order to get rid of the researcher.
- Unfortunately some 'teleselling' is disguised as research, so giving this form of marketing research a bad reputation and leading to complaints about 'intrusion of privacy'.

With the advent of flexible monitoring systems and phone charges, it is increasingly common for TV programme producers to ask viewers to phone in and vote on some particular issue or other. There are companies that will provide this telephone service on request.

Person-to-person interviewing.   Personal interviewing might be considered to be the most effective form of primary research collection, and is the method most readily associated with the commonly held perception of market research. Personal interviewing can take place in the street, in a shopping centre, in the home, at work, etc. We have all seen (and avoided?) a person in the street with a clipboard waiting to pounce on a selected respondent. The interview may take five minutes if carried out in the street, or as much as an hour if conducted in the home.

The principal advantages of person-to-person interviewing are as follows.

- The desired respondent can be easily identified, and persuaded if need be, to answer questions.

■ The process is interactive, body language and verbal nuances can be read and the respondent can be guided through the questionnaire and helped wherever there are difficulties or misunderstandings, invaluable when the answers sought are complicated.

■ The questionnaire can be longer (up to one hour is probably the maximum time), and explanations given if there are sensitive areas. Because of the increased available length, 'omnibus editions' can be developed in which interested organizations can buy in two, three or more questions to be asked.

The main disadvantages are that the personal survey can be very expensive, suffer from interviewer bias (intensive training can help to minimize this) and take a long time from inception through to analysis and use.

QUANTITATIVE AND QUALITATIVE METHODS OF RESEARCH

It is possible to distinguish two distinct types of primary research methods:

1. quantitative;
2. qualitative.

QUANTITATIVE METHODS.   Most questionnaire surveys will use questions that have been rigorously tested before use, are structured, and the answers can be quantified into clearly defined, coded compartments. This facilitates the collection, classification and analysis of the data and allows computer and statistical techniques to be used. Most government statistics are collected and presented in this form.

All the questions on the questionnaire are arranged so that any answer that is given can be coded and recorded in mathematical form. To facilitate the process the questions tend to take the form of closed-ended, yes or no type questions (see the discussion below on closed and open questions). This allows the statistics to be presented in terms of percentages, and trends across all areas and past years can be compared.

From the point of view of advantages, the quantitative method is attractive because the process can be undertaken in a quasi-scientific manner and the results presented in a detached and objective statistical form. Quantitative research attempts to discover the needs and wants of the customer in as objective a way as possible, eliminating researcher bias and subjectivity.

However, there are inevitably some disadvantages and in this case there is little doubt that this method has its limitations. Understanding the consumer also involves seeking out opinions, emotions, 'gut' feelings and latent or subconscious thoughts. These needs do not lend themselves easily to the 'scientific' approach inherent in the quantitative method.

QUALITATIVE METHODS.   To overcome the problems with the quantitative approach identified above, marketers, working in conjunction with psychologists, have developed a group of techniques known collectively as the 'qualitative approach'. Through the use of these techniques researchers hope to get at customers innermost thoughts and feelings, often unobtainable in other ways. These techniques include the following methods:

1. focus or discussion groups;
2. in-depth interviews;
3. shadowing;
4. psycho-analytical techniques.

Focus or discussions groups.   Probably the most used, and the most successful of all these techniques is the informal discussion or focus group. An organizer is employed by a market research agency to select and invite a representative number of individuals (usually any number between five and twenty) to an informal discussion evening at a hotel or a specially prepared venue. A facilitator then presents the group with a discussion topic. This will be some sort of problem that requires information on customer reactions. It might be a firm bringing out a new drink wanting to have feedback on taste, brand name, bottle shape, colour or overall price levels. Another company might want its clients' and customers' inner-most thoughts on its corporate image.

The sessions may be semi-structured or unstructured and many different techniques can be used to stimulate discussion including TV films, magazines and sound equipment. The session can be recorded by tape, by video or by written word for later expert analysis. The facilitator is present to guide and give direction to the discussion. This form of research is now being used much more often as consumers become more complex and individualistic in their needs and wants.

This method has the great advantage of allowing participating group members to relax in a sympathetic and relaxing environment (often encouraged with a liberal supply of refreshment) enabling them to express thoughts and feelings that they would otherwise not be able, or want, to articulate.

A further advantage is that a group can be quite easy to set up and it is a good method to use if time is short. The costs involved can be relatively low (£1000 per session if using a professional agency). Much important research has been obtained by large client companies using as little as five or six groups strategically organized around the country.

It is not uncommon for a frequently occurring issue or concern, expressed during the discussion groups, to be subjected to further investigation using one of the quantitative methods detailed above.

There are disadvantages with the focus group method, as the following points illustrate.

- The method is open to abuse by an organizer who does not rigorously select a representative sample of participants.
- Inexperienced facilitators can inadvertently lead the discussing and so influence the participating consumers' opinions rather than sitting back and guiding what goes on with a few, well timed but limited, interjections.
- As with all forms of qualitative research the interpretation can be highly subjective even if undertaken by an expert.

The in-depth interview.   If a problem is complex and solutions difficult to come by, it may be necessary to conduct a series of 'one-to-one' in-depth interviews with selected customers. These should be undertaken by experts able to manipulate the technique so as to elicit the most useful information. The interviews may be structured, semi-structured or unstructured. This method has the benefit of collecting deeply ingrained information on customers' inner-most beliefs, attitudes and desires. However it should be used in conjunction with other methods as it is very narrow in its application.

The advantages and disadvantages are very similar to those identified for the focus group.

Shadowing. In a variation of the in-depth interview the company researcher will spend a day with a chosen customer who will be representative of the target market. This would typically be a housewife going about her daily task. The 'shadowing' process would begin in the kitchen where the customer would be asked about the various household products she has bought (and has not bought) and why. She would then be accompanied as she went around the supermarket, notes would be taken about behaviour and questions asked about reasons for the purchase and non-purchase of various products. The researcher must be skilled in inter-personal behaviour, observation and analysis.

The advantages and disadvantages, once again, are similar to those identified above in the discussion of focus groups.

Psycho-analytical techniques. Market research analysts have adopted many psycho-analytical techniques from the discipline of psychology to help in understanding consumer behaviour. This form of research works on the theory that people are not able to express many of their real thoughts and concerns through more overt research methods because of subconscious constraints (interested students might visit the more accessible writings on the subconscious by Sigmund Freud). Psycho-analytical methods include the following:

- *Creative imagery* – using creative imagery, representative consumers are asked to draw, paint or use moulding materials to describe their feelings about a subject, for example the brand name of a bank, a beer, a car, a box of chocolates, etc. They are encouraged to be as imaginative as possible using colour, shapes and images. The resultant, often abstract, images are then psycho-analysed by an expert to 'uncover' the real repressed thoughts of the participants (Guinness launched a whole promotional campaign partly using this method).

- *Cartoon story* – a similar method to the above but in this instance the participants are given a basic story in cartoon form and asked to draw their thoughts and desires on how the story might finish. The concept behind this method is that the consumer can express values through the cartoon story they might be unable to take responsibility for in a more direct way.

- *Word association* – with word association a sequential list of words are presented and the respondent asked to say what these words remind him or her of. The word 'beer' might be given followed by the reply 'lager' or 'spirit' followed by the word 'gin' or the brand name 'Gordons'. Of course Allied Lyons, the beer manufacturer, would hope that the word 'lager' would prompt the unthinking reply 'Fosters'. This could then indicate that their marketing was working.

■ *Electronic research methods* – there are many forms of electronic gadgetry that are used in this search for consumer reaction to company products. A galvanometer measures the strength of a subject's interest or emotions aroused by an advert or picture. It picks up changes in sweating that accompanies emotional arousal (it is the same method as the one used for lie-detectors).

Subconscious consumer reactions can also be gauged through eye-blink measurement. Images of products or brand names are presented by the use of a tachistoscope and the depth and level of effect measured by eye-blink reaction on an eye camera. Increased eye movement indicates high levels of recognition and interest. These techniques are often used to measure the effect on consumers of particular TV and newspaper adverts. It is a way of measuring the success or otherwise of an advertising campaign mounted to increase the awareness of a particular brand or product.

The objective of the above techniques is to get at consumers' inner-most, often subconscious, thoughts and attitudes. This is a very specialized area requiring highly trained operatives and all the methods identified above are dependent on specialist agencies setting up and running the programme and then classifying, interpreting and presenting the results.

The disadvantages with psycho-analytical techniques fall into the following categories.

■ Like all qualitative methods, the use of psycho-analytical techniques can be relatively expensive if used on a large sample.

■ Consequently, the sample studied tends to be very small and may therefore not be representative.

■ The interpretation of results, whilst undertaken by an expert, is still subjective.

Taking this subjectivity, and the smallness of the sample into account, the results should be handled with the utmost caution.

However, as with other forms of qualitative research, the big advantage is the richness of the information that can be obtained. To paraphrase the lager advert: 'it gets to the parts that other forms of research cannot reach'.

QUANTITATIVE AND QUALITATIVE METHODS COMBINED. A research programme will often include both quantitative and qualitative research. A discussion group, in-depth interview or shadowing exercise might throw up a consistent factor needing more information which can then be tested by a more extensive quantitative survey.

Market research survey design

The market research survey is probably the method of collecting information that has the highest profile amongst the general population. It is also the method most likely to be used by students or small companies undertaking their own research. For this reason it is worth spending a little time on the concepts behind good survey design (the whole process is shown in diagrammatic form in Figure 2.8).

Good survey design is much more difficult than it first appears (the Office for National Statistics (ONS) has taken years perfecting its General Household Survey) and it is a task that should be approached with caution. On the surface it would appear that all that needs to be done is to find out what information is needed, from whom, and then go out and collect it. In practice the process is more exacting and there are many examples of time, money and effort being wasted because of misunderstood and badly planned survey activity.

Identifying the problem

Identifying the nature of the problem can be the most difficult and the most contentious part of the whole process but if this is not achieved the whole process will be confused and the end results disappointing and even unusable. All interested parties must be involved at the earliest stage including the marketing research agency if one is to be used. Many organizations, recognizing the importance of good problem identification and analysis, will often take all involved personnel to a neutral and peaceful country hotel for a few days discussion away from unnecessary interruption and distraction. It is hoped that this will initiate intensive and unrestrained debate so that the very essence of the problem needing research can be identified.

Primary and/or secondary research

Secondary research sources should be investigated to see whether any research exists that could be of use in solving the identified problem. Most survey research will include some form of background secondary research to establish a framework for the primary research, for example identifying market size or customer numbers.

Establishing objectives

As with the whole marketing research programme, survey objectives must be clearly established and agreed at the very beginning of the process and obviously must link in with the problem to be solved. Whenever possible these objectives should be as specific and exact as possible, that is quantified over time, so that performance indicators can be set for every part of the process and then success or failure measured, both as the research programme progresses and at its completion.

Set the budget

A budget must be set indicating overall and intermediary costs. The method used for budget allocation should preferably be by the objective and task method discussed earlier on the different methods for setting the budget.

Sampling methods

Rarely will a company need information from everybody in the whole *population* or *universe* (both words mean the total number of people relevant to a particular survey, for example students in Colchester or CD buyers in Chelmsford; it does not mean the total population of the town or the country) so most marketing research will be aimed at a selected target market segment.

However it would be hideously expensive and impractical to interview all the members of the selected target market. It is also not statistically necessary to interview everybody and a representative sample can be used. A metaphor might be in the baking of a cake; as long as it is *mixed properly* tasting a small piece will supply information on the taste of the whole. This is known as the sampling frame or unit.

SAMPLING FRAME

The sampling frame is the sample that is chosen to represent the whole. The size and how the sample is chosen plus who is chosen is therefore crucial. An example of different sampling frames and their characteristics might be:

- middle-class people between the ages of 50 and 55;
- female students between the ages of 16 and 18;
- men, aged 25–35 who are interested in cars.

It is self-evident that if the wrong people are selected, the information collected will, at best, be of no use and, at the worst, cause important decisions to be made on inappropriate evidence.

If you wanted to select 100 people to represent the student population of a university of 10,000 it is crucial that the individuals chosen for the survey match the percentage of the chosen criteria types in the population. If the sample criteria considered important are:

- sex: male or female;
- full- or part-time students;
- non-mature and mature students;

and the student population at the college consists of:

- 6000 women and 4000 men;
- 3000 full-time and 7000 part-time students;
- 1000 mature students and 9000 non-mature students;

then the chosen sample of 100 must reflect the general population of 10,000 and should be:

- 60 women and 40 men;
- of these 30 would be full-time and 70 part-time;
- and 10 mature and 90 non-mature.

Simply choosing 100 students at random might cause the sample to be unrepresentative, consisting perhaps of all women or all full-time students or with no mature students.

The sample selected must be representative of the total market.

SAMPLE SIZE

The number of people who need to be interviewed will depend on the costs involved, the size of the market, the need for exactitude and the intensity of the problem that has to be solved. Large samples will give greater reliability than small samples, but the cost and the time involved increases as more people are interviewed. Statistically it has been shown that questioning a given percentage of a market can give quite accurate results when the collected information is extrapolated to the whole of that market, as long as the sample chosen is fully representative.

NOP, Marplan and Gallop Poll, are market research companies that regularly carry out voting intention polls for political parties, newspapers, TV and radio companies. They maintain that a poll sample of approx. 1500 people (if correctly chosen) can accurately reflect the views of the whole of the voting population (40 million). Similarly a sample as small as twenty can be statistically significant if chosen properly.

SAMPLING PROCEDURES

Once the sample target and size is known, decisions must be made about how the respondents are to be chosen. To obtain a representative sample a probability sample of the population should be drawn.

Probability sampling allows the mathematical calculation of 'confidence limits' and so results can be closely measured against pre-determined criteria. Non-probability sampling error cannot be measured but under certain circumstances it can be more convenient. (It is not intended to go into probability theory in any depth, but interested readers should consult the relevant literature.)

PROBABILITY SAMPLING. Probability sampling can be broken down into three different forms, each of which will be discussed in turn:

1. simple random sample;
2. group random sample;
3. area random sample.

Simple random sample. To be statistically sound there should be an equal opportunity for every person in the selected population to be chosen. A method often used, for example, is to select for interview every tenth person off the Post

Office Address File (the Post Office Address File is used by the postman or the postwoman to find and deliver mail and it consists of every possible household and small business address in the UK. The file can be used by any other organization prepared to pay a rental charge. Another similarly useful listing is the Electoral Role, consisting of all names and addresses of UK citizens able to vote). If the tenth address is unoccupied or an interview is refused, the interviewer cannot knock next door as this would distort the randomness of the survey. The unresponsive address just falls out of the survey. Bear in mind, however, that too many refusals could dilute and eventually invalidate the final results.

The BMRB National Readership Survey uses a method similar to this when setting out its sampling procedure.

Group random sample. This method is very similar to simple random sampling (and for this example will still use every tenth entry on the Post Office Address File), except that the selected population is divided into groups that reflect the different characteristics of the sampling frame. This could be age or occupation or lifestyle, etc., but for this example the type of house the respondent lives in will be used.

There are literally hundreds of headings in use but as an example the following may be identified: better-off retirement areas; agricultural dwellings; less well-off council estates; high status non-family areas; poor quality older terraced housing; multi-racial areas; etc. (house types enable research companies to estimate other characteristics as age, income, social class as these factors often correlate with house type).

One person can now be sent to interview all retirement homes, another to agricultural dwellings, another to the council houses and so on. This can make operating the survey simpler and more efficient.

Area or cluster sampling. Still using the random selection technique, area or cluster sampling divides the population up into separate geographical areas and the sample to be interviewed is then drawn from the separated areas. Using our example above, one interviewer may be given all the different households to interview within each given geographic area that make up the sampling frame, for example ten less well-off council houses; five in better-off retirement housing; five agricultural dwellings; five high status non-family homes. Each area chosen will come together to meet the demands of the overall sampling frame. This is the method used by the ONS in its general household survey.

NON-PROBABILITY SAMPLING. Non-probability sampling is probably the way that most students will undertake their research because of cost and time factors. This form of sampling lays little or no claim to any form of scientific validity and so its limitations must be clearly recognized. Non-probability sampling can be broken down into three simple types:

1. convenience sample;
2. judgement sample;
3. quota sample.

Convenience sampling. Using this method the easiest and most convenient people are selected for interview. This might be family, friends, acquaintances, or work colleagues, fellow students or people in the street. If people passing by in the street are selected care should be taken, as this method could cause problems. If, for example, a coach has just disgorged 60 old-age pensioners in the town for a day trip, alongside where the interviews are taking place and the interviewer is unaware of this, then it is possible that all those selected to be interviewed would be old-aged pensioners. This would severely skew the results.

Judgement sampling. Similar as convenience sampling except that the interviewer decides on the different types of people who need to be interviewed. This might be done intuitively or on some sort of agreed and relevant criteria such as sex, age or occupation.

Quota sampling. This time the sample is subjectively divided into groups and numbers that are considered to be representative of the population as a whole, for example twenty women, thirty men, ten students, and each quota is then interviewed.

On the question of statistical validity, it should be remembered that probability sampling can be statistically measured while non-probability cannot. Any marketing research will only be as good as the representative sample chosen for interview. If this is flawed then the whole process will be invalid.

Method of collection

The type of survey to be used will have to be decided. The choices identified earlier were postal, telephone or person-to-person. It will also have to be agreed whether to make the survey quantitative or whether to include some qualitative questions. The survey method chosen will be influenced by the objectives of the survey, the costs involved and the amount of time available. In this case the person-to-person survey method has been chosen as an example.

The questionnaire construction

Once the objectives have been drawn up, the target respondents selected and the sampling method and the method for collection agreed, the questionnaire itself can be constructed.

When constructing a questionnaire different types of questions will be used, dependent on the information required, the size of the sample, and the number of interviewers to be used. One of the biggest problems with interviewing is the influence that interviewer bias can have on the way the questions are asked and the way the replies are recorded. The overall results will be severely impaired if the same question is interpreted in different ways by different respondents.

This concern forces the questionnaire designer to make the questions quantitative, unambiguous and straightforward. Interviewer instructions should precede each question and they should be simple to ask, simple to answer and simple to record. Many research companies now use lap-top computers which the interviewer will use when conducting the interview. The replies are fed into the lap-top and then the results can be sent directly to the head office central computer through the use of a telephone link.

Qualitative questions can be asked, but they are more difficult to classify and code. Questions can be classified in two forms:

1. closed questions;
2. open questions.

CLOSED QUESTIONS

Because of the demands and limitations identified above most questionnaires are quantitative and use some form of closed question that asks for simple facts or answers in the 'yes', 'no' or 'don't know' form. This allows for little or no room for unwanted manoeuvre and distortion on the part of interviewer and interviewee.

THE CARDED QUESTION.   In some cases the question to be asked may possibly cause the respondent embarrassment. Instead of asking a person's age he or she can be shown a card and asked to state which category number they fall into, as illustrated in Figure 2.2.

THE DICHOTOMOUS QUESTION.   The dichotomous question is really just a basic yes, no, or don't know (dk) response (the 'don't know' should always be included to provide a 'home' for the uncertain, the confused or the intellectually challenged). An example is shown in Figure 2.3.

MULTIPLE CHOICE.   The 'multiple choice' question is more flexible than the dichotomous question but still only allows a selection from a list of pre-determined options. An example is given in Figure 2.4. This forces the respondent to answer with one (or more) coded examples.

SEMANTIC DIFFERENTIAL.   The semantic differential question asks respondents to mark, with a cross, along a horizontal scale of 1 to 5 how they feel about descriptive opposites. Using as an example, a group of hotels, the customer is

| **Figure 2.2** | *The carded question* |

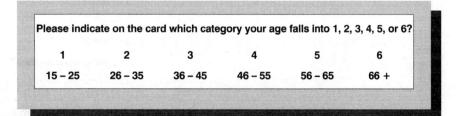

Please indicate on the card which category your age falls into 1, 2, 3, 4, 5, or 6?

1	2	3	4	5	6
15 – 25	26 – 35	36 – 45	46 – 55	56 – 65	66 +

| **Figure 2.3** | *The dichotomous question* |

	Yes	No	Dk
'Do you smoke?'	✓		
'Have you ever eaten chicken?'	✓		
'Have you a motor car?'		✓	

asked to fill in the survey question across the following sets of opposites; old-fashioned or modern; welcoming or unwelcoming; high price or low price; easy to get to or hard to get to; good service or bad service. All the crosses can be joined up revealing a company profile. This is shown in Figure 2.5.

The customer can be asked to go through the same process by looking at the nearest competitor to the initiating hotel group. Comparisons can then be made and improvements carried out if the company is found to be lacking in any important customer service areas.

IMPORTANCE SCALE. On a scale, this time of 1 to 7, with most important at one end and least important at the other, respondents are asked to mark off their preference as illustrated in Figure 2.6.

| **Figure 2.4** | *Multiple choice* |

'How did you come to work this morning? was it by'

1 car?
2 bus?
3 bicycle?
4 train?
5 walking?
6 or some other method?

Figure 2.5 | *Semantic differential*

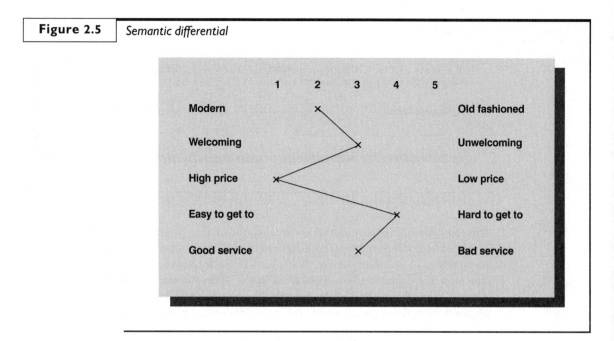

SATISFACTORY SCALE. The satisfactory scale is similar to the importance scale, but the term satisfactory is used instead. Figure 2.7 shows a typical satisfactory scale card.

CODING THE ANSWER. The closed-ended question forces the respondent to answer within well restricted parameters. This enables the market researcher to code the replies into statistically usable categories, essential if computers are to be used for storage and analysis. If we take a simple research question on smoking and ask whether the respondent smokes or not, categorizing the answer into 'yes', 'no' and 'don't know' gives us results which can be easily quantified. For example out of 1000 people who were interviewed, the following results were obtained:

- 700 (70%) said they didn't smoke,
- 200 (20%) said they did, and
- 100 (10%) said they didn't know.

Figure 2.6 | *Importance scale*

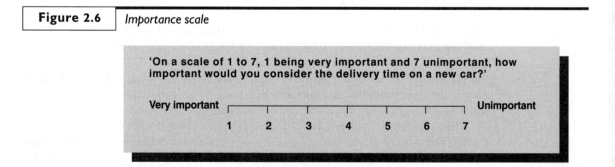

Figure 2.7	*Satisfactory scale*

'On a scale of 1 to 7, 1 being highly satisfactory and 7 unsatisfactory, where would you put the overall service of Barclays Bank?'

Highly satisfactory   Unsatisfactory

       1   2   3   4   5   6   7

This can now be extrapolated to the whole of the population and the results reported and compared with past figures, giving an increase, a decrease or a static comparison in statistical form. If we wanted to introduce other factors into the equation, for example the occupations of the different smokers and non-smokers, then it is possible to do this by putting in a question about the occupation of the respondent and assigning a code by some predetermined formula.

THE USE OF COMPUTERS. If the research analysis is to be complex one of the many available computer research software programs can be used to assist in the process. All questions are coded in the questionnaire design. When the collection is complete the coded replies are put into the computer program. The program will then allow storage, and all manner of complex cross-referencing to be done and comparisons to be made using the various coded pieces of information in many different ways.

BRMB, who undertake the National Buying Survey (this consists of over 80 pages of questions on everything including grocery purchase, DIY and gardening products, confectionery eaten, lager drunk, insurance used and holidays taken), store enormous amounts of information on computer programs obtained from the 25,000 people who answer the questionnaire every year. Such is the sophistication of the software used that if a client wishes to know the number of men in the UK who eat Jacob's Cream Crackers, whilst drinking Carling Black Label, go for their holidays in Torremolinos and think that a 'real man' is someone who can drink ten pints of beer at one session, The National Buying Survey will probably be able to tell them (at a price of course).

OPEN-ENDED QUESTIONS

There are severe limitations to the use of closed questions. In restricting the answers to yes or no, or a limited choice of a few options, the respondent is forced to answer in a manner determined by the research designer. This is unavoidable if the results are to be coded. However, people are more complex in their views and customers have opinions, feelings and attitudes about products and services that will affect the products and services they purchase.

This complexity will not be reflected by the closed question. If more information was wanted about smoking we would need to ask 'what do you think about smoking?' or 'why did you stop smoking?'. These open questions allow the respondent the opportunity to offer more information in the form of opinions, beliefs and values.

Open question are of the qualitative type identified earlier in the chapter and should be used sparingly in a questionnaire because of the difficulties in recording and classifying the answers into a usable statistical form. It could be possible to ask 100 people an open question and receive 100 different replies. The market researcher also has the difficult job of trying to write the answer down verbatim, crucial if there is to be no interview interference and meaning injected into the answers and if the analysis is to retain credibility.

CODING OPEN QUESTIONS.   One method that is used to overcome the problem of many different answers to the open question is to try to classify the multifarious results into smaller more usable categories. If we take the question 'what do you think about smoking?' it is possible to categorize maybe five different types of replies. All *similar* answers are then placed in one category or another. Where there is uncertainty, the category that comes nearest to the answer is chosen. In this way the information can be coded and used in the same way as for closed questions.

Pre-testing and implementation

All questionnaires should be pre-tested on at least ten people for ease of understanding before the survey proper is undertaken as it is inevitable that it will not work effectively first time without refinement. Experience has shown that questions, if not tested first, will be misunderstood or be seen to be unanswerable in the yes/no/dk form by some respondents within the sampling frame.

To test first allows the questionnaire to be adjusted and refined so that it works easily and effectively when used in the full sample. To print 500 questionnaires only to find they are flawed is a waste of precious time and money that could have been avoided with a little more thought and pre-testing.

IMPLEMENTATION

There comes a time when the questionnaire will be ready to be implemented. Factors to be considered here will include the following:

- the period of time for which the survey will run;
- training of interviewers;
- the actual time of day surveying will be carried out;
- the location where surveying will take place;
- informing the authorities.

TIME PERIOD OF THE SURVEY.   This might be one day, a week, a month or six months depending on the number of interviewers and the amount and type of information to be collected. The longer the length of the survey the more expensive it will probably be. The information will also take longer to analyse and digest; this could be critical if speed is of the essence.

INTERVIEWER TRAINING.   There is quite a skill in first selecting the correct person to interview and then persuading him or her to stop and answer questions. Refusal rates can be high and this can affect both interviewer morale and sample validity. Similarly the question must be asked in a consistent and uniform way between interviewers to eliminate questioner bias. So training will be needed to ensure all interviewers reach the necessary standard.

SELECTING THE CORRECT TIME AND THE CORRECT DAY.   The time of day – morning, afternoon or evening – and the day of the week – mid-week or the weekend – can affect the smooth running of the survey if time and day considerations are important. An example might be a survey with businessmen as the sampling target. In this case lunch-time during the week might be the best time to catch the required interviewees.

SELECTING THE RIGHT LOCATION.   The location selected for the interviewing must self-evidently be where the respondents are available for interview. Even so, some places are better than others and some thought should be given to this problem. In the case of the businessmen mentioned above, the location would probably be in the commercial sector of the city centre.

INFORM THE POLICE.   It is always wise to inform the police that interviewing is to take place on a certain day in a certain location. This is especially necessary if going from house-to-house. This will reassure any members of the public who might phone the police to report suspicious activity.

The questionnaire analysis

When the programme has finished the questions must be classified and analysed. If a simple questionnaire has been used this should be fairly straightforward. If it is more complex then enough resources should be allocated to make certain that every scrap of value is realized and the original objectives are met. Computer progamming will greatly assist in this task.

It is at this stage that the value of the questions will be appreciated. If the initial problem has been wrongly or inadequately diagnosed then this will now be revealed by the quality and the relevance of the results. Similarly if there has been uncertainty or misunderstanding about the appropriateness of a particular question it will be reflected in the answers that have been given. The results should be measured against pre-determined standards and their validity assessed.

PRESENTING THE FINDINGS

The findings of a research programme will need to be presented to the initiating body in both written and verbal form. Marketing research knowledge and attention span will vary from one group of people to another and this must be taken into account when offering the marketing research results to the client or company board of directors. There should be more detailed information in the written report than in the visual presentation.

The final visual presentation should be kept as simple, as interesting and as enlightening as possible, but without underestimating the intelligence of the audience. Diagrams, pie charts and bar charts should be used wherever possible and these should be colourful and simple with the minimum, but optimum, information included. This can be important because when there are competing projects within a large organization the quality of the presentation can often swing success one way rather than another.

Monitoring and control mechanisms

As with all forms of planning, control mechanisms, consisting of allocation of responsibilities and feedback reports should be built in to monitor, regulate and keep on course the marketing research programme. There should be contingency provisions allowed within the whole programme for unexpected problems that might arise. This will probably be in the form of extra budget money or more people. The overall results can finally be measured against clear, specific objectives to ascertain the success or failure of the survey.

SURVEY RESULTS NEVER USED

Despite the amount of professional support available in survey design, there exist marketing research reports commissioned by directors which are gathering dust in boardroom cupboards and which for one reason or another have never been used. The possible causes for this are many but they could include the following:

- The wrong problem was identified and the wrong objectives set at the beginning of the process, therefore nullifying the results.
- There was uncertainty about how to use the data once it was collected.
- Chief executive officers may have refused to accept research findings that contradict their pre-conceived assumptions about the market.

THE USE OF 'TEST' MARKETS TO AID MARKET RESEARCH

The 'test' market is used by different industries in different ways to help solve problems and reduce uncertainties that cannot be overcome within the organization. The market chosen to test out some aspect of the product, for example the taste, the packaging, a new brand name or the level of potential sales, should reflect the total market in every way possible, but in microcosm, that is a small exact version of the larger.

 The test market chosen must be representative of the market as a whole.

Test markets are used to attempt to eliminate the risk involved when the time comes for a full product launch. Test marketing is becoming more difficult as large supermarkets refuse to cooperate by allowing space in localized areas for this form of research. They argue that it interferes with both their corporate product range planning and the need to obtain optimum sales from every foot of display space.

Figure 2.8 illustrates in diagrammatic form the survey design process which we have just considered in detail.

THE MAJOR CONSIDERATIONS ON GOOD MARKETING RESEARCH

The following five sections discuss the major considerations that need to be taken into account when attempting good marketing research.

COSTS.   Financial considerations are major constraints on good market research. If a company has a limited amount of money to spend it should make certain that it will obtain value for money. There is also a cost–benefit consideration because there is little point in undertaking rearch at great expense if the end results do not justify the initial financial outlay.

IN-HOUSE OR OUT OF HOUSE.   Whether to buy in from an outside marketing research agency or undertake the research programme internally will depend on company resources and expertise. A marketing research agency can offer knowledge, skills and a professional approach in specialized areas unavailable to the lay-organization, and should be used if at all possible.

ACCURACY.   It can be difficult to maintain the right level of accuracy in marketing research as there are too many imponderables for the process ever to be totally objective and scientific. If the quantitative method is used only limited information can be obtained, and if the qualitative method is used there is an over-reliance on subjective collection and interpretation.

When secondary research is used time should be spent in examining, first, the survey objectives to see that these are relevant to the company's needs and, second, that the procedures used by the organization which originally collected the information match the required standards of accuracy.

Figure 2.8	*Survey design process*

```
1  Problem identification
2  Primary and/or secondary research
3  Objective setting
4  Budget
5  Sampling procedure:     sample frame
                           sample size
                           probability/non-probability
6  Methods of collection:  postal
                           telephone
                           person-to-person
                           quantitative/qualitative
7  Questionnaire design:   closed questions
                           open questions
8  Pre-testing and implementation
9  Analysis and presentation of results
10 Monitoring, feedback and control mechanisms
```

Primary research commissioned through an agency will be as reliable as the integrity and efficiency of the agency which undertakes it and this should be verified before agreeing the contract.

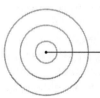 **The rule of thumb with all marketing research information is that it should be treated with caution and not a little scepticism, be used in conjunction with other techniques and should aid, not replace, the decision-making process.**

TIME.   All forms of marketing research are time consuming, some methods more so than others. Often the market can move so quickly that there is not time to spend weeks and months on endless research trying to be absolutely certain before launching a new product. This can force the marketing manager to make a decision between launching early with inadequate information, and perhaps gaining the element of surprise, or launching late with more information and risk losing the 'first to market' competitive advantage.

SECURITY.   Marketing research can create security problems and this will be more critical in some industries than others. If a firm discovers that a competitor is researching a new product that could threaten its market position, it will move heaven and earth to pre-empt or damage that launch.

The use of information technology in marketing research

The growth in information technology has given the marketing research department a powerful weapon in collecting, classifying, analysing, holding and presenting marketing information. A computer the size of a TV can now store, and use more effectively, the same amount of information that 20 years ago would have needed a computer the size of a large room.

Companies now have access to billions of items of data on every consumer and potential consumer in the country. Direct marketing companies have information on every family in the country including their address, social class, ages, dates of birth, sex, occupations, spending patterns, earnings, leisure pursuits, debts and county court judgements. With this information they are able to make contact with both their existing and new customers. They are now able to personally address and post all kinds of promotional material direct to tightly segmented interested parties as well as steering clear of those that have acquired a reputation for indebtedness.

Speed of information access is increasing with mind-numbing persistency. If we phone the Automobile Association and give them a car registration number, the operator can look at a VDU screen and call up all the relevant information on that car immediately. Barclaycard can call up an instant customer profile the moment the operator is given the card number.

Even smaller companies can buy in, rent or lease information storage and retrieval facilities on large global computer networks. The retail industry, through the use of EPOS and EFTPOS (Electronic Point of Sale and Electronic Fund Transfer Point of Sale) now have the capability to collect, analyse and store the name and address and purchasing information obtained as the customer moves through the checkout; information which can be used in future stocking, distribution and promotional activity. The major marketing research companies now have information on almost every consumer in the UK and this is increasing constantly.

Market research as a basis for decision making

There is common agreement that good marketing research is essential for making sound commercial marketing decisions. Despite this there are numerous examples of capital investment being made in projects without the support of adequate research. At the time of writing this book a private hospital costing £180 million to build has gone into liquidation only five months after opening because there was insufficient international demand for its services. This seems to be a prime example either of inadequate market research or of a mis-interpretation of the results.

Marketing research is important and no decision should be made without a healthy understanding of the factors that will influence that decision. However, to repeat the truism spelt out earlier, the marketing manager should always have a healthy scepticism towards any statistical data and should be prepared to recognize their limitations. Data should be used in conjunction with other management techniques, as an aid to decision making, not as a substitute.

Summary

Marketing information is vital to the marketing manager in making strategic and operational decisions. Too often, such information is not available, comes too late or is unreliable. Evidence that information gathering is happening in a coordinated and systematic way in a company is the existence of a Marketing Information System (MkIS). This can operate in a formal or an informal way depending on the size and the wealth of the company.

The Marketing Information System consists of four parts, internal information, marketing intelligence, marketing research and storage and analysis. All four parts coordinate so as to provide a constant supply of relevant up-to-date information about the organization's markets to the marketing manager.

Marketing research is research undertaken for a specific purpose and we looked at this process in some depth, including the difference between secondary and primary research. The sources of secondary research and different forms of primary research were then examined.

Quantitative and qualitative methods were identified and the strengths and weaknesses of the different methods available were analysed.

The factors in the marketing research survey process were identified and evaluated including problem identification and evaluation, the use of secondary as well primary information, the setting of objectives, the budget level, sampling procedure, method of collection, the structure of good questionnaire design, pretesting and implementation, analysis and presentation, and monitoring and control mechanisms.

Finally costs, whether to run the programme in-house or out-of-house, accuracy, timings, and security were identified as major concerns in the management of the marketing research process.

Questions for discussion

1. Many would argue that we now live in the 'information age'. What do you understand by this statement?

2. Give examples of the part that information will play in good marketing decision making. How would the Marketing Information System aid this process?

3. What do you consider the value of secondary research to be? Why is so much now available and what are the many sources?

4. How might competitive advantage be gained by the use of marketing intelligence?

5. What information might qualitative research obtain that quantitative research might not? Give examples.

6. Identify all the factors involved in a marketing research programme that asks you to identify why student numbers are reducing at a sixth form college.

7. What part do you see database marketing playing in the future development of marketing research?

8. Why do you think there has been a growth in the use of discussion groups in marketing research? What factors need to be considered in setting up this type of research and how valuable is it?

9. Many FMCG producers now launch a new product on to the whole market rather than first through a test market. Why do you think this might be so?

10. What kind of research would be appropriate in the following situations?

    (a) Sainsbury's exploring areas to open a new store.
    (b) An advertising agency gaining a new account working for a company that manufactures fashion clothing for the youth market.
    (c) A financial services company wanting to develop a new product for the over-fifties.

Case study

At the beginning of the year John Smithers decided that he really was fed up to the back teeth with his job on the money market and he would like to work in an area more akin to the subject of his business degree taken at Boxford University. He had left university at 22 and was lucky enough to find temporary work as a security guard in London. Although he found the job boring he really was grateful to be earning some money at last which enabled him to begin to pay off the huge mountain of debt he had accumulated through his years of study.

Then, quite out of the blue, he accidentally ran into a friend from his early school days who happened to be working for Justin and Taylor, one of the many financial institutions in the city of London that specialized in the buying and selling of currency. The outcome of this chance encounter was that John went for an interview and was offered a job as a money-broker. That was three years ago and in January he decided he had had enough and wanted out.

His degree had been in marketing and his particular interest had been in marketing research. Whilst at college he had worked for a short while for a marketing research company, standing in the local shopping centre asking selected individuals specific questions about their shopping habits. Although he had found this particular activity narrow and restrictive he had gained an insight into the overall workings of the research agency and in retrospect now felt that he would like to work in this area.

He had registered with an employment agency and after two unsuccessful interviews had managed to obtain a position as a junior research assistant with Abcock and Brown, a medium-sized research agency based just outside of London in Croydon. John was to work with a research team headed by Barbara Lacy, a partner in the organization, who had been with Abcock's since its inception.

The company specialized in all forms of marketing research, including both secondary and primary activity, and its mission proclaimed that no research task was too small, and that all undertakings would be given the same assiduity, integrity and dedicated commitment. Strict adherence to this policy had earned the organization a high reputation in the marketing world. Much of the work undertaken was for new products being launched into the retail trade and the company had gained quite a reputation in this area for the thoroughness of its methods and the integrity of the results obtained.

The first client that John was involved with was Norbury's, who happened to have its head office based in Croydon. Norbury's was an internationally recognized manufacturer of chocolate and chocolate type products. Abcock and Brown had undertaken many research projects for this company including the initial behavioural research needed before the successful launch of the now famous, niche product, 'Nigglets, toffees for people with dentures'.

The chocolate market is tremendously competitive and there is a continuous demand for new products and new markets. This imperative for new innovative products demands constant quality marketing research about both markets and customers. If the research is misguided, unrepresentative or inadequate then millions of pounds can be lost either through the launch of products that are unwanted or poorly targeted or due to the non-launch of products because the demand has been unrecognized. Abcocks is there to ensure that this problem is either eliminated or minimized.

Because of this need Norbury's had become one of Abcock's best clients and this mutual trust and respect had led to this latest research brief on customer reaction to the concept of a revolutionary new global chocolate countline (individual chocolate bar) product to be aimed specifically at pregnant women. This was the brief that John was first involved with.

The project was to cover a six-month period and would involve both secondary and primary research. A budget had been set for £250,000 and this would have to cover research undertaken in the UK and around the world. Abcock's had reciprocal agreements with foreign research agencies under which work would be undertaken on a low cost basis.

It was known that pregnant women liked chocolate but that a small percentage felt it to be unhealthy, and harmful to the baby and so had feelings of guilt when driven to consume. Norbury's had concrete scientific proof that this new chocolate product would have absolutely no harmful effects whatsoever and they would of course like this information to be eventually transmitted to the customer.

Jane Bostock was the new product development manager at Norbury's responsible for this project and John would be working with her. She had collected very little information on this particular market and so the research programme would be starting at the very beginning of the new product development process and be concerned with testing the legitimacy of the overall concept. If this initial research indicated the non-existence of a viable market then the project could be rejected before too much money was wasted. It was known that some secondary research existed on the food likes and dislikes of pregnant women, being the result of research undertaken by the US marketing research company Lawson and Cutler five years ago.

If the research seemed to identify the possibility of a market then the product development programme could proceed but in a more focused way. Under the watchful eye of Jane Bostock, the new product development team at Norbury's would develop the product further by identifying relevant benefits and alternative brand names. This second stage would need to be tested for customer acceptability as the programme rolled on, adjustments made where necessary to the product and then re-tested until it was certain (as far as this is possible) that all product developments had customer approval.

Jane Bostock needed two research briefs, one for the first stage of the process and one for the second stage. It was agreed that the brief should include, amongst other things, clear identification of the problem, research objectives, a budget, target market, methods to be used and why, timings, and monitoring and control mechanisms. She would supply a draft positioning statement for both the concept and the product. This would set down, in outline form, such things as possible product benefits, needs of the target market, how it might be promoted and so on.

Barbara Lacy felt that this new research project with Norbury's was an idea vehicle for John to test out his marketing ability and so she set him the task of coming up with answers to the following questions.

Case study questions

1. What secondary information is needed in this first stage of the marketing research programme for the new chocolate countline bar? What alternative methods might be used to obtain this information and why? What are the strengths and weaknesses of each?

2. Put together a draft brief for both stages of the research programme identifying all the factors that must be considered. Clearly relate the process to information needed by Jane Bostock. What other information might be needed by you from Norbury's to help with your task?

3. It is anticipated that both qualitative and quantitative research will be used. The qualitative research method selected will probably be the use of focus group discussions. How might you go about organizing this and what are the pitfalls you might encounter?

   The quantitative methods selected will include the use of the person-to-person survey questionnaire. Identify the process involved here, including targeting and sampling procedures, and then go on to construct an imaginary questionnaire that could be used.

4. What other factors must Norbury's consider when undertaking this form of marketing research?

Further reading

Anderson, A.H. and Chansarkar, B. (1994) *Effective Market Research*, Blackwell, Oxford.

Crouch, Sunny (1992) *Marketing Research for Managers*, Heinemann, London.

Gorton, K. and Carr, I. (1984) *Low-Cost Marketing Research*, Wiley, London.

Kent, Raymond (1994) *Marketing Research in Action*, Routledge, London.

References

AC Nielsen research: www.acnielsen.com

British Market Research Bureau: www.bmrb.mediatel.co.uk

Dun and Bradstreet (UK): www.dunandbrad.co.uk

Gallup (UK): www.gallup.com

IPSOS-RSL Research: www.rslmedia.co.uk

The Market Research Society UK: www.marketresearch.org.uk

Millward Brown: www.millwardbrown.com

Mintel: www.mintel.co.uk

MORI: www.mori.com

National Readership Survey: www.nrs.co.uk

NOP Research Group: www.nop.co.uk

Office for National Statistics: www.ons.gov.uk

The Post Office: www.postoffice.co.uk

Ray Wright: www.raynetmarketing.com

Research International: www.research-int.com

Taylor Nelson, Audits of Great Britain: www.agb.mediatel.co.uk

UK Government sites: www.open.gov.uk

3

Consumer behaviour

AIMS AND OBJECTIVES

By the end of the chapter the student should:

1. be able to identify the social, cultural, psychological and personal factors that play a part in human behaviour and appreciate how and why they influence the consumer in the purchase of products and services;

2. be aware that the reasons why people buy products and services are often complex and varied and are not always those that are first articulated;

3. recognize that the decision to buy will often involve more than one person and that each contributor must be given due consideration;

4. evaluate the need to understand the process involved in decision making so as to be able to influence and help the customer toward purchase.

Introduction

Understanding customer behaviour

In the preceding chapter we looked at the importance in marketing of marketing research. It was established that without knowledge of the outside world good marketing decisions cannot be made. Inherent in this is the need to have reliable and comprehensive information about the customer.

Complicated reasons for purchase

If an organization is to offer a product or service that customers will want to purchase, the marketing researcher must first try to discover what exact benefits will be needed. This is much harder than it first seems. People buy products for all sorts of reasons, some obvious and others not so obvious.

Customers might state that the reason they want one particular motor car rather than another is because of better petrol consumption or that they only see a motor car as a means to transport, that is to get them from A to B. However extensive research has shown that the real reason for purchase may well be more complicated than these simple functional reasons. It seems that other factors such as the need for 'status' or 'belonging' linked to deep-rooted feelings of inferiority or insecurity must be considered. If this is correct, then only if these more abstract reasons are understood can the real benefits required be clearly identified and products and services offered in the most appropriate and satisfying way.

NECESSARY TO GET AT UNDERLYING NEEDS AND CONCERNS

In order to understand the real reasons why people buy one product rather than another or one brand rather than another it is necessary to get at their underlying needs and concerns. To do this we must try to understand the many factors that influence human behaviour and which in turn will influence the buying decision. If patterns of behaviour, resulting from particular influences, can be established then this can be exploited and manipulated by the marketer to produce marketing mix offerings that exactly match the benefits required by the target market.

GENETIC AND ENVIRONMENTAL INFLUENCES

Factors influencing behaviour can be both genetic and environmental. The degree to which genetic factors, inherited ways of thinking and acting, affect personality and behavioural traits is controversial because it is so difficult to separate the genetic influences from the environmental. It is not intended to enter the debate here except to say that marketers have attempted to use categories of inherited personality types, developed by academic psychologists – introverts, extroverts, etc. – in segmenting the market and we will look at this in more detail in the next chapter.

Environmental influences on behaviour begin from the moment we are born and continue through the whole of our lives, although their effect is much weaker as we become older and more set in our ways.

 Purchase decisions are complex, multi-layered and the reasons behind them are often not immediately obvious. Adequate and sophisticated market research must be undertaken so as to discover both overt and latent underlying needs.

Factors influencing behaviour

The factors that influence consumer behaviour will now be examined under the following headings:

1. cultural influences;
2. social influences;
3. personal influences;
4. psychological influences.

Some of these influences might be considered to be environmental, cultural and social, whilst others might be considered to be a combination of both external and genetic, that is personal and psychological.

Cultural influences

The culture of a society consists of the common attitudes, beliefs, ways of living, thinking and acting, and language which are passed on from one generation to another by way of social institutions such as the family, schools and the workplace. Taken together with the infrastructure, buildings and artefacts handed down from generation to generation, this all contributes to an overall common perception of the world that will vary from ethnic group to ethnic group and from nation to nation.

SUB-CULTURE

Sub-cultures can exist within the overall culture of a society. They are manifested by a minority way of living and behaving, adopted by groups of people, that is in some way different from the accepted widespread culture of the majority of the population. The sub-culture can be a more or less permanent way of living, can affect just a small or a larger part of a group member's life and tends to be open to change, as customs and practices change, to meet and adapt to new circumstances.

This is why we hear sociologists talk of a 'youth culture', with values which are different from the rest of society and which young people adopt, in common with others with similar needs, for short or longer periods in their lives; examples of this include such groups as Rockers, Skinheads, Crusties, Skins, Goths, and New Age Travellers. Students can also be said to have their own sub-culture which they adopt whilst at school, college and university. Other examples of sub-cultures with their own beliefs and values include gay and lesbian groups; black groups; vegetarian groups; Freemasons; ballroom dancing groups; etc. – all examples of like-minded people coming together and developing their own sub-cultures.

RELIGION

To a lesser or greater extent, religion imposes certain ways of living and behaving on its followers that could be considered to be sub-cultures. Christianity, Buddhism, Islam, Hinduism, Judaism, as well as religious sects such as Rastafarianism, the Church of Scientology and Hare Krishna, all have codes of behaviour its adherents are expected to abide by. Research shows that religion is less influential in Western society than in the past, especially among the young.

CULTURE, SUB-CULTURE AND MARKETING

Marketers need to understand the culture and sub-culture of different societies because people from different cultures and different religions will often want vastly different product offerings to satisfy similar needs. A thirsty woman in England may want a cup of tea, in France a bottle of Perrier water or glass of wine, in Italy a small cup of coffee, in Australia an iced lager, in the USA a Coca-Cola and so on.

In some cultures and sub-cultures products may only be acceptable if presented in a particular form, or made available in a certain way, for example tea without milk or sugar, baked beans in a jar rather than in a tin, curry with chips, raw fish, ice-cream in a bread roll, or meat only in soya bean form. Other products may be acceptable in one culture but not in another, for example pork, men's magazines, Kosher food and marijuana. This can go so far as to include product content, colours, packaging, brand names and wording, and the form of promotion undertaken.

Sub-cultures are a fertile area for selective 'niche' marketing and many forward thinking companies have successfully taken advantage of this (the idea of the 'niche' market will be discussed later, but basically it is a small, specialized portion of the market. Examples are the growth of the so called 'Pink Market' for gay and lesbian products, which can now be seen at their own exhibition held at Earls Court, or the marketing of specialized hair products for young black people.)

In marketing abroad a company has to make decisions on whether to sell its products in the same way in every country or adapt each product to the possible disparate cultural demands of each country. The sale of alcohol is forbidden in many Muslim countries so this would restrict any form of direct entry. In other countries beer is not the traditional drink. Draught bitter, while popular in the UK, is almost unheard of in Germany where bottled lager is the largest seller. In France some female sexual stereotypes, unacceptable in the UK, are used to advertise products. In the UK beer drinking takes place mainly in the traditional 'pub', in France it is in a bar or restaurant, whilst in Sweden most drinking is done at home.

Social influences

There are a wide range of social influences that will affect customer behaviour. We will begin by considering social class, before going on to look at institutions, norms, life groups, roles and status.

SOCIAL CLASS

Although becoming much less of a controlling influence than it used to be, the social class we are born into will have an effect on the type of person we are and the sorts of products and services we like to purchase. In the UK three broad areas can be identified – working class, middle class and upper class (a more detailed classification is given in the next chapter).

It is argued that the class system is historically much stronger and more pronounced in England than elsewhere in the world. This may well be true but social class in some form or other exists in most countries around the world. Social class, in simple terms, puts people into categories by their occupation, the level of income earned, the amount of capital they have been able to accumulate and the type of lifestyle they lead.

SOCIAL CLASS AND MARKETING

At each social class level prospective consumers will probably be born with different advantages, motivated by different needs, and driven by different expectations. This in turn can lead to a demand for different products, bought according to class, that will satisfy these needs. Likewise the same product may be demanded by both the working and the middle class but for different reasons. This will affect both the type of product produced and the way that it is distributed and promoted.

Although gradually diminishing, there are many products and services that are still marketed according to social class. This includes tobacco, alcoholic drinks, holidays, groceries, entertainment and newspapers.

SOCIAL INSTITUTIONS

Social institutions exist whatever the level and development of the society. These include basic social institutions like the government, family, school, college or university, church and place of work, as well as voluntary institutions such as social clubs, the Boy Scouts or Girl Guides, a football club or golf club and the Woman's Institute. All impose ways of thinking and forms of behaviour on their members.

The most important of the above is the influence of the family and especially the mother. Many behaviourists argue that early upbringing, from birth until seven, is the period when personality and attitudes are predominantly formed.

SOCIAL NORMS

Social 'norms' are expected ways of living and behaving that are imposed on the members of a social group or sub-group by the social institutions identified above. Methods of indoctrination used range from, the informal forms that might take place within the family, to the formal forms that happen at school or college. The mass media is also seen as a major player in this process.

Refusal to conform to the expected norms (normal way of living) of the group can lead to many different levels of reproach ranging from mild disapproval to indictment under the law leading to a term of imprisonment. In the main, coercion is not necessary as most people would rather feel part of a group and conform than not conform and risk being isolated or ostracized. People will want to purchase products that reinforce this sense of 'togetherness'. The skill on the part of the marketer is to achieve this whilst still allowing the customer a sense of their own individuality.

REFERENCE GROUPS

As well as the influence of the institutional factors above; we tend to develop attitudes and ways of living which are the same as groups of people, known as reference groups, that we would like to be associated with. This might be the group of friends we always hang around with, the middle class people next door, the members of the squash club, a group of friends at university or the people we drink with at the pub. People will often want to purchase products or services to conform to, or to impress, a particular reference group.

LIFE ROLES

We adopt or are ascribed many roles in life including: son or daughter, father or mother, sister or brother, husband or wife, lover, bread winner, team captain, worker or manager and so on. In any one lifetime many roles will be played, either concurrently or consecutively, as we grow older and move into different relationships. All roles have ways of behaviour attached that will affect consumer purchase patterns and so must be of concern to the marketing manager.

STATUS

The position held in relationship to others can confer elements of power, privilege and respect. Different status will be associated with particular types of behaviour. So the secretary of the golf club will be expected to dress and behave in a certain way as will the student who becomes elected union president. The sales manager has a higher status than the ordinary salesman or woman and he or she would expect this to be reflected in the type of car driven, for example a BMW for the sales manager and a standard Ford Mondeo for the salesman. The bank manager might go on holiday to the Bahamas whilst the bank cashier might go to the Costa Del Sol.

There is no doubt that all the institutions and concepts identified above will have, to a lesser or greater extent, an affect on human development and so will greatly influence both the reasons behind the purchase as well as the actual products and services purchased.

SOCIAL INFLUENCES AND MARKETING

As with culture, social institutions (family, school, work, etc.) and social constructs (norms, reference groups, roles and status) create the basis for present and future patterns of behaviour. Knowledge and an understanding of these influences is essential and will help the marketer develop products and services desired by the consumer and thereby influence both immediate and future behaviour. Membership of the more informal institution can shape and change behaviour as belonging imposes some form of conformity demand. Again knowledge of this will assist the company in the identification of wanted benefits and product development.

There are many products where market research has shown that the purchase has been influenced by the factors we have just identified. Examples include:

- *Family upbringing* – soap powder: women will loyally continue to buy Persil because it was the washing powder always used by their mother.

- *Reference groups* – fashion clothes: Levi 501s and Doc Martin Boots are purchased because these may be associated with the reference group most admired.

- *Different role needs* – chocolates: different types are bought as presents for others dependent on the particular role being 'acted' out, for example the role of husband – 'Black Magic' for his wife; the role of son – 'Milk Tray' for his mother; the role of father – 'Smarties' for his daughter; the role of office manager – 'Quality Street' for the staff.

- *Status needs* – cars: as identified above, different types of cars reflect different levels of status. For some customers Rolls Royce and Bentley will have a higher status than BMW, Mercedes and Jaguar and for some, these latter makes will have a higher status than Ford, VW and Lada. For many salesmen and sales-women the type of company car they are given is a very contentious issue being the most important indicator of both their status within the company and their status compared with salespersons in other companies.

So it can be seen that all these products – soap powder, fashion clothes, choco-lates and cars (and most other products too) – must be produced and marketed in a way that reflects all the different customer needs otherwise there is every prob-ability that the product will not be purchased, or will be purchased from a more enlightened competitor.

Personal influences

There are many personal influences and circumstances that will affect our buying behaviour in an ever-changing pattern. This will include such things as:

- *Age* – 1, 5, 10, 20, 30, 40, 50, 60 or 70 yrs old.
- *The stage in our life cycle* – whether we are a teenager, living with a partner, married, have children, retired, etc.
- *Occupation* – teacher, banker, machine operator, solicitor, etc.
- *The type of life style we pursue* – home loving, out every night, sports fanatic, health freak, etc.

- *Our personality* – out-going, reserved, introspective, obsessively tidy, depressive, etc.
- *Level of education and intellect* – Low, medium or high.

PERSONAL INFLUENCES AND MARKETING

Most of the personal factors identified here will develop and change as we move through life, leading to the demand for different products and services as our individual circumstance change. Below are a few examples:

- a skate-board at 15 years compared to a wheelchair at 80 years;
- disposable nappies when the baby first arrives;
- more expensive holidays for parents, Hawaii rather than Butlins when the children eventually grow up and leave home;
- technical books for a teacher, sports equipment for someone working in the leisure industry;
- the home-lover will spend more on DIY products for the house, the socialite more on entertainment and eating out and the obsessively health conscious more on health products.

Psychological influences

As well as cultural, social and personal factors, the marketing practitioner must also take into account individual and group psychological factors (here psychology being defined as a study of the mind or the 'psyche'). This will include complicated concepts such as personal motivation, emotions, perception, beliefs, attitudes, interests and opinions as well as concepts of what constitutes 'Self'.

MARKETING AND PSYCHOLOGICAL CONCEPTS

As competition has increased and more products have appeared on the market the customer has become ever more demanding in the type of products and services he or she is prepared to purchase. It has been argued throughout this chapter (and throughout Chapters 1 and 2) that the marketer has to keep pace in understanding and anticipating these demands or be overtaken by the competition.

However this task is now more difficult than ever before. This is because the reasons behind these different demands have become much more complex than they were in the past. Once upon a time influencing factors such as social class, family background and religion were strong indicators behind the reason for purchase. So a working class daughter would be happy to use the same brand of nappy because mother had used it or a son would drink the same brand of bitter as his father. Similarly a Jewish boy would eat the same things as his father or a Hindu girl would dress the same way as her mother.

However, over the last few decades factors such as social class, family background and religion have become much less important as influencing factors behind consumer behaviour. Increased affluence has led to a blurring of the social class divide so that less people now see themselves as working class than in the past, thus minimizing the affect that this might have had on product and service purchase.

Likewise, as society has become more secular, religious demands no longer have the same control over children as it did over their parents, for example a Muslim boy will want to dress in the same way and go to the same night spots as his Protestant friend and a Hindu girl will want to eat the same food and play the same music as her Roman Catholic boyfriend.

This has led the marketer to look toward psychological factors, both conscious and unconscious, as determinants of purchasing behaviour. Many marketing techniques have now been developed to get to a root understanding of concepts such as attitude, motivation, perception and inner-most thoughts and desires. Some of these were discussed in the chapter on marketing research under the heading of 'qualitative research'.

FREUD AND THE THEORY OF THE SUBCONSCIOUS.   Although much of what Sigmund Freud wrote is now open to criticism, his basic concept of a subconscious area of the mind that can affect behaviour in an indirect way still enjoys enormous influence amongst marketing academics and practitioners alike. Marketers trying to understand the reasons why people act the way that they do (often in contradiction to what they say) will now often look for answers in that part of the mind, below the level of conscious thought, that may influence behaviour in a manner unknown to the decision maker.

THE SUBCONSCIOUS AND MARKETING.   To try to help the reader to understand how subconscious drives can affect product purchase decisions we can apply the theory to the following marketing example.

A consumer wanting to buy a gold watch states the reason for the purchase is the need to tell the time. Now the salesperson can accept on face value that this is the reason for purchase and sell the benefits of the watch in terms of its accuracy and ease of use in doing just this.

However, followers of Freud might want to argue that this overt and seemingly obvious reason for wanting to buy the watch may not be the real reason behind the desire for purchase. They might forward the proposition that the real reason for the purchase was not the superficially apparent one given in good faith by the customer, that is to tell the time, but a more entrenched, subconscious-driven reason, of image-enhancement to boost a deep-rooted sense of inferiority and low self-esteem.

If this sub-conscious reason were the real benefit demanded then this would of course affect the way in which the product would need to be promoted and sold. The salesperson would have to impress the customer with the idea that to wear the watch would lead to the benefit of image-enhancement and status recognition by others rather than accuracy in telling the time. Doubters in this theory might want to look at how some watches are advertised, for example Ellesse watches have been advertised with a young, attractive man and woman in one another's arms, attired only in swimwear, with the slogan 'designed to perform' (what has this got to do with telling the time, we might ask).

INTELLECTUAL, EMOTIONAL AND INSTINCTIVE INFLUENCES

Public commentators, as long ago as the Greek philosopher Plato, have considered the different ways that people have of 'thinking' about their needs and wants and desires. This is because people do not all seem to think in the same way when coming to decisions. Some people take their time and ponder long and hard before deciding, whilst others take no time at all and act almost on impulse. As with other influences, marketers are interested in the thinking process because they want to try to understand what is going on so that benefits can be offered that take these processes into account.

In a simple and very general way these concerns discussed here can be condensed into a theory that, when making decisions, people 'think' at three different levels (Figure 3.1):

1. *intellectual and rational thought:* thinking with the use of the brain and so might be considered to be the highest level of thought;
2. *emotional thought:* 'thinking' with the heart and might be considered as mid-level thought;
3. *instinctive thought:* 'thinking' with the gut and might be considered the lowest level of thought.

PEOPLE THINK AT DIFFERENT LEVELS. It can be argued that individuals think and act using varying degrees of intellect, emotion and instinct. Some people think and act more at the highest level, some at the mid-level, while others think and act more at the lowest level. The level of thought employed will depend on both genetic and environmental factors as well as the importance of the decision itself.

INTELLECTUAL, EMOTIVE AND INSTINCTIVE INFLUENCES AND MARKETING. We would all like to think that we make decisions based on pure rational analysis, but research shows

| **Figure 3.1** | *The three levels of thought* |

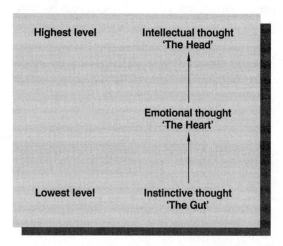

this not to be so. In fact it is argued that most consumer decisions are made for emotive rather than intellectual and functional reasons. Examples of this can be shown by taking three disparate products, a motor car, perfume and chocolates.

- A *motor car* might be bought for purely rational functional reasons – as a means of transport to get from A to B. In the case of a company purchase this will probably be the case. However, the evidence seems to show that a consumer purchase of a car is based more on emotive factors such as status and sex appeal, known collectively as 'feel good factors'.

- *Perfume* is purchased by women for predominantly emotional reasons. It offers a woman high status among friends of her own sex and makes her feel that she is more attractive to the opposite sex. A woman may well have different types of perfume for different occasions – a utility perfume for everyday use and a deluxe version for special occasions.

- *Chocolates* are often purchased instinctively while passing through the super-market checkout. It is because of this 'impulse' factor that parent pressure groups have succeeded in persuading some of the large supermarkets to remove sweets from the checkout areas and out of the reach of demanding children.

MASLOW'S HIERARCHY OF NEEDS

Management and marketing practitioners have adopted and adapted the concept of a hierarchy of needs originally developed by the American writer Abraham Maslow. In simple terms it is posited that people are motivated by different needs depending on personality type, the decision that has to be made and the situation pertaining. The categorized needs are identified in rank order from the lowest to the highest. These are, at the lowest level, bodily or physiological needs, then safety or security needs, social or belonging needs, status or power needs and, at the highest level, self-becoming or spiritual needs.

The theory is that needs must be satisfied in ascending order from the lower level to higher. Higher order needs cannot be addressed until lower order needs are satisfied (Figure 3.2). Individuals, groups and countries will be at different motivation levels dependent on the level of economic development, industrial activity, political stability and social and cultural demands. This graphical repre-sentation of Maslow's theory is also known as the triangle of needs.

MASLOW AND HIS INFLUENCE ON MARKETING.   Whilst not fully accepting the notion of a priority needs hierarchy, research undertaken by many advertising agencies has shown that there are groups of people who make purchasing decisions based on the need to satisfy some form of basic emotional need. The different need cate-gories are stronger in some consumers than others.

Therefore, some consumers with a strong basic safety or security need will want one type of product offering, for example a Volvo or Guardian Insurance, while others with a strong basic status or recognition need will want another, for example a Porsche or American Express Card. In the same way, some consumers, driven by basic physiological needs, will want one type of newspaper, for example the *Sun* or *Sunday Sport*, while, others driven by self- becoming or spiritual needs, will want another, for example the *Guardian* or the *Catholic Herald*.

Figure 3.2	*Maslow's triangle of needs*

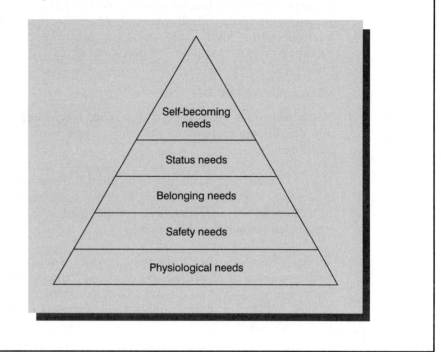

Similarly, countries may be at different levels of need on the Maslow hierarchy and so, for the marketer, either the emphasis will have to be on different products or the product will have to be sold differently to address these different needs. An example might be a bicycle sold for its environmental benefit in the UK (a self-actualizing need), whilst in China, where it is an essential form of transport, it might be sold for its dependency benefit (a security need).

The importance of understanding all the influences on buying behaviour

Marketing is about understanding customers so as to produce products that will satisfy their needs and wants. Superficially this might seem to be simply a case of talking to consumers and asking them questions. However the process is much more complicated than this because people tend to display complex, deep and, at times, seemingly irrational modes of behaviour.

Consumers may well say one thing and do another. One product, assured of success by research, for example Cadbury's boxed chocolates for men, will fail while another launched with relative disinterest will be spectacularly successful, for example Philias Fogg Exotic Snacks.

If an organization is to be successful in marketing the behavioural influences identified above, cultural, social, personal and psychological factors must be investigated, analysed and related to buying behaviour. This analysis must be undertaken through the use of the most sophisticated and professional methods of marketing research available. Only when the importance of carrying out this analysis thoroughly is understood can meaningful products and services be produced that really satisfy root needs and wants.

NEEDS, WANTS AND DEMAND

Needs, wants and demand tend to be used interchangably throughout this book and the differences between the three terms as used in marketing will now be identified.

NEEDS. 'Needs' are basic inputs required to restore equilibrium to the human condition. Needs will include physical needs such as hunger, thirst, cold reduction, social needs such as comfort and love, or spiritual needs such as knowledge and self-enlightenment.

WANTS. Wants are the products or services required to reduce and satisfy the need requirement identified above. The specific 'wants' required to satisfy the basic need will vary from country to country, from region to region and person to person. Wants tend to be driven by the influencing factors discussed throughout this chapter. Examples are:

- I am hungry, I want a bowl of rice; a McDonald's Hamburger; a Chinese take-away; pie and mash; a dinner at the Savoy.
- I am thirsty, I want a glass of water; a Pepsi; a Holsten Export; a Pina-Colada; a pint of scrumpy; a glass of Champagne.
- I am cold, I want a Paka-mac; a new coat from Next; a Christian Dior dress.
- I need company, I want to go to the market cafe; the Red Lion; Stringfellows Night Club; Caesars Palace, Las Vegas.
- I need spiritual uplift, I want to read Jeffrey Archer's new novel; Listen to Rod Stewart or Cliff Richard; go to the Royal Opera House.

Confusion between needs and wants can cause a company to imagine that their product is needed, rather than just wanted as a 'need satisfier'. If a better 'need satisfier' comes along then the customer will move from one product to another.

A classical marketing example of this is typewriter companies which thought that people 'needed' typewriters when what they 'needed' was something to write their letters. This left them unprepared for competition in the form of the computer word processor. Similarly the need is for a 'hole maker' not a Black and Decker electric drill.

DEMAND. Effective demand only exists when there is money available to pay for the product. Many people in under-developed countries 'need' basic commodities such as food, shelter and clothing. Many people may want a Rolls-Royce or an eight-bedroom mansion but few can actually afford one. Ultimately it is 'effective' demand that the marketer is interested in, not needs and wants.

Other factors influencing behaviour

There are other influences on buyer behaviour, especially at the decision-making stage and these will now be discussed.

The decision-making unit (DMU)

As well as considering all the many factors already identified that will affect buying behaviour it is important to realize that there is often more than one person involved in the decision-making process. In fact a whole string of people may be involved. It is all very well identifying the needs of the end-consumer and then marketing the product with benefits to meet those needs, if that end-consumer is the one who is going to make the decision to purchase. However, products are often bought by one person and used by another.

THE CUSTOMER AND THE CONSUMER MAY WELL BE DIFFERENT PEOPLE

An organization must identify all of the people who might be involved in the decision to purchase one of their products. They must then prioritize and decide who will be the target of its marketing effort. Using the example of children's toys, who should this be? Should it be the end-user – the child – or the person who makes the purchase decision – the mother or father – or should it be a combination of both child and parents?

The answer is that marketing research must be undertaken to discover who will have the most influence on the final decision. This will vary from product to product and industry to industry. In the case of children's toys there tends to be an element of both child and parent participation, dependent on the product and the age of the child. Legislation also restricts how products are marketed to children.

OTHER PEOPLE INVOLVED IN DECISION MAKING

To complicate the matter even further the customer may not be the purchaser and there might well be a number of others involved in the process. The group of people who might possibly be involved in the decision-making process are known as the decision-making unit (DMU).

The decision-making unit (DMU) consists of the following categories:

- the *suggester*: the original person or group suggesting the product or service;
- the *influencer*: any person or group who can in any way affect the purchasing decision;
- the *decision maker*: the person or group who has the power to make the actual decision to purchase;
- the *buyer*: the person or group who actually makes the purchase;
- the *end-user*: the person or group who will use the product.

The idea of the *gatekeeper* might be added to this list. This term is used for anybody who stops the marketing person getting to others in the decision-making unit. This might well be a doctor's receptionist, a parent of a child or a managing director's secretary.

All the roles listed above, known collectively as the decision making unit, could be carried out by one person or they could be played by a number of people.

Only if all the contributors to the decision-making process are known can the marketing department, after marketing research, identify needs and offer different benefits to satisfy these needs.

The decision-making process (DMP)

Throughout this chapter it has been argued that to be competitive a professional organization must understand, as far as possible, all the influences on buyer behaviour and also be able to identify the many different people involved in the decision-making process. With this understanding the marketing manager will be able to develop products and services that, theoretically, are tailored to satisfy needs at whatever level of consciousness. But the buyer also goes through a process of stages as he or she moves from product unawareness through to purchase. Again this process must be identified so that the marketer can offer help and support to the customer at every stage, moving them towards purchasing a relevant product or service from the company product portfolio.

The decision-making process (DMP) moves the buyer through six stages, from a state of unawareness through to purchase and post-purchase feeling, and this can be seen in Figure 3.3.

As customers move from one stage to another, different resources can be allocated so that the customer is moved forward again to the next stage in the process and so on to a successful conclusion. The company should be aware that its different consumers may be at different stages and so different approaches may be necessary.

THE DMP AND THE PURCHASE OF A NEW WASHING MACHINE

The DMP should be understood so that the company can manipulate and allocate the correct resources, hopefully persuading the customer to buy its products. How this process is put into practice is now shown with regard to the purchase of a new washing machine.

STAGE 1: PROBLEM RECOGNITION. The movement from problem unawareness to problem awareness can be stimulated either by the producer or the customer. Initially there is problem unawareness until:

| **Figure 3.3** | *The decision-making process (DMP)* |

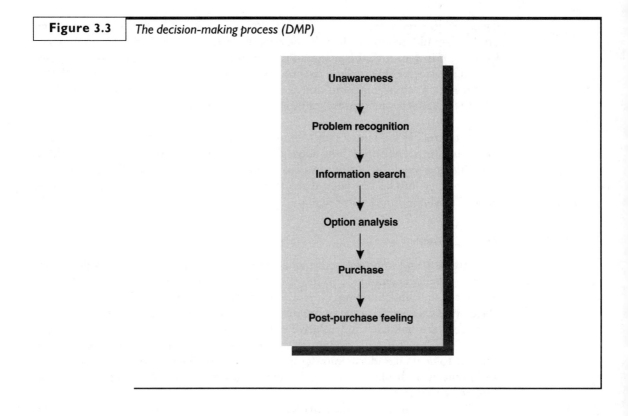

1. the washing machine breaks down and is too expensive to repair, or
2. the prospective customer feels that the washing machine is outdated and a newer model is required. In either case the manufacturer can influence the situation by some form of promotion.

STAGE 2: INFORMATION SEARCH.   The customer searches around for product information. The task for the company here is to make certain that current and adequate information is available. This may be by TV or press advertising or point-of-sale material.

STAGE 3: OPTION ANALYSIS.   At this stage the prospective customer will require more detailed information. The company task here is to make certain that this information is readily available when and where the customer wants it. This can be achieved by a head office information service, leaflets and point-of-sale material available at the retail outlet, and product knowledge training for retail staff so that they are able to inform and persuade the customer who is shopping around for information.

STAGE 4: PURCHASE.   When the customer is prepared to purchase, the required product must be available in the form required. It must also be adequately demonstrated and delivered on time if required.

STAGE 5: POST-PURCHASE FEELING OR COGNITIVE DISSONANCE.   Once delivered the product should be easy to install and seen to function as promised by the manufacturer. If it does not, this can lead to 'cognitive dissonance' which is a negative post-purchase feeling, giving rise to customers asking 'Why did I pay all this money for a washing machine that is sub-standard? I want my money back.' Fast, effective after sales service can minimize this negative reaction.

It is also possible for a customer to move back through the DMP if problems arise, for example a customer may have collected information on a new washing machine, analysed the options available and decided on a particular make only to find that that model has been discontinued. This might cause the customer to begin the whole process over again.

TYPES OF DMP

The intensity and importance attached to the DMP will vary across products and services. As decisions made in life will vary from the trivial and mundane to the important and life-changing, so product and service purchase decisions can take place across the same range of importance levels. Some decisions, like buying tea or coffee, are habitual and relatively unimportant whilst others, like buying a house, are almost unique and much more important. Frequency of purchase, the amount to be paid and the knowledge (or lack of knowledge) of the product class and brand will all play a part in deciding the importance level attached by the consumer to the DMP.

This level of importance attached to a buying decision must be known because this will affect the level of consumer problem solving involved. This in turn will influence the way the product should be marketed. The different importance levels attached to the decision-making process, with the attendant customer problem-solving task are identified in the discussion below.

THE DECISION-MAKING PROCESS, LEVEL OF IMPORTANCE AND PROBLEM SOLVING INTENSITY

LOW IMPORTANCE; VERY LITTLE PROBLEM SOLVING.   This situation will be the case for products bought on a regular basis, probably out of habit. Products in this category will include FMCG goods such as the weekly groceries, newspapers and cigarettes. The customer expects these types of products to be readily and easily at hand and may get upset if the layout position is changed or the product is out of stock (this is especially true in supermarkets where customers can get very upset if layout changes mean that he or she can no longer easily find a particular tomato ketchup or hair shampoo).

MEDIUM IMPORTANCE; LIMITED PROBLEM SOLVING.   At the second level of importance higher priced products, bought less frequently than FMCG goods will be included – such items as clothing, electrical products, furniture, etc. There will be much less of a problem if the purchase is a straightforward replacement of an existing product and brand rather than a new product or an unknown or little known brand.

HIGH IMPORTANCE; INTENSIVE PROBLEM SOLVING.   At this level are products bought very infrequently, perhaps only once or twice in a lifetime. The products are probably very highly-priced, with longer term repercussions. Examples include the purchase of financial services, such as life cover or a pension, a house, a new car or even a holiday.

OTHER CONTRIBUTORY FACTORS.   The level of importance and the problem-solving intensity will vary from customer group to customer group. Some people change their cars every year, others buy only once every ten years. A *new* product being bought at any level will cause increased problem solving, as will the introduction of a new brand.

   Only if the complexities and subtleties of the process are understood (as they relate to specific products) can the marketing department know its task and develop strategies to deal with the process. This will include making information available at the right time and in the appropriate manner.

Organizational buying behaviour

Throughout this chapter on influences on buying behaviour we have tended to concentrate more on consumer markets rather than on business markets, where one business sells products or services to be used by another. This area of marketing is known as 'business to business marketing' or 'industrial marketing'. This definition does not include companies that sell to retailers or wholesalers for onward sales to the end-customer, for example Kelloggs; Mars; Hotpoint; Procter and Gamble.

   Examples of business to business organizations include: Rank Xerox business systems; ICI who, amongst other things, develop and market a whole range of chemicals for use in industry; TNT, the worlds largest transport business; Continental Can who make all kinds of packaging for industrial use; Pilkington, the manufacturer of glass related products.

SOME BASIC DIFFERENCES

Many of the concepts identified here will relate equally to a buyer in a business organization as they do to consumers. However, many of the influences are not the same because there are some basic differences between consumer and organizational buying behaviour. The main differences are now briefly considered.

RATIONAL REASONS.   In an organization a buyer is purchasing products or services for the company rather than for themselves, family, friends or relatives. The reasons for the purchase therefore should be *rational* and linked to the clear operational needs of the organization.

EMOTIONAL REASONS.   In consumer marketing the reasons for purchase tend to be based more on *emotional* needs such as the need for security, the need to feel wanted or for status needs. This is not the case in organizational purchasing.

SELLER/BUYER RELATIONSHIP CLOSER.   In business to business marketing the relationship between the buyer and the seller will be closer as they are fewer in number, the products bought will tend to be more expensive and they will probably see one another on a regular basis as contracts for purchase are established.

EASE OR DIFFICULTY OF IDENTIFYING THE DMU.   In consumer markets the DMU is usually easy to establish, for example if a husband and wife enter a shop to buy a new bed the skilled salesperson should have little problem identifying which of the two is the decision maker.

In business markets the DMU can be much more complex and difficult for the salesperson to unravel, for example if National Westminster wanted to buy a new computer system for its invoicing process the DMU could involve many different people within the organization including the users of the system, the budget holder, advisors and designers, the board of directors, etc.

Summary

People buy products and services for many reasons. Initially we might believe the obvious reason, that is for the function the product performs. A motor car is purchased as a means of transport to take us from A to B, clothes are bought to keep us cool in the summer and warm in the winter, and drinks to satisfy us when thirsty. However experience has shown the marketer that there are many reasons, other than the functional, why a customer will want to buy one product rather than another.

The modern consumer is a complicated human being purchasing products so as to satisfy a multiplicity of needs. To be able to sell its products a company must produce benefit offerings that match these differing needs. The needs may be overt and easily identifiable or latent and more difficult to comprehend.

This calls for an ever more sophisticated understanding of consumer behaviour and the many factors that have influenced this behaviour in the course of individual development and growth from childhood through to mature adult. Culture, sub-culture, social class and religion all exert the broadest and deepest influence, indoctrinating the attitudes and beliefs and ways of living of the society and sub-groups we are born into. Family, school, reference groups, work groups, roles and status all work to inculcate particular ways of viewing the world. Other influences include age, occupation, lifestyle, economic circumstances, person- ality, motivation, perception, learning and individual attitudes and beliefs. All of these factors will affect and influence the products and services we may wish to purchase.

The concept of thinking at three levels was discussed and the levels identified as the rational, the emotional and the instinctive. Product choices will be made with the emphasis on any one of these three levels, or on a varying combination of all three. Generally, an organizational buyer will purchase for rational reasons and a consumer for emotional. It was recognized that the strength and relevance of these influences will probably vary from individual to individual, from region to region and from country to country.

The differences between needs, wants and demands were then identified.

It was recognized that the decision to purchase may be made by one person or, as is more likely to be the case, by more than one person. This was introduced through the concept of the decision making unit (DMU).

As well as understanding the DMU the marketer also needs to understand the complex and intricate processes the customers go through when making decisions. This was discussed using a decision-making process model (DMP).

Finally we looked at the different levels of importance that are attached to different forms of buying decisions.

Questions for discussion

1. Jesuit priests have a saying: 'Give us a child to the age of seven, and we will have that child for life'. What do you think that they mean by this and how does this relate to marketing?

2. Do you think that social class still exists? What do we mean by social class? Do you think that all countries have some form of social class and if you do what are the underlying similarities?

3. How might the upbringing we had affect the type of products we purchase?

4. What do you understand the following terms to mean: roles; norms; status; reference groups; sub-groups. How do they relate to marketing?

5. What do you understand by the theory of the unconscious? Why is this concept important in marketing and how might it be used?

6. Can you identify different reasons why we might want to purchase products and services? Use different product/service groups when giving your reasons.

7. What types of cultural differences would a food company need to consider if marketing products around the world?

8. How many different people might be involved in the purchase of the following products:

   - a house;
   - a new sewage works for the local community;
   - a family holiday;
   - an ice-cream?

   How is this linked to the concept of the DMU and why is it important to identify and understand these different groups?

9. The prospective customer may be at different levels on the DMP. How will this affect the different elements of the marketing mix? How valuable are these types of models?

10. People purchase products for functional reasons and the marketing behavioural specialist unnecessarily complicates the buying process. Discuss.

Case study

O'Henry's had been manufacturing children's products for over 35 years and now marketed a whole range of products in over 20 different countries. The organization was renowned for the variety, quality and the craftmanship of its products and wherever in the world children's products were discussed O'Henry's was inevitably mentioned. The total group turnover in 1998 had been over £35 million.

The company came from very humble origins, beginning in the backroom of a cottage in the Yorkshire village of Smetton, the home of Sheila and Henry Trollop. Sheila Bassford had always seemed to have a creative and imaginative nature from a very early age and her parents and school teachers had encouraged the natural talent she seemed to have in painting, needlework and later on in sculpture. She seemed to have a flair for any form of design and could turn her hand to almost any form of creative activity.

As she grew older she would spend more and more of her time making various artefacts for friends, relatives and the different institutes that she was involved with. This would include such things as paintings for friends at Christmas, dolls' houses for the Oxfam shop, dolls' prams for the church raffle and the scenery for the local drama group.

However it wasn't until she courted and married Henry Trollop that she turned her hand to making children's toys in any form of commercial way.

Henry was a typical Yorkshire man, dour, plain speaking, hard working and as honest as the day was long. He was the son of the village blacksmith and had acquired the business when his father had retired.

As the traditional blacksmith's work with horses diminished Henry steered the business more towards areas where he wisely believed that demand would grow. This covered all kinds of products that could be made using the forging skills he had learnt as a boy. So he made iron gates, fencing, arches and plant climbing frames and soon gained quite a reputation for the quality of his work.

It was through working together on a stage setting of Romeo and Juliet for an amateur drama production that Henry and Sheila met. She was designing and making the backdrop and he was constructing the metal balcony that was to fix to the side of Juliet's bedroom. Three years later they were married and living in a cottage in two acres of land on the edge of the village.

It was from the backroom of 'Rose Cottage' that Sheila started to make and sell her range of 'Yorky' dolls, initially to people in the local village, and then further afield to retail outlets selling children's toys and art and craft products. With Sheila's natural imaginative and creative talent and Henry's practical and business acumen the enterprise went from strength to strength and soon they where making a whole range of children's products from the original Yorky doll, to prams, houses, scooters, model cars and animals.

During this time they had registered the name of 'O Henry' (Sheila insisted on this as the company name as a sign of her love for Henry), moved out of the backroom of Rose Cottage and into a large warehouse on a newly built industrial estate. No longer working alone they now had a board of directors and a general manager, Tim Withers, and employed over 100 workers to help in the manufacture of children's products. Although no longer making all the products themselves, Henry and Sheila insisted that the organization must not lose its well deserved reputation for honest, solid, Yorkshire reliability and value for money.

Over the years two children were born, a girl Annette and two years later, a boy Samuel. Samuel entered the business at sixteen whilst Annette, always more ambitious, had decided to stay on at school, obtain her 'A levels' and go on to take a business degree and then an MBA specializing in marketing.

In 1987 O'Henry's expanded further when Tim Withers recommended that they make a bid, which was successful, for Scrattons, an old established company now facing hard times, that manufactured a range of children's products that could be seen more as educational rather than purely play toys. This included such offerings as metal and plastic globes of the world, maps with capitals cities that light up when the correct button was pressed, children's board games, as well as a range of different play activity toys branded under the fairly well known name of 'Playlearn products'. In buying Scrattons they also acquired a small publishing company, Dinosaur Publishing that dealt solely with children's books, and Scrattons (models) Ltd that specialized in manufacturing model plane and boat construction kits.

In 1990 Henry and Sheila decided to retire and take a back seat in the business and Tim Withers became managing director with the young Samuel Trollop as general manager. Business was still good, although the competition was becoming more intense, especially from AJB Corporation, a US multinational manufacturing educational toys, and Jager Arts and Crafts a small UK company specializing in manufacturing toys from traditional materials.

However by 1995 the organization was beginning to experience difficulties with static sales and falling profit. It was at this time that Annette, having gained her business degree and MBA, decided to come into the business as marketing director at the invitation of the board of directors. After spending two weeks acclimatizing herself with the business, Annette decided that she needed to look at the business from very basic marketing concepts as she felt that the organization had lost direction over the last ten years. This intuitive view was confirmed after conducting an initial marketing audit.

Annette found that the organization now manufactured many different forms of children's products for sale to many different customers and many different markets. They sold everything from children's books, traditional 'art and craft' type toys, model construction kits, educational children's products, board games and modern popular products such as plastic guns, footballs, scooters, etc. A great number of the products they manufactured themselves but some they bought from elsewhere (mainly from the Far East) either in complete form, and they added the O'Henry name, or as individual parts which were then used in conjunction with their own manufactured parts to make up a whole product.

After digging a little deeper Annette found that most people, at all levels within the company, were both uncertain about who the different customers were for the different products the company manufactured and were also unsure about the real reasons behind the purchase. Most argued that this wasn't a problem as the company manufactured toys and the customers were obviously children, buying because they wanted to have immediate enjoyment.

However, from her knowledge of marketing, Annette knew that this approach to the customer decision-making process was far too simplistic and in reality the process was far more complex and involved. She knew that unless every manager within the organization understood both who the customers were and why they bought the company's products they would not be able to develop marketing mix programmes that would specifically satisfy the different customer benefits demanded.

To help the company to come to terms with these very basic concepts she decided to call in a marketing research company specializing in customer behaviour. The questions that she needed to find answers to are listed below.

Case study questions

1. Looking at the whole range of products offered by O'Henry's, can you evaluate the different reasons behind the purchase? It might be useful to use the model of Plato's Divided Soul as a starting point for the examination.

2. Do you think that upbringing, for example culture, social class, religion, race, family circumstances, peer group pressure, etc. will influence both parents and children in their choice of toys? Can you give examples of how and why this might happen?

3. In this chapter we discussed the decision-making unit (DMU). How might this apply in the purchase of the sorts of products manufactured by O'Henry's? Will the DMU be the same for all the children's products identified? What are the different benefits demanded by the various members of the DMU and can these all be allowed for in the development of the marketing mix?

4. Identify the buying stages involved in the decision-making process for the purchase of educational toys to be used in a primary school? How might the producer profitably influence this process?

5. Would the organization be able to market its products in the same way all around the world? Give examples of where differences might exist.

Further reading

Argyle, M. and Coleman, M. (1995) *Social Psychology* (Longman Essential Psychology Series), Longman, London.

Foxhall, G. and Goldsmith, R. (1994) *Consumer Psychology for Marketing*, Routledge, London.

Howard, J.A. and Sheth, J.N. (1969) *The Theory of Buyer Behaviour*, Wiley, New York.

Reis, A. and Trout, J. (1980) *Positioning; The Battle for your Mind*, McGraw-Hill, New York.

Reis, A. and Trout, J. (1986) *Marketing Warfare*, McGraw-Hill, New York.

Stevenson, L. (1974) *Seven Theories of Human Nature*, Oxford University Press, New York.

Wells, W.D. and Prensky, D. (1996) *Consumer Behaviour*, John Wiley, New York.

Williams, K. (1986) *Behavioural Aspects of Marketing*, Heinemann, London.

Worchel, S. and Shebilske, W. (1955) *Psychology, Principles and Practice*, Prentice Hall (UK), London.

4

Segmentation, targeting and positioning the product

AIMS AND OBJECTIVES

By the end of the chapter the student should:

1 be able to define segmentation and recognize why companies need to analyse and classify markets and consumers;

2 be able to identify the ways that markets can be segmented while appreciating the strengths and limitations inherent in the process;

3 describe how products can be positioned and targeted to meet identified segmentation criteria.

Introduction

Why segment the market?

In the preceding chapter the many influences that may affect the buying decisions of existing and potential customers were examined in some detail. It was argued that these influences will cause people to want to buy different products and services to satisfy individual needs and wants. In this chapter it is argued that only if these concepts are understood by all marketing personnel can clear marketing strategies be planned and developed that will exploit these influences. This will be done by providing products and services that offer precise benefits to meet whatever may be the major driving need in each particular consumer.

With most products it would not be practical or economical to produce different customized products for every single person in the market. However there are always exceptions and some organizations actually gain competitive advantage by producing customized products for individual customers. In fact almost any *product* – cars, boats, houses, fashion clothes – or *service* – interior design, landscape gardening, computer software, hair cutting, pension or health plan – can be customized if the buyer is prepared to pay the asking price.

However for most products and services it would not be profitable to sell different offerings to every individual in the market. Conversely it would be unacceptable from the point of view of the customer to sell exactly the same product to everybody, as needs and tastes vary from individual to individual and from country to country.

The marketer must therefore break the market down into manageable and profitable groups, clusters or segments in which people have the same or similar characteristics and will demand the same or similar product benefits. To facilitate the process a realistic basis for dividing the market must be established. The way the market is split becomes a balancing act that must take into account the needs of the consumer and the resource and profit needs of the organization.

One of the earliest forms of market split would have been between male and female, because of basic differing needs. Although there are 'unisex' products, it is still one of the major forms of segmentation.

A working definition of segmentation can now be given:
Segmentation is dividing the market into groups, or clusters of customers based on realistic and meaningful criteria so as to offer targeted benefits.

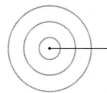

Market segmentation

This imperative to divide the market into different segments in order to offer products that match different consumer needs and wants is at the very heart of marketing and is known as market segmentation. Only if the varying and diverse benefits demanded by different groups in society are known can products and services be developed with benefits that will satisfy these many disparate needs.

STRATEGIC IMPORTANCE OF SEGMENTATION

It should be self-evident that if the organization is uncertain about who its customers are it will not be able to offer products and services that precisely meet these customer needs. However there are many examples of companies losing contact with the needs of their customer base, offering unsuitable products leading inexorably to falling sales (IBM, Next and KwikSave are examples). Progressive managers now realize the long-term strategic importance of detailed knowledge of customer segments as one the most important factors in the planning process affecting the whole of the marketing mix. Also running through the process should be an understanding that segments, and customers within those segments, evolve, develop and change, so demanding ever-different product service offerings.

The first step in the process is to identify a basis for the segmentation. The basis chosen can be as simple or as complex as market circumstances demand, for example in terms of industrial or consumer markets; age, sex, employment, lifestyle; or by size, geographical location and so on. This will be investigated in more detail as we move through the chapter.

Once the basis of segmentation has been established further investigation is needed to determine the most important and relevant characteristics of each segment. Individual segments can be evaluated to ascertain their business worth, for example market growth, level of competition, profit potential, company product viability, etc. and then the most attractive segments selected. These become the segments to be targeted for development.

MARKET RESEARCH AND SEGMENTATION

It is worth emphasizing that the process of segmentation will begin with marketing research to seek out the different benefits demanded by various groups. Seldom, if ever, will a producer offer the same product to the whole mass market.

Factors determining the approach to segmentation

How a company will segment its market will depend on many different factors. These will include the following:

1. the size, objectives and resources of the company;
2. the type of product and market;
3. the competitiveness of the industry.

THE SIZE, OBJECTIVES AND RESOURCES OF THE COMPANY

The size of the company and the resources it has available will dictate to a great extent how it segments its market. For example the Ford Motor Co. will want to sell to the world and so segment on a global scale whilst the local hairdresser will service a very small catchment area and segment accordingly.

THE TYPE OF PRODUCT AND MARKET

Some companies have a simple product portfolio that lends itself to easy segmentation, for example bread, potatoes, petrol, industrial cleaning products; whilst others have a more complex product mix making it much harder, for example catering and hospitality services, financial services, fashion clothes.

THE COMPETITIVE STRUCTURE OF THE INDUSTRY

In the main the more competitive the market the more each organization will look toward differentiating their product so as to gain competitive advantage. The greater the selection on offer the more consumers will demand choice and the greater will be the need for tight segmentation. An example of this might be the change that has happened with the traditional English pub. Competition and the need to attract more customers has led to the theme pub offering an ever greater choice of food and real ales. In the past a pub might have offered a choice of two different beers and a salad sandwich or a sausage roll. Now many pubs offer a choice of over 20 different beers and food as diverse as Italian, Thai, French and American to be eaten as a snack, at lunch time or as a full three or four course dinner, all at prices that match their targeted customer's expectations.

The viability of segmentation

Not all identified segments will be acceptable and for a segment in the market to be viable for an organization the customer group chosen as the market for a product must be:

1. profitable;
2. measurable;
3. within resource constraints;
4. ethically and legally acceptable.

We can look at each of these areas in turn.

LARGE ENOUGH TO BE PROFITABLE

To be attractive for an organization, the identified market segment must be large enough to be profitable. Market research could well identify a market for 'iced soup on a stick' or 'corduroy walking sticks' but it would not be profitable for a large company to manufacture and sell to these markets if they only consisted of 100 people.

THE 'NICHE' MARKET.   However what is unprofitable for a large company may be more profitable for a small one, creating what is known as a 'niche' market. An example of this was when Ford stopped producing a soft-top sports car because the market was too small. This left a market 'niche' for smaller manufacturers such as Lotus and Morgan to move into and exploit.

MEASURABLE

When a company is looking at potential markets it must be able to measure the size of the various customer groups and assess what the possible demand might be, that is whether there are 1000, 1 million or 100 million potential customers. If this cannot be done then a sales, cost and profit forecast cannot be undertaken and so a planned approach will not be possible.

WITHIN RESOURCE CAPABILITY

A company will have finite resources depending on its size and asset base. Segment opportunities may be identified but the company finds itself unable to take advantage of them because of resource limitations, for example research might indicate a possible demand for a more luxurious and expensive type of carpet which the company cannot produce because it does not have the financial resources to purchase the more sophisticated equipment needed to manufacture the carpet (an example of 'resource driven marketing').

ETHICALLY AND LEGALLY ACCEPTABLE

The identified market segment must be both ethically and legally acceptable to the organization. The mission statement or other form of corporate declaration may spell out the ethical basis on which the organization intends to undertake its business, and so constrains it from expanding into selective areas. At the time of writing, the Co-operative Bank is running a series of adverts stating that it will not invest clients' money in areas that it considers are politically and morally suspect. This would include not investing in companies that might cause rainforest destruction or ozone layer damage as well as avoiding countries such as China or Burma that are considered to have undemocratic or oppressive regimes.

Similarly legal consideration will always preclude entry into certain defined market segments, although what may be unlawful in one country may be lawful in another (marijuana can be bought legally in Holland but not in the UK). Ethical and legal constraints may restrict an organization in other areas including selling alcohol and cigarettes to children; drugs other than for medical or industrial use; furniture or clothing that is highly combustible; or where animals have been used for medical or cosmetic research purposes.

Basis for segmentation

There is no single way to segment a market and the alternatives are legion. Through the use of research a marketer will try to identify how, where and why products are purchased and base their segmentation on the method most likely to produce the best results. This basis for segmentation will undoubtably vary from product type to product type as well as from customer to customer and some of these different forms will be identified as we move through the chapter.

FRAGMENTING BASIS FOR SEGMENTATION

With an ever-increasing demand by the customer for choice, coupled with the growth in the ability of companies to provide personalized products to satisfy this choice, the basis for segmentation is continually fragmenting and changing into ever more categories. Examples of this will include the following.

- The market for financial services for a large banking organization was once divided into four or five simple segments; now over 150 exist.

- Whereas, at one time, bread was only available in white and brown, a multitude of forms are now marketed including: frozen, chilled or ambient temperature; different colours, as well as white or brown; bread from France, Italy or Germany; natural and organic bread; bread with little stones in; bread for toasting; bread you can bake yourself; bread for the weight conscious; bread in all different shapes and sizes; the choice seems limitless.

- Even bottled water is now divided into markets for still and fizzy, sophisticated and utility, flavoured and unflavoured, fancy or plain bottles; and water from a Welsh, Scottish or Swiss mountain stream.

Whilst there well may be the odd example of a company unilaterally producing a new type of bread, bottled water or financial service product in the hope that it might sell, the overwhelming reason for the growth in these new markets is because of increased customer demand identified through the use of both informal and formal market research.

MORE THAN ONE VARIABLE

Only with very basic, commodity type products, will one method alone be used as a basis for segmentation. An example might be the market for coffee beans where the market will probably be segmented by geographical location, for example London, New York or Paris. A company manufacturing nothing but industrial clothing such as donkey jackets or dungarees might segment only by size but will be quite likely to use sex (male and female alternatives) as well.

The more sophisticated the product and market the more likely that two, three or more variables will be used in the segmentation process although, depending on the product or market, one variable will probably be more important than another. If we consider the market for cars we will find that it will probably be segmented by age, income, sex and lifestyle and different car products and different car product benefits are offered to match the different demands of each market.

In Figure 4.1 examples of markets segmented by 1, 2 and 3 variables are shown where 1 might be age, 2 is age and sex, and 3 is age, sex and income. Market 1, segmented only by age, might be the market for childrens' reading books; market 2, segmented by age and sex, might be the market for disposable nappies; and market 3, age sex and income, might be the market for shoes.

We can now look in more detail at the many different ways that are used to segment the market, beginning with the split between industrial and consumer markets.

| **Figure 4.1** | *Examples of markets segmented by 1, 2 or 3 variables* |

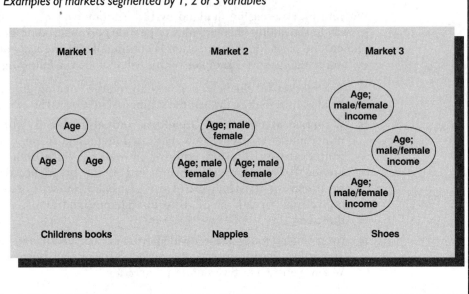

Industrial and consumer markets

A major distinction to be made is between selling to the trade (industrial markets) and selling to the end-consumer and so most organizations will clearly distinguish between marketing products and services in:

1. industrial markets;
2. consumer markets.

This distinction is made because the processes in selling to one market rather than the other are so different. We will look in turn at the important characteristics of each market and show how each of these two areas can be segmented into smaller and more precise groups.

Industrial markets

Industrial marketing (or 'business to business' marketing as it is sometimes called) is when one producer sells products to another producer for own consumption, usually to be used in some way in the production of products or services. A company will need to know whether it is marketing to an industrial or consumer market as the approach that needs to be taken is different (an example was given in the preceding chapter which discussed a customer buying for his or her own use being driven by emotional needs, whilst a customer buying for a company's use is motivated by rational needs). The industrial market can be broken down and segmented in the following ways;

1. size of the company;
2. density of the companies;
3. whether a manufacturer or a service provider;
4. whether in the private, public or not for profit sector.

SIZE OF THE COMPANY.   The purchasing company may be large, medium or small (the criteria used here will vary according to the needs of the segmenting company but it could be in terms of numbers of employees, sales turnover, market capitalization).

DENSITY OF COMPANIES.   Companies in the same industry often cluster together in geographical areas, for example shoe industry in Northampton; cars in the Midlands; clothes in the east end of London; pottery in Staffordshire, etc. A large company which puts down roots in one area will then attract other associated businesses.

WHETHER A MANUFACTURER OR SERVICE PROVIDER.   Whether the purchasing company is a manufacturing organization or a service provider will allow for differentiation of the markets. Manufacturing industries will include areas such as: packaging; chemicals; pharmaceuticals; while examples of services are: financial; retail; leisure and computer software.

PRIVATE, PUBLIC, OR THE NOT FOR PROFIT SECTOR.   More and more companies are moving from the public to the private arena but the distinction is still important. Private companies will include such giants as Cadbury Schweppes, GEC, Bass, Granada, as well as BT, Yorkshire Water, Transco (gas), and National Power in the private but regulated sector.

The public sector will include areas such as: the National Health Service, local and national government, defence, etc. The not for profit sector covers such organizations as charities, museums, places of public interest, and the Boy Scouts and the Girl Guides.

The industrial market can be further segmented into three product areas:

1. capital equipment – buildings, machinery, vehicles, etc.;
2. running services – heating, lighting, stationery etc.;
3. component products – products that go into making up a finished product, such as nuts and bolts, raw materials, packaging, etc.

These are just a few of the many ways the industrial market can be segmented and the most profitable and realistic method will depend on the resources of the organization and the demands of the market identified earlier. Any method of segmentation will be legitimate as long as it simplifies and generates an understanding of the market.

WHY SEGMENT INDUSTRIAL FROM CONSUMER MARKETS?

Industrial markets are segmented from consumer markets because the needs of each are different and so the marketing approach has to be different. The industry market is further broken down and segmented because, again, there are varying needs demanding different approaches within each industry. In this way the public sector has different needs from the private sector, manufacturing has different needs from the service sector and selling capital equipment is different from selling component parts. Once these various needs are understood, specialized skills can be developed within the organization so that the exact benefit can be offered to match the demanded customer need. It is also a way of bringing some semblance of order to a seemingly amorphous and confusing market. This is crucial when planning and implementing the marketing and sales effort.

Consumer markets

We can now look at the basis for consumer market segmentation under the following headings:

1. geographic;
2. demographic;
3. socioeconomic;
4. behavioural;
5. psychographic;
6. lifestyle.

GEOGRAPHIC SEGMENTATION

As with industrial markets, there are many ways of segmenting consumer markets. Geographic segmentation is separating the market in terms of geographic location. These locations can be identified under the following headings.

INTERNATIONAL (GLOBAL) SEGMENTATION. A multinational company (British Airways, BT, British Aerospace) would need to segment its markets according to global trading areas, for example The European Union, The Pacific Rim, The North American Free Trade Area; or it might want to segment according to individual countries such as China, Australia, France, etc. Other organizations (e.g. charities, government agencies) might want to segment in terms of first, second and third world countries, developing and developed countries or the north/south divide.

SEGMENTATION AT A NATIONAL LEVEL. Another company might need, or want, to segment within its own national boundaries in terms of its cities, towns, villages, regions and districts.

Sainsburys, when deciding where to locate a new store, will look to be on the edge of all large cities and towns above a certain size and a direct selling double glazing company might want to segment its markets according to regions and districts.

CLIMATE. Some international organizations, because of the products manufactured, might segment their global markets geographically by climate, infrastructure and topography. Examples might include: ice-cream, refrigerators (hot climate), electric blankets (cold climate), umbrellas (wet climate), bottled water (dry climate). (Although it must be said that some UK companies have made money by 'carrying coals to Newcastle' – selling sand to the Sahara, fridges to Iceland and pizzas to Italy.

DEMOGRAPHIC SEGMENTATION

Product/service sales are dependent on population numbers and movements. So an understanding of demography, the study of population, is essential in segmentation. Demographic variables used for classification include:

- The overall size of the population, growth, densities and movement trends.
- The breakdown of the population in terms of sex, age, family size and life stage. Of particular interest at the present time is the fact that people are living longer, the old are becoming more populous in relation to the young and more couples are living together rather than getting married.

SOCIOECONOMIC SEGMENTATION

Demographic variables can be divided further into groups based on social variables such as social class, culture and sub-culture, leisure pursuits, family life stage, education and literacy levels, occupation, club membership, religion, race and nationality.

The market can also be profitable segmented using socioeconomic data such as disposable income, per capita income, income spread and income levels.

GEOGRAPHIC, DEMOGRAPHIC, SOCIO-ECONOMIC COMBINATION. As stated earlier, very rarely will only one variable be used. It is much more likely that two or more would be used. Possible combinations might be geographical location, age and income, or location, age, disposable income and social class. The variables are integrated to build what are called consumer profiles.

CONSUMER PROFILES. A company, such as Tesco, will employ a marketing research agency to undertake research and combine geographic, demographic, socioeconomic segmentation data so as to develop consumer patterns and profiles for selected areas where they intend to open a new superstore. This will allow Tesco to predict (usually with unnerving accuracy) the level of consumer flow through their stores and the amount of money the consumer will be prepared to spend.

With a little imagination we can make up the following typical customer profile for a new store:

- Woman/man; married; 2 children; shops once a week; disposable income £15,000; spends on average £100 on groceries; lives within a 10 mile radius of the new store;
- potential size of market, 250,000 and growing.

Figure 4.2 gives some more detailed examples of the major socioeconomic segmentation variables that might be used.

SEGMENTING BY INCOME. As an example Ford have developed a range of cars at prices to suit different income levels. From the lowest to the highest, Ford produce the Fiesta, Escort, Mondeo, Scorpio and to cover the higher levels it bought Jaguar. There are extras that can be purchased on each model allowing for every pocket. But remember, Ford will use other variables as well as income.

SEGMENTING BY AGE AND SEX. Mothercare, part of the Storehouse, BHS group, segments its markets according to age and sex. Its customer profile is children from birth until 11 years old and pregnant women. Mothercare therefore produces a range of products, including clothes, toys and foods for different ages for both baby boys and girls within this age range as well as clothes for pregnant women. Through the use of research, Mothercare designs and offers product benefits that match the changing demands of parents as their children grow and develop.

Figure 4.2	*Socioeconomic segmentation*

Age
0–12, 13–20, 21–35, 36–50, 51–65, 66+

Sex
Male, female

Disposable income
Under £10,000; £10,000 – under £20,000; £20,000 – under £30,000;
£30,000 – under £50,000; £50,000+

Family size and make-up
Pre-teenager; teenager; independent; co-habiting; married;
married with children under 5; over 5; single parent; married,
children left home; retired

Education
Level of literacy; primary; secondary and tertiary education; mature student

Religion
Protestant; Roman Catholic; Muslim; Jewish; Hindu

Ethnic group
Indian; Pakistani; Welsh; black; white

Nationality
English; Welsh; West Indian

Social class
Upper; middle; lower

Disposable nappies. An interesting development where baby and toddler age and sex has been used to segment the market is in disposable nappies. In response to market research Pampers, for example, now offers a range of disposable nappies to meet the changing needs of mother and baby from first born through to four years old.

The range includes different nappies for boys (blue label) and girls (pink label); different nappies for different ages and weights – mini, 3–6 kgs, midi, 4–9 kgs, maxi, 8–18 kgs, maxi plus, 10–20 kgs, Junior, 12–25 kgs; and nappies with different benefits including ultra dry, with waist elastic, and super absorbent. There are over a dozen different disposable nappy products to meet the needs of identified, different segments where once there was only one. In fact this whole market hardly existed 30 years ago when women had to re-wash and re-use the Terry towelling nappy.

SEGMENTING BY FAMILY CIRCUMSTANCES AND LIFE CYCLE STAGE. There is no doubt that different products will be needed at different stages of our lives. Research has shown that the consumers will require different products dependent on family circumstances and the particular stage they have reached in their life cycle (from birth to death). Segmentation categories and relevant products might include:

- *pre-teenager* – toys, sweets, comics;
- *teenager* – CDs, lipstick, clothes;
- *independent* – alcohol, perfumes and male fragrances, designer clothes;
- *co-habiting, married* – furniture, mortgage, electrical products;
- *married, children under 5* – baby products, DIY products;
- *single parent* – nursery facilities;
- *married, children over 5* – educational products, books, children's clothes;
- *married, children left home* – holidays, financial products;
- *retired* – gardening products, books, winter holidays.

In all probability these segments could be broken down even further, for example take the last category – retired. This could be broken down further into middle class, under 60, plays golf, vegetarian, fun loving, gregarious and so on. This form of greater fragmentation allows products to be developed that have ever-more precise benefits.

SOCIAL CLASS. Social class (see Figure 4.3) is still an important method used in segmentation and it is worth expanding on this method. A person's social class is still considered by some organizations as a worthwhile indicator of the sorts of products that might be purchased (although this is becoming increasingly less so as the social class divide becomes more blurred).

Newspaper readership, TV viewing, fast food purchase, holidays, alcohol consumption, etc. are all areas where this form of segmentation is often used. There are slightly different methods used and Figure 4.3 illustrates an example of one type of social class grouping.

The groupings and percentages given in Figure 4.3 should be treated with care, not only because of the assumptions made when putting people into categories, but also because of the changes that are continually taking place.

Figure 4.3	Social class grouping

Socio economic group	Occupation	Approx. percentage of population
A	Upper middle class; higher managerial, administrative or professional.	6
B	Middle class; intermediate managerial, administrative or professional.	10
C1	Lower middle class; supervisory or clerical, junior managerial, administrative or professional.	28
C2	Skilled working class; skilled manual worker.	25
D	Working class; semi-skilled and unskilled manual worker.	18
E	Those at the lowest level of subsistence; state pensioners, casual or lowest grade workers, the unemployed, students (assumed to have little money.	13

Using the social class classification identified in Figure 4.3, newspaper readership could be classified into the following:

A Bs,	*Financial Times*
A B C1s	*Daily Telegraph*
C1 C2 D Es	*Sun* or *Daily Mirror*

There are, of course, some A Bs who read the *Sun* and some C1, C2, D, Es who read the *Financial Times* but the concept is based on majority figures. Social class is linked very closely to income as well as to status and style of living. It tends to be used less and less as a method of segmentation as social divides become blurred.

BEHAVIOURAL SEGMENTATION

Using behaviour as a means of segmentation, buyers are divided into groups according to their attitudes and behaviour shown towards products and companies. Some of the behavioural categories that are used include:

1. existing users;
2. heavy users;
3. brand switchers;
4. role play users;
5. past users;
6. complimentary product users;
7. value-sensitive users;
8. end use users.

EXISTING USERS.   There are some c
perhaps buying the company product
attempt to measure the degree of loyalty
By clear segmentation and targeting, level
inforced and customers encouraged to move

Loyalty encouragement might be consi
argued that it costs over five times more to att
an existing one. Through the use of a sophisticate
referencing, loyal customers can also be cross-s
products from the company product portfolio.

HEAVY USERS.   It may be important to know whether t
medium or heavy user of the product. The 'Pareto rule' sta
ization, 80 per cent of sales come from 20 per cent of custome
then the main thrust of the marketing effort should be aimed at
that is at 20 per cent of the customers. An example might b
drinkers: research shows this group to comprise mainly young wome
ages of 18 and 30 and so this should be the segment targeted.

BRAND SWITCHERS.   Some customers have a repertoire of products (perhaps
five different brands) switching from one favoured brand to another dependi
price, availability, promotional incentive or personal inclination. Market rese
should indicate the size and value of this segment and, if it is large enough, acti
should be taken to increase loyalty.

ROLE PLAY USER.   Research has shown that many consumers purchase products
according to the role they are playing at the time of purchase. A typical example
might be a women buying yoghurt. If in the role of mother, she might purchase a
pack of children's fun-flavoured yoghurts; if in the role of PTA committee member
buying for the school fair, it might be own-label products; and if in the role of 'self-
indulgent me', she might purchase a more sensuous, up-market brand.

As with the brand switcher, the size of the market must be researched and if
large enough a range of products produced to cover all contingencies.

PAST USERS.   Again a more sophisticated database should enable a company to
segment and target past users. With a little prompting and some form of incentive
they might very well be encouraged to purchase again. An example at the end of
the 1990s is BT's enticement back campaign, aimed at customers 'poached' by
the competition.

COMPLIMENTARY PRODUCT USER.   The market may be segmented by targeting the users
of similar types of products, and again the ability to cross-fertilize customer information makes this increasingly possible. So the users of one health product might
very well be in the market for another type of health product. Likewise the owner of
a Barclay's bank account may well be in the market for a longer term loan.

In selling complimentary products the reliability of the information, the
accuracy of the targeting, and the timing of the offer are central to the success of
the segmentation project.

service-sensitive the customer is can
rch shows that the level of after sales
may be the way for a company to
Many products are price-sensitive
mpetitive market, can put a heavy

may vary and, if known, new
uses. Manufacturers of tinned
ent consisting of customers
dishes. Similarly, the manu-
ket when retailer feedback
young girls. (There are
like a student

customers who are more loyal than oth
for many, many years. Many organizat
exhibited by one customer over ano
of loyalty can then be rewarded ar
up the loyalty scale.
red especially important as
act a new customer than to
marketing database and
old a whole range of

e customer is a li
es that, as a general
s. If this is the case
hese heavy users,
the heavy gin
between the

four or
ng on
rch

GMENTATION

saw the growth of psychographic segmentations based on consumer
attitudes. Marketers have recognized the limitations of demographic and
nomic grouping in segmenting particular markets, realizing that consumers
y for emotional reasons linked to individual inner-needs. These needs are not
ys apparent and, more importantly, they will cross socioeconomic barriers such
as social class, income and education. They can be 'discovered' through the use of
qualitative research methods written about in the chapter on marketing research.

PERSONALITY TYPES.   There are many theories on personality types and the different
emotional needs of each type. Marketers will segment these many different types
into meaningful groups and attempt to develop product 'personalities' that match
these different needs. Some of the many categories identified by different
commentators include the following:

- introverted, extroverted;
- sensitive, insensitive;
- power seeking;
- gregariousness;
- compulsive;
- obsessive;
- insecure;
- guilt-laden;
- high-achiever,
- low-achiever.

Personality type segmentation may also be used with Maslow's triangle of needs,
as these could all be classified in terms of personality types.

The various personality types will want products with benefits that satisfy
their major needs. If the need for security is the overriding need then the major

product benefit should reflect this, for example the Volvo motor car is marketed with safety benefits. If the overriding need is compulsive cleanliness then the same would apply, for example 'Domestos kills all known germs'.

LIFESTYLE SEGMENTATION

As consumers have become more educated, more affluent and more sophisticated they have tended to purchase products and services less in term of religion, race, social class, etc. and more in terms of lifestyle aspirations linked to personality characteristics.

With this form of segmentation, consumers are divided into groups that reflect common attitudes, interests and opinions. This has led to advertising agencies identifying and grouping consumers under a whole range of colourful acronyms such as; Yuppies (young, upwardly mobile, professional); Buppies (black, upwardly mobile, professional); Dinkies (double income, no kids); Woollys (well-off oldie, with lots of lolly); Lombard (lots of money but a real dickhead). This list is only restricted by the limits of imagination.

Many advertising agencies have developed their own lifestyle clusters relating to specific products and markets and listed below are the sorts of descriptive ways they segment the market, according to both the product and target market characteristics:

- *Go-getters*: aspire after status and recognition, upwardly mobile, materialisitic, will always seek the newest and the most conspicuous product; eat out two to three times a week, have a dozen credit cards and probably drive a Porsche.

- *Quietly-comfortable*: oldest of all the groups, large disposable income, confident; will be attracted by 'conservative' luxury products; three holidays a year; probably own a BMW.

- *Middle-of-the-roaders*: conformists, conservative, want security, believe in old-fashioned values; eat out once a month, will use branded products, drive a Ford Mondeo; holiday in France.

- *Spiritualists*: inner driven, non-materialistic, worry about 'green' issues, prodigious readers, go to the opera/classical music/theatre once a week; will use own-label grocery products, walk and cycle wherever possible and have abandoned the Citroen 2CV and VW Beetle for environmental reasons.

SEGMENTING THE WOMEN'S MARKET. The women's market for a particular product, for example perfume, fashion clothes, alcohol, might be segmented in the following way:

- *Environmentally aware woman*: married, living with someone; liberal-left opinions; adopts fashionable causes; outgoing, active in the community, gregarious.

- *Business woman*: married, or living with someone; 30–40 years old; does not want children; independent and self-centred; high-flyer at work; affluent; fashionable; visits opera and theatre.

- *Part-time working older women*: married, children over 11 years old, reasonably affluent, buys value for money products; traditional, conservative opinions; enjoys eating out, going to the theatre.

■ *Live-for-today, fun loving woman*: single, 20–30 years old; sensual, material-istic and ambitious; goes out four or five times a week, clubs and pubs; high disposable income; 'snappy' dresser; three holidays a year, singles.

(If you don't see yourself never mind there are many other ways the market can be segmented, perhaps you would like to have a go.)

Segmentation methods change and shift

Lifestyle segmentation classifications will be constantly shifting and changing as attitudes, interests, opinions and lifestyles change. The various categories can also be intermixed if this is found to be profitable.

Lifestyle methods can be used with age, income, behaviour, geographic vari-ables, etc. It can also be used for categories other than humans and a good example of this is the dog food market. Take a trip around the local Sainsbury or Tesco and you will discover a plethora of products on sale for the following market segments:

■ puppies;

■ adult dogs;

■ overweight dogs;

■ older dogs;

■ pedigree dogs;

■ surrogate 'child' dogs;

■ ill dogs.

Marketing research should be used constantly to identify new ways of classifying viable customer groups.

The marketed product must match the characteristics of the lifestyle, age, income, behaviour group it is aimed at. The consumers in the selected group must want to be associated with the product and feel that it reflects their chosen lifestyle.

As we have discussed the basis for segmenting the market can be chosen in many ways. We have identified:

■ industrial and consumer

■ geographic

■ socioeconomic

■ behavioural

■ psychographic and lifestyle

There might be other ways of segmenting the market and each company must decide which is the most appropriate method for them. It is not always an easy task but, because of its importance, persistence should be encouraged.

Targeting the market

Once an appropriate basis has been selected and the important characteristics determined the company must choose which segments to attack and which to ignore.

Evaluating the segments

In the segmentation process each identified segment now needs to be analysed so as to evaluate its attractiveness to the organization.

The fundamental questions that need to be answered would include the following:

- *The markets*: questions to be asked would include: market size, growth, potential and cost and profit levels as well as the amount and size of the competition, the availability of raw material supplies and the role, if any, of a middleman in the supply chain.

- *Company resources*: questions here would focus on internal strengths and weaknesses and include such areas as: availability of capital, skills of the workforce, existing product portfolio synergy and its market 'fit', price suitability and ability to deliver in the most appropriate manner.

SELECTING THE SEGMENT

After evaluation, the organization can now select one or more of the most attractive segments at which to target its products. A clear customer profile should be developed for each segment so that nobody should be in any doubt about the needs and wants of each market. Below are two customer profile examples, a simple one for the clothes industry and a more complex one for the holiday market.

- Customer profile for a clothes industry segment: sex, female; age, 35–50; income, £35,000; family stage, married, no children; lifestyle, business woman.

- Customer profile for the holiday market: male, single; age, 22–35; social class, ABC1; income, £25,000–£35,000; drives an Escort GT; works in financial services; extrovert; enjoys the 'good life'; drinks upmarket, branded lager; gregarious; enjoys active organized holidays with people of the same age. Size of market in the UK: 1,000,000; segment static.

Product positioning

Having identified, evaluated and selected the most attractive segments and spelt out a clear customer profile for each buyer group, the marketing manager must decide where in the market his or her products should be positioned.

The 'position' held by a product/service in the market will be how the organization wants the product/service to be perceived by the consumer in terms of factors such as brand image, value for money, price availability, etc. This will always be in relationship to the competition.

POSITIONING AND CUSTOMER PERCEPTION

Where a product is perceived to be 'positioned' in the market will be in the mind of the target consumer and not necessarily in the product itself. A company might believe it has a high value, well regarded product, but if the customer is unconvinced it will not sell. A white T-shirt costing £3 bought for the writer's son was considered unacceptable, whilst one with a crocodile on the front costing £20 was acceptable.

There are many alternative market positions and working from the customer profile, the company should develop and market a product that is different, better or cheaper than competitive products and matches the exact requirements of the customer group to be targeted within the selected segment.

Depending on the researched customer needs, the product for the selected market can be positioned in the market *against the competition* according to the following alternative criteria:

- of high, medium or utility value; reflected by high, medium or low price;
- having a USP (unique selling proposition) centred on tangible factors such as quality workmanship or ease of use and/or intangible factors with an emotional appeal such as 'if you love your family protect them with Dettol';
- being available through direct or indirect methods of distribution.

PRODUCT POSITIONING STATEMENT

Where the company intends positioning the product in the market will be formalized by the marketing department issuing what is called a product 'positioning statement'. This will spell out, in written detail, all the attributes of the products selected from those discussed above.

The positioning statement would then be made available to all departments and agencies that might be involved in the development of the product. This is to make certain that customer needs are considered at each stage in the process and that the final product offering – including its content, design, packaging, quality, brand name, price and distribution channel – will match customer expectations and be promoted in the most favourable way so that it occupies the desired position in the market.

Using the example of the customer profile for a segment in the holiday market above (male, 22–35, single, ABC1, etc.) a product positioning statement can be constructed. It might include the following information:

- High priced but 'value for money', mixed sex, adventure, discovery holiday, crossing Africa on a Jeep safari, part camping, part hotel.

■ Promote on excitement, sex, once in a lifetime, get away from the normal tourist routes.

This would be very much a niche market.

PRODUCT POSITIONING MAP

A product positioning map is often used in the positioning process. Using the holiday as an example we can take the many different types of holiday packages and, using a two-dimensional scale with opposites at each end of the poles, identify where each type of holiday might be positioned (Figure 4.4).

The selected criteria can be whatever is considered important in any particular market. Using the example of the holiday market the criteria of low/high price has been chosen for the vertical axis and conservative/adventurous activity for the horizontal. After undertaking market research, the holiday company and its main competitors are plotted. It is also a useful method for identifying a 'gap' in the market where there seems to be little or no competitor activity.

Developing a marketing mix for each selected segment

With the help of market research, a customer profile and product positioning statement can be developed for each individual market. A relevant and

| **Figure 4.4** | *The holiday market* |

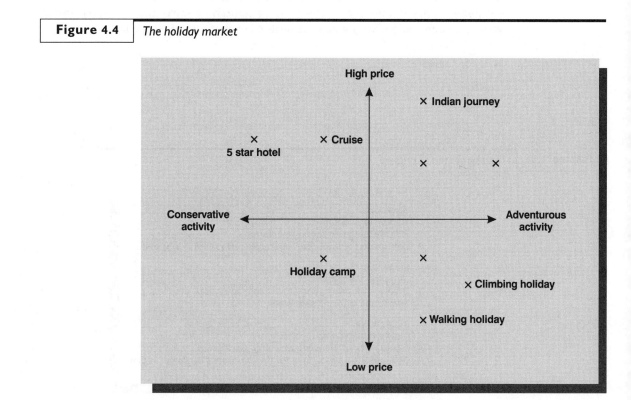

customized marketing mix offering can then be developed for each identified segment. The whole segmentation process is set out in diagrammatic form in Figure 4.5.

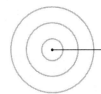

Benefits of segmentation

The overall benefits to the organization in clearly segmenting its markets can now be identified.

1. It enables the company to focus on clearly identified individual needs.
2. A product portfolio can be developed offering clear, targeted, product and service benefits tailored to these needs.
3. This should lead to greater customer satisfaction.
4. It encourages the relevant staff to develop a greater awareness of customer profiles and the different markets (especially the niche market).
5. Overall it should make the company more competitive.

Having looked at the benefits of segmentation it is worth remembering the alternative. If segmentation is not undertaken then clear, focused individual benefits will not be offered and the customers, demanding choice and unhappy about what is on offer, might very well vote with their feet and go elsewhere.

Figure 4.5	*The segmentation process*

Stage one
Market segmentation
1 Identify the basis for segmentation
2 Determine the important characteristics of each segment

Stage two
Targeting the market
3 Evaluate the marketing attractiveness of each segment
4 Select one or more segments

Stage three
Product positioning
5 Identify where the product will be positioned
6 Develop a marketing mix for each targeted segment

Market segmentation strategies

When deciding on its approach to segmentation the organization has three basic options:

1. undifferentiated marketing;
2. selective marketing;
3. concentrated marketing.

We will look briefly at each in turn.

Undifferentiated marketing

Undifferentiated marketing is selling the same product to the whole market. It was argued earlier that, generally, it is no longer possible for most companies to do this because of the customers' demand for a customized product. However, many large organizations would like to sell the same undifferentiated product to the whole of the market because by manufacturing, distributing and promoting one product to the whole market they could gain economies of scale and learning curve cost savings and also avoid the extra costs associated with changing manufacturing methods to produce different product offerings to different market segments.

EXAMPLES OF UNDIFFERENTIATED MARKETING

Some companies come very close to undifferentiated marketing. McDonald's have opened more or less the same outlets in New York, Croydon, Tokyo, Istanbul and Moscow (although there are slight variations in the food presentation). Although Coca-Cola offers the same product to a mass market it still produces Diet-Coke for weight-watchers.

However, for most products, customer demand for individual choice linked with such things as cultural and infrastructure differences make undifferentiated, mass marketing possible for only a minority of companies (Figure 4.6).

SELECTIVE MARKETING

More often organizations select the market segments where they feel that they will have a competitive advantage and offer specific product benefits tailored to meet consumer needs in each selected segment (Figure 4.7).

CONCENTRATED MARKETING

The competitive activity, the size of the company and the resources at its disposable might determine that the organization concentrate its effort in one clear market segment. This should enable the organization to develop specialist knowledge and skills and so give it a competitive advantage over a more broad based and often much larger rival.

Figure 4.6	*Undifferentiated marketing*

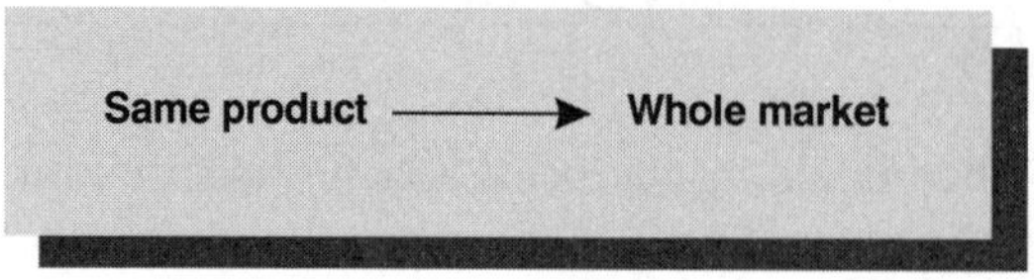

Same product ⟶ Whole market

Figure 4.7	*Selective marketing*

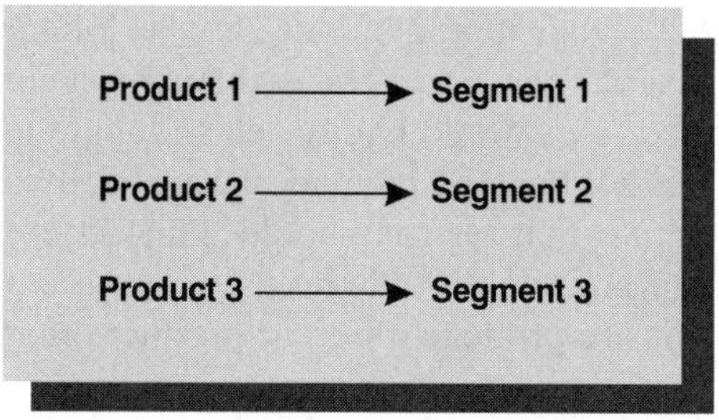

Product 1 ⟶ Segment 1

Product 2 ⟶ Segment 2

Product 3 ⟶ Segment 3

This concentrated form of segmentation tends to lend itself to the concept of niche marketing discussed earlier in the book. Examples might be Sock Shop selling only socks; Knickerbox, selling only underwear; Tie Rack, selling only ties (Figure 4.8).

SELECTING A STRATEGY

The choice of strategy – undifferentiated, selective or concentrated – will depend on the following:

1. company objectives and resources;
2. the type of product;
3. the type of market;
4. the activity of competitors.

COMPANY OBJECTIVES AND RESOURCES.   A company manufacturing a very small range of basic commodity products with little or no added value – like wood screws – may well only produce for one or two companies and have no need for segmentation. Also, it might not have the resources to develop into other markets and so continue to make either for a very small market or for own label sales.

Figure 4.8 | *Concentrated marketing*

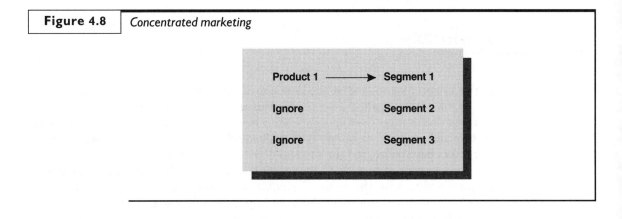

THE TYPE OF PRODUCT.   Some products do not lend themselves to strong differentiation. This tends to relate to the amount of value that can be added to the product. As a rule of thumb the greater the added value (branding, innovation, packaging, service, etc.) the more the market can be differentiated, for example watches, cars, clothes, confectionery.

Conversely the opposite is true, so with basic commodity products – for example petrol, sugar, salt – there is less opportunity for differentiation (although we have to be careful about claims that products cannot be differentiated. Water was once seen as a product allowing little differentiation but now we have a whole range of segmented bottled water products. Even the humble paper clip has its different segments.)

THE TYPE OF MARKET.   As with products, in some markets it is more difficult to create any form of differentiation than it is in others. Financial services is an example of a market where it is difficult to differentiate one company product from another (although by no means impossible) as life insurance, pensions, overdrafts, etc. tend all to be the same. Any differentiation tends to come through corporate image and branding, attractiveness and service.

The position of the product in the distribution chain also affects ability to differentiate. Again, as a rule of thumb, the more middlemen there are between the product and the customer the less likely there is to be differentiation.

COMPETITIVE ACTIVITY.   A large amount of competitor activity in a market will force an organization continuously to look for some way to gain competitive advantage and this might very well be through differentiation.

Summary

In this chapter we looked at the concept of segmentation. Competition and the inexorable drive toward ever more consumer choice demands products and services that match customers' desired benefits. It is not practical to produce customized products to satisfy every individual need, so to overcome the problem marketers have developed the process of market segmentation.

This consists of breaking the market down into viable and realistic groups of customers who have the same or similar characteristics. Marketing research is used to identify and prioritize the most important of these groups.

We then went on to identify the many different criteria that can form a basis for segmentation. These included, industrial and consumer purchasers, geographic, social, economic, psychographic and lifestyle classifications. Some criteria for segmentation selection and evaluation were identified covering both company resources and the demands of the market.

It was shown that, having decided on the basis for the segmentation, evaluated the alternatives and chosen the most attractive, the organization can develop product or service offerings that match and satisfy the needs and wants of the selected segments. This process was identified under the concept of product positioning.

The benefits of segmentation were discussed and finally three strategic approaches to the market, undifferentiated marketing, selective marketing and concentrated marketing were outlined.

Questions for discussion

1. To gain economies of scale a company must try to create homogeneous products. Do you think that this is possible on either a national or international scale?

2. More and more customers demand choice at an ever lower price. How can a manufacturer manage this problem? Use the car industry as an example.

3. Do you consider that social class can no longer be considered a reliable method of segmenting the market? Give reasons and examples.

4. Using your imagination, develop market and customer profiles for the following products:
   - lager;
   - car insurance;
   - water;
   - confectionery.

5. Discuss the criteria that must be considered in the process of segmentation and targeting.

6. Why is research so important in segmentation? What information would be needed by an insurance company wanting to segment the market in Poland?

7. Write a product positioning statement for the following products:
   - office furniture;
   - children's toys;
   - training course;
   - crockery.

8. Imaginatively segment the following markets using your own lifestyle categories. Give at least five lifestyle characteristics to each of your chosen groups:
   - airline;
   - leisure centre;
   - tea;
   - holiday;
   - chocolate.

9. Using the strategic approach to segmentation give examples of organizations that could operate, and products that could be sold, in an undifferentiated market, a selective market and a concentrated market. Give reasons.

10. Discuss the fragmentation of the mass media, especially TV and radio, and the effect this might have on the ability of a company to segment effectively.

Case study

Market segments waiting to be discovered

As markets continue to fragment and consumers want ever more choice there are more and more market segments waiting to be discovered and exploited by the more imaginative and creative type of organization. An example of this can be shown by the recent development of the so called 'third age' market (young age!, middle age!, third age!).

The population explosion at the end of the Second World War, caused by couples wanting to have a family after years of hardship and deprivation, combined with the subsequent improvement in health, welfare and medical services has resulted in a large section of the population now being between the ages of 50 and 65. In 1961 there were 16 million people over 50 in the UK. By 2021 there will be 22.5 million accounting for 37 per cent of the population. This an increase of 40 per cent against an overall population rise of 15 per cent.

Two-fifths of these over-50s are from the middle-class, white-collar, ABC1 social groups with paid-up mortgages (66 per cent are owner occupiers), have double incomes (husband and wife both working), and children no longer living at home. Therefore many people in this so-called 'third age' group have large amounts of income at their disposal and so constitute a huge and affluent market. Even many of the older skilled workers, the C2s, have considerable disposable income with lower outgoings and insurance and endowment policies coming to fruition.

A market research report by the market intelligence group, Maps, shows that this age group is becoming more mentally and physically active and are spending more time and money on holidays, eating out, visiting friends, gardening and home improvement. The report also makes the point that they are one of the biggest buyers of winter sun holidays

Over the last few years other market research has begun to identify this relatively untapped source of consumers with unsatisfied needs looking for product benefits that are targeted specifically at them, making the point that people within this group have complained for years that they could not get products and services tailored to meet their own specific requirements.

In the past older people have argued that the reason that they could not get the sorts of products and services that they wanted was because many organizations were so focused on the younger market, in the belief that 'young was beautiful', that they were unaware of this growing potential. Many producers in reply argued that the reason for concentrating on the under-50s, -40s, -30s, -20s, was because market research has shown that this was where the demand existed.

Although complaining, the older market consumer was prepared to accept products and services that did not quite match his or her needs, as in most cases there was little or no alternative. So the older woman would accept a dress or coat, and the older man a suit or shirt, not quite in the modern style and both would be prepared to pay the same for car insurance as the more riskier younger man or woman. But now these 'third age' segments have been discovered and customized products are being offered at an ever-increasing rate.

Fashion clothes, leisure pursuits, holidays, financial services, etc. for the over-50s and over-60s are now available and new market segments are being identified and products developed continuously.

Case study questions

This 'third age' segmentation is an example of the different ways the market can be segmented if the marketer is not restricted by conservatism or lack of imagination.

1. Why do you think that it seemed to take so long for this market to be discovered? What do you think the organization should do to make certain it stays ahead of the competition in the search for new markets?
2. How many ways might this market be segmented?

Further reading

Argyle, M. and Coleman, M. (1995) *Social Psychology* (Longman Essential Psychological Series), Longman, London.

Bass, F.M., Tigert, D.J. and Lonsdale, R.T. (1968) 'Market segmentation: group versus individual behaviour', *Journal of Marketing Research*, 5, pp. 264–70.

Foxhall, G. and Goldsmith, R. (1994) *Consumer Psychology for Marketing*, Routledge, London.

Gunter, B. and Furnham, A. (1992) *Consumer Profiles; An Introduction to Psychographics*, Routledge, London.

Howard, J.A. and Sheth, J.N. (1969) *The Theory of Buyer Behaviour*, Wiley, New York.

Reis, A. and Trout, J. (1980) *Positioning; The Battle for your Mind*, McGraw-Hill, New York.

Reis, A. and Trout, J. (1986) *Marketing Warfare*, McGraw-Hill, New York.

Stevenson, L. (1974) *Seven Theories of Human Nature*, Oxford University Press, New York.

Wells, W.D. and Prensky, D. (1996) *Consumer Behaviour*, John Wiley, New York.

Williams, K. (1986) *Behavioural Aspects of Marketing*, Heinemann, London.

Worchel, S. and Shebilske, W. (1955) *Psychology, Principles and Practice*, Prentice Hall (UK), London.

5

The marketing mix:
the product

AIMS AND OBJECTIVES

By the end of the chapter the student should:

1 evaluate the role of the product in the marketing mix;

2 be able to identify the many different forms of product classification, including the differences between products and services;

3 be able to identify, describe and evaluate all the elements that go to make up the product and apply this to the concept of added value.

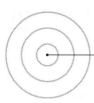

Introduction

The marketing mix

In Chapter 1 we looked at the concept of the marketing mix and identified in outline form the roles of the product, price, place and promotion in marketing products and services that would satisfy the needs of selected markets.

Commonly known as the 'marketing mix', or the 4 Ps, the product, price, place and promotion are the 'controllable tools and techniques' that the marketing manager must use to manipulate, hone and shape in order to satisfy the consumer needs that marketing research should have identified.

It was argued that all four elements of the mix must come together in an integrated and effective way so that the optimum customer-satisfying solution is achieved. Over this and the next four chapters we will be looking at each area in some detail and examining the part that each plays in successfully creating a good relationship between the organization and its customers and then bring them together in the last chapter on planning.

Figure 5.1 shows a copy of the marketing model involving the marketing mix shown in Chapter 1. We examined market research in Chapter 2 and the target market in Chapters 3 and 4. Now we will look at the marketing mix: product, price, place and promotion. The first element of the marketing mix to be examined is the P for product.

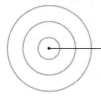

The product

It might arguably be said that the product or service that the organization offers for sale is the very reason for its existence. Without a product there is no company.

Figure 5.1	*The marketing model*

Marketing research

Marketing mix

The Company → Product Price Place → Promotion → Target Market

Revenue

As marketing puts the customer at the very heart of its activities the product or service must be developed and offered in conjunction with the customer's and the market's needs.

The product eventually marketed will consists of many elements – some tangible and some intangible. Some of the elements will be intrinsic to the product and others will exist only in the mind of the customer. To help in understanding all these elements it is helpful to break the product down into its constituent parts and examine each part in turn. However, a simple working definition of a product is needed before we begin.

Product definition

Taking a very wide definition:

A product can be anything that satisfies a need or a want in exchange for some form of payment (where the payment may sometimes be some benefit other than money).

A product may be:

- *A product, a service or a combination of both* – It can be a product, e.g. a bar of soap, a desk, a road bridge; or a service, e.g. an education course, an operation, a massage; or a combination of both, e.g. a meal in a restaurant, a holiday, a visit to the cinema, a plumbing repair (although bear in mind that nearly all products now combine some element of service).

- *An idea or a concept* – It can be an idea or a concept; e.g. genetically engineered food, hair removal by electrolysis, some form of consultancy.

- *A process* – It can be a process, e.g. the running of a marketing information system, bad debt collection, a current bank account.

- *A person or a place* – It can be a person or a place, e.g. a politician, a pop singer, Windsor Castle, Colchester Town.

- *Written, sung, played or performed* – It can be a book, a song, a tune or a play.

- *A smell or a taste* – A perfume, a unique recipe (even this can now be patented).

- *The whole organization and/or its products* – The product can also be seen as the whole organization e.g. Abbey National or Debenhams and/or the particular products that it markets, e.g. mortgages or clothes.

Product classification

Products are classified by academics and practitioners alike into groups according to the function they perform for both the company and the consumer. This is important to understand because different products will need to be marketed in different ways. This will vary according to the type of product and the market at which it is aimed. The product classifications named below are not mutually exclusive and many products will appear in more than one category. There are three main categories to be considered:

1. consumables;
2. durables;
3. services.

CONSUMABLES

Consumables (or non-durables) are those products that are bought and consumed in their usage. This will include products such as food, groceries, drink, toiletries, newspapers (consumed in the sense that they are read and thrown away), cigarettes, petrol, oil, etc.

DURABLES

Durables are products that have a longer life than consumables. This will include products such as cars, houses, furniture, both brown (TVs, hi-fi, radios, etc.) and white (washing machines, tumble dryers, fridges, etc.) electrical goods, carpets, lighting, etc.

SERVICES

There is no doubt that services are different in character than the type of goods identified above. All goods have some form of service involved, albeit merely in the transaction involved. However many other benefit offerings involve very high levels of service in some form or other and these need a different marketing approach. Services include:

- *retail services*: shops, departmental stores, supermarkets, etc.;
- *leisure services*: meals out, accommodation, holidays, entertainment, recreational, cultural, etc.;
- *financial services*: money management, mortgages, pension plans, insurance, personal equity plans, etc.;
- *medical services*: hospital, doctor, physiotherapist, cosmetic, etc.;
- *communication services*: entertainment, telephony, computer networks, etc.;
- *energy services*: gas, electric, nuclear, coal, etc.;
- *motor vehicle services*: repairs, leasing, renting, etc.;
- *household services*: cleaning, repairs, painting, building, etc.
- *education services*: schools, colleges, universities, etc.

Services account for over 60 per cent of all spending and so their importance cannot be over-estimated. Some of the services are in the public sector and some in the private. Such is their importance that any of the above could be studied as a separate discipline.

DIFFERENCES BETWEEN SERVICES AND PRODUCTS

When marketing in the service sector the following types of differences between services and products should be noted:

1. inseparable;
2. intangible;
3. perishable;
4. variable;
5. ongoing.

INSEPARABLE.   With a tangible product the benefits are encapsulated in the product itself and cannot be separated from the actual delivery. Marlboro cigarettes, Kodak film, Waddington's Monopoly, Reader's Digest, the Ford Escort have intrinsic benefits which should remain constant wherever the consumer actually buys the product. With a service the manner and way the product are delivered are part, if not all of the product and cannot thus be separated. Its intrinsic value is dependent on how it is offered at the point of delivery (we look for physical evidence (another 'P'?), image, cleanliness etc. as a sign of acceptable service). A service can:

- take place at the same time as the purchase, e.g. a meal in a restaurant or a haircut;
- be sold and then produced later, e.g. a holiday or a pension scheme;
- be an ongoing process, e.g. schooling or treatment by a doctor.

INTANGIBLE.   A service, unlike a product, cannot be touched, only described. The customer can see, try, feel the product when buying a car or a TV. However, when buying a holiday, a personal equity plan, an operation or an education for the children, the benefits have to be described by the producer and imagined by the customer. For this reason the sales and promotion process can be more difficult and demanding than selling a tangible product.

PERISHABLE.   Unlike a product (cars, drinks, furniture) a service cannot be put together, packaged, stored and used on a later occasion. The product finishes with each offering and starts again with the new. Even with some form of guaranteed service contract, for example on a gas boiler, or a computer system, this will still apply as the value perceived by the customer is dependent on the level of the service given in response to each customer and organization contact.

VARIABLE.   Each service offering is only as good as the last performance (a lecture one week may be magnificent and dreadful the next). A meal in a restaurant is only as good as the last offering and one bad experience can destroy the reputation created by all past good ones. Similarly the service in one town or country may differ drastically from the service in another. This has severe organizational problems for some companies, for example KFC, Wimpy, Harvester, Comet, Post House, Prudential, where the quality of service given is crucial to maintaining competitive advantage. This is especially relevant when the company expands abroad.

ONGOING.   Many services consist of some form of ongoing benefit that can last a lifetime. This puts an enormous pressure on the producer to maintain an acceptable level of service.

McDonald's sell a product, the hamburger, but the 'product' could be said to be the whole experience which would include the ambience of the outlet including the decor, the food and the service given by the staff. It can be argued that, because of consumer demand, most products must now incorporate some element of service both at the time of purchase and after purchase.

FURTHER SUB-DIVISION

Consumables, durables and services can be broken down into two major areas:

1. industrial products;
2. consumer products.

It it important to understand the distinction between the two product areas, as significant differences in the respective markets will call for different marketing approaches. You may recall the following differences discussed earlier:

- industrial markets have less buying points than consumer markets;
- industrial products are consumed by organizations, consumer products by individuals;
- industrial buyers buy for rational reasons, consumers for emotional reasons;
- in industrial markets each transaction tends to contain more worth than in consumer markets.

INDUSTRIAL PRODUCTS/SERVICES.   Products/services that are sold by one organization to another, *for that organization's own use*, can be classified as 'industrial products'.

Industrial products can be further sub-divided into three major areas. Again, the reason why this distinction is made is because each area will demand a slightly different marketing approach:

1. *Materials and parts* – Materials and parts are all those things that a company will purchase for use in producing the end product. In the car industry this will include such items as: nuts and bolts; electrical wire and terminals; glass for the windows; metal; tyres; seat coverings; engine parts; and so on.
2. *Capital items* – Capital items will cover all those items that would be seen as fixed assets on the company balance sheet. This will include: land; factories; machinery; IT; office equipment; transport etc.
3. *Supplies and services* – Supplies and services are all those products and services that will be consumed by the organization in the running of the business. This will include: energy for lighting, heating, operating the equipment, e.g. gas, electricity, oil, coal; water; administration products and services, e.g. paper, files, pens; services such as: management consultancy, advertising agency; payroll systems, costing systems, etc.

CONSUMER PRODUCTS/SERVICES.   Consumer products and services can be divided into a number of categories. It should be noted that the categories are not mutually exclusive and that some products will be included under more than one heading.

Fast moving consumer goods (FMCG). FMCG are all goods that have a very quick turnover. All the products sold by Sainsbury, Tesco, Gateway, Asda, etc. would be classified as FMCG. They tend to be consumables but can be non-consumables.

Convenience goods. These goods are so-called because they are readily available at a convenient time and place. This might be any time of the night or day. In return for this 'convenience' the customer is prepared to pay a premium price. Convenience goods will probably all be FMCG. Examples will include such items as bread, milk, groceries, batteries, toilet paper, disposable razors, newspapers, fast food, confectionery and, in some cases, National Lottery tickets.

The 1980s and 1990s have seen the growth in convenience stores such as T&S Stores, which trade under the names Supercigs and Dillons, Seven to Eleven and Spar, 'eight till late'. However by far the biggest growth in this sector has been the convenience store on the petrol station forecourt. All the major companies, Esso, Shell, BP, Q8 (often in partnership with the large supermarkets) now have some form of convenience store in all their major outlets and in many cases it has become the most profitable part of the business. Recent changes in the law now allow some of these stores to open 24 hours a day, seven days a week.

Staple goods. This classification covers basic products that will be consumed on a regular basis. Staple goods will probably be both FMCG and convenience goods. What is a staple may vary between different groups of consumers. It will include products such as bread, potatoes, milk, margarine or butter, beer, tea, breakfast cereal, toilet rolls, etc.

Distress goods. Distress goods are those products that people have to buy and so do not have to be convinced they need (except in being persuaded to buy one brand rather than another). This will include such products as car tyres, batteries, toilet rolls, razors, female hygiene products, etc.

Impulse goods. These are groups of products that are purchased on impulse, that is on the spur of the moment. Many different types of products may be purchased on impulse including food, confectionery, clothes and even more expensive items such as TVs and cars. If products are known sometimes to be bought on impulse, the retailer will often aid the process by displaying the product within easy reach.

Own label goods. These are products produced for a retailer by a manufacturer and sold under the name of that retailer. There has been an enormous growth in own label products over the last 20 years notably through outlets like Tesco, Sainsbury, Marks and Spencer, B&Q and Homebase. Own label products are seen to be in direct competition to the manufacturer's own branded goods because many consumers perceive them to be of equal or better value.

Shopping goods. Shopping goods are products that the consumer will want to take time to chose. The buying process will involve looking around and visiting different outlets. It includes products and services such as furniture, cars, cookers, bicycles, washing machines, carpets, double glazing, insurance, mort-gages, holidays. The seller would need to make certain that point-of-sale information is made available in all of the relevant forms so as to aid the prospective consumer toward purchase.

Speciality goods.   Speciality goods are products that serve a speciality market. They could include products such as cameras, computers, fishing tackle, golf equipment, cowboy accoutrements, etc. These products tend to be sold through specialized outlets with a deep assortment of one type of product.

Unsought goods.   Some products and services are needed but not actively sought out as the need:

■   may not be recognized by the customer;
■   may take place some time in the future;
■   may be painful to contemplate.

With these types of goods the producer will need to market the products in a pro-active manner by actively seeking out the customer and persuading purchase. Unsought goods might be life insurance, a funeral cost payment plan, a will making service, extended warranties, etc.

Product classification and the DMP

Product classifications have been developed to help in the marketing process as different classes of products will probably demand a different marketing approach.

In the decision-making process (DMP) customers looking to buy a shopping good will follow one process (extensive problem solving) while in purchasing FMCG goods (routine buying) they will follow another. Similarly convenience goods will be marketed with a different marketing mix emphasis than will be unsought goods.

As the market changes new product categories are identified to cater for these changing circumstances as marketing managers recognize the need for a new specialized and consistent marketing approach (the convenience goods market hardly existed 20 years ago). An organization unaware of movement in the market affecting the decision-making process will lose competitive advantage.

INTERNAL METHODS OF PRODUCT CLASSIFICATION

For planning purposes an organization may classify products internally under the six categories explained below. It should be appreciated that these classifications must be treated with some care as one company may have a slightly different interpretation of them than another.

PRODUCT RANGE.   The product range is the full list of products that a company offers for sale. This is usually available on a leaflet or brochure.

PRODUCT WIDTH.   The product width is the number of products offered for sale compared with other similar companies. So a company may have a small product width or a large product width.

PRODUCT LINE.   In each product line the items have some common characteristics, customers and/or uses.

■ Hotpoint offers different product lines that include washing machines, fridges, tumble dryers, vacuum cleaners and cookers.

■ The Ford motor company offers many different product lines including the Fiesta, Escort, Orion, Mondeo, Scorpio as well as Jaguar cars and Ferguson tractors.

■ Procter & Gamble markets (amongst other things) detergents, toothpaste, deodorants, disposable nappies, hand soap, shampoos and face and toilet tissues.

PRODUCT LINE LENGTH.   Product line length looks at the number of different products in each product line.

■ Hotpoint produces different types of washing machines including a front loading automatic, a top loading automatic and a twin-tub.

■ It also produces freezers and fridge-freezers as well as fridges.

■ In the cooker product line it offers microwave ovens, built-in ovens and hobs, and free-standing cookers.

■ Under the detergent product line Procter & Gamble sells many different brands including Ariel, Bold, Daz, Breeze, Fairy.

PRODUCT LINE DEPTH.   Product depth refers to how many versions are available in each product line.

■ Hotpoint offers a choice of front loading automatics under the following model numbers; WM 12, WM 13, WM 22, WM 31, all at different prices, offering a lesser or greater level of benefits including variable spin speeds, number of wash programmes and in white (WM 31W) or almond (WM 31A) with brown trim, or all white.

■ Procter & Gamble offer Ariel in many different sizes and different forms.

■ The Ford Fiesta can be purchased in basic form or with a choice of bolt on extras.

PRODUCT MIX OR PRODUCT PORTFOLIO.   The product mix, or product portfolio, is concerned with the relationships, harmony and synergy between product lines in the mix as well as product lengths and depth. There needs to be a balance struck between the dis-economies of scale associated with offering too many different product lines and product depths and the need to offer the customer adequate choice.

Too many products being offered can lead to the marketing effort being diluted across too many areas working against a focused approach. An organization will have core business skills built up over many years. This experience and knowledge in one area (e.g. frozen foods) may not be readily transferred to another (e.g. snack foods) and so competitive advantage may be lost.

When the market is growing there is a tendency for companies to grow also. In the optimistic 1980s companies grew by acquisition, taking over other companies producing both similar and dissimilar products. Retailers took over other retailers, manufacturers bought other manufacturers, retail clothes businesses went into property development and brewers bought retail takeaway outlets. A buoyant market hid the dis-economies of scale weakness (identified above) in the product mix.

The downturn in the economy and increased competition exposed these weakness causing organizations to take stock and rationalize their product range. Ideally an analysis of the whole product portfolio should take place on a regular basis.

A product mix can be such that seasonal demands for one product are offset by those of another. In theory an example might be marketing ice-cream in the summer and umbrellas in the winter.

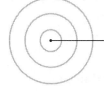

Building customer benefits by adding value to the product

People buy products because they hope that the benefits gained from the transaction will satisfy some outstanding need. So another way of looking at the product is as 'a bundle of customer benefits' put together by the producer hopefully to perform this task. As the consumer becomes more sophisticated, more benefits are demanded. To maintain a competitive advantage the organization must continually offer more. This process of continually upgrading product benefits is called 'adding value'.

Therefore marketing and selling products and services in the modern market can be seen as a process of continually adding value in response to the ever-changing demands of the targeted consumer. Because of the added value the customer will often be prepared to pay a higher price.

There are many different ways that an organization can add value to its products in response to customers' demands for choice and ever better value, and the progressive organization will always be looking for more innovative ways.

The functional and the symbolic attributes of the product

Added value can be categorized under two general areas corresponding to the types of benefits demanded by the customer. These two areas can be identified as:

1. the functional;
2. the symbolic.

THE FUNCTIONAL

Most of us might argue that the main reason we would want to purchase a product is because of its functional properties. This is the overt purpose of the product and the reason for purchase seems to be self-evident. As an example can you think for a moment about the functional reasons why the following products might be bought:

1. a watch;
2. bottled water;
3. a pen.

Of course the answers would be:

1. to tell the time;
2. to quench the thirst;
3. to write with.

Most products have some sort of functional purpose. Cars are for transport, clothes to keep us warm, shoes protect the feet, the theatre entertains, food satisfies hunger and insurance protects in case of mishap.

THE SYMBOLIC

Of course we do buy a watch to tell the time, water to quench our thirst and a pen to write with. But continuous, in-depth market research and practical experience, has shown that people also buy products for reasons other than the functional – they buy them for symbolic reasons. By symbolic we mean as a representation of some other, sometimes deeper and less transparent, emotional or instinctive need. This concept fits in with the buyer behavioural models identified earlier in Chapter 3, for example the three thinking brains; Maslow's hierarchy of effects; Freud and the theory of the subconscious.

Using the behavioural models developed in Chapter 3 and taking the example of the watch, the bottled water and the pen less obvious *symbolic* reasons, rather than functional, for why the customer might want to purchase these products can be identified.

- A gold watch may be bought to inform others how successfully rich we are (status needs), a mickey mouse watch to show how fun loving and unmaterialistic (social needs), a 'chunky' divers watch with a 100 functions gives 'street cred' to the owner (security needs).
- Scottish spring water in a premium priced designer blue bottle at a dinner party, informs our guests that we are avant-garde (status needs).
- An expensive 'Parker' pen associates the owner with having a knowledge of quality and comfortable wealth.

All these symbolic reasons for purchase, other than the functional reasons, satisfy some form of emotive need.

A COMBINATION OF FUNCTIONAL AND EMOTIONAL BENEFITS

It seems that products are purchased for both functional and symbolic reasons and so when designing, developing and promoting a product both functional and symbolic needs have to be catered for. The importance of each can be discovered by customer behavioural research. With some products the reason for purchase will lean more toward the functional (double-glazing, sugar) and with others more toward the symbolic (perfume, fashion clothes).

Most consumer products are bought to satisfy an emotional need (research has shown that over 75 per cent are bought for symbolic reasons) and so symbolic benefits will be most important. On the other hand, most business to business products are bought for functional reasons and this should be recognized when developing the marketing mix (although there is evidence that even these products are, at times, bought for symbolic reasons).

The unique selling proposition (USP)

The idea of the Unique Selling Proposition (USP) was first introduced by Rosser Reves in the USA. Reves argued that all organizations, if they want to succeed, should offer the customer some form of unique benefit not offered by the competition. It should be based on an organizational strength and could be either functional or symbolic. It could be to do with the corporate image, in the product itself or in the after sales service.

A USP is particularly important when introducing a new product to the market, especially if heavy competition already exists. If the new product has nothing to differentiate itself from existing products then there is no reason why the customer should switch.

USP AND THE OPENING OF A NEW RESTAURANT

An example might be in the opening of a new restaurant. If 50 restaurants already exist in the town there must be a very good reason, a USP, why the customer should choose to go to the new one rather than stay with the old tried and tested restaurant. In this case the USP offered could be in the depth of service offered, the uniqueness of the food, the location, the price charged and so on.

PRODUCT STRATEGY AND THE USP

It can be argued that there are three simple approaches in developing a USP product strategy and the organization should choose one or more if they are to successfully sell their products (this is linked into product positioning and those uncertain about the connection should refer back to the previous chapter on segmentation). The three approaches are outlined below.

1. make the product cheaper;
2. make the product better;
3. make the product different.

If the organization cannot adopt one of the above approaches to its product offering there might be little reason why their product should be bought. We will now look at each approach in turn.

MAKE THE PRODUCT CHEAPER. If an organization sells in the whole market and decides to use price as the product USP, and many similar products exist in the market, it would have to be a price that is lower than the competition. It could achieve this in two ways, either working on a lower profit margin or producing the product more cheaply. It could only adopt the former method in the short term because the competition could always respond and a price war may well develop.

To maintain price leadership in the long term, the organization would have to have lower costs than the rest of the competition. This would probably mean it had achieved market leadership, because only by selling more products than any other company can greater economies of scale lead to lower costs, and so allow the leader to continually charge lower prices across the whole of the market.

However a smaller company could use a low price as its product strategy by contracting to manufacture own label products for a large retailer, for example ASDA. Although not having the economy of scale benefits of the larger company, lower costs may be achieved if the large retailer guarantees a certain level of purchase and undertakes most of the marketing costs.

MAKE THE PRODUCT BETTER.   Some companies gain competitive advantage by making the product better than the competition in some significant way. This could be better in content, performance, appearance, delivery, or after sales service. Marks and Spencer would argue that they gain competitive advantage using this strategy.

MAKE THE PRODUCT DIFFERENT.   Other organizations look for advantage by adopting a USP that offers the customer something different to that being offered by the competition. It is worth repeating that this 'difference' need only be in the mind of the target consumer and can be functional and/or emotional. The way a company may choose to differentiate its products can take many forms including quality, branding, service, etc. and these elements will be examined as we move through the chapter.

Product differentiation can be used to sell across the whole market or it can be used to sell in a small market niche. An example of product differentiation across the whole market might be Coca-Cola. The manufacturer of Coca-Cola claims that it has a secret recipe that makes its drink different from all other colas. It also uses the emotive appeal of being 'the real thing', that is all that is good about America can be associated with Coca-Cola. Other companies using the same approach include: Heinz, 'Beanz, Meanz, Heinz'; Kalibur, the alcohol free lager; Campbell's condensed soups; Reckitt & Coleman, Down to Earth, 'Green' household cleaner.

Examples of product differentiation in a market niche include: Phileas Fogg with its 'Fine food from around the world', a range of exotic and unusual snack foods; Waggle Dance, 'the Original Honey Bottled Beer'; *Private Eye*, the satirical magazine; all of which are aimed at a specific, narrow, target market.

We can now look in more detail at the many other ways that value can be added to the product.

The added value process

The idea behind the concept of value added is that there is a basic core to all products around which benefits are then added in response to consumer demand. The process will be examined under the following headings:

1. the core product;
2. primary added value;
3. supplementary added value.

THE CORE PRODUCT

All products and services have some basic form or core and this is the starting place for the added value process. This core might be tea, potatoes, milk or coffee beans or it might be somewhere to sleep, a week's rest from work, or a financial loan (all organizations must be clear about the nature of their core product otherwise confusion can cause the wrong benefits to be promoted).

In the past the consumer would buy unlabelled tea loose and by the scoopful from a large tea chest. Potatoes were only available in the form they came out of the ground (including the mud), milk was sold by the jugful and coffee beans were sold loose, to be ground down for use by the consumer. A bed for the night would be in some local hostelry, a week away from work might be a holiday in a tent on a farmer's field and a loan might be through some form of mutual loan club (often based in a pub).

COMMODITY PRODUCTS. Many of these basic core products, often described as commodity products, are still traded in the city on what is known as the 'commodities market'. This market would come under the umbrella of business to business marketing.

ADDING VALUE IS A CONTINUOUS PROCESS. Increasing consumer affluence, more awareness, the demand for more choice, and greater competition, forced companies to add ever more added value to this basic core product.

PRIMARY ADDED VALUE

In response to customer demand most, if not all, consumer products will now have some form of added value and this will be examined using the idea of primary and supplementary added value benefits.

Primary added value consists of all the benefits that are attached in an immediate sense to the product and are there before purchase, whilst supplementary added value consists of the benefits offered that follow on after the purchase.

We can now look in more detail at all the added value options collectively known as primary added value beginning with innovation and design.

INNOVATION AND DESIGN. Product and service innovation and design are crucial if competitive advantage is to be maintained and many commentators and practitioners argue that it is *the* essential ingredient to success. In response to demand, the core product can be continuously developed and offered in ever more attractive, progressive, convenient or different forms. The development of new technology is forever aiding this process.

The potato may become crisps, oven ready chips or powdered mash potatoes; tea may be sold in tea bags (square or round) or as instant granules. Coffee can be bought in liquid or powdered form and colour may be added to improve appearance. The bed for the night can be in a number of different purpose built hotels (according to taste) with TV, video, in-room bar, showers and bidet; the holiday can be on a cruise liner or in a chalet in the Australian Blue Mountains. The financial loan can be taken up in a hundred different forms.

QUALITY. Alternative quality levels can be offered according to demand. This might be high, medium or low quality according to use, price and industry norms.

PACKAGING. The packaging can add value in many different ways including protection, design, appearance, information giving, and ease of use. We will return to the role of packaging in more detail later in the chapter.

BRANDING. Giving the product a name enables consistent quality, taste and performance to be recognized and it can come to mean something very personal to the customer. The product can also be requested by name. As with packaging, branding will be discussed in greater depth later.

FEATURES AND BENEFITS. Many different features can be added, all giving greater benefits to the product. Looking at the different products listed below, features can be identified that could be added so as to enhance presentation and performance.

A basic music system can have added value through quadraphonic sound, remote control, tape to tape facility, TV linkage. A motor car can have high quality radio, air bag, power steering, leather seats. The value added benefits of a house may include a fully fitted kitchen, carpets, curtains, landscaped garden.

All the other elements of the marketing mix, price, place and promotion, will also affect customer perception of the product and will be seen as either adding or taking away value.

PRICE. The price charged for the product will be seen as part of the product and reflect the overall sense of value for money felt by the customer. Too high or too low a price will confuse customer perception of added value.

PLACE OF PURCHASE. Where and how the product is made available for sale will also reflect on the image of the product and so should compliment all the other elements of the product. Premium priced, quality lingerie would create a negative customer reaction if sold from a stall in the market.

PROMOTION. Through the use of promotion (e.g. advertising) a product, brand image and reputation can be developed and reinforced.

If all the factors identified above are to add value to the finished product they should be developed in conjunction with the customer through the use of marketing research.

SUPPLEMENTARY ADDED VALUE

Such is the nature of the competitive marketplace that the search for improvement is never ending. The supplementary layer of added value includes those factors that can be added to offer benefits *after purchase*. Supplementary benefits might include: after sales service, service contracts, delivery and installation, guarantees and warranties, and returns policies. These can be examined in a little more detail.

AFTER SALES SERVICE. Most products will have some form of after sales service especially through the guarantee period. An imaginative marketing approach would offer a comprehensive service incorporating all the actions necessary to keep the customer satisfied. This would include such areas as prompt reaction to complaints, friendly telephone manner and informative and helpful staff. It might also include taking a pro-active view on future customer needs and wants. All the other factors categorized below might be seen as an integral part of an all-round, customer-centred approach, to after sales service.

SERVICE CONTRACT. More important in some industries than others, a service contract offers an extension of the basic guarantee in return for a sum of money, for example four years extra cover on a TV, washing machine, video recorder, for a payment of £100.

DELIVERY AND INSTALLATION. If appropriate, delivery might include installation and a demonstration. For the marketing driven company this would be at the convenience of the customer and not the company. Whether or not to charge will vary according to the product and the competitive norm. Some companies attempt to gain competitive advantage by giving this service free of charge.

GUARANTEES AND WARRANTIES. Guarantees and warranties are now seen as very much a part of the product. A guarantee can cover all of the product or just selected areas, for example parts only. All products are covered by some form of legal protection but many organizations choose to offer additional benefits. A company cannot afford to appear to have an inferior guarantee and may have to offer the same extra benefits offered by the competition unless its product is perceived to be superior in some other way.

RETURNS POLICY. The conditions under which a company is prepared to take a product back if the customer is dissatisfied can influence the initial purchase and persuade the customer to purchase.

Marks and Spencer has an enviable reputation as a leading retailer in the UK. Its no-quibble returns policy has been a major factor in building this reputation. Many customers will purchase products knowing they can take them back if not suitable.

Figure 5.2 summarizes the added value process described in this section in diagrammatic form.

PRIORITIZING ADDED VALUE

We have identified the many ways that the organization can add value to its products and have seen that, from a basic core commodity, the marketing

Figure 5.2	*Added value*

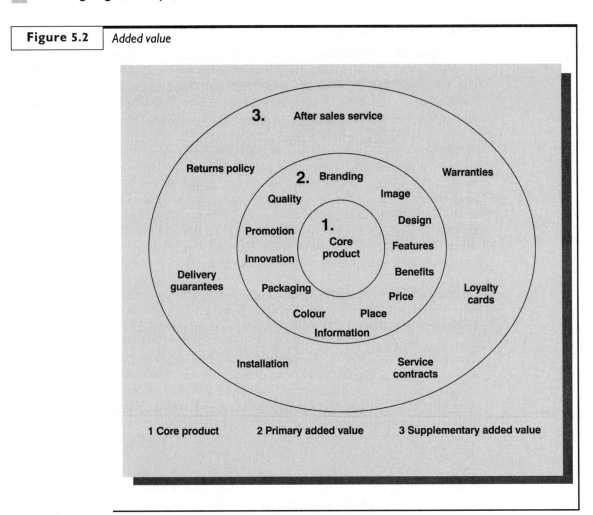

manager can build competitive advantage by adding any number of the factors identified under the concept of primary and supplementary added value.

Which of these added value factors should be prioritized in developing the product and the marketing mix will vary from one product or service to another and from one market to another. In some industries it might be the after sales service that is the most important (computer systems), in others it might be the brand name (confectionery countline bars). With cars it might be a six-year guarantee (Daewoo) and for a takeaway meal it might be the quality (Waitrose). In one area it might be the functional products (DIY) that must be emphasized in another the symbolic (beauty and skin care). Inherent in the concept of good marketing is the realization that the correct areas must be identified and the relevant benefits offered.

ADDED VALUE AND PRICE

In very general terms, the more value a company can add to its product the more (all other things being equal) the customer might be prepared to pay. In this way more profit might be made. An example might be a commodity product like frozen chicken. The basic product might be sold on average for 70p per lb/45p per kg. It might be a little cheaper at Tesco and a little more expensive at Marks and Spencer. However, add more value, for example tandori chicken slices, or chicken cooked in orange, and double, treble or quadruple the price per lb/kg can then be charged.

ADDED VALUE AND CHANGE

Organizations cannot afford to become complacent as customer added value priorities change and become ever more demanding. In the affluent 1980s, branding was seen as the overriding consumer purchase stimulus. In the more frugal 1990s concern about the price is top of the agenda.

As a result of competition, what was considered as an extra and happily paid for a decade ago is now expected to be included in the basic product, as is ever better quality and overall value for money.

Due to their importance we will now look at again at two areas, packaging and branding, in much more detail. We begin by looking at packaging.

Packaging

The importance that packaging can often have in adding value to products and services cannot be over-estimated. In many cases the packaging is not only an essential part of the product, it is the very reason why the product is actually purchased.

Research has shown that bottled water is often bought for the cache that comes from the name on the bottle (Perrier), the bottle shape and the bottle colour (blue or green). People like to put it on the table when entertaining guests for dinner or when running a company meeting. A box of chocolates is often bought for others because of the message that the packaging sends out as well as for the chocolates inside (Black Magic).

How packaging is used

Before discussing the actual role the packaging performs we will briefly look at the different types of packaging used. These fall into three levels:

1. primary;
2. secondary;
3. tertiary.

PRIMARY PACKAGING

The primary packaging is the first layer of packaging that surrounds the product. It includes boxes, bags, bottles, tins, cartons and other various forms of wrapping made in many different sorts of material. Some products will only have this one layer of packaging. Drink in a bottle (whisky), toothpaste in tube, a chocolate biscuit snack in a silver wrapper. Some products will have more than one layer of packaging.

SECONDARY PACKAGING

Secondary packaging is the next layer. This will include the same types of packaging identified above but used as an additive to the primary packaging. The whisky bottle in a presentation box, the tube of toothpaste in a cardboard package and the chocolate biscuit grouped with others in see-through foil.

TERTIARY PACKAGING

Tertiary packaging is the third layer and is used mainly for delivery purposes. Bottles of whisky will be delivered to the retailer or the wholesaler in an outer package as will toothpaste and chocolate biscuits. It can be used by the retailer for storage, delivery and display purposes or discarded.

The role of packaging

Packaging can perform many roles in the marketing of both products and services including the following.

PROTECTION. Some products travel farther and are more easily damaged than others. The layers of packaging will act as protection, especially if the product is going abroad.

Many years ago washing machines and refrigerators were delivered in square, brown cardboard boxes. Despite using stronger and stronger cardboard, reinforced with supports on all corners, too many machines were found to be damaged by the time they were unpacked in the consumer's home. More information was added to the outside of the boxes, stressing the fragility of the contents, all to no avail. Extensive research identified the root cause of the problem. Although the delivery people could read the information and knew what the contents were, they habitually treated the items as cardboard boxes, not as washing machines or refrigerators. The cardboard gave a false appearance of high strength, so the boxes tended to be thrown around, stacked and unstacked with too much vigour. Also the contents could not be examined at each delivery stage because of the time taken and the damage done to the appearance of the packaging by unpackaging every item.

A domestic appliance company came up with the answer. See-through plastic bubble pack with polystyrene corners. The interior could be seen at all times so that nobody was in any doubt about the contents. Any damage could also be seen quickly and without having to unpack every package. A clear example of innovation applied to packaging.

EASE OF USE. Ease of use is a way a company can gain competitive advantage. This affects all layers of packaging. A retailer must have packaging that fits in with its methods of storage, movement around the warehouse and display. A triangular shaped package may look attractive but will be unacceptable if it does not sit comfortably, or if it takes up too much room on the retail shelf.

Ease of use for customers includes packaging that is easy to carry, easy to store, easy to open, easy to use and re-use and easy to dispose of. Persil now have a pull tape at the bottom of their large powder boxes which allows the square box to collapse for easy disposal.

INNOVATION AND DESIGN IN PACKAGING

Many companies have gained competitive advantage through the development of innovative packaging. Examples are toothpaste in a push-top container, a widget in a beer can, wine in a box, whipped cream in a press-top container, tetra-pak for longer life liquids, tea in pyramid shaped tea bags.

DESCRIBING THE PRODUCT

A great deal of information can be placed on the packaging. This can be about the contents, instructions for use, sales promotions, special offers and information about other company products. It is also a way for the manufacturer to by-pass the retailer and conduct a dialogue directly with the customer and companies such as Heinz and Kelloggs are now taking full advantage of this opportunity to develop longer term relationships with their customers.

MAKING THE SALE

In some areas of retail, with the development of self-service, the packaging has come to be known as 'the silent salesman'. Research shows that over 70 per cent of products in the supermarket are chosen on impulse and colour, pictures, words, sales promotions, etc. used skilfully on the packaging can 'talk' to the customer and hopefully persuade purchase.

At any one time over 15 per cent of supermarket products will have some form of money-off, extra content free, competition opportunities and two-for-the-price-of-one sales promotion incentives printed on the packaging to encourage purchase.

PACKAGING: PUBLIC POLICY AND CONSUMER PROTECTION

GREEN ISSUES. The environmentally-aware caring 1990s have seen pressure brought to bear on companies to be more concerned about 'green' issues such as waste, use of finite resources and pollution and many organizations now take this responsibility very seriously.

Procter & Gamble offer Bold in re-usable boxes and sells the refills; Persil writes on the packet that its ingredients are biodegradable and the packaging is made from 80 per cent recyclable materials; Sainsbury offer shoppers one penny back whenever the customer uses their own shopping bags. Many supermarket car parks now have recycling bin facilities with separate compartments for used bottles – green, brown and clear – and for tins and cans.

FAIR PLAY.   Consumer pressure groups have instigated protection legislation covering such areas as fair packaging and labelling. The product contents must be accurately described and the packaging must not attempt to deceive by either giving information that is not true or by creating an illusion of more content than actually exists.

The socially aware marketing company will have developed policies and codes of practice to cover these areas, without waiting for legislation, driven by the desire to satisfy customer needs.

Branding

Such is the value of a brand name that one company taking over another is prepared to pay many times the quoted market price for the company in order to obtain well-known, market brand leaders. Old, well-known brands are so valuable because new brands are extremely costly and difficult to establish in the market.

Ford bought Jaguar paying over double the share price to obtain a famous name associated with quality and luxury. Nestlé did the same in buying out Rowntree with famous brand names like Aero, Kit-kat, Smarties, Quality Street, Rolo, Yorkie and Black Magic and the toy makers Mattel (Sindy Doll) and Hasbro (Barbie Doll) became locked in an escalating takeover battle for J.W. Spears the makers of 'Scrabble'.

The value of the brand

So what are the benefits of a brand and why are companies prepared to pay over the odds? Originally products were sold in commodity form. There was nothing to distinguish one offering from another. However, because of confusion and coun-terfeiting some producers started to 'brand' their product in some way to denote the place of origin (e.g. gold and silver, furniture, clocks). In this way, as repu-tation spread, a higher price could be charged for superior workmanship and resale values were maintained.

LIFE BEFORE BRANDING

Most grocery products were originally sold loose in an unpacked and unnamed form either by the pound, by the pint or by the length. The author has memories of visits to a large grocery store in the 1950s in the east end of London. The shop would have been about 100 feet long. A large marble counter ran the complete length of the shop on both sides. There seemed to be about 50 people on each side, consisting of servers, cutters, weighers and packers. There was no such thing as self-service. Most of the products seemed to be sold in loose form.

The customer would go to the appropriate counter – meats, butter and margarines, tea, milk, cheeses or vinegar. The meats and fish were unpacked on steel trays, butter, margarine and cheese were in slab form, tea was loose in tea chests, milk in large metal containers and vinegar sold from wooden barrels with taps on. Some of the products were identified by country or district of origin but there were no markings (except the price) other than this.

The customer would order by weight, size, scoop or returnable container. The product was then cut to size, weighed, poured or scooped, packed and wrapped in plain paper, or put in an unmarked container. Much of this was skilled work and the store would have employed trainees as well as experienced staff.

Product quality could vary from one week to another as the customer had no way of maintaining continuity of purchase. To ask for the same product as last week would have to have been very much a 'hit and miss' affair. Purchase quality could often only be identified with the naked eye and this often meant the housewife visiting shop after shop, looking for the best possible buy. Branding and self-service has now radically altered this retail approach.

Interestingly enough, a company now exists, Weigh and Save, that has returned to this non-brand formula using it as a USP to differentiate the market. Products – sweets and some grocery items – are presented on the shop floor loose and in containers. The customer takes a plain paper bag and fills as much as they need using the scoop supplied. This is then taken to the counter for payment. It is supposed to be cheaper in price than the branded equivalent.

The benefits of branding

Producers soon began to recognize the benefits that could accrue to the customer, to the retailer and to their own company by putting some form of recognizable name or mark on their products and widespread branding took off.

CUSTOMER BENEFITS OF BRANDING

Branding brings a number of benefits to the consumer.

- *Recognized quality*: having used a product once and liked the experience, the customer can recognize the brand and so be able to purchase the exact same product again.
- *Consistent quality*: branding promises the same level of quality wherever the product is bought. A Mars bar will be the same in Tokyo, Moscow or Croydon. Similarly Heinz baked beans will taste the same whether bought from the corner shop, the garage forecourt or the supermarket.
- *Time saving*: recognized and consistent quality saves the consumer time in not having to personally search out and test variable and unknown quality levels.
- *Provides information*: the brand becomes a receptacle for a vast amount of information about both the company and the product.

- *Identifies function*: a well known brand and its function can be immediately recognized. Persil washes clothes whiter, Weetabix is a healthy breakfast food and Gillette supplies shaving products to 'real men'.
- *Satisfy emotional needs*: in earlier chapters it was argued that customers buy products for reasons other than functional. Brand names like Porsche, Microsoft, Kodak, Maxwell House, Johnny Walker, Levi, the Prudential, satisfy emotional needs such as status, recognition, companionship, security, etc.

SELLER BENEFITS OF BRANDING

The advantages are not just for the consumer; producers can also benefit.

- *It gives legal protection*: the brand can be registered and any competitor infringement prosecuted. Harrods, the Champagne Association, Boss, Nintendo, will attempt to prosecute infringement anywhere in the world (although this is difficult in some developing countries without reciprocal brand registration agreements).
- *Builds loyalty*: customers become attached to a brand because of both perceived functional and emotional reasons. Brands develop recognizable personalities and research has shown generations of mothers and daughters buying Persil, Oxo or Hovis out of a sense of loyalty. People will stay with the same bank or building society for years, this strong sense of loyalty preventing change.
- *Power with the retailer*: a strong brand will persuade the retailer to stock the product because of consumer demand. Despite the growth of own label brands, products like Mars, Milky Way, M&Ms, Penguin, Kelloggs, Pedigree Chum, Bird's Eye, HP sauce, Sony, National Panasonic, Hotpoint, etc. will always be stocked for as long as the brand demonstrates strength with the consumer.
- *Helps segment the market*: different brand benefits can be specially developed and aimed at different segments. Procter & Gamble makes Daz, Ariel, Bold and Fairy bio and non-bio soap powders, offering different benefits to different segments of the market.
- *Repel competition*: brand reputation and customer loyalty can keep out competition. As with Procter & Gamble above, many different brands in the same market will force other companies to compete on many fronts.
- *Build corporate image*: respected brands will be associated with a quality company. Corporate image is important in maintaining the support of investers and keeping the share price high.
- *Easier to process orders*: clear brand identification reduces confusion when ordering.
- *New product launches*: a well-known brand name will aid the launch of a new product as there is every chance of it being tried and tested by the consumer because of past reputation. Microsoft Windows 98 is an example and, despite some pre-launch criticism, sales of £5 billion are expected around the world.

■ *Strategic planning*: established brands tend to have a regular pattern of sales and so make strategic forecasting and planning more reliable. It also enables brand values to be calculated and used in estimating the worth of the company.

OVERALL WEAKNESSES OF BRANDING

Branding has its critics and there are those who argue that branding is unnecessarily, expensive (adding on average over 65 per cent to the price through advertising and promotion) and an offensive waste of precious resources when millions in the world are starving.

Others argue that customers want branded products, are prepared to pay extra and feel that they offer real value for money. The growth in own label products (accounting for something like 35 per cent of all products sold) is at present testing the validity or otherwise of this argument. This is a complex and complicated area worthy of more discussion and interested students should investigate the reading material further.

It is also argued that some brands lose power because the name becomes too well-known and is seen as a generic term. The customer may ask for a Hoover and be prepared to accept any type of vacuum cleaner, Sellotape for sticky tape, Rizla for tobacco paper and Biro for a pen.

Some brand definitions

The following list includes some of the brand definitions in use plus other related terms.

■ *Brand*: name, term, sign, symbol or design e.g. Kellogg's cockerel; Marlbrough's cowboy; Coca-cola's white wavy line and the bottle shape; Shell's shell; Lloyd's black horse; Legal and General's brolly; Guinness's harp.

■ *Corporate brand*: the company itself can be seen as the brand. BT has the prancing trumpet player; The Prudential has the androgynous head; Apple computer, the apple; and Esso, the tiger.

■ *Brand name*: can be spoken.

■ *Brand mark*: can be seen.

■ *Trade mark*: gives legal protection (seen as TM). Under an addition to the Trade Marks Act which came into effect in November 1994, businesses will now be able to register three-dimensional shapes, sounds and smells for protection under law as well as brand names and brand marks.

■ *Copyright*: gives a legal right to produce. This includes music, videos and books.

■ *Brand equity*: is the value of the brand both in terms of customer loyalty and estimated money worth.

■ *Brand awareness*: percentage of consumers who express awareness of a brand as revealed by an opinion poll.

■ *Brand stripping*: acquiring a company for its brands.

Brand decisions

There are many alternative decisions that need to be made when looking at branding policy. A number of examples will now be discussed.

MANUFACTURER'S BRAND

The producer may decide either to develop its own brands or to acquire existing brands through purchase or merger. Strong brands demanded by consumers create a power position *vis-à-vis* the middleman. Own brand names can also be franchised or licensed out for others to use. Virgin franchises with City Jet, flying out of the London City Airport, and licenses the name for use on Vodka and PCs. It has also used it to launch a new cola in a joint venture with Canadian company, Cott.

OWN LABEL

Alternatively a manufacturer can choose to make products for other companies. This could be in areas as diverse as soups under the Sainsbury name, underwear under the Marks and Spencer St Michael label, or dishwashers under the Zanussi name. This gives little or no power to the producer in the relationship with the retailer as they can easily contract to manufacture elsewhere if the terms and conditions are better.

Companies that have made own label for others include, Cross and Blackwell, Golden Wonder, Heinz and Hotpoint. Some companies refuse to make own label goods for others feeling that it might devalue their own branded products, for example 'If it doesn't say Kellogg's on the outside then it's not Kellogg's in the inside.'

OWN LABEL AS A BRAND

CORPORATE BRAND. With an increased higher profile and enhanced reputation many corporate own label products, once seen as low value and anonymous, have now become serious brands in their own right, able to challenge the might of the largest manufacturer brand. Tesco's wine, Sainsbury's cola and Marks and Spencer's suits are all seen by some targeted customers as on a par with comparable manufacturers' brands.

CORPORATE SUB-BRAND. As well as corporate own label some retailers have developed their own sub-brands. Sainsbury have Novo washing powder; the Co-op have '99' tea; Dixons have Matsui TVs.

GENERICS

We have also seen the re-appearance of generic staple products like lemonade, bread, margarine, etc. in no-frill packaging at rock bottom prices. Whether this is just a symptom of an economic downturn (the consumer is more price conscious because of a lack of the 'feel good factor') or more structurally embedded only time will tell.

A COMBINATION OF OWN BRAND AND OWN LABEL

There might be more customer benefit if manufacturer and retailer come together and use their combined resources in jointly branding the product. This form of relationship marketing could be the way forward for some companies. Tesco's champagne is a fact but will we see it on future labels: Heinz soups made for Sainsbury, Johnny Walker for Asda and Sony for Comet.

BRAND EXTENSION, BRAND LEVERAGE

Brand extension is taking the brand name and reputation and using it across other product areas – Bugatti into mens toiletries, Bic into disposable razors, Mars into ice-cream and Honda into lawn mowers. However experience has shown that companies must be careful about how they exploit the brand equity. In many cases the consumer will associate a brand with a particular product group and be uncomfortable if the name is used elsewhere. Examples of brand extensions that have failed include Levi into men's suits and Bic into perfume.

Branding strategy

There are different organizational approaches to branding strategy across all the organization's strategic business units (SBUs) with their own corresponding strengths and weaknesses. In many cases the adopted method has been as much by chance as by intention. The different approaches employed include:

1. individual brand name;
2. blanket company name;
3. separate company name;
4. a combination.

We will look at each in turn.

INDIVIDUAL BRAND NAME

Adopting this approach the parent company has a range of products branded and marketed as separate entities. If the overall company name is mentioned it is only on the margin. An example is United Biscuits with products mentioned earlier such as Penguin, United, Bandit, Tuc, Tartan shortbread, Ross, Wimpy. Likewise Procter & Gamble markets its product under the brands of Ariel, Bold, Fairy, Breeze, Comfort, etc.

STRENGTHS OF INDIVIDUAL BRAND NAMES. Each brand is a strength in its own right as segment personalities are developed. This allows the market to be tightly and individually segmented, thus preventing an attack across the whole market, as rivals can only come in on each segment. The failure of any one product will not necessarily spread to other areas.

WEAKNESSES OF INDIVIDUAL BRAND NAMES. On the downside, each brand must be promoted separately which is not only more costly but also develops little or no synergy across all areas that might come from the projection of an overall corporate image.

BLANKET PARENT NAME

Almost directly contrary to the approach taken above is the use of the parent company name across all the products. Sony will be on all TVs, music systems and radios. Heinz uses the same approach with products like Heinz soups, Heinz tomato ketchup and Heinz baked beans.

STRENGTHS OF BLANKET NAMING.   The advantage with this approach is that the kudos emanating from the Heinz name is used on all the products. In promoting the name of Heinz promotion money will work harder as it spreads across all products.

WEAKNESSES OF BLANKET NAMING.   The disadvantages might include not being able to selectively promote individual product benefits to each target segment and problems with one product might affect the image of them all.

SEPARATE COMPANY NAMES

Many conglomerates may well have separate family names for the different SBUs in its business. The parent company acts almost as a holding company. Examples of organizations taking this approach are:

- United Biscuits (the parent company) owning subsidiaries McVities, Ross, K.P., Pizzaland, Wimpy, Callard and Bowser (separate company names).
- Unilever (parent) owning Bird's Eye, Wall's, Fray Bentos, Lipton's, Persil (separate company names).
- Sears (parent) owning Dolcis, Hush Puppies, Shoe Express, Shoe City, Saxone, Freemans, Selfridges, Miss Selfridge, Millets, Olympus, Richards, Wallis, Sportsworld, Adams (separate company names).

STRENGTHS OF HAVING SEPARATE COMPANY NAMES.   Each family company has a reputation in its own right and is a specialist in its chosen market. This would have taken many years to build up and the use of the parent name could well cause this goodwill to be lost.

WEAKNESSES OF HAVING SEPARATE COMPANY NAMES.   The disadvantages are the same as those identified earlier. Each company must be promoted separately, so losing any economy of scale gains.

The unknown parent may also cause the overall strength of the company to be undervalued and under-estimated on the stock market. This lack of corporate awareness worried United Biscuits in the takeover crazy 1980s causing them to promote the parent corporate image more vigorously.

A COMBINATION OF THE ABOVE

Maybe in the quest of going for the best of all worlds some organizations will opt for a combination of the above. Examples of this are products which use both the parent name and the brand name: Kellogg's (parent) Coco Pops (Brand), Kellogg's Rice Crispies, Kellogg's Fruit 'n' Fibre.

THE BEST METHOD

It should be appreciated that, as with many areas of marketing, no one way is correct and what might be right for one company may be wrong for another. The situation is also fluid and constantly changing. As environmental circumstances change, firms get taken over, new ideas are mooted and so the emphasis for the organization will also change.

Summary

In this chapter the concept of the 4 Ps as an acronym for the marketing mix was reintroduced and the 'P' for product was examined in detail.

A 'product' was identified as any form of demanded benefit offering. The generic use of the term included the idea of a corporate product as well as sub-products and services. The many different methods for classifying products were identified.

The functional and symbolic properties in products were identified and it was argued that consumers will purchase products for both rational and emotive reasons building on models developed in the chapter on consumer behaviour.

The many properties that go to make up a product were then explored, beginning with the idea of a product core and adding consumer driven added value. This included primary elements like innovation, quality, branding, packaging, promotion, price and distribution channel as well as supplementary benefits such as after sales service, deliveries, guarantees and a returns policy.

Finally, packaging and branding were examined in more detail.

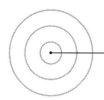

Questions for discussion

1. What are the differences to be taken into consideration when marketing services rather than products? Give examples.
2. All products now contain some form of service in their value added make up. Comment.
3. Identify the functional and symbolic reasons that might cause the following products to be purchased:
   - a sports car;
   - an industrial water sewage system;

- men's fragrance, women's perfume;
- a holiday;
- life insurance.

4. How might value be added to the following products: a bank account; water; bread; holiday? Is it true that the consumer will always be prepared to pay more for added value?

5. Take the different consumer and industrial product categories and outline the different marketing approaches that will be needed for each. Use actual examples.

6. What is meant by innovation and design in marketing products and services? Why is it important?

7. Identify the many aspects of packaging. What part does it play in the marketing of products and services? Give examples.

8. What do you think will be the outcome in the battle between own label and branded products? Do you think that the concept of a producer's brand is declining?

9. What do you consider to be the best strategic corporate approach to branding: individual brand names or a blanket parent name across all products?

10. What part do you think that relationship marketing can play in the successful development of products and services? Relate your answer to financial and leisure services.

Case study

The value of the brand

At the time of writing this book the Accounting Standards Board, which represents the whole accountancy industry, has recently published a discussion document tacitly accepting the principle that the value of acquired brands should be recognized on company balance sheets. Up to this time intangible assets such as brands, licences and patents, that were acquired when one company took over another, were included as 'goodwill', and counted separately on company balance sheets.

The problem with trying to estimate the value of brands is one that has caused difficulties for some organizations for decades. A company with many brands may be under-valued because this value is not realized. This can then create an opportunity for the company to be purchased at less than its market value. Conversely, a company overvalued because an optimistic price has been given to its brands could create the opposite situation causing stakeholders to think that the company was in better shape than it really was.

It is this very problem that the Accounting Standards Board will attempt to address. There is no doubt in most people's minds that brands do have some form of value. The only problem is that this 'value' is intangible. What price can you actually put on well established brand names such as IBM, Sony, Bovril, Smirnoff, Guinness, Gillette, Playtex, Bird's Eye, Wrigleys, Hovis, Pedigree Chum etc. Almost ten years ago, Ford was prepared to pay nearly three times the market share price to acquire the Jaguar brand name because of all the magic attached to this premium product. Similarly Nestlé were prepared to pay over double the market share price for Rowntree because of the many well established confectionery brands in its product portfolio.

A study by the US business magazine *Financial World* has identified what it considers are the ten most valuable brands in the world. It is no surprise that it finds McDonald's and Coca-Cola brands the two most valuable worth over 70 billion pounds between them. These are followed by such brands as; Disney, IBM, Kodak, Microsoft, Motorola, Hewlett-Packard, Marlboro, Mercedes, Kellogg's, Sony and so on.

The study comes from research undertaken by an international company called Interbrand. Overall brand value figures are calculated using a formula based on the worldwide sales of products carrying the brand name and the brand's operating income.

It has been argued that the growth in value of the hi-tech brands, IBM, Motorola, Hewlett-Packard and Microsoft is due to customer ignorance in this field and so there is an increasing reliance on brand names in order to make buying decisions.

However the value of a brand will shift from year to year with the value of Bass falling 18 per cent, Smirnoff 9 per cent, and Benson & Hedges 26 per cent between 1998 and 1999.

Despite the values put on the brands identified above the growth in own label products in the UK over the last decade has stirred up a debate about the long-term future of a brand because of this head-on competition by the retailer's own products. The giant supermarkets now stock over 50 per cent own label products and many lesser brand names have been delisted from some supermarket shelves (Cherry Blossom boot polish, Cross and Blackwell tinned products, Smith's Crisps). Many retailer own label products are now seen by the customer as brands in their own right with all the imagery that this prospect conjures up. It is now acceptable for Tesco's own label wine to be seen on the table at middle-class dinner parties whereas ten years ago this would have been seen by many as definitely *infra dig*. Marks and Spencer, arguably the number one retailer in the UK has always stocked own label products under either the M&S or St Michael name.

No brand name seems safe from own label competition. Soap powder, coffee and tea, cleaning products, alcoholic and soft drinks, food, electrical goods, clothes, furniture, carpets, fabrics, DIY, footware, car products, holidays, etc. have all spawned retailer own label products. Nowhere is the battle more apparent than in the premium cola market, worth a cool £430 million in the UK. The last two years has seen the market swamped by own label products attacking the might of Coca-Cola and Pepsi-Cola, the market leaders. Asda, Tesco, Sainsbury, Safeway and the Co-op, are now joined by the latest contender, the Spar retail group who are spending £2 million on a TV campaign to launch their own cola across Europe. Sainsbury's own label cola, Classic Coke, took over 25 per cent of the UK market from the giant Coca-Cola Corporation when first launched and looks certain to increase this share over the next year.

Nevertheless market research has shown that people are still prepared to pay a premium for branded products as long as there is real perceived added value. Customers are prepared to pay over £50 in the UK for Levi jeans because of the prestige and status attached to this USA marketing phenomenon. This is despite the fact that they sell for a third of this price in the home country. Tesco scored something of a publicity coup by buying pairs abroad at the cheaper price and selling them in their stores for £30. Levi management were not amused.

Branded names, thought to have been moribund or finished have reappeared as marketing managers realize the value of well-known names still remembered with affection by many customers. In fact many of the top selling brands in the UK have been in existence for over 50 years and are still going strong, for example Persil, Bovril, Bisto, Oxo, Hovis, Mars, Kit-Kat, Kellogg's, Weetabix.

Triumph Motorcycles, one of the market leaders in the 1950s and 1960s (selling over 250,000 bikes a year) has re-emerged in the 1990s after virtual extinction, now has a waiting list, and is expected to increase production five-fold over the next three years. Even the Reliant Robin three-wheeled motor car is attempting to make a comeback after similarly almost disappearing. This brand resurgence has been helped in no small way by all the free publicity engendered by the TV series 'Only Fools and Horses' where the hero 'Del-Boy' drives one of these strange forms of transport.

Spangles sweets, Action Man toys, Double-Diamond beer are brand names once finished but now resurrected. Some famous brands have been purchased from defunct companies and used to market products purchased from all around the world. The right to use the name of 'Bush', once a UK company brand synonymous with quality TVs, radiograms and radios, was sold-off over 20 years ago for over £2,000,000 and now appears on TVs, radios and video tapes that have been manufactured from all over the world, mainly in the Far East.

It is argued that brands will always be wanted because they offer the consumer choice and consistency. A few years ago Dixons, the brown goods electrical retailer, suffered falling sales. It had decided on a product strategy which relied on stocking a large amount of own label product lines. TVs, videos, radios, hi-fi equipment, were bought in from manufacturers around the world and offered to the customer under the Dixons own label name, Matsui. The products could be purchased from whichever factory offered the best value for money so allowing Dixons to make a better profit mark-up than on the branded products sold.

However, in response to the downturn in sales, research was undertaken which indicated that the product mix they had on offer leant too much toward own label products. Their target customer was more discerning than initially thought and wanted to see a bigger range of products from well respected manufactures such as Sony, Technics, National Panasonic, Hitachi and Sharp. Dixons have since reversed their earlier product mix strategy and now stock more branded products.

Case study questions

1. How do you think the manufacturer should protect their brand equity? Why do you think that brands can be so valuable?

2. Do you think that Sainsbury, Tesco, B&Q, Boots, W.H. Smith will ever be powerful enough to stock all own label products? Do you think that some product categories are more susceptible to own label encroachment than others? Give examples.

3. How might an argument be developed on the need for manufacturer's branded products? Give actual examples.

Further reading

Anderson, A.H. and Woodcock, P. (1994) *Effective Entrepreneurship*, Blackwell, Oxford.

Bloom, R.H. (1981) 'Product redefinition begins with the consumer', *Advertising Age*, 26 October.

Chernatony, L. and McDonald, M. (1992) *Creating Powerful Brands*, Butterworth-Heinemann, London.

Foster, D. (1972) *Planning for Products and Markets*, Longman, Harlow.

Heller, R. (1989) *Unique Success Proposition*, Sidgewick and Jackson, London.

Kotler, P. and Armstrong, G. (1980) *Principles of Marketing*, Prentice Hall, London.

Lancaster, G. and Massingham, L. (1993) *Essentials of Marketing*, McGraw-Hill, Maidenhead.

References

7-Eleven: www.7-eleven.com

The Chartered Institute of Purchasing and Supply: www.cips.org

Dixons: www.dixons.co.uk

Franchise handbook: www.franchise.com

Interbrand Consultancy: www.interbrand.com

Marks and Spencer: www.marks-and-spencer.com

Competition Commission (formerly Monopolies and Mergers Commission): www.mmc.gov.uk

Nestlé: www.nestle.com

Office of Fair Trading: www.oft.gov.uk

Proctor and Gamble: www.pg.com

Retail week: www.retail.co.uk

Sainsbury: www.sainsburys.co.uk

Tesco: www.tesco.co.uk

Unilever: www.unilever.com

Walmart: www.wal-mart.com

Wolff Olins, corporate/brand identity agency: www.wolff-olins.com

6

Product models and product development

AIMS AND OBJECTIVES

By the end of the chapter the student should:

1   be able to identify various models used in marketing including the product life cycle, the BCG portfolio model, new product development and the new product adoption process;

2   describe how these different models are used, how they interrelate and their limitations;

3   evaluate the importance of continuous new product development to many organizations.

Introduction

Product models

In this chapter a broader overview of products and markets is taken by examining some theoretical models used by the marketer in attempting to profitably manage the company's range of products in a turbulent competitive environment. All the models used in this chapter are inter-linked and should therefore be used interactively. New product development will be examined, but we begin by looking at the model of the product life cycle.

The product life cycle

Central to good product planning is managing the product in the marketplace from its introduction, growth (hopefully) and probable eventual decline. A helpful model that can be used in this process is the concept of the product life cycle, PLC.

The theory behind the concept is very simple. It argues that all products have a life cycle much the same as human beings. Using the human analogy, products are born, develop and grow through childhood, adolescence, adulthood, old age, and then decline and eventually die. As with man/woman the product will have different demands at different stages in its life and so different marketing approaches will be needed at these different stages. The life cycle concept can be applied equally well to products, product ranges, brands and markets.

THE VALUE OF THE PLC

However it is important to realize that the concept of the PLC is a theory and not all practitioners adhere to its basic tenets. As with all models its value is in its use by managers when discussing and analysing their own and competitors' products in trying to understand markets, market share, and growth and decline (there are many examples of managers not knowing that the market for a particular product was declining until it was too late). However its importance should never be over-estimated and it should only be used as an aid to understanding and not as a predictive tool or substitute for decision making.

Why a product life cycle?

The main arguments for the product life cycle are as follows.

- The continuous development of new technology is making existing products obsolete ever more quickly. It also means PLCs are getting shorter.

■ Consumers become increasingly bored with existing products and demand new innovative benefits and choice.

■ Increased competition forces companies to look for competitive advantage through new product launches.

In the PLC diagram shown in Figure 6.1, sales is used on the vertical axis to measure life stage and time is used on the horizontal axis to measure the period. The stages used are:

1. research and development;
2. introduction;
3. growth;
4. maturity;
5. decline.

As well as a sales line there is also a profit line over all the stages. The PLC time period will vary from product to product and could be seen in terms of months, years or decades.

Using the model of the PLC marketers attempt to describe what will happen to:

■ sales;
■ price and profits;
■ customers;
■ competition.

| **Figure 6.1** | *The product life cycle* |

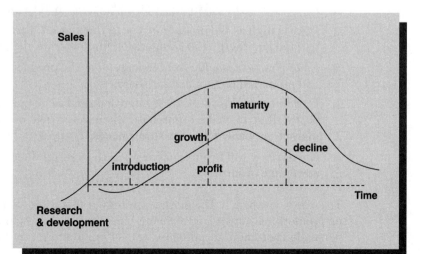

The marketing manger will be concerned about how these factors are affected and interact across the PLC from product introduction through to its removal from the market. The PLC can be used to describe one product or the whole market.

Each stage in the process can now be examined, identifying the different marketing approaches needed.

RESEARCH AND DEVELOPMENT STAGE

It can be seen from the model that the process begins with research and development. At this stage there are no sales and so profit is negative, as the product is not yet on the market and any money spent is a pure cost.

The strategy here should be to ensure that there are enough relevant products in R&D waiting to come to market. The number of products in the R&D stage at any one time will vary from company to company and from market to market. More products will be needed in R&D under the following circumstances:

- Where the product life cycle is short and new products are continuously demanded. Areas of the FMCG market tend to fall into this category.
- Where new technology plays an important part. This would include areas such as IT, electronics and the motor trade.
- Markets with strong competition as organizations attempt to gain competitive advantage through innovation and product development.
- High fashion markets where customer demand continuously changes.
- Industries that have a long lead time from R&D to launch. In the pharmaceutical industry products can take 20 years from inception through to market launch.

INTRODUCTION STAGE

There will come a time when the product is ready to launch on to the market. This is the introduction stage and is characterized by the following factors:

- *Low sales* as the customers wait to be persuaded to purchase.
- *Price* is high as the product is new to the market, R&D costs need to be recuperated and there is no competition forcing down the price.
- *No profits, no cash flow, and high spend* as the product is vigorously advertised and promoted to gain market share.
- *Customers* at this stage are limited and tend to be innovators who will want to be the first to make a purchase whenever a new product comes on to the market, probably to satisfy status needs.
- *Competition* will be minimal or nil as the new product launch should have the advantage of surprise.

THE MARKET STRATEGY.   The market strategy at this stage should be to spend heavily on promotional activity (advertising, sales promotions, selling, etc.) to inform and persuade customers to purchase and so build and expand the market as fast as possible before the competition can enter.

GROWTH

Hopefully sales should start to take off and increase. This is the growth stage. The growth stage is characterized by the following factors:

- *Sales* are fast growing as customers become aware of the benefits on offer and purchase the product.
- *Price* is still high but under threat as competition starts to enter.
- *Profits* begin to appear and the cash flow is getting better as sales increase, but costs are still high as heavy promotion continues.
- *Customers* are increasing and are known as 'the early majority'.
- *Competition* is now growing as competitors catch up and enter the market. They do, however, help to expand the market as they will also be spending on advertising, sales promotion and selling.

THE MARKET STRATEGY.   The market strategy at this stage should be to go for market penetration (heavy sales) and market leadership. Being leader in the market should give economies of scale difficult for the competition to match. This should lead to lower costs and therefore higher profits, even as prices are forced down.

MATURITY

Eventually market potential will have been reached and the market will be in the maturity stage. This is characterized by the following factors:

- *Sales* will level off as the market reaches a plateau.
- *Price* is forced down as more competitors fight in a market that is levelling off.
- *Profits* are probably at their highest as promotion spend will be minimal (all customers are now aware of the product) and costs are at their lowest (high economies of scale and benefits of the learning curve mean that the product can be produced for ever lower costs).
- *Customers*: the majority of the customers are now in the market and it reaches saturation.
- *Competition* is intense as more organizations fight for less market.

THE MARKET STRATEGY.   The market strategy is to defend market share by offensive methods, often price cutting and sales promotions.

DECLINE

Eventually the market starts to decline. This is characterized by the following factors:

- *Sales* are falling as customers move on to other products.
- *Price* is falling as customers leave the market and late buyers need to be enticed in.
- *Profits* are falling as price is forced down.

- ■ *Customers* will be the laggards who only buy when the price has reached rock bottom.
- ■ *Competition* is at over-capacity and companies gradually leave.

THE MARKET STRATEGY. The market strategy at the decline stage is to maintain share, harvest by spending little but taking out as much as possible; it is important to know when to terminate and leave the market.

Managing the product through the life cycle

The characteristics of the life cycle need to be known and understood so that the product can be managed at every stage by the marketing manager, manipulating the elements of the marketing mix so as to meet the changing circumstances. Available options might well include the following:

- ■ Lowering the price (or in some cases raising the price).
- ■ Increasing, or decreasing the number and type of distribution channels (shops, departmental stores, superstores, etc.).
- ■ Enhancing the product in some way by adding more primary or supplementary value, e.g. more features, making larger/smaller, better quality, different packaging, repositioning, etc.
- ■ Increasing/decreasing the advertising, changing from TV to the press, putting on some form of sales promotion, e.g. a competition or 10 per cent extra for the same price.

Of course what needs to be done will depend on all of the marketing circumstances, especially the reaction of both the customers and the competition.

DIFFERENT TYPES OF PRODUCT LIFE CYCLES

Not all products will follow the classical life cycle shape moving through the stages of introduction, growth, maturity and decline described above and shown in Figure 6.1.

A number of different types of PLC can be identified. Each will be discussed in turn.

CLASSIC STYLE PLC. There are some basic conservative classic styles that always seem to be on sale, purchased by a sizeable solid group of minority consumers. Then, for whatever the reason, there is a large increase in sales as a particular style becomes fashionable and is demanded by a larger, often mass market. After an amount of time the fashion subsides and the style goes back to its original market and level of sales. This might then be repeated after a period of time and so the process will begin all over again. Classic style products include: brogue shoes, short or long dresses, suits, duffle coats, tweeds and brogues, the Aga Cooker, pine wood furniture, etc. (Figure 6.2).

FASHION PLC. The fashion PLC is experienced by a product which becomes extremely fashionable and achieves a good level of sales, before dropping off when the product goes out of fashion. The shape of the graph is similar to that of the

Figure 6.2 | *Classic style PLC*

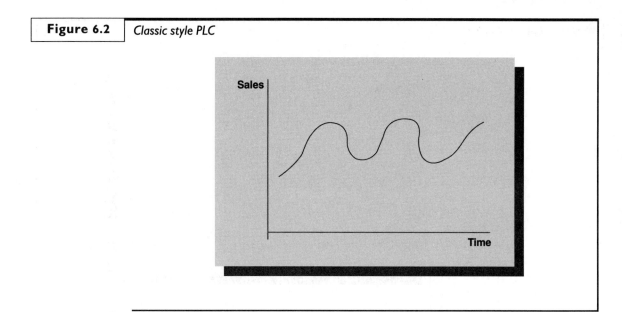

classic product; the difference is that this product does not repeat its fashionable performance (Figure 6.3).

FAD PLC.   The Fad PLC is that group of products that seem to burst on to the market, achieve stunning sales over a very short period but then decline as quickly as they come. Chidren's products feature heavily in this market and include products like the Rubic's Cube, Cabbage Patch dolls, skate boarding, Hula hoops, etc. (Figure 6.4).

Figure 6.3 | *Fashion PLC*

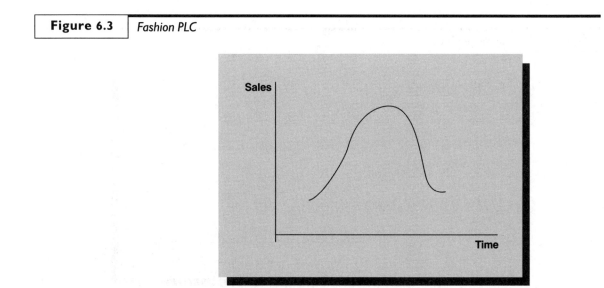

Figure 6.4	*Fad PLC*

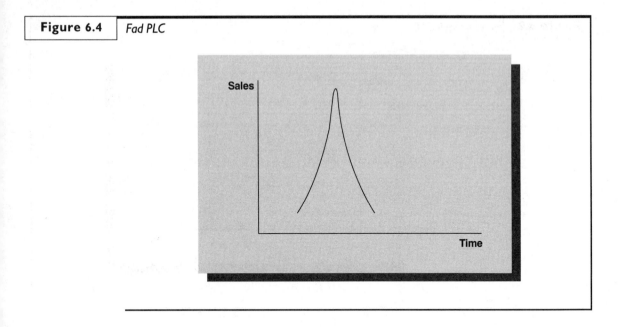

SCALLOPED PLC. Many well-managed products such as some soap powders or chocolate bars tend to follow a scalloped process. As the product starts to decline further added value is injected to revitalize sales. This process can seem to go on almost indefinitely, for example Mars bars; Kit-Kat; Persil; Bold (Figure 6.5).

More value could be added by, for example: a change of packaging; increased performance; new, blue whitener; size increase; different forms such as mini/bumper sizes, all to maintain and increase sales performances.

Figure 6.5	*Scalloped PLC*

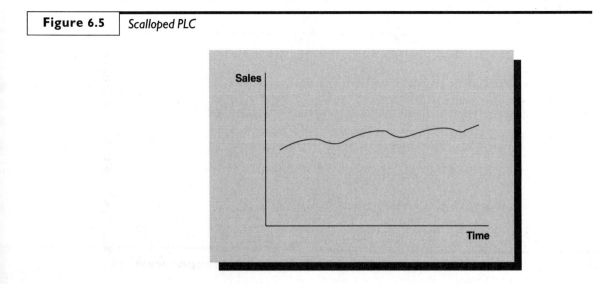

| Figure 6.6 | *Humped-back PLC* |

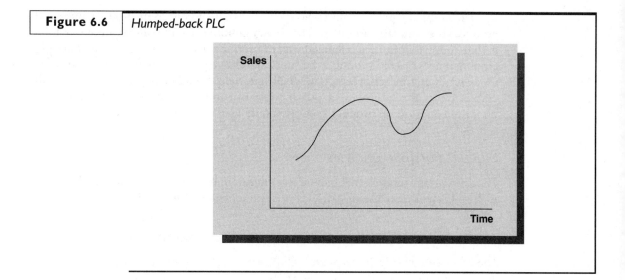

HUMPED-BACK PLC.   When products are in decline the choice must be made whether to liquidate or inject new life by *repositioning* the product. By repositioning the product we mean shifting how it is seen in the marketplace from a market in decline to a new market with growth. Examples of products where this has been successfully achieved include Lucozade moving from a product positioning as a health drink for old people and children to one where it is seen as a drink for young sports people (Figure 6.6).

THE VALUE OF PLC MODELS

Models of the PLC can help the marketing manager when evaluating product policy in the following ways:

- help to identify, contrast and compare where each company product/service is on its product life cycle compared with the competition;
- help to understand the factors involved in the life of a particular product/market and so aid the forecasting and planning process;
- help in the use of different forms of promotion as the product/service moves through the life cycle.

If the PLC for the industry is growing and the PLC for the particular product is in decline, then questions need to be asked and relevant action taken. Similarly if the PLC for the industry is in the decline phase but the company product or brand is still growing then, again, an analysis should be undertaken to discover the reasons.

The product portfolio

The product life cycle can now be developed by using it with the theory and modelling associated with the concept of the *product portfolio*.

The company product portfolio consists of all the different product lines and products the company produces. The theory behind the company product portfolio is that there should be a balanced mix of products to cover various and changing circumstances. As old products die there should be new products coming through; if one product area is in recession, ideally another should be in growth. This way all company resources are utilized to their optimum level, costs are kept at a minimum and overall product synergy should lead to company success.

Product portfolio analysis

There are many models that can be used in product portfolio analysis and here the Boston Consultancy Group (BCG) portfolio matrix is discussed.

BOSTON CONSULTANCY GROUP (BCG) PORTFOLIO MATRIX

The BCG 2×2 matrix looks at the relationship between market share and market growth. Products, product lines or SBUs (a strategic business unit is a term used for anything from a product through to a company division or subsidiary that is strategically important to the health of the organization) are then plotted on the matrix according to market share and market growth.

In Fig. 6.7 the left vertical axis measures the rate of market growth, the top horizontal axis measures relative market share. The rate of growth measure to be

| **Figure 6.7** | *BCG portfolio matrix* |

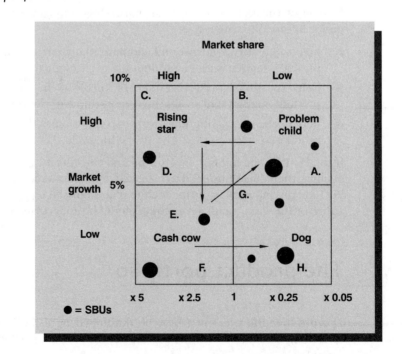

used will be any rate considered relevant by the practitioner. In our example it will be seen that 5 per cent and 10 per cent market growth measures are used. As you will see there is a high growth box and a low growth box.

The SBUs are designated by circles and the size of the circle will indicate the amount that the product contributes to product portfolio overall company revenue.

The bottom horizontal axis measures market share in relation to the nearest competitor. A figure above 1 indicates market leadership and market share above the nearest competitor, for example × 5 = 5 times market share compared to the nearest competitor. A figure less than 1 indicates non-market leadership and sales in relationship to the market leader, for example × .05 = 5 per cent of sales compared with the market leader. Again there is a high and a low box (as with market growth the figures used are relevant and can be decided by the marketing manager).

With all the products plotted on the the matrix grid an overall picture will appear covering company products in terms of:

1. whether a particular product (SBU) has high or low market share;
2. whether the market for that product has high or low market growth;
3. the contribution that product makes to overall revenue;
4. the position each product has in the market compared with the major competitor;
5. where each product is on its PLC.

BCG PORTFOLIO MATRIX REVENUE AND COST INDICATOR

The BCG matrix can also be used to indicate the organization's cost and cash flow position (Figure 6.8) where x indicates the level of revenue costs, and 0 = zero.

So, in the problem child box, revenue = 0, indicating little or no sales and costs = x, indicating heavy costs either because of research and development or, if the product has been launched, heavy distribution and promotion costs.

In the rising star box revenue = xxx, indicating increasing revenue as sales take off in a growing market and costs = xxx, indicating heavy costs as money is pumped in to gain market share before the competition arrives.

In the cash cow box revenue = xxx, indicating heavy sales and optimum revenue as market leadership is exploited and costs = x, indicating low costs because of economies of scales and learning curve savings.

In the dog box revenue = x, indicating low sales and revenue as the market is in decline and costs = x, indicating low costs, just enough to support existing sales.

BCG MODELS EXPLAINED

The organization's products will all be plotted on the grid according to their market share and the growth in the market (Figure 6.7).

The process is circular, moving from the top right hand square to the top left hand square mirroring the PLC. The hope is that the problem child will become a rising star. Eventually the market will mature and the product will move toward

| Figure 6.8 | *BCG portfolio matrix revenue and cost indicator* |

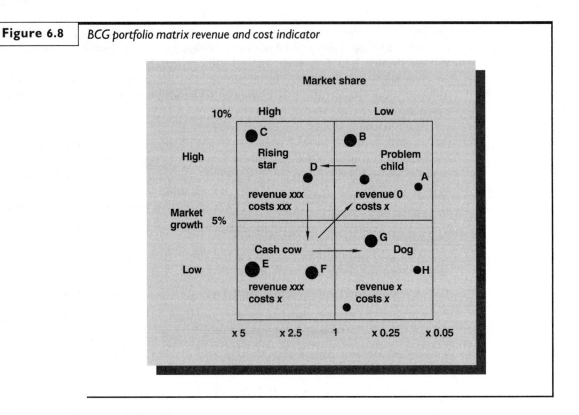

the cash cow and eventually finish in the dog segment. If the product can be repositioned (like the example of Lucozade mentioned above) it would re-start the whole process.

THE PROBLEM CHILD SQUARE. Product A, a 'problem child', has a low market share in a high market growth industry. But it is at the bottom end of the market growth (5 per cent). Product B is doing better, being higher in the segment. It is called a problem child or question mark because there is doubt about the product's ability to increase sales and move into the rising star box.

Finance. Costs are high as money is ploughed into research and product development. Sales are virtually non-existent and so revenue is nil and the cash flow is negative (see Figure 6.8).

Product strategy. The product strategy here is to make 'drop' or 'go' decisions backed by good market research. If the decision is 'go' then adequate resources must be made available to move the product into the rising star square.

THE RISING STAR SQUARE. A product located here will have a high market share in a high growth rate market (hence rising star). It can be seen that product C is better placed than product D.

Finance. Costs are high as the company vigorously promotes to gain market share and maintain market leadership. Sales are taking off, cash flow is good (see Figure 6.8).

Product strategy. Continue to promote in aggressive product support to maintain leadership position and earn more market share.

CASH COW SQUARE. Can you now study the 'cash cow' square and identify the market and product characteristics and why it is called a 'cash cow'.

It should first be seen that there is high market share but low market growth. This indicates products in a maturing market. Again product E is better positioned than product F. Called a 'cash cow' because spend is little, as the products are well established, there are economies of scales and learning curve advantages and revenue is at its highest although the market is slowing down.

Finance. Revenue is high, profit is high, cash flow is good and costs are low (see Figure 6.8).

Product strategy. The product/market strategy to use here would be to maintain market position and stimulate consumer interest for as long as it is still profitable to do so. This might include a small amount of advertising to remind customers about the product, sales promotions as an incentive and price cutting and continuous product improvement to stimulate sales (as in the scalloped PLC identified earlier).

High profits gained here should be re-invested to support new, problem child products coming through.

The product could be re-positioned as life expectancy moves the product in the direction of the dog square.

DOG SQUARE. The dog square is characterized by low market share and low market growth, hence the adjective 'dog'. The market is in decline and it can be seen that both products G and H have a low market share. However G is in a better position than H.

Finance. Products here are bringing in relatively little revenue. Similarly there might be very little cost involved. However care should be taken in analysing the true cost of products in the 'dog' box as this can often be much higher than a cursory look might imply. The analysis should also include 'opportunity costs', such as time spent on marketing that could be more effectively spent concentrating on products with more potential (see Figure 6.8).

Product strategy. The alternative strategies here would be to harvest, to divest, to liquidate or to reposition.

To *harvest* means to take as much revenue out of the product while spending as little as possible. Product G could be a candidate for harvesting. The price could be drastically reduced to take advantage of lower income buyers, distribution increased and/or the product sold through distributors not normally associated with the product. The product could be *divested*, sold off to another company or *liquidated* (shut down). If the product still has some form of credible brand equity left (Lucozade) then *repositioning* would be a possibility.

 However, care must be taken to see that, whatever action is taken in harvesting, divesting, liquidating or repositioning the product, short-term considerations do not harm the long-term future of other products.

Balanced portfolio

Ideally a company would maintain a balanced portfolio of products. In theory, if the company had 100 products there would be 25 products in each square with a continuous anti-clockwise movement of products, old products ending (dogs) and new products coming through (problem child) supported by revenue and profits generated by the cash cow (Figure 6.9).

In practice the number of products in each square will depend on both the type of product and the demands of the particular industry. In some industries more products would need to be in the problem child square than in others. This might be because of the long lead time taken in research and development, for example pharmaceutical products that can take 10–20 years coming to market or because customers demand a continuous supply of new products, for example the film industry.

| **Figure 6.9** | *A balanced product portfolio: 100 products* |

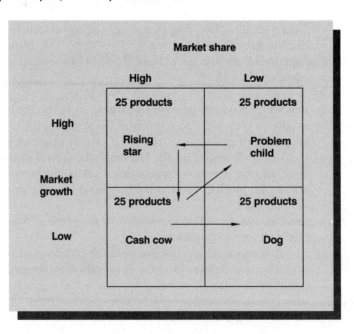

The situation all companies must avoid is a market position where all, or most of the products are in the cash cow or dog square and there are no new products in the problem child or rising star squares waiting to come through (Figure 6.10).

Limitation of product portfolio models

The process described above tends to be arbitrary and very theoretical. Products are allocated to squares based on questionable and limited knowledge. Models should therefore not be used as a method for predicting future product direction but there is a value in a more limited way. This is as a method of concentrating and focusing the attention on the importance of portfolio analysis. Being aware of product trends and relationships is crucial to a company's survival.

Portfolio modelling forces organizational staff to examine and compare their range of products both internally and also with those offered by the competition. In this sense 'actively taking part in the process' is probably more important than the end result. The models do not have to be used in the way described and they can be adapted and used by practitioners in any way considered helpful.

| **Figure 6.10** | *An unbalanced product portfolio: 100 products* |

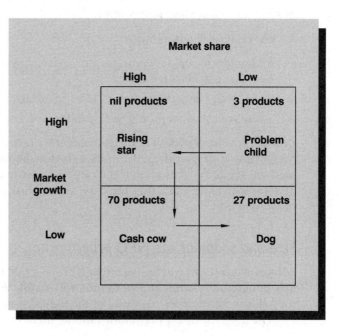

New product development

It was argued earlier that product life cycles are getting shorter as new technology outdates products at an ever-increasing rate, customers demand more choice and are bored much quicker and competition grows as trade barriers come down and markets open up. This imposes the need on many organizations to have a strong new product development (NPD) programme.

Why there is a need to develop new products

An organization might have a NPD programme for the following reasons:

- maintain its position and reputation as an innovator;
- defend its market share;
- be in the forefront of the development of new markets;
- take advantage of new technology;
- optimize resources, including production and distribution strength.

These and many other factors identified earlier put enormous pressure on companies to be continuously bringing new products to the market in order to maintain market share and competitive advantage.

DEFINITION OF A NEW PRODUCT

A 'new' product might be:

- a change or replacement to an existing product, i.e. added features and benefits, e.g. Mars ice-cream;
- an existing concept but new to the organization, e.g. Virgin selling insurance;
- a totally new concept, e.g. the Mondex cash card system.

How the customer perceives the product state is the most important factor for the marketing staff to take into consideration because this will affect how the product/service is marketed. If the targeted customer *perceives* the product to be new (or not new) then this must be taken into account when developing the marketing mix.

Size and scope of the NPD programme

Some organizations will have a larger NPD programme than others. The size of the new product development programme will mainly depend on the type of products it produces, the market structure of the industry and the level of the competition.
   The need for NPD programmes will be higher where:

- customer demand is for new, progressive, hi-tech products (electrical, engineering, computerized goods);

■ the company maintains competitive advantage through continuously bringing new products on to the market (Sony, Philips, 3M);

■ there is a tradition in the market for new products (pre-cooked meals, children's toys);

■ where there is intense competition (toiletries, airlines, financial services).

INTERNAL NEW PRODUCT DEVELOPMENT. If a company is to maintain competitive advantage then it must apply the concept of new product/service development internally – that is to how it actually runs its own business – as well as externally – that is to how it markets its products. If it still uses outdated machinery, processes and systems then it will not be able to compete with its more up-to-date and forward thinking competitors.

Internal new product development will embrace such concepts as internal marketing, 'total quality management', 'just in time' materials management, 'activity based costing', 'benchmarking', employee 'empowerment' and so on.

SOURCE OF NEW PRODUCT IDEAS

New product ideas are the life blood of new product development and some markets (toiletries, confectionery, grocery) need hundreds of new products every year to satisfy customer demands. Ideas for new products can come from both within and without the organization and we can look at both these sources in turn.

SOURCES OF IDEAS WITHIN THE ORGANIZATION

■ Employee suggestion schemes from different departments including: sales, production, finance and complaints.

■ The deliberate and planned use of creative group thinking techniques, such as brainstorming and mind-mapping.

■ The research and development/new product ideas department.

■ Ideas can also come about by accident (this was how penicillin was discovered), by luck, or even by dreaming.

SOURCES OF IDEAS WITHOUT THE ORGANIZATION

■ Customer suggestions, customer complaints, customer needs identification, market research.

■ Suppliers' and intermediaries' suggestions and needs.

■ Examining competition and competitors' products including reverse-engineering (breaking down competitors' products to see how they are manufactured).

■ Research and development taking place in universities and colleges. Companies will often sponsor this type of activity.

■ From reading patent publications, trade journals and other media, including trade exhibitions where different products will be on show (ideas can come from areas not necessarily directly related).

■ New product idea agencies exist which employ creative and imaginative staff who will come up with new ideas in almost any area on request (at a price of course).

■ New technology, e.g. mobile TV telephones; word processors that are voice activated; e-mail.

■ As a by-product or spin-off from other areas including: the space programme, e.g. Teflon used on non-stick frying pan; from new legislation, e.g. the catalytic converter to minimize exhaust fumes; from changes in social customs and practices, e.g. take away meals; draught beer in a can.

Formalizing NPD

Many companies will formalize the NPD process recognizing its importance as an integral part of the long-term strategic planning process. This will involve the following:

■ commitment from top management;

■ setting up a focused department or project team with clear objectives and a budget;

■ allocating clear responsibilities including appointing 'product champions' at every stage of the NPD process to see that momentum is maintained;

■ creating communication channels to funnel new ideas through;

■ creating an innovative culture where new ideas are encouraged.

COST OF NPD

Understanding the NPD process is imperative as the costs involved are high and no revenue comes in until well after the launch, and no profit until often years later. Of course the money spent on products that are never launched is unrecoverable and so the pressure is always on to monitor and control the process effectively and efficiently.

The new product development process

NPD can be seen as a series of stages culminating in the launch of the product. Different research has shown that many product ideas are developed but very few actually reach full product launch. And of those that are launched, very few can be considered a success by reaching sales targets set for them by one year later.

The NPD process can be seen as a funnel with as many as 100 product ideas put in at the top and the bulk of the ideas being discarded at different stages, until only two or three are actually launched on to the market (Figure 6.11).

STAGES OF NPD

The new product development process can be examined through the following seven stages:

1. idea generation;
2. idea filtering;
3. concept testing;
4. business analysis;

| Figure 6.11 | *The NPD funnel* |

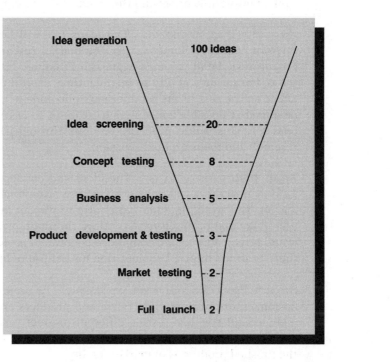

Idea generation   100 ideas

Idea screening - - - - - - - - - 20 - - - - - - - -

Concept testing - - - - - - 8 - - - - - -

Business analysis - - - - 5 - - - -

Product development & testing - 3 -

Market testing - 2 -

Full launch 2

5. product development and testing;
6. test marketing;
7. full launch.

STAGE 1. IDEA GENERATION. At this preliminary stage, the project group coming together to generate ideas would look for quantity rather than quality and the methods used should be geared to achieve exactly this. We looked earlier at the many areas that new ideas can come from, but it can still be difficult to get people to break from traditional ways of thinking and allow their minds to move into the more imaginative and creative realms needed for the generation of new product ideas.

Many companies now take their managers away, isolate them in country hotels and involve them in creative idea courses trying to generate forms of lateral thinking that will come up with a new idea to match the success of 'Trivial Pursuits', 'Shake 'n' Vac', the pyramid tea bag, or 'Direct Line' car insurance. This area is vast and those interested in the subject should consult one of the many books written on creative management.

STAGE 2. IDEA FILTERING. The quantity of ideas developed at stage 1 are distilled until only the most attractive are left. This may involve some informal research but often can be undertaken through discussion and argument within the project group. The vast majority of the ideas will be discarded at this stage as impracticable, unworkable or beyond the scope of the organization.

STAGE 3. CONCEPT TESTING.   The ideas left will be moulded into realistic and relevant concepts. Some *inexpensive* market research can now be undertaken to broadly test viability. Internal questions that need to be asked here would include the organization's ability to manufacture, capital outlay, the costs involved, the effect on the rest of the product portfolio and so on. Externally, questions would be aimed at possible consumers to attempt to assess superficial reactions to the concept. This would probably be done through the use of limited qualitative research and focus group discussion.

STAGE 4. BUSINESS ANALYSIS.   The ideas and concepts that have survived stage 3 (and by now there will only be a few) are given a more thorough business examination. This would include some form of project analysis and projected pricing, cash flows and profits forecasts. More thorough production and marketing costs would be considered and comparisons between projects would have to be made as there is always internal competition for the use of limited resources.

STAGE 5. PRODUCT DEVELOPMENT AND TESTING.   As projects become accepted as viable options, more work is undertaken and products are developed further. This will include adjusting and testing different product variations including ingredients, packaging, branding, pricing, making prototypes and testing and re-testing until the finished product is of market quality.

   At all stages the target customer will be involved using the many, relevant, marketing research methods identified in Chapter 2. At the end of this stage the final decision on market launch would more or less be made.

STAGE 6. TEST MARKETING.   Before deciding on a full launch, a small representative sample of the whole market might be chosen in which to test market the product. The test market, perhaps containing 5–10 per cent of the target consumers, should be as representative of the whole market in every way possible. It would include the socio-demographic mix, geographical spread, distribution and promotion methods. If the results, in microcosm, are good then full launch can proceed. Because of the difficulties involved with test-marketing (costs, security, un-cooperative intermediaries) this stage is sometimes ignored and the new product goes straight to a full launch.

STAGE 7. FULL LAUNCH.   The last stage for the product that has successfully overcome all the preceding obstacles is its full launch on to the market. From the 100 ideas that began probably only two or three will have reached this final stage. For every launch only one out of three will still survive after 2 years.

NPD and risk

In Figure 6.11 it is shown that of 100 product ideas generated only two are launched. For every launch only one out of three products recuperate their costs. NPD is a risky business for the following reasons:

- The cost involved: it is extremely expensive developing and marketing new products especially in terms of advertising and promotional costs. The global launch of Micosoft Windows, Win 95, is reputed to be costing $1bn. The Rolling Stones alone are alleged to have been paid $7 million for the use of their song 'Start Me Up' as a voice-over to the TV commercial

- The amount of competition, all launching new products and fighting for a share in the market. New players from all around the world are continually entering (in 1992 nearly 1000 different new soft drinks were launched on to the Japanese market of which only approximately 10 existed one year later).

- Customers can be wary about trying new products and brands, preferring to stay with those that they know and trust.

- Despite increasingly sophisticated market research, expensive mistakes can still be made, wrong benefits identified, and products launched that do not sell or do not reach the sales and profit figures predicted (the Channel Tunnel and the Walt Disney theme park in France are examples where marketing research can go drastically wrong causing billions of pounds to be lost).

Product innovation and adoption

Marketing people are interested in both the process of new product adoption and the time that it takes for the product to be purchased by the bulk of its customers. The speed of new product adoption is of interest for the following reasons:

- The speed of product adoption equates to product sales, revenue and profit returns.

- Before the onset of a new project, investors will want to know how long it will take before they will get their money back (the payback period). Inevitably one project will be competing with another and this payback period will be a major consideration.

- The new product adoption process will involve different groups of customers at different stages and at different times. Each group will probably be buying for different reasons and so will need a different marketing mix approach.

IDEA ADOPTION AND CULTURAL CHANGE

The concept of new product adoption was actually taken and adapted from the work undertaken by an American sociologist, Carl Rogers, who was interested in the way that culture alters and new ideas are adopted by society. In simple terms, Rogers wanted to know both how long it took for different beliefs and attitudes to permeate down through the whole of society and the way that it happened. The following example can be used to illustrate the sort of cultural change that interested Rogers.

In 1966, when the author married, there was no thought given to co-habiting rather than marriage and despite courting for six years this option was never considered. At this time, family and friends would have frowned on this form of behaviour and research from that time shows that less than 2 per cent of the population saw co-habitation as a viable alternative. If couples did live together without the formality of marriage they would tend to keep very quiet about it because of the fear of social opprobrium.

Now, however, 30 years later, the propensity is for couples to live together rather than getting married and in research undertaken recently over 75 per cent of the population see this as an acceptable and viable alternative.

So over a period of 30 years we have seen a radical cultural change take place pertaining to the institution of marriage. Questions to be asked about the process would include such things as: how did it happen?; why did it happen?; what, if any, were the major influences? In this particular case government institutions would very likely need this information because of the effect that marital changes might have on social policy.

IDEA ADOPTION AND MARKETING

Marketers have taken this idea adoption model and adapted and related it to the customer adoption of new concepts and new products. Matters of particular interest will include the following:

- How long is the time period involved; do some beliefs and attitude changes take longer than others to permeate and so will some products be more readily assimilated than others?

- What can speed up/slow down the process and how does the process actually work?

- Are there certain groups of people who believe first and then pass the new concept on to others? How does this process work?

- And most importantly of all: how can the organization advantageously influence and manipulate the process?

These questions and others are at the heart of innovation and adoption theory.

The product adoption innovation curve

GROUP TYPES AND CHARACTERISTICS

Using a 'bell shape' normal distribution curve, the process can be broken down into five distinct groups and types of customers. The percentage number indicates the percentage of the buying population.

Innovators (2.5 per cent); early adopters (13.5 per cent); early majority (34 per cent); late majority (34 per cent); and laggards (16 per cent) (Figure 6.12). The adoption process starts with the innovators and moves through, in turn, the other groups. The laggards will be the last to purchase.

Each group will have different characteristics and needs that demand specific benefits. It is the marketing department's task to understand and develop marketing mix packages that cater for the separate needs of each group. The aim is to move product sales from the beginning to the end so that (in theory) 100 per cent of the target population has purchased.

| **Figure 6.12** | *The adoption curve* |

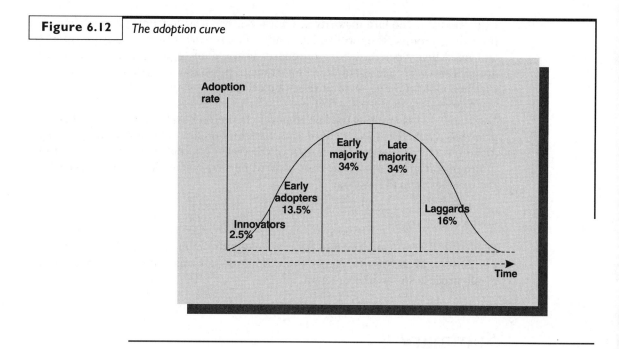

At any one time the company could be marketing to one group rather than another, or to more than one group. But the company must know where their product is on the adoption curve otherwise an inadequate or the wrong marketing mix will be offered.

INNOVATORS.   Innovators or opinion leaders are seen to be important in beginning the process, because unless they purchase the launch will fail. This accounts for approximately 2.5 per cent of the target population. This group is motivated by status and recognition and must have the very latest in new products. They are willing to purchase if these needs are satisfied.

EARLY ADOPTERS.   Early adopters have similar needs to the above, but are a little more wary. They will wait to see if there is an initial take-up by the innovators or opinion leaders they respect and will not buy products that they feel will only have a short life. They will also wait for 'new product bugs' to be ironed out. As 13.5 per cent of the population, they are a substantial group and purchase by them will indicate that sales are moving in the right direction.

EARLY MAJORITY.   For a mass market product, entry by the early majority is crucial as they account for 34 per cent of the population. Only if they enter can economies of scale be gained and prices reduced to bring in the whole of this group as well as enticing the late majority. The early majority are a little more cautious and will buy when a product is seen to be well established and they are convinced of quality and value for money.

LATE MAJORITY.   The late majority are conservative, less consumer driven than the preceding groups. They will reflect and compare with the competition offering and need heavy persuasion to purchase. Price is an important factor with this group. However, once again, it is important to persuade this group to purchase as they account for 34 per cent of the population.

LAGGARDS.   This group is the last to enter the market and will purchase when the price has reached its lowest point. They look for bargains and end-of-product lines. Although accounting for 16 per cent of the target population they are a relatively unimportant group insofar as they tend to purchase at rock-bottom prices when the product is on the way out.

REPEAT PURCHASE

Once the laggard market has been reached the company will be into repeat purchases and the development of new product features and benefits, and so the whole process starts all over again.

Summary

In this chapter we examined some marketing models used in helping to evaluate product portfolio development. The first model introduced was the the product life cycle. The thinking behind this concept is that all products are born, grow, mature and eventually die. Products in the portfolio will probably be at different stages. As the product enters different phases, different forms of marketing are needed. It was argued that if the organization is to be successful it must look and plan across the whole life time of a product.

Different types of product life cycles were then identified, all demanding different marketing mix approaches. The need to manage all products through their life cycles was examined using the Boston Consultancy Group product portfolio matrix.

The increasingly strategic importance of new product development was then discussed. Finally the reaction of the customer to NPD was examined through the use of the product adoption innovation curve.

Questions for discussion

1. Discuss the many ways that the model of the PLC can help marketers in making both tactical and strategic decisions. What concerns must be paramount in using the model?

2. There is nothing the manager can do once the product has reached the decline stage on the PLC. Discuss.

3. Where might the following products be on the PLC: Mars bar, digital TV, the MBA, dishwashers, home computers, the high street bank, alcoholic lemonade, the milkman, the Internet?

4. Describe how the BCG matrix operates. What do you think is the value (if any) of this sort of model to practical product portfolio management?

5. What are the benefits of a balanced product portfolio? Discuss the financial implications.

6. Identify the various consumer group characteristics in the Roger's innovation new product adoption curve. What might the different marketing approaches be to each segment?

7. Discuss the importance of new product innovation, design and development to an FMCG organization.

8. How might an organization instil a culture of innovation into its organization and where might new product ideas come from?

9. Adapt the new product development process to one of the following industries: leisure, groceries, financial services, toys.

10. How might the product life cycle, the Boston Consultancy Group matrix, new product development, and the product adoption curve models all be linked together and be of use in looking at a strategic approach to product planning?

Case study

Most products will begin their lives as some form of idea gaining form and developing within the research and development department of the organization. It is here that most product life cycles begin, some going on to make a fortune for the company, whilst others peter out and become nothing other than an expensive cost on the profit and loss account.

Some products will reach the market and have a long, almost endless product life, some will hit the market, shine brilliantly for a split second and fade away without trace, and some will hit the market, have little or no response and expensively fizzle out.

In some markets there is the expectation, learnt through knowledge and experience, that product life cycles will be short whilst in others there is the hope that the product will last for such a time that research development and launch costs will quickly be covered and the product will then go on to earn the company substantial and continuous profits.

In some cases the product life cycle predictions turn out to be accurate and product rewards will equal expectations, but in others market research and subsequent sales forecasts can be hopelessly wrong, causing high costs, little revenue and so profit losses. The secret of success, for which all marketing managers seek, is the ability to be able to predict which product idea will succeed and which will not. This becomes more imperative as the costs involved for a full product launch escalate to frightening proportions.

The real secret to success rests in gathering as much detailed knowledge as possible of customers' likes and dislikes, their needs and wants, and an in-depth understanding of their propensity to purchase.

However, despite greater and more sophisticated forms of research developed over the last 35 years, problems still keep surfacing and no new product launch can be deemed to be a cast-iron certainty. It seems that some new products are more readily adopted by the consumer than others and some new products are taken up much more quickly than others.

In theory marketing research should identify whether or not there is a need for a product and if the customer will purchase with little or no trouble. However experience has now shown marketing managers that problems can arise when least expected especially when the concept is so different from what already exists and offers benefits that to many potential consumers seem to be esoteric and hard to imagine in practical usage.

One historical example that illustrates the problem was the introduction of the automatic washing machine in the early 1960s. Research undertaken by Hoover, the domestic appliance manufacturer and market leader at the time, seemed to indicate quite conclusively that there would be a market for a washing machine that just needed to be fitted to the taps, plugged in, loaded with washing, soap added and then left to get on with the washing. All the housewife needed to do when the wash-cycle was finished was to empty the machine and hang the washing on the line. In some cases she did not even have to do this as the clothes would be spun dry enough to iron straight away. Nobody need be there while the machine was in operation and it could be set working on any day of the week and even during the night time while the whole family was asleep.

This probably seems to be no big advancement to most readers in the new millennium but this was an enormous improvement on the way that the washing was done at that time. Most housewives would have been using a single tub washing machine with a paddle in the middle or wheel at the back to agitate the water back and forth and round and round.

Each load of washing was manually put into the tub, the heater switched on and when the water was hot enough the paddle or wheel set in motion. When the agitation was finished the hot soapy water was emptied and cold rinsing water was added. Finally all the washing was squeezed through a roller wringer, either manual or electric, fixed to the back of the machine and then hung up to dry. If the family was reasonably affluent they might have had a spin dryer instead of a wringer and, if really modern, a twin-tub, combining both washing machine and spin-dryer in one appliance, would have been in use.

Hoover launched the Hoover 'keymatic' automatic washing machine with great expectations followed by automatic machines from Hotpoint, Bendix, Parnell, Servis and GEC. Even at a price of over 120 guineas compared to 77 guineas for the twin-tub (one pound, one shilling in old money, and many products were priced in guineas as the producer received a little more and the buyer thought they were paying a little less) sales of automatics were expected to take off.

However the product encountered much more resistance than research had indicated. Customers did not flock to part-exchange their old single-tub and twin-tub machines for this new wonder product and the pace through the product life cycle took much longer than anybody had anticipated. The consumer resistance encountered turned out to be for reasons that the limited amount of research had failed to pick up.

Wash-day had traditionally taken place on a Monday and the housewife would put this time aside and spend all day washing and ironing the family wash. Starting early in the morning, manually loading each wash load into the machine, standing by while it washed, rinsing it in the sink and then putting it through the wringer or into the spin dryer, our hardworking mother was often not finished until late into the afternoon; and this drudgery would take place week in and week out. Common sense would surely predict that a product that could eliminate this burdensome task would be welcomed with open arms.

However, what the research failed to pick up, was the overall feeling of involvement experienced by the housewife as she undertook the weekly wash. As arduous and time consuming as it may have been, washing was linked very closely at this time to the role the woman had to play in the running of the household and her part as a good wife and a loving mother. The automatic washing machine would take this away and she would feel guilty if she no longer had this task to perform.

Other problems causing resistance were to do with feelings of uncertainty about the ability of the automatic machine to wash as cleanly and as quickly as the manual method. With the automatic each wash would take as long as two hours and with as much as six loads to wash this would amount to ten or twelve hours in total. Of course the operator need not be there whilst the machine was washing and it could be set into action anytime of the day or night and any day of the week.

Unfortunately this was more difficult to understand than first thought and there were many examples of housewives, having been persuaded to purchase this new wonder machine, still saving up the whole of their washing for Monday and then standing about all day, not daring to leave the kitchen in case the machine did something it ought not to have done, until the whole of the weekly wash had been done. Many could not conceive of leaving the machine on all night for fear of breakdown or flooding. Washing on other days of the week was also conceptually problematic.

Because of these problems the domestic appliance manufacturers had to undertake a huge customer education programme and despite this belated attack the automatic washing machine took nearly 20 years to be bought by the mass of the population against a pre-launch prediction of 5–7 years. In 1997, 95 per cent of all households had an automatic washing machine, most users could not dream of managing without it, and it is used as much by men as by women and the market is now well into repeat purchases.

Another example that highlights the difficulties involved with product life cycle prediction and new idea adoption is the case of Dixons, the electrical retailer, and Sega and Nintendo computer games. At the launch in 1992 Sega Megadrives and Super Nintendo packs were selling for £169 each, Dixons adopted the product as a strategic part of its portfolio, and the market was expected to have a life of at least ten years. However during 1998 prices have fallen to £129, then £99 and now £89, as the product moved through its life cycle much quicker than most pundits had forecast.

Now Dixons have had to acknowledge that game consoles are toys and not brown goods and consequently do not have the longevity associated with adult products.

Dixons made a similar mistake with product adoption prediction over the sale of satellite dishes, but this time failed to stock enough supplies and so were unable to take advantage of the war that broke out between BSB and SKY for satellite customers.

Case study questions

1. Using the example of the automatic washing machine, describe how you might manage the product through all the product life cycle stages from research and development through to decline if the product were to be launched on to the market now. Link the process to the product adoption curve describing the various groups of customers and how you might entice them to enter the market. Do you think the PLC for automatic washing, in the form that we now recognize, might disappear; if so what might replace it?

2. The dishwasher has caused all sorts of problems for manufacturers as it appears to be rigidly stuck at the early adopter stage despite periodic attempts to promote it heavily over the last 25 years. Investigate why this might be and develop a programme that could overcome the problem.

3. The story of the automatic washing machine is an insight into family role stereotyping as well as a reflection on the process of new product development and launch. Discuss the cultural change that has taken place within the family since the early 1960s, especially with regard to the role of the housewife, relate it to the innovation adoption curve and the overall implications for marketing.

4. New product development is crucial in many product areas. What factors would need to be considered if developing a new product development programme for a large organization in the grocery or confectionery trade? How important might be the brand?

Further reading

Booze, Allen and Hamilton Inc (1982) *New Products Management for the 1980s*, Booze, Allen and Hamilton, New York.

Doyle, P. (1976) 'The realities of the product life cycle', *Quarterly Review of Marketing*, summer.

Henry, J. and Walker, D. (1991) *Managing Innovation*, Open University Business School, Sage, London.

Levitt, T. (1965) 'Exploit the product life cycle', *Harvad Business Review*, November–December.

Rogers, E.M. (1983) *Diffusion of Innovations*, Free Press, New York.

Tushman, M.L. (1988) *Readings in the Management of Innovation*, Ballinger Pub. Co. London.

7

Price

AIMS AND OBJECTIVES

By the end of the chapter the student should:

1 be aware of the part that price plays with the product in the marketing mix;

2 be able to identify and evaluate all the factors that must be considered when pricing the product;

3 be able to identify and evaluate the different methods by which an organization can price its products;

4 identify and analyse the many alternative ways that pricing can be used in supporting the product and marketing mix success.

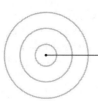

Introduction

The role of price

Price is the element of the marketing mix that seems to be most misunderstood by students and practitioners alike. Most approaches under estimate the all-round contribution that pricing can make to the optimum use of marketing resources. This is not only because of revenue and profit contributions but also because of the many other functions that price can perform in developing successful marketing mix strategies. So let us start with a definition.

PRICE DEFINITION

Price is the value (usually measurement in monetary terms) that the seller agrees to sell a product or service for and the value at which the buyer agrees to purchase.

This exchange transaction can either be:

- *fixed*: the price is given and the buyer either agrees or disagrees;
- *negotiable*: buyer and seller bargain until a mutual price is agreed;
- *a variation*: one element may be fixed and other elements negotiable.

The method used will vary from product to product and from market to market. With some products the price is fixed and no negotiation will take place, for example the products in Sainsbury or Tesco, whilst with other products or services the price can be negotiated as there is often room for manoeuvre, for example double glazing or antiques.

In some countries it is traditional to negotiate on almost any price, for example Turkey or Greece, whilst in others to do so is considered highly irregular and frowned upon, for example the UK or France. However, as markets have become more competitive more price negotiation seems acceptable, even in the UK.

Price and the marketing mix

THE RELATIONSHIP WITH THE PRODUCT

There is a continually shifting customer relationship between the price of the product and the added value elements such as branding, packaging and quality. When looking around and comparing different products the customer will be continuously balancing price and product to arrive at what they consider to be the best overall value.

With most products price will always be a factor although its importance will vary.

As a rule of thumb, in times of economic well-being (high 'feel good' factor) consumer demands might be said to move towards added value factors (branding, added features, quality, etc.) and away from price and conversely during times of economic stringency (low 'feel good' factor) demands move towards price and away from added value (see Figure 7.1).

With most products the producer will try to move the consumer toward added value and away from price because this can lead to greater product differentiation *vis-à-vis* the competition and a higher profit. So during the economic boom of the 1980s producers were able to move consumers toward demand for highly fashionable brands and away from price considerations. This was achieved mainly through the use of heavy TV and print advertising. The whole process was exemplified by the growth of the so-called 'yuppie' culture. Wild young men working on the London money market, earning lots of money and spending it on Porsche cars, designer clothes, Champagne, Caviar and Barratt type executive houses. The downturn in the economy of the early 1990s swung the pendulum from brand back to price considerations.

PRICE AND PROMOTION

Price is seen as an essential ingredient in the promotion of a product. As a form of sales promotion it is used to offer such incentives as short-term discounts and money off (groceries and alcohol); easy credit terms and interest free (cars); and 'buy now, pay six months later' (brown goods) type of offers.

Care should be taken in using price for promotion purposes. Some practitioners argue that an organization should be wary about using price reductions as a form of promotion because it encourages the purchaser to concentrate on price rather than added value. It might also lead to a customer only being willing to purchase when prices are reduced and for them to view the retail outlet as a cut price operation (Debenhams always seems to have some form of the 'blue cross' sale operating).

| **Figure 7.1** | *Price and added value relationship* |

Economic circumstances

Low 'feel good' factor   High 'feel good' factor

Concern with price -- -- -- -- -- -- -- -- Concern with added value

◀ -- -- -- -- -- ▶
Constantly shifting consumer relationship

PRICE AND PLACE

Depending on the type of product or service, the price charged will often be linked to the channel of distribution (the P for place) and different prices can be charged for the use of different channels.

For example products purchased at a convenience store (petrol station) will cost more than those purchased at the local hypermarket (you pay more for the 'convenience' of buying out of normal shop hours or from the shop on the corner), chocolate bought from a vending machine will cost more that chocolate bought from a sweet shop, and the price of drink at a theatre or night-club will be more expensive than at the local pub.

Factors determining price

We will now look in some detail at some of the many factors that will determine the final price of the product or service that the consumer will eventually pay. Some of these factors will be internal to the organization and some external. The organization should be able to control the internal factors whilst most external factors are market driven and are generally outside the control of the organization. The factors to be considered are:

1. price objectives;
2. costs;
3. market structures;
4. level of demand;
5. competitors' prices.

Objectives

The price approach adopted by the management will depend ultimately on what the organization hopes to achieve, its pricing objectives. Pricing objectives will vary not only from industry to industry and company to company but also from product to product.

There is also a difference in kind between:

1. long-term (strategic) pricing objectives;
2. short-term (tactical) pricing objectives.

These will both now be explained in more detail.

LONG-TERM OR STRATEGIC PRICING OBJECTIVES

Ultimately the price that the organization sets for its products must link back through agreed marketing sales and profit objectives to the overall corporate objectives. The corporate objectives will be set in terms such as return on capital employed or return on investment and this will have some sort of affect, albeit indirectly, on the pricing policy eventually adopted.

The long-term, or strategic, pricing objectives will also be linked to overall marketing policy, and the needs of the product portfolio and individual products.

Allowing for the need to price within the umbrella of marketing and corporate objectives, the alternative strategic pricing approaches discussed below can be identified.

MARKET PENETRATION PRICING.   If the marketing objective is to increase sales within the existing market (market penetration) then the price must be pitched at a level that will achieve this. This would normally be a price set below all other competitors in the market that offer a similar and comparable product offering. Many Japanese manufacturers (Hitachi, National Panasonic, Honda) had a reputation for taking this approach when first entering the UK market. The large supermarkets were able to 'steal' over 20 per cent of the petrol market by rigorously undercutting the major participants such as Esso, Shell and BP.

MAINTAIN/GAIN MARKET LEADERSHIP PRICING.   If the objective is to maintain or gain market leadership then the relevant price action will need to be taken. The form this takes will be dependent on the market conditions but will usually mean matching or undercutting the market leader or nearest main competitor, for example Direct Line car insurance gained market leadership by selectively undercutting all others in the market. However it is now losing market share as the other players in the car insurance market react by adopting aggressive pricing themselves. A reinforcement on the truism that marketing is a dynamic process and never stands still.

MARKET ENTRY PRICING.   Market entry pricing will vary according to existing market conditions. If the market to be entered is new or the product is new then there will be no competition and a high price can be set. On the other hand if competition is rife the price set must be low to match the price levels already pertaining. Hitachi were able to charge over £500 for the first CD player, being one of the first on to the market; but they eventually had to lower the price as competition grew.

COMPETITOR HARMONY PRICING.   Although active price collusion between companies is illegal, competitive harmony pricing (sometimes known as 'passive shadowing'), that is charging the same price as the competitors, is not. If market structures are favourable, for example oligopolistic, then tacit agreements to compete on added value (e.g. free gifts, competitions, extra amounts, service, etc.) and not price may 'evolve' between companies. Many petrol companies tended to adopt this approach for years until their market share was so severely eroded by the large supermarkets (described above) that they had to react with aggressive price reductions themselves.

MARKET DISCRIMINATORY PRICING.   Market discriminatory pricing is deliberately charging a range of prices for the same product in different markets. This might be on a regional, national or international level. As with most pricing strategies, the opportunity to do this will depend on many different market conditions.

Examples where this might happen include a supermarket chain charging more in country districts, where there is little competition compared to in town, or a car manufacturer charging less in one country and more in another because of different consumer pricing expectations.

The UK car industry was accused of following this latter practice but argued that prices charged for the same vehicle were different in one country rather than another because of exchange rates, tax and other costs. Because of this practice a new market developed as it was cheaper for a UK customer to buy a British car in Denmark or Belgium and import back into the UK rather than purchase in the home market. Consumer pressure groups have criticized some of the large super-markets (and warned consumers to be aware) for charging more for the same product in different outlets.

The Monopolies and Mergers Commission, in fact, found no evidence of any anti-competitive behaviour or wrong-doing on the part of the car manufacturers, but as this book goes to print the newly named Competition Commission is reinvestigating.

CUSTOMER DISCRIMINATORY PRICING.   Customer discriminatory pricing is the charging of different prices to different customers and tends to be limited to trade customers. A company may charge one price to the wholesaler and another to the retailer and one price to a major customer and another to a smaller one (because of this many small companies now band together into voluntary buying groups to gain greater power and lower prices e.g. 'Spar' for grocers, 'Combined Independent Holdings' for electrical independent retailers).

Some organizations will offer lower prices to such groups as AA members, students, old age pensioners, Ford employees and so on. Customer discriminatory pricing can cause customer conflict if one customer finds out that they are paying more than another and so feels unfairly treated.

Many stores now offer price reductions to customers who are prepared to buy in bulk and some outlets now exist solely for this purpose.

PROFIT MAXIMIZATION PRICING.   If profit maximization is the objective then one of the following approaches might be adopted.

- *Charge a low price with a low mark-up* (the 'mark-up' is the difference between the cost of the product and the selling price). The profit on each product will be low but volume sales might lead to a higher overall profit. This strategy will only work with products that have a quick sales turn-around, e.g. grocery products (known as 'pile it high and sell it cheap' when this objective was operated, successfully, by Tesco in the 1960s and 1970s).

- *Charge a high price with a high mark up*. In this case sales will be less but each product will be making more profit. Used as a strategy where the product is of high value, rarely purchased or has some form of unique attribute, e.g. Rolls-Royce, Rolex watch, Armani suit.

- *Restrict supply and so maintain a high profit margin*. However this approach would only be possible if there were few or no competitors (a monopoly), no substitute products or some form of collusion (legal or otherwise). The European Common Agricultural Policy works in this way with products taken off the market if the price falls below an agreed level.

The organization will need to work out which approach suits it best and this will depend on how sensitive the price is in relationship to demand (known as demand/price elasticity, discussed later in the chapter) and the interrelationship between fixed and variable costs, sales volumes and overall profits.

PREMIUM PRICING.   If the product strategy is differentiation through a quality 'up market' brand image then the pricing strategy would be to price high so as to reinforce the desired image. Givenchy, Yves Saint Laurent and Elizabeth Arden are examples of companies that set high, premium prices for products, in this case perfume and fragrances, to compliment and enhance an image of product luxury.

A few years ago a group of these companies successfully stopped Superdrug from stocking and discounting its products because it was argued that the downward interference with price, as well as the cut price image of Superdrug, caused damage to their luxury product image.

With a high quality product too low a price will detract from the product image and send out the wrong customer benefit messages.

OVERALL MARKET LOW PRICE.   With an overall market low price approach (also appearing as 'everyday low prices') the organization markets its products across the whole of the market on the continuous promise that its prices will never be undercut. This approach will probably only be open to the rich and/or the powerful. To be successful the organization adopting this approach would probably need the economies of scale concomitant with market leadership. Examples of companies able to do this might be: B&Q, the DIY organization; News International with the *Sun* and *The Times* newspapers and now Esso in the selling of petrol.

NARROW MARKET LOW PRICE.   A company might look for low price leadership in smaller, niche markets where specialization and differentiation can lead to cost savings. An example might be the grocery chain Aldi able to undercut the large grocery majors by formulating a low price strategy across a limited range of selected products. This purchasing policy allows the company to gain the economies of scale associated with bulk buying across a limited assortment of food and non-food products.

Similarly Kwik-Fit, the car exhaust fitting company was able to undercut the larger parts and service suppliers by specializing in this one area, buying in bulk and gaining both economy and fitting skill advantages and eventually becoming the market leader in this one area.

SYSTEM PRICING.   Many companies adopt a systems approach to pricing. With this approach prices will not be given for the individual items that go to make up the whole product or services. Only a complete price is offered. This approached is often used in the marketing of products such as fitted kitchens and bedrooms, computer systems or packaged holidays.

CUT PRICE PRICING.   Another strategic approach is to offer seemingly continuous price cuts on all products. An arch proponent of this approach is the furniture company MFI. At any one time price cuts, for example 40 per cent, 50 per cent, 60 per cent off the normal selling price will be on offer on selected products. This strategic approach to price should not be confused with the tactical promotional price offer approach taken by a company to increase sales at certain times of the year, for example in a winter or spring sale.

It should be noted that there are strict laws about what can be offered as a price cut and what cannot and MFI has successfully argued that it does not infringe any price law by seeming to offer continuous cut prices through out the year.

SURVIVAL PRICING. There could be times of low sales when the survival of the company might depend on the pricing policy adopted. This would probably take the form of pricing to encourage cash flow or pricing to cover immediate, variable costs until the market picks up. Many retailers had to adopt some form of survival pricing in the late 1980s early 1990s, to combat the downturn in retail sales associated with the economic difficulties at this time, by reducing stock levels and increasing cash flow (usually through the use of almost continuous sales periods).

TRADE PRICING. An organization selling products through intermediaries, that is wholesalers and retailers, as well as direct to the consumer, will have to develop separate pricing policies to allow for differing and additional needs and for the tasks that the intermediaries perform for the producer.

Intermediaries hold stock for resale and not for their own consumption and the price that they are charged for the products will have to reflect the many tasks that they undertake for the producer. These tasks will include the following:

- holding and paying for stock;
- offering the customer a selection of products from which to choose and giving advice on the most beneficial choice;
- undertaking various promotional activities as well as delivery and installation and possibly after sales service.

In return for undertaking the tasks outlined above, the intermediary will expect the price that they are charged by the producer to offer additional or different benefits than those expected by the end-consumer. These expected benefits will include:

- agreed profit margins;
- bulk discounts;
- discounts for earlier payment;
- extended credit;
- joint promotion help;
- a 'fair' product returns policy.

SHORT-TERM OR TACTICAL PRICING OBJECTIVES

There will be many occasions when a need will arise to react, tactically, in the short term to market and environment circumstances. These will include the following:

■ loss of market share;

■ defend against increased competition, e.g. the *Daily Telegraph* had to reduce its price as a response to price cutting by *The Times*;

■ discount pricing as a form of promotional incentive, e.g. £2 off for a short period, for quantity purchases, for prompt payment;

■ guaranteed pricing, e.g. in times of high inflation a guarantee to maintain and not to increase the price can be seen as a worthwhile sales incentive;

■ to get rid off excess/end of range stock;

■ overcome cash flow difficulties;

■ loss-leader pricing, e.g. a supermarket pricing its bread below cost price to induce customers into the shop where it is hoped they will purchase the rest of their weekly shopping;

■ pricing for product trial, e.g. when introducing a new product to the market the producer might offer it at half its normal selling price to persuade the consumer to sample and hopefully re-purchase.

There is academic argument about when an objective is strategic and when it is tactical (survival could be seen as both a strategic and a tactical pricing objective). It could be argued that there is no right or wrong answer to this as, whether an objective is tactical or strategic, will depend on market circum-stances, individual organizations and personal predilections.

Costs

The cost involved in producing goods and services must play a major part in deter-mining the final price charged for a product. Any fool can manufacture a product and sell below cost. However, to do this would very quickly lead to the company going out of business. So cost must be covered and a percentage added to allow for a reasonable profit to be made.

There are two ways the company can increase its profitability. Increasing the price and/or reducing its costs. In many markets it is impossible to do the former and so the latter becomes a major consideration when looking at the pricing of the product. Because cost plays such an important part in deciding the final price (and determining the profit to be made) it is necessary to look at this area in some detail.

DIFFERENT SORTS OF COSTS

To begin with we will look in simple terms at two different types of costs – fixed and variable – and the relationship that these have with the product portfolio mix, volume of sales and levels of profit.

Fixed costs (FC).   These are the costs that are incurred whether the company produces products or not. FC will include outgoings like rent, rates, loan interest payments, administration, wages for employees working on a full-time basis and any form of long-term contract such as a three-year sponsorship deal.

Variable costs (VC). These are costs that are incurred only when products are produced, so VC will be linked directly to the product or service itself. VC will include outgoings like raw materials, packaging, point-of-sale material and forms of energy expended on the production such as electricity, heating, oil, etc. and any other form of cost that arises as a direct result of service, product or sales creation such as advertising, sales promotions, exhibitions and sales commission.

THE RELATIONSHIP BETWEEN COSTS, VOLUME AND PROFIT (CVP)

Product portfolio analysis (using the BCG portfolio matrix discussed in Chapter 6) should be undertaken so as to develop the most favourable cost, volume and profit mix across all the products.

As fixed costs must be paid whatever the production, it is to the benefit of the organization to spread these as widely as possible so all resource capability is used to its optimum level.

There are many ways that marketing can contribute to greater cost/price effectiveness. These will include an analysis of the following three options:

1. overall cost efficiency;
2. relating costs to the product portfolio;
3. break-even analysis.

Overall cost efficiency. As with all other departments, marketing can look towards its own cost and accountability structures, eliminate waste, set clear performance indicators, allocate levels of responsibilities and implement value for money programmes. This can be achieved in one of two ways:

Going for a lower price. There is a temptation to believe that the best approach is to go for the highest possible price. But the following advantages can accrue by lowering the price:

- lower profit mark-up but an increase in the volume demanded; as sales turnover increases (dependent on the price sensitivities of demand) *overall* profit could be higher (remember Tesco and 'pile it high and sell it cheap').
- more sold should lead to greater economies of scale because of bulk purchase, greater use of floor space and better distribution efficiencies;
- if there is spare capacity, increased sales will absorb this slack and so contribute and spread the overall fixed cost.

Going for a higher price. In some market circumstances it is possible to raise price and therefore profit margins without affecting sales. This will depend on the type of product, the alternatives available, the competition and the level of demand. A 10 per cent price increase adds directly to net profit whilst a 10 per cent increase in sales would contain a large element of costs.

The product portfolio and costs. All products in the portfolio need constant scrutiny to assess overall cost demands and revenue contribution. This especially applies to those products in the 'problem child' and 'dog' squares and these areas can be examined in a little more detail.

Problem child square. Cost decisions in the problem child square (low sales in a growing market, high costs, little or no revenue) are predominantly 'go' or 'eliminate' decisions. If 'go' then the commitment should be wholehearted. If in doubt the product should be eliminated because of the drain on both variable and fixed costs.

Dog square. Cost decisions in the 'dog' square (low sales, low growth market) are reposition, maintain, harvest or eliminate decisions.

- *Repositioning* (remember Lucozade?) a 'go' decision, demands total resource commitment if it is to be successful.

- *To maintain* a product's current position will depend on the interplay between its drain on resources and its contribution to fixed costs. If in doubt it should be eliminated.

- *To harvest* (little or no spend, while obtaining as much revenue as possible before elimination) the product should be managed in a controlled and planned way with concern given to the effect on the other products in the portfolio and the whole of total cost.

- *Product elimination* decisions should be taken earlier rather than later as there are inevitably many hidden costs across the whole portfolio associated with 'dog' products. This will include opportunity costs such as the salesperson spending valuable time attempting to sell non-viable products when their time and energy could be spent more effectively elsewhere.

- *For survival* purposes production can continue for a short period as long as variable costs are covered and a moratorium is temporarily called on the fixed costs.

BREAK-EVEN ANALYSIS. Break-even analysis looks at the number of sales needed to cover both fixed and variable costs (total costs). This is a function of fixed costs, variable costs and price. The lower the price the more sales are needed; the higher the price the less sales are needed. This relationship can be shown in diagrammatic form (see Figure 7.2) or by a simple formula:

$$\text{Break-even point} = \frac{\text{fixed costs}}{\substack{\text{selling price} - \text{variable cost} \\ \text{per unit} \qquad \text{per unit}}} = \substack{\text{number of units} \\ \text{to be sold}}$$

Selling price – variable costs = contribution

If the fixed costs are £2000, the variable costs for each product are £3 and the selling price is £5 per unit, that gives us the following break-even calculation:

$$\frac{\text{£2000 (FC)}}{\text{£5 (SP)} - \text{£3 (VC)}} = 1000 \text{ units}$$

If the selling price were dropped to £4 then the number of units that would need to be sold would be:

$$\frac{£2000}{£4 - £3} = 2000 \text{ units}$$

Likewise if the price were raised to £8 then the number of units that would need to be sold would be:

$$\frac{£2000}{£8 - £3} = 400 \text{ units}$$

The question might be asked that why not just raise the price to £13 and then only 200 units need to be sold? From the discussion earlier it should be remembered that price relates to volume as well as to costs. If we raise the price to too high a level the customer will resist and may even refuse to purchase. The price which it is possible to charge will therefore depend on the price sensitivity of the market.

The break-even chart

■ Break-even analysis can be shown in graph form, which will identify the break-even point and the profit levels for different levels of output (Figure 7.2).

■ Different break-even charts can be constructed for different price/costing levels.

■ Sales forecasting should give an indication of how many sales can be achieved each week, month and year. This way the output and the break-even point can be linked to a specific period of time. This is crucial when attempting to identify when a particular project will start to make money and begin to repay its start-up costs (especially for the bank which is lending you money. The bank will expect to have a break-even sales figure and the time in which it is expected that this will be achieved).

The organization has fixed costs of £2000 for the year. If variable costs are £15.00 and the selling price is set at £35.00 then the break-even point will be at point x, 100 units (the break-even amount can be plotted using different price levels).

Market forecasting should indicate the level of sales expected per week. The number of units to be sold to reach the break-even point, divided by the sales expected per week will give the time when the break-even point will be reached, in our example above, if an organization is selling 5 units a week on average, then it will break-even after 20 weeks.

Market structures

The structure of the market will also affect the ability of the organization to set and control the price and the following market structures can be identified:

1. free monopolistic;
2. controlled monopolistic;

| **Figure 7.2** | *Break-even chart* |

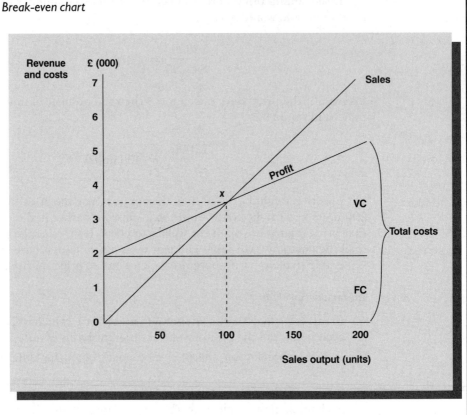

3. oligopolistic;
4. perfect competition;
5. adulterated competition.

FREE MONOPOLISTIC

In theory a monopoly market is a market with only one player, but in practice an organization is said to have a monopoly where it controls over 25 per cent of the market (this definition varies and the reader should not be too concerned as long as the concept is understood). If the company has a monopoly for its products it can be said to be a 'price-setter' and can (in principle) charge any price it wants as consumers can either buy more or less, or go without.

There is a trade-off, however, between a high price, high mark-up but less sales, or a low price, low mark-up and more sales. The company accountant and sales and marketing director should be able to estimate the optimum profitable relationship.

The government attempts to restrict the growth of monopoly companies through the use of the Competition Commission as it is considered to be inimical to the development of competition and a healthy market. Organizations thought to have a monopoly might be Tate and Lyle, the sugar company, because of historic market share, Tetra Pak, because of patent rights on a unique packaging material, and Thorn EMI with copyright on the many artists whose work it sells on CD.

CONTROLLED MONOPOLISTIC

Similar conditions apply in a controlled monopoly to those above, except that the prices charged must conform to guidelines set down by the government or government appointed bodies (known as regulators). Many of the newly privatized industries – BT (the regulator is Oftel) – and the old utilities – water (Ofwat), electricity (Offer) and gas (Ofgas) companies – have to set their prices within strictly (or no so strictly) controlled guidelines.

OLIGOPOLISTIC

An oligopolistic market structure exists where a few large companies (the market 'players') control the market. Under these circumstances competitive 'harmony pricing' often dominates.

Competitive harmony pricing was defined as a tacit agreement between the market players on the price to be charged whilst competing on other forms of added value, for examples prizes and competitions. Each organization understands that to unilaterally lower its prices will not gain any advantage as the other players will immediately follow suit and unless the market expands all will be worse off as the same amount of products will be sold but now at a lower price.

Petrol companies might be seen as an example where this could happen. Another example might be the grocery supermarket business dominated by Tesco, Sainsbury, Asda, Safeway and Gateway. A price war almost developed when Tesco attempted to gain market share by dropping its prices. Sainsbury immediately followed and both stores gained little. Tesco subsequently regained market share by moving from price and concentrating on its loyalty card scheme.

PERFECT COMPETITION

Perfect competition could be seen as an idealized form of market structure existing only in the mind of the economist. With the theory of perfect competition there are infinite numbers of competitors in the market all able to leave and enter the market freely, each individual firm unable to affect both the price and the total level of supply. In this type of market the price is decided by the interaction of supply and demand and all organizations concerned are 'price-takers' rather than 'price-setters'.

ADULTERATED COMPETITION

It must be argued that perfect competition does not exist and all markets in the industrialized world are a combination of all the market structures described above and that structure could be described as one of adulterated competition.

Some markets and industries lean more toward the monopolistic (gas, water, petrol, pharmaceutical), and others more toward the competitive (DIY, food products, financial services). The situation might also vary from the home market, where an organization might be said to have a monopoly, to the international market, where competition will exist (BT, British Airways, British Aerospace).

The last decade has seen a movement around the world from monopoly to competitive markets, especially since the ending of the Russian Empire. Capitalism and some form of competitive market now exist in countries such as China, Vietnam, Poland, Hungary, the Czech Republic, Slovakia and Bulgaria, where none existed before.

In an adulterated competitive market situation a company may be either a price-setter or a price-taker dependent on the competitive structure of their particular industry. This could be a price-setter in the home market and a price-taker in the international market.

Level of demand

The level of demand in the market will obviously have a bearing on the price the company is able to charge. The marketing manager will want to influence the price at which the product or service is sold, so there must be an effort made to measure the relevant level of existing or potential demand.

Expected demand must also be known, as an aid to the whole planning process beginning with an expected sales forecast.

MARKETING RESEARCH AND THE MEASUREMENT OF DEMAND

One important way to identify the potential sales for a product is through the use of marketing research. Both primary and secondary forms of research can be used in attempting to forecast levels of demand for a product or service. Secondary research can be used to examine past market activity in the same, or similar product areas. If trends or patterns are evident these can then be used to predict future sales.

Both quantitative and qualitative primary research methods can also be used. This will involve surveys and/or question and answer sessions with customers, intermediaries, suppliers, sales staff, etc. about their views on the direction of future sales.

THE ECONOMIST'S VIEW OF DEMAND

The economist's view of demand and its relationship with price must also be considered. Economists will argue that for most products (all things being equal), the following will apply:

- the higher the price the lower will be the demand and conversely the lower the price the higher will be the demand;

- an excess supply (a glut) at any one time will cause prices to fall while a shortage of goods at another time will cause prices to rise;

■ similarly the more demand in the market for a product the higher is the price that can be charged and the lower the demand for a product the lower is the price that can be charged.

This leads us to outline the economist's general view of the relationship between supply and demand. The first point states that the higher the price is the lower the level of demand for that product. Conversely, the lower the price, the higher the demand. This gives us a simple demand curve as illustrated in Figure 7.3.

At a price of £6 only four products will be demanded, but at £4, ten products will be demanded.

Conversely, with supply, economics tells us that the higher the price in the market the more the producer will be prepared to supply (more profit) but the lower the price the less the producer will be prepared to bring to the market (less profit). This gives the supply curve shown in Figure 7.4.

At a price of £6 the producer will be prepared to supply ten products but if they are offered £4 the producer will only be prepared to supply four products.

We can now put the demand curve and the supply curve together to give us the demand and supply curve and the price that will eventually be charged for the product (Figure 7.5).

| **Figure 7.3** | *The demand curve* |

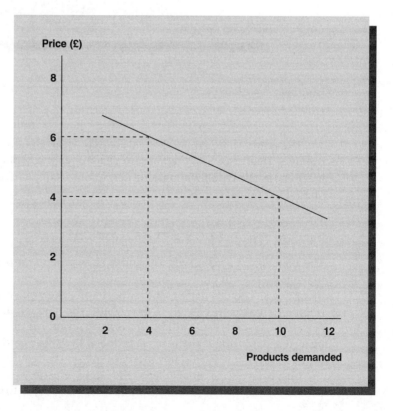

| **Figure 7.4** | *The supply curve* |

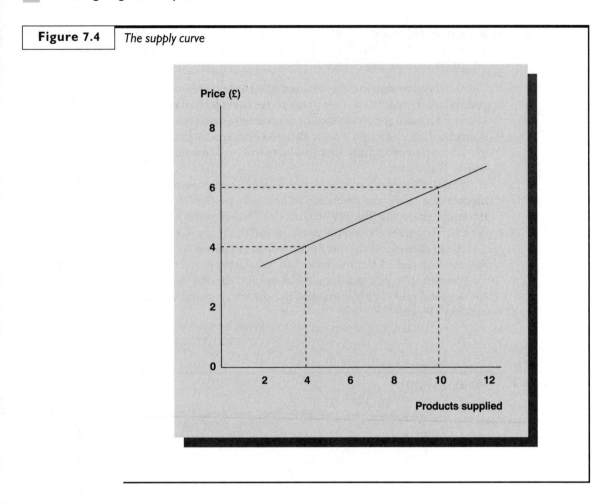

The point where demand equals supply is the amount consumers are prepared to buy at that price and the amount the supplier is willing to make available. This is known as the equilibrium point (*x*). In our example the price is £5 and the level of goods supplied is seven.

DEMAND AND THE CONCEPT OF ELASTICITY

The concept of product elastic and inelastic demand is important to marketing managers as it will impinge on their ability to move the price of the product either up or down. There is little point in increasing the price of a product by 10 per cent hoping to make more profit if, as a result, the demand for that product falls by 50 per cent. The end result will be *less overall profit*. On the other hand the result will be as disappointing if the price is reduced by 10 per cent hoping to increase sales only to find that sales did not increase. Again the result will be *less overall profit*.

So products (or goods) are said to be elastic or inelastic; where elasticity measures the sensitivity of the demand for the product relative to a price change.

| Figure 7.5 | *The demand and supply curve* |

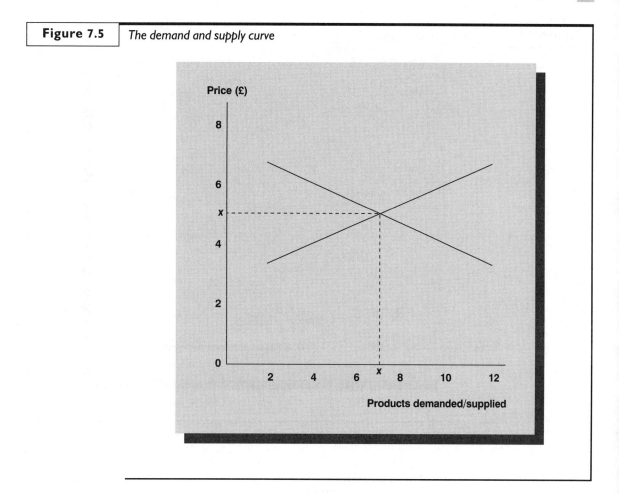

The more price elastic the product is said to be, the more responsive demand is to price change. Similarly the more price inelastic the product is said to be, the more unresponsive demand is to change. We will look in more detail now at both elastic and inelastic demand.

ELASTIC DEMAND. A product is said to have elastic demand if the price goes down by, for example, 10 per cent and there is *more* than a 10 per cent increase in demand or if the price goes up by 10 per cent and there is *more* than a 10 per cent decrease in demand. This can be shown by the elastic demand curve (Figure 7.6).

At £10, 100 units are demanded, but a 10 per cent reduction to £9 leads to an increase in demand of 50 units, an increase of 50 per cent. Alternatively if the price were £9 a 10 per cent increase in price to £10 would reduce demand from 150 units to 100 units, a decrease of 66 per cent. This product would be said to be extremely sensitive to a price change.

THE CHARACTERISTICS OF ELASTIC PRODUCTS. Products or goods that are said to have elastic demand will have the following characteristics:

| Figure 7.6 | *An elastic demand curve* |

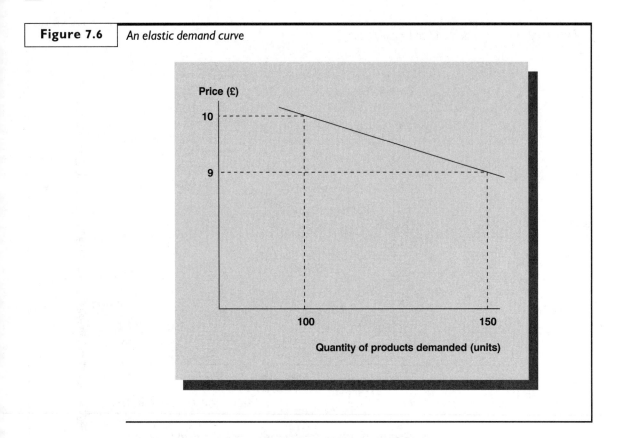

The following text appears in the figure:

Price (£)

10

9

100

150

Quantity of products demanded (units)

- They will have little or no consumer perceived added value, e.g. a commodity or staple product, and will be sold solely on the price, e.g. milk, bread, cheese, squash.

- They will be in plentiful supply and there will be many competing brands on the market. This will allow the customer to switch easily to another brand if there is a price increase from his or her existing supplier or a price decrease from a competing supplier, e.g. switch from Maxwell House to Nescafe coffee or from Ruddles to Theakstons beer.

- Elastic products are easily substituted one for another. So as the price increases the customer switches away from one product to another that is similar. An example would be the movement from one holiday to another, from coffee to tea or from one method of crossing the English Channel to another.

The grocery trade and the holiday and leisure industries have all grown enormously over the last 25 years by reducing prices and subsequently increasing sales by a far greater amount.

UNDERSTANDING ELASTICITIES OF DEMAND. The large supermarkets have learnt that by working on very small profit margins they are able to turn their stock around twenty or thirty times in one year thus making far greater profits overall.

INELASTIC DEMAND. Conversely a product is said to have inelastic demand if the price goes down by, say, 10 per cent and there is *less* than a 10 per cent decrease in sales, or if the price goes up by 10 per cent there is *less* than a 10 per cent increase in demand (Figure 7.7).

An 11.1 per cent increase in price from £9 to £10 leads to a negligible drop in demand from 105 units to 100 units, a 4.7 per cent decrease. Alternatively a decrease of 10 per cent in the price from £10 to £9 would lead to a very small increase in demand from 100 units to105 units, an increase of 5 per cent.

THE CHARACTERISTICS OF INELASTIC PRODUCTS. Inelastic products might have one or more of the following characteristics:

- Be in short supply, available only in limited amounts, or scarce, e.g. gold, cocoa after a bad harvest, fish on the day of a poor catch, or cigarettes on the Falkland Islands.

- Where one company, or group of companies or countries act together to control the supply, e.g. in the EU with the CAP, the OPEC countries and the supply of petrol, cement manufacturers and the supply of cement.

- Where supply is restricted because of some form of legal restriction, e.g. patent or copyright.

- Where the product is unique, e.g. a painting or a one-off exhibition or concert.

| **Figure 7.7** | *An inelastic demand curve* |

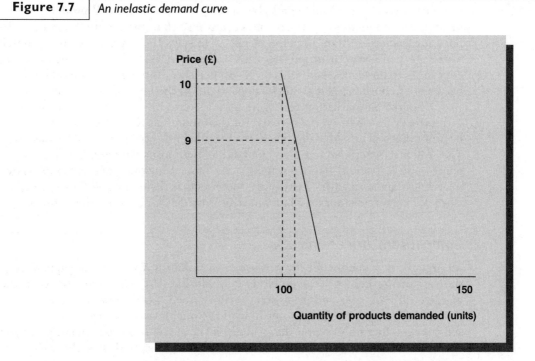

- Where there are no substitute products, e.g. electricity, water, bread at 2.00 am or a drink at the theatre.
- Addictive products, e.g. cigarettes or alcohol (although the consumer can always move to another brand).
- A low priced product where price movements have relatively little effect on disposable income, e.g. salt, matches, potatoes.

Understanding demand inelasticities, the music industry has been able to hold the prices on new compact discs of popular performers way over the £10 level because of the level of consumer demand and the exclusive contracts they have with the artists (despite manufacturing costs of allegedly below one pound). The MMC has examined this industry and found that there was no case to be answered.

MEASUREMENT OF ELASTICITY.   Business managers will attempt to measure levels of elasticity across all of a company's products. It is necessary to know the level at which a price rise might cause a greater fall in sales than is compensated for by an increase in the profit margin, leading to an overall drop in profits.

There are sophisticated computer models that will attempt to measure this elasticity at different price change levels. An example is the tax on cigarettes which is a large tax revenue earning inelastic product. Too high a price increase could lead to an overall fall in tax revenue as smokers abstain. Government economists will therefore need to, and do, work out the overall revenue which will be received at different levels of price increase.

ELASTICITY AND MARKETING.   Elasticity is important to marketers because they need to know the affect on sales of both a price increase and/or a price decrease. In this way they are able to manage and plan pricing policies across all products in the most profit enhancing way. If demand is elastic so that putting up the price by 10 per cent leads to a 20 or 30 per cent fall off in sales the company could be much worse off than before it raised the price. Likewise if a decrease in price of 10 per cent leads to an increase in sales of 20–30 per cent, the company could be much better off. In both cases it would be dependent on the level of profit margin.

Of course all marketing managers would like to be able to increase the price with little or no effect on the demand for the product as the increased revenue will be profit that will be added directly to the bottom line of the profit and loss account. They will attempt to achieve this by branding and promoting and hopefully developing more inelasticity by encouraging a consumer perception of product or service uniqueness and exclusivity. Luxury products such as diamonds, perfumes, designer clothes, gourmet restaurants, fine wines, etc. are developed using this principle.

Competitors' prices and offers

An organization cannot set its own prices in isolation from what is happening in the rest of the industry (as much as it would like to). The competitors in the market will have cost and price structures that will need to be investigated and analysed. There is very little point in working out the price at which you wish to sell your product only to find that when you try to sell it on the open market you are above the price of identical or similar products. If this is the case your products will not sell.

It should also be appreciated that in most markets price movements instigated by one company will cause corresponding movements by the competition and this should be borne in mind when playing around with product prices. An alert manager should attempt to predict the reaction of the competitor whenever he or she instigates a price increase or decrease.

To what degree one price change will affect another will depend on the prevalent market structure (e.g. monopoly, oligopoly, etc. as discussed earlier).

PRICE PROMISE

As a result of difficult market conditions and increased competition many companies now offer the price promise that if the same product can be purchased more cheaply elsewhere then they will refund the difference if notified within seven days, for example Comet, Dixons, Co-op, Do-It-All, Homebase, Powerhouse, etc. This tends to encourage the use of own-label or products made exclusively for one retailer (on which, of course, price cannot be compared).

Methods of selecting the price

The factors that affect the pricing of the product need to be considered and a pricing method chosen. There are many different methods available and the following ones will be discussed:

1. cost-plus pricing;
2. going-rate pricing;
3. break-even and target-profit pricing;
4. what-the-market-will-bear pricing;
5. customer-driven pricing.

Cost-plus pricing

This method of pricing has an immediate attraction because of its apparent simplicity. The cost of the product is worked out by allocating a portion of the fixed costs to each product and then adding it to the variable costs. This gives the total cost of each product and the percentage profit desired can be added to give the selling price. The following calculation provides a practical example:

	(£)
Fixed cost allocation	10·00
Variable cost	5·00
Total costs	15·00
Desired profit, 50%	7·50
Selling price	22·50

DISADVANTAGES. In using cost-plus pricing there is an assumption made that having established the total cost price the product manager need only add the desired mark-up, in this case 50 per cent and then offer the product at the resultant selling price. But this does not take into account the fact that the competition may be offering a similar product at a lower price, because of greater productivity or a willingness to work on a lower mark-up.

Similarly the customer may be unwilling to pay this price either because they can go without or they can purchase the same or a similar product from the competition.

However cost-plus pricing might be a viable proposition in some industries, for example the basic utilities, for the reasons associated with product demand inelasticities described above.

Going-rate pricing

In most industries the structure of the market will decide the general level of prices. As discussed earlier, in an unregulated monopoly almost any price can be charged bearing in mind the trade-off between profit and sales, whilst at the other end of the market – perfect competition – the price will be decided by the interplay of supply and demand and be outside the control of the organization. However most companies will be setting the price somewhere between these two extremes.

Adopting the 'going-rate' concept the company will set the price according to price rates that are used in their particular markets. These price rates might have come about through tacit agreement, through similar cost and profit needs, through customer demands or by competitive market interaction.

A pattern of different price bands tends to develop, with each price band aimed at different target groups. A company launching a new product will price and compete within these bands (or price plateaus).

An example might be TVs with price levels at approximately £300, £400 and £500. If we take the £300 level, the product might be aimed at the C2DE market and sold on utility value. The price asked might vary say between £289 and £309 dependent on market circumstances. The £400 market might be aimed at the C1C2 markets, have a few added benefits, and have price movements between £385 and £410. Finally the £500 priced band might be aimed at the ABC1 market, have full added benefits and be priced between £490 and £520.

A TV manufacturer might compete in all three bands or chose only one or two in which to compete. When pricing the marketing manager will be aware of the bands within which to price.

ADVANTAGES. The advantage in adopting going-rate pricing is that there is little or no effort needed in deciding product cost and selling price. The market will have set the parameters. This is particularly helpful if the going rate allows for high profit margins due to little competition or a concentration on added value rather than price. It also reduces the prospect of a competitor reacting aggressively by lowering the price in response to a new market entrant setting a price below the going rate, and perhaps causing a downward spiralling of prices in some form of price war (as in the petrol price war described earlier in the chapter).

DISADVANTAGE. The disadvantage of going-rate pricing is that it can lead to complacency and inefficiency. Almost any market is now open to invasion from competitors prepared to ignore custom and practice and set their price according to a lower cost base or more customer demanding criteria and so steal market share.

Break-even and target-profit pricing

In the section on break-even analysis the relationship between fixed and variable costs was discussed demonstrating that there is a certain level of sales at which total cost are covered and profits can be made. If a higher price is charged then total cost recovery will be quicker. Conversely if a lower price is charged then total cost recovery time will be longer.

In some circumstances there could be time demands made on a company, for example by a bank or finance house, in terms of payback periods and profit targets. If this is the case then the price charged would need to conform to agreed revenue and profit targets.

Break-even pricing is often used when a voluntary group such as the students union or an amateur theatre group decide to put on a disco or some form of concert or play especially if the project is non-profit making and only total costs need to be recovered. A limited amount of tickets are priced to cover both fixed and variable costs on the understanding that all will be sold. Of course problems will arise and a loss made if the requisite amount of tickets are not sold.

The flexibility to do the above would of course depend on the same market and product conditions identified earlier in the chapter.

What-the-market-will-bear pricing

Pricing by what the market will bear, is to take advantage of market conditions such as shortages, scarcity or a product uniqueness and the price is set at the highest figure the customer is prepared to pay.

This may seem, on the surface, to be an attractive method because optimum profits can be achieved. However a word of caution. There are times when higher prices can be charged and customers have little or no choice but to purchase, but in doing so ill-will might be generated which could have long-term detrimental affects. Also charging too high a price can leave room for competitors to come in, undercut, and steal the market. It has been argued that this is similar to the pricing policy pursued by Rank Xerox with its photocopying machines in the early 1980s, allowing the Japanese, notably Cannon, to move in with a lower priced, better value offering.

Customer-driven pricing; the marketing approach

Taking a marketing approach, the selling price should be set at the level the customer is prepared to pay.

 In most cases the price the customer will be willing to pay can be established through the use of marketing research.

VALUE-ADDED DRIVEN PRICING

The price the customer is prepared to pay and the importance that price will play in the purchase compared with other elements of the marketing mix will vary according to perceptions of added value:

■ The higher the perceived added value the more the customer will be prepared to pay (Mercedes). The lower the perceived added value the less the customer will be prepared to pay (Ford Scorpio).

■ Similarly the higher the perceived added value of the product the less important price becomes compared with the other elements of the marketing mix. The lower the perceived value the higher the importance placed on price becomes as an element of the marketing mix.

These will include all the factors identified earlier such as the amount of competition, levels of supply and demand, product enhancements, time, economic and personal circumstances, etc.

PSYCHOLOGICAL PRICING

Research has identified ways of tactical price presentation that the customer feels more comfortable with than others. The most notable of these is pricing within price band parameters. So we see prices at £4.99 rather than £5.00, £99 rather than £100 or £999 rather than £1000. The argument is that the price is perceived by the customer to be within the lower price band rather the higher, that is in the nineties rather than the hundreds. Marks and Spencer railed against this practice arguing that it was meant to deceive and was therefore not conducive to good customer relations and it now sells its products at the rounded price.

Psychological pricing also includes the following methods of which examples are offered.

■ Advertising a product as costing only 99p a day to run (less than a pint of beer) rather than £30 a month.

■ Advertising the product at £999 and in very small print adding that this is exclusive of VAT. The price including VAT being £1173.82 (a much less attractive looking price don't you think?)

■ Quantum pricing is the point above which sales might be radically affected. Cigarettes priced below £2, e.g. £1.70 for 20 might be seen by the customer as costing £1 plus some lose change. Move to over £2 and the effect can be dramatic in sales down-turn as the customer is now aware that the price is £2 – 'two whole' pounds.

■ Rather than breach a quantum point (e.g. £1 for a chocolate bar) a producer might prefer to keep the price at 95p and reduce the amount offered.

■ Using the number '8' rather than a '7' as it looks more attractive.

The procedure for setting the basic price can now be set out in diagrammatical form as a basic model for setting the price (Figure 7.8).

| **Figure 7.8** | *Procedure for setting the basic price* |

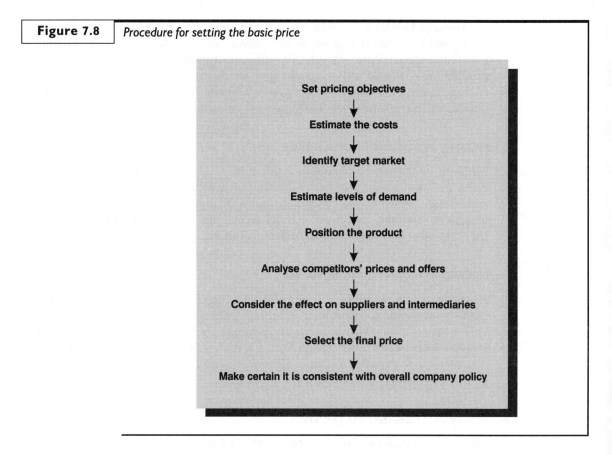

Marketing and the flexibility of price

Price can be used in many different and flexible ways so as to enhance the product offering and segment the market. A number of the alternative methods that can be used are now briefly considered.

PRICING BY BEHAVIOUR

Many companies will price by customer behaviour offering the heavy or regular user a loyalty bonus or price discount off products purchased, for example the Tesco loyalty card, now used by 6 million customers. Past users of a product might also be targeted and offered price reductions for re-using the product, for example re-ordering *The Economist* magazine at a 50 per cent discount if contracting for three years.

PRICING BY TIME

Different prices can be charged for the product or service at different, under-utilized, times of the day, night, week and month of the year. Thus railway companies charge lower prices outside of the rush hour, in the evening, on weekends and at bank holidays.

Package holidays, air flights and ferry crossings offer lower prices for night travel, weekday travel and off-season travel and the electricity and telephone companies charge different prices at different times optimizing the use of their product mix. Phone calls are cheaper in the evening and on Sundays and customers can purchase a 'white meter' which charges a lower price for electricity if used between the hours of 12.00 pm and 7.00 am.

PRICING BY SOCIO-DEMOGRAPHICS

Different prices can be charged for different sized groups, for clubs and institutions, for families, for children, for old aged pensioners, students, between men and women, and between business and individual use. Discos, theme parks, museums, cinemas, the cross channel ferries are all examples of organizations that take advantage of this form of flexible pricing.

PRICING BY QUANTITY PURCHASED

Many organizations will offer lower prices for larger quantities purchased. This is used to encourage the purchase of more products or a range of products. Some organizations are making this facility increasingly available to the consumer, for example Sainsbury's buy three and get one free or Bottoms-up offering an extra 5 per cent off ten bottles of wine. However quantity discounts tend to be used predominantly in business-to-business and trade negotiations.

PRICING BY DELIVERY METHOD

Some organizations will price by the method of delivery, for example if you collect and install you pay one price, if we deliver and install you pay another. This could lead to the growth of the 'cash and carry' type of retailer where the customer could choose to collect at a lower price all sorts of products from computers and fridges to garden sheds and houses. The seller would offer delivery and installation but at a stipulated price.

PRICING BY DISTANCE

The price charged will often vary according to the distance between the supplier and the customer, for example radius bands of 5, 10 or 50 miles from the outlet; the greater the distance, the higher the price. When selling abroad different prices may well be charged depending on where responsibility for the product is taken on. This might be at the factory gate, at the docks before shipment, at the docks after shipment, when delivered to the customer and with or without insurance. The customer is able to choose, or often negotiate the best method for them.

PRICING BY METHOD OF PAYMENT

Price can be used as an incentive to encourage payment by a method favoured by the producer. This might be a discount for cash or for early or immediate payment.

Similarly extra might be charged for the use of a credit card, cheque book or credit terms. Price, as a form of extended credit, is also used to encourage purchase. This might be interest free credit or 'buy now and pay in six months time'.

SOME GENERAL PRICING TERMS

As well as the terms used throughout this chapter, there are many different pricing terms that are used and a number of them are now given brief explanations.

SEALED BID PRICING. With some contracts, sellers are invited to tender a sealed bid price to undertake or purchase some form of product or service. Each bidding organization will not know the price tendered by its competitors and usually the lowest price will win. This forces all participants to identify the client needs, examine their costs in minute detail and set their keenest price. This method of pricing tends to be used in areas such as building and civil engineering contracts. It can be open to abuse from unscrupulous participants colluding with one another and fixing the price.

PRICE SKIMMING. An initial inelastic market allows a high price to be charged before the competition enters and drives down the profit margin. Hitachi was able to price skim the market and charge over £500 for the first CD player until competition from all over the world forced the price down to lower levels, in some cases, to below £100.

PRICE CREAMING. Price creaming is the ability to ask a premium price because of a perceived high added value on the product or service, for example a Blur or Rolling Stones concert, a Bentley, or a bottle of Moet and Chandon Champagne of a particularly good vintage.

PRICE LEADERSHIP. Price leadership is attributed to the company that is dominant in the market and which is able to dictate the market price that all the others will follow. This tends to be the market leader operating in an oligopolistic market structure, for example Esso or Shell in the petro-chemical industry or Time Warner in the cinema business.

PREDATORY PRICING. With predatory pricing a more powerful company will loss lead on its prices to drive out or destroy the competition. It can be illegal if seen as anti-competitive, that is if the intention is to drive out the competition and then put the price back up. The ubiquitous Japanese car and electrical manufacturers where continually accused of this in the 1970s and 1980s as they moved in and undercut home markets.

Predatory pricing has also allegedly been used in the newspaper industry where intense competition for readership persuaded Rupert Murdoch to lower the price of *The Times* and the *Sun* below cost to attempt to gain market share from the *Daily Telegraph* and the *Mirror*.

INFLATIONARY PRICING. During times of high inflation, pricing can become extremely difficult, especially on longer term contracts, and the marketing department will need to work very closely with the finance department if costly pricing mistakes are to be avoided. If inflation is at 30 per cent and the product mark-up is 15 per cent a price charged today will be below cost price in six months time.

Ideally the seller would like to link the prices charged to some form of retail price index, raising them at the same level as inflation. This can be acceptable to customers, and can even be used as a sales incentive (e.g. buy now as it will be more expensive next month) if they become used to paying an increase each month. An example of this was in the late 1970s and early 1980s when high inflation enabled Barrett, the house builder, to increase house prices by 3 or 4 per cent virtually every month.

PRICE HAVEN.   A product will be considered to have a price haven if it is able to hold a high price because of inelastic demand, customer loyalty, a brand, patent or some other form of unique advantage. This obviously has a great attraction for companies and is one of the reasons that one company will pay over the odds for another if it has many well respected brands.

PRICE RANGE.   This is the range of prices that are offered across a product line.

PRICE SENSITIVITY.   Price sensitivity is linked very closely to price elasticity. If a product is price sensitive then either an increase or a decrease will lead to large movements in demand. Products that are price sensitive will cover many different industries and include such products as beer, holidays, electricity charges, bread and cars.

PRICE AWARENESS.   This is the extent to which consumers react to price and price differences across the market when looking to purchase products. In times of economic down-turn customers will shop around and price becomes a major factor. At other times, price becomes less important as customers look for other forms of added value. In most cases the seller would prefer to market products that were not bought solely on price considerations.

PRICE STRUCTURE.   This is the detailed price structure, including discounts for different amounts and for different customers, prepared by an organization for both the trade and the end-consumer.

RECOMMENDED RETAIL PRICE.   A producer might issue a price that it feels its products should be sold at and this it calls its recommended retail price. One might speculate where this price is supposed to come from and the cynic might argue that it is nothing other than a vain expression of the price at which the producer would like to see the product sold. To be fair, the producer might argue that the recommended retail price is a useful guide for the retailer when pricing his or her products for resale and it is often used by the retailer as a benchmark from which discounts are offered and readers will no doubt have seen many adverts that follow this pattern, for example: 'Recommended retail price £100, our price £80, save £20'.

Under consumer law recommended retail prices have little or no validity and the retailer can ignore this recommendation and sell the said product at whatever price he or she considers profitable.

PRICE MIX.   This is the pricing policy adopted by a company across all its products to meet both the demands of its customers and the threat of the competition.

A company might offer a range of utility products at a low price to meet the needs of one market and a range of higher valued products at a higher price to meet the needs of another. The trick is to have a price mix that meets all the needs of the customer otherwise he or she might buy one product elsewhere and then be seduced into buying all their products from the new supplier, for example Waitrose not selling low priced milk causes the customer to buy this, and eventually all other needed products, from Tesco.

PRICE INDEX (USUALLY USING THE RETAIL PRICE INDEX, RPI).   Price changes on an agreed range of products are measured against a base index (usually 100) set in a particular year. It is used, amongst other things, to measure levels of inflation.

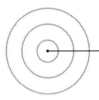

Summary

In this chapter we have looked at the use of price in the marketing mix. It was argued that it is the most mis-understood and underutilized of all the tools in the marketing mix.

The relationship between price and the other elements of the marketing mix was considered and the need for a coordinated relationship between price and the other three elements emphasized. The many factors, both internal and external to the organization, that affect the pricing of products were then examined beginning with the different types of price objectives that could be set both at the strategic and tactical level.

The importance of fixed and variable costs, and the need to manage these costs in the pricing of products was discussed and the relationship between costs, volume, profits and the product portfolio examined.

The effect that different market structures – free monopolistic, controlled monopolistic, oligopolistic, perfect competition and adulterated competition – will have on the pricing of products was then examined.

The many aspects of demand and its relationship to pricing were explored including: demand and the role of research; demand and the interaction of supply and demand; demand and the different forms of elasticity. The part that the competition might play in the pricing of company products was also outlined.

Some of the different ways that organizations are able to price their products were then reviewed including: cost-plus pricing; going-rate pricing; break-even and target-profit pricing; pricing by what-the-market-will-bear, and customer-driven pricing. The many different ways that price could be used to enhance the attractiveness of products and services were explored before finishing this chapter on price by looking at the range of different pricing terms used in marketing.

Questions for discussion

1. It could be argued that price is the most important element of the marketing mix. Would you agree or disagree? Give your reasons.

2. How important is the relationship between supply and demand and price elasticities in the pricing process? Give examples of products or services where price is affected by the interrelationship between supply and demand.

3. What factors must be considered when looking to price a new product/service?

4. Why is it that some products are much more prone to price competition than others? Give examples.

5. Identify the different methods of pricing products. Give examples of products and markets for each method.

6. What is the relationship between costs, volume, profit and pricing? How might this be exploited across the product portfolio matrix?

7. Identify and discuss the different ways that price might be used in the following industries:

   ■ cars;
   ■ holidays;
   ■ water;
   ■ financial services;
   ■ computers and computer services;
   ■ pharmaceuticals.

8. Some companies are price-takers and others are price-setters? Why might this be? Give examples.

9. How important is price in grocery retailing? How does it affect the relationship between the large hypermarkets, the discounters, the small retailers, well-known brand manufacturers, own label manufacturers and consumers?

10. It is argued that, unlike a UK company, a Japanese company looks at the cost of the product as the last element in the chain. First they identify the quality of product demanded by the target market, then they identify the price that the customer is prepared to pay. They then, lastly, seek to manufacture the product at the price demanded. Discuss.

Case study

There had been a zoo in Lexden for well over 100 years. It is set in open countryside, surrounded by farmland about seven miles outside the main town of Strasford. It was originally owned by the Hungerford family who started with a small collection of animals in 1887. Sir Cecil Hungerford had been in the diplomatic service most of his life and had spent a good part of it serving in the British Empire, first in India and then in Africa. A man of independent means, he had inherited a large amount of money and a medium sized mansion in Lexden including 5000 acres of some of the best farming land in the county of Suffolk.

He was persuaded to follow his father and go into the diplomatic service when he left Oxford University but his overriding passion had been in the study of animals in the wild and his degree had been in zoology, being the science of animal life, botany and biology.

As a diplomat Sir Cecil went to serve in India as first secretary in Bombay, then Delhi and Calcutta. After ten years he was moved to Africa to become the foreign consul in Nairobi. Working on both these continents enabled him to indulge his passion for studying wild animals. Whilst in India he married Penelope Barstock and between them they produced a family of three boys.

His personal wealth enabled him to ship a number of animals back to his country mansion in Lexden. Cages were built and to begin with small animals such as monkeys, lizards, snakes and exotic birds were collected, but gradually Sir Cecil became more ambitious and larger animals such as tigers, lions, deer and chimpanzee were added.

Originally the collection of animals was for his own pleasure and study although he would often invite friends, acquaintances and scholars to come along for a private viewing. On retirement he kept in contact with like-minded people from around the world, buying, selling and breeding animals until he was the proud owner of one of the largest privately owned collection of animals in Europe.

On his death the collection passed to his eldest son, George Hungerford, who had inherited his father's passion for wild animals. After George's death his son, Harold, and daughter Barbara took over the management of the zoological programme and, because of increased costs and national demand decided to open the zoo to the public in 1950. It was an immediate success; it prospered and grew and, by the mid-1960s, was attracting over 1,000,000 visitors a year. By this time part of the land had been sold off and the zoo operated within 1000 acres. Some animals were kept within conventional cages whilst others were allowed more freedom to roam in large, purpose built paddocks.

Harold and Barbara had never married and as the company moved into the last decade of the twentieth century they decided to sell and retire to the south of France. They had accepted an offer from Tim Wright holdings, a privately run company that had interests in holiday camps and golf courses.

Harold and Barbara had instigated a modernization programme four years before the sale of the zoo, in an attempt to improve revenue and increase the level of customer visits to the zoo. Attendances had stayed static during the 1980s at around 650,000 visitors a year, the majority coming from London and the Home counties, and the rest from East Anglia, the Midlands and a few from Europe.

In the centre of the zoo stands the old mansion house which now performs many functions. Upstairs on the first floor, in two large rooms, are the company's offices and Elaine Martin, the managing director, works from here helped by five office staff. The other rooms on this floor are taken up by a small library, research and development resources and a fully-equipped animal hospital and laboratory where minor ailments can be catered for and research undertaken. The whole of the top floor, formerly the servants quarters, is now used by six of the zoo trainers and helpers as individual bedsits and by the rest of the employees as a staff restroom. The ground floor has a reception area for enquires, an area for mothers and babies and a large ex-dining room that can be used for conferences and lectures. Alongside the mansion is a large single storey building in red brick, with a tiled hip roof, constructed five years ago in a style that was in keeping with the old house, and purpose-built to be used as a restaurant and snack bar.

Elaine Martin, has continued the modernization programme, working in conjunction with animal welfare specialists to enlarge and improve both the breeding programme and overall animal conditions and welfare. She has appointed a marketing manager, Stuart Barren, with instructions to put together a marketing plan that would attract more visitors and improve revenue, cash flow and eventually profit.

Stuart Barren has set to with a will and has already developed many customer-centred ways of making the animals more approachable to their audiences. A marketing information system is in the process of being installed and will be up and running within two months. He has taken on an assistant, Fleure Paddock, to look after the promotional activity and they are both working on the budget at the present time.

Stuart's immediate concern, however, is with the development of a pricing policy. He has a degree in marketing from the University of Harlesden and under-stands fully the importance that the correct pricing policy will play in a business such as this.

At the moment the zoo charges £6.50 for adults and £4.00 for children under twelve. Parties over 20 are given a 10 per cent discount. This brought in a revenue last year of just under £2,500,000. Overall costs were £2,450,000 giving a net profit of £50,000. The zoo employs 50 full-time staff and 100 on a part-time basis. The business is seasonal with very few customers visiting in the late autumn and the dark days of winter.

Case study questions

1. What further information needs to be collected before a clear pricing policy can be implemented?

2. Discuss the alternative pricing strategies and tactics that might be used by the Lexden Zoo to encourage both greater customer attendance and higher revenue.

3. How important are costs in this type of business and how might they be contained/improved?

4. Using as a guide the model in Figure 7.8 'Procedure for setting the basic price' on p.217 put together a simple pricing policy document that would match the needs of the zoo.

Further reading

Rogers, L. (1990) *Pricing for Profit*, Blackwell, Oxford.

CIM study text (1991) *Certificate Economics*, BPP publishing, London.

Crissy, W. and Boewadt, R. (1971) 'Pricing in perspective', *Sales Management*, 15 June.

Bird, M. (1991) *Improve Your Profits*, Piatkus, London.

Gabor, A. (1988) *Pricing; Concepts and Methods for Effective Marketing*, Gower, Aldershot.

8

Channels of distribution

AIMS AND OBJECTIVES

By the end of the chapter the student should:

1. understand what is meant by channels of distribution and appreciate the part they play in the marketing mix;

2. be able to identify and evaluate the different channels used by companies to make products and services available to the customer;

3. to be able to identify the criteria for channel selection and outline the different strategic approaches used by companies in channel decision choices;

4. examine the contribution that effective and efficient physical distribution can make to the overall marketing effort.

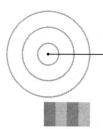

Introduction

The P for place: channels of distribution and physical distribution

In the preceding chapters we have looked at the P for product and the P for price. In this chapter we will look at all the aspects that relate to the P for place. It is worth repeating here that care should be taken when using acronyms for the purpose of memory enhancement. It was argued at the beginning of the book that the use of the 4 Ps acronym as a shorthand way to describe all the tools and techniques available to the marketing manager had its limitations and so should be approached with caution. This is especially true when using 'place' as an abbreviated way of describing the complex process of making products or services available to the end consumer.

This element of the marketing mix, for ease of understanding can be broken down into two clear categories:

1. distribution channel options;
2. physical distribution.

Each of these categories will be examined in detail, but it is crucial that the distinction and the differences between the two areas is understood as they often seem to be a cause of confusion.

Distribution channels are the alternative methods that might be chosen in making the product/service available to the customer for purchase.
Physical distribution is how the product/service actually gets to the customer once the choice of channel has been made.

As with the product and price (and later on promotion) the place – how, where and when the product is made available – is linked inextricably with all the other elements of the marketing mix and so cannot be seen in isolation. This theme will be developed as we move through the chapter. We begin by looking first at channels of distribution.

Channels of distribution

In simple terms the channel of distribution is where the customer will expect to see, and be able to purchase, the product or service.

It is worth while breaking channels of distribution down further into two major areas:

1. direct distribution;
2. indirect distribution.

This distinction is illustrated in Figure 8.1, where it can be seen that distributing direct makes the product available direct from the producer to the customer without any intervening organization in between. Selling indirect, on the other hand, involves channelling the product through an intervening organization who will then make the product available to the customer.

A producer can choose to sell direct, indirect or via a combination of both depending on certain criteria that will be identified and discussed as we move through the chapter. The method eventually chosen will have long-term strategic implications for the organization and so the process should be treated as being of the highest importance.

We will begin the discussion by identifying and evaluating the factors involved with distributing products direct to the customer.

Direct channels of distribution

Many companies choose to distribute their product directly to their customers without the use of an intervening organization, known alternatively as an intermediary or middleman, and they will do so for the following reasons outlined below.

MAINTAINING CONTROL. The major advantage in selling direct is that full control can be maintained over all elements of the marketing mix. This will include the way the product is presented, its selling price, where the product is offered for sale and how the product is promoted and sold. A carefully crafted, tightly targeted brand image might need special nurturing and care and a producer might feel that this could not be left to the uncertainties of an unappreciative intermediary.

COSTS. Whether there are cost savings in marketing directly rather than indirectly will depend on product and market circumstances. Superficially there appears to be a saving as selling direct eliminates the need to pay a percentage amount, in terms of a reduction on the expected selling price, to the intermediary for undertaking some of the marketing tasks.

The amount the producer will have to discount from the expected selling price will differ according to the type of product and industry but it can vary from

| **Figure 8.1** | *Direct and indirect distribution* |

Direct distribution
Producer ────────────────────────────────▶ Customer

Indirect distribution
Producer ──────▶ Intervening organization ──────▶ Customer

approximately 10–15 per cent on groceries, 20–35 per cent on electrical goods and 50–60 per cent on household furniture.

However this saving must be weighed against the cost to the producer of having to undertake all of the marketing mix tasks that would have been borne by the intermediary, for example advertising, promotion, display, selling, delivery, installation and after sales service.

GUARANTEED OUTLET.   Selling direct should ensure a guaranteed outlet for the company's products (as long as the customer wants to buy) as there are no intervening bodies between the organization and its customers, refusing to take stock or taking stock from elsewhere, and so restricting supply. This can be important because of growing competition and increased intermediary strength.

At any one time a producer could be in danger, if selling through an intermediary, such as Tesco or Safeway, of having their profit margins squeezed (if the retailer insists on a price reduction), having their product space reduced or even having their products delisted (taken off the shelves), because the retail buyer feels he or she can achieve better sales by stocking a competitors' products. It is self-evident that without a way of getting the products to the market a company will go out of business.

BUILDING CUSTOMER RELATIONS.   Dealing direct with the end-consumer enables the producer to communicate and build a very close relationship with the customer. This close relationship, unfettered by an intervening organization, can facilitate greater continuous and long-term satisfaction, supported by the use of market research and database analysis (relationship marketing).

FOCUSED, SPECIALIZED ATTENTION.   A company selling direct can present its product or service in a concentrated and focused way to the customer unhindered by immediate competitors' products. Product benefits can be matched to customer needs using the specialized knowledge and experience that only comes from selling one's own company products. This is especially relevant when selling complex and high valued products such as pensions, unit trusts, and health insurance.

A middleman, on the other hand, will be offering a whole range of products from many different companies, with only a general knowledge of the whole and limited knowledge of each individual product range. There is also no reason why the retailer staff, for example, should wish to push one company's products rather than another, unless there are incentives involved. In many cases the salesperson will be offered an incentive but it will probably be on the retailer's own label products and not the product of the outside producer.

METHODS USED IN DIRECT CHANNELS OF DISTRIBUTION

There are many ways to make a product directly available to the customer, including the following:

1. direct salesforce;
2. house parties;
3. customer collection, factory outlet;

4. own retail outlet;
5. mail order;
6. print;
7. TV, telephony and computers;
8. radio.

These various methods will now be looked at in more detail.

DIRECT SALESFORCE.   The most common form of direct distribution is through the use of a company's own salesforce. The salesforce can be full-time, part-time, employed or self-employed. The salesperson might call on the customer in person or use the telephone (telesales) or employ a combination of both methods, for example using the telephone to obtain an appointment followed by a personal visit to achieve the sale.

Examples of companies that use a direct sales force include:

■ *Betterware Household Products*: a salesperson will call on a regular basis door-to-door taking orders for household products such as furniture polish, dish-cloths and washing liquid, and returning a week later delivering the order.

■ *Direct Line Insurance*: one of the great successes of the last decade has been the Direct Line Insurance company, selling insurance over the telephone direct to the end customer and by-passing the insurance broker (middleman). Until this company was launched it was always argued that this service could not be offered directly over the phone, as the discerning car owner would want the choice and expertise offered by the insurance broker in policy selection. This method has since spawned a whole range of imitators including Virgin, Kwik-Fit and Churchill.

■ *Avon Cosmetics*: the 'Avon Lady' calling direct on the customer's home selling a range of cosmetics has become a business legend. Each sales representative will recruit other saleswomen, building up a very effective salesforce.

■ *Anglia Double Glazing*: all of us must, at some time or other, have been called to the telephone (usually at an inconvenient time) only to find that a double glazing or building manufacturer's salesperson was on the telephone asking if we wanted to purchase any of their products. Anglia have successfully used this method for many years. The telephone call will be followed up with a personal visit.

HOUSE PARTIES.   Part-time sales people (usually women) are recruited to organize sales 'parties', in their own or other peoples' homes. Friends, relatives and acquaintances are encouraged to attend, usually with the offer of some small incentive. The salesperson is then paid a commission, 10–15 per cent on all sales made. Products sold in this way include; shoes, cosmetics, clothes, household products and wines. Companies that use this method include:

■ *The Tupperware Company* markets a range of plastic type household products using a network of part-time agents.

■ *Anne Summers* sells adult erotica in the same way as the above.

■ *The Dee Corp.* sells childrens clothes and toys again in the same way as above.

CUSTOMER COLLECTION. Another form of a direct distribution channel is persuading the customer to come along to the organization or factory to purchase the product (usually through some form of factory shop). Products sold in this manner include furniture, clothes, vegetables and fruit ('pick your own'). The Falmer Jean company has successfully run an outlet at its factory shop in Essex for over ten years where it sells stock that is no longer in fashion. However, when it first opened, there was some consternation amongst local Falmer dealers affected by the cut-price operation.

PRODUCERS OWN RETAIL OUTLETS. Some manufacturers open their own retail outlets through which they sell their products (this will be examined in more detail later in the chapter under the heading of vertical integration). Examples of companies that have chosen to do this include: The Singer Sewing Machine Co.; many of the large petrol companies such as Q8, Esso and BP; financial services such as Abbey National, Barclays and M&G.

MAIL ORDER. The big growth area in direct channel distribution is through the use of mail order. Product and service offers are sent out by post and customers are invited to respond direct (this should not be confused with the mail-order catalogue, for example Littlewoods, which is an indirect form of distribution). In theory almost any product can be sold through mail order and examples include: books, magazines, clothes, compact discs and financial services.

PRINT. Some companies choose to sell their products direct through magazines and newspapers. Products and services such as furniture, clothes, electrical goods, financial services, etc. will be advertised (called off-the-page advertising or direct response) with a response coupon or telephone number and the customer is invited to send money (or credit card number) and purchase direct.

TELEVISION (TERRESTRIAL, SATELLITE, CABLE), TELEPHONY AND COMPUTERS. Business to business and retail products are sold individually or by a combination of the above. On TV this might be by individual ads or through a retail channel such as QVC. Response can be by telephone or e-mail. Increasingly the Internet is offering products through company owned web-sites such as Dell Computers (www.dell.com). Enormous growth is expected especially when TV and computer combine and offer multi-media inter-active opportunities to purchase direct into the home of the customer. It would appear that almost any class of product or service can be distributed in this way.

RADIO. This is similar to the use of TV. There has been a big growth in the number of different radio stations catering for specialist audiences, making it particularly attractive to companies selling products or services to tightly targeted markets. The use of this medium is on the increase. Classic Radio is a good example – with its ABC1 audience it attracts adverts from companies such as Health Craft vitamins and minerals, Royal Mail delivery service, Marshall Cavendish specialist magazines and the Royal Bank of Scotland.

NETWORK MARKETING

Over the last few years we have seen the development of so-called 'network marketing' which is really a form of direct distribution through a network of self-employed sales people. Each participating member will be given a region, district, or area in which to take orders for products. He or she can then recruit others to work for them. These others can then also recruit others to work for them and so on down the network.

The person at the top of the network may get 2 per cent of all sales at every level, the next 5 per cent from their level downwards, the next 10 per cent of their level downwards and so on. Only a small amount of display products need be bought and customers' orders are fulfilled from centralized warehouses and the customer charged direct.

The USA company Amway markets its household products in this way and has salespeople working at the top of the network earning over $250,000 a year in commission. This is not the same as pyramid selling which is now illegal.

PYRAMID SELLING. In pyramid selling each sales level from the top down acts as an intermediary and actually purchase the products for resale from the level above to sell to the level below, after being persuaded that it is a business opportunity that cannot fail. Often there is no end-consumer purchase and the middleman is left holding stock he or she cannot sell. This practice was made illegal after a spate of complaints in the 1980s from a whole series of participants left holding a garage full of worthless washing-up liquid or dog food they had paid thousands for and could not sell.

DIRECT SELLING. Direct selling is self-evidently selling products directly to the end-customer. The direct selling association (DSA) exists to promote companies that use direct distribution to channel their products to the end-customer. Member companies include, Amway (UK), Betterware; The Tupperware Company; Kleenezee Homecare; Ann Summers (Sales); Avon Cosmetics; The Dee Group.

DIRECT MARKETING

A definition of direct marketing is any marketing activity that exploits the direct relationship between the producer and the end-consumer and can include all of the elements of the marketing mix. In the sense that 'direct distribution' must take into account all the other elements of the marketing mix it could be easily identified under the label of 'direct marketing'.

So the concept of direct marketing would subsume all the factors identified above under direct distribution as well as all forms of direct selling (it could be argued the Direct Selling Association should be called the Direct Marketing Association). Therefore direct distribution, that is own retail outlets, promotion and sales, leaflet dropping, mail order, teleselling, TV, Internet, direct response etc. are all forms of direct marketing, if part of the marketing effort is aimed directly at the customer.

A company might undertake some of its marketing activity by indirect marketing (distribution through an intermediary) and some of its marketing activity by promoting direct to the customer (see Figure 8.2) although there would have to be care taken to see that one method does not intrude on the other and so cause disruption and conflict.

Figure 8.2	*Direct and indirect marketing*

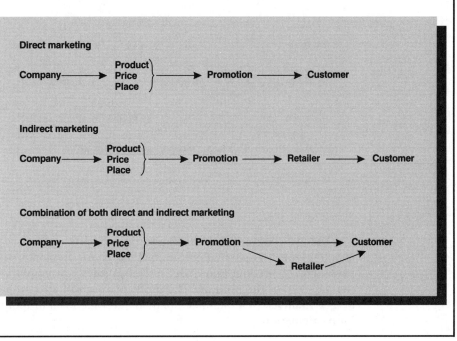

Examples of organizations that use both methods include: British Airways, direct (direct mail) and indirect through travel agents; Barratt the house builder, direct (salesperson in a show house, or advertisement in the paper) and indirect through an estate agent.

Indirect distribution

Many companies choose to use middlemen or intermediaries to bring their products to the market. An intermediary is an organization or an individual which acts as a conduit for product or service delivery, between the producer and the end-customer.

There can be one, or more, intermediaries in the distribution chain from the producer to the end-customer and each may purchase the goods either for resale to the end-customer or act as some form of agent, passing on the product to another intermediary.

Figure 8.3 illustrates the different types and lengths of distribution channel involving one or more intermediary.

LONG AND SHORT DISTRIBUTION CHAINS

It can be argued that the longer the distribution chain the greater the loss of control over the elements of the marketing mix as the end-customer becomes ever more detached from the producing organization.

| **Figure 8.3** | *Different types and lengths of distribution chain* |

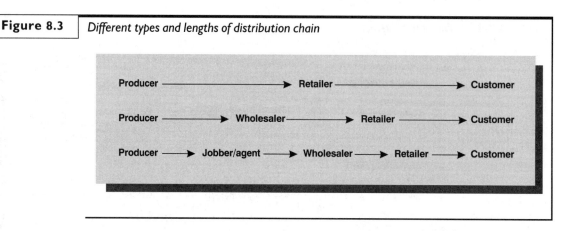

This will be more relevant to some products and services than others, but channel length is particularly important where elements such as brand image, presentation, product knowledge and after sales service play an important part in the make-up of the product. The profit margin will also probably be lower with a longer chain as each member will demand some form of monetary compensation for participation.

NUTS AND BOLTS. It might be the case that as the product moves through the distribution chain each member will add some form of value to the product. Let us consider, as an example, basic car nuts and bolts bought in bulk by an agent from a manufacturer in South Korea. This intermediary breaks the mass of nuts and bolts into smaller amounts (added value); these are then sold on to a wholesaler who sorts them into different categories (whitworth, AF, etc.) and puts just a few nuts and bolts in small cellophane packets and staples them to a display card (added value).

These cards are subsequently sold on to an agent with a delivery van who drives around all the motor spare shops (added value) in his or her area and sells to the owner or manager. The manager then puts the display card on show and sells the end-user one packet at a time (added value). Of course the price will have risen during the whole process from a few pennies to probably over one pound.

ADVANTAGES OF INDIRECT DISTRIBUTION. Having discussed some of the reasons why a company might sell direct to its customers, we need to identify why, in other circumstances, companies might chose to abandon the certainty of a guaranteed market and pass control of its marketing mix to somebody else by selling indirect through the use of an intermediary such as a wholesaler or retailer. A number of these reasons will now be evaluated.

Existing dealer/customer networks. Most producing companies lack the necessary resources to get their products direct to the customer even if they wanted to. Retailers such as Burtons (the menswear retailers), Iceland, the Co-op, John Lewis and wholesalers such as Edmunsons (electrical wholesalers), Jewsons (builders merchants) have outlets across the country and in most cases it would not be feasible, in terms of time, costs and knowledge, for a producer to develop its own networks from scratch when it is much easier to use those already in existence. This is especially apposite when marketing abroad for the first time, as lack of market knowledge is great and customer awareness poor or non-existent.

Location. Linked to the previous reason is the importance put on the location. Many retail organizations have excellent site locations built, developed and refined over the years through the use of professional marketing research and constant customer contact. It would be too expensive for a producer to develop the right site even if it could be found.

Targeted customers. Intermediaries will have developed their own customer profiles, understand the benefits sought, and have instant contact with specific target markets. This guaranteed reach is invaluable to a producer, especially if their market is highly specialized.

Knowledge of the market. A middleman with years of experience in the trade can offer a wealth of knowledge about suppliers, competitors, customers and markets. They are also in the position of being able to undertake marketing research, so keeping abreast of developments in the market. This information is especially important where the market is some distance from the product or service base.

Specialized skills. Many producers have made the mistake of thinking that they can retail products or services as well as developing products and services. In the 1980s many financial service organizations moved into estate agency only to find they lacked the necessary retail skills to keep the outlets turning over a profitable amount of business.

Retailers such as Bairstow Eves (estate agents), Tesco, Dixons, Next, Marks and Spencer, offer specialized retail skills developed and refined over years of practice in such areas as branding, product knowledge, range planning, stock presentation, selling, promotion, delivery and installation. All this acts as a form of added value to the product which the newly entering producer is unable to replicate.

Offer customer choice. In most cases the customer wants to see a range of different products before making a choice. For example, before buying a vacuum cleaner a customer might want to see the product offerings from Hoover, Electrolux, Hotpoint and AEG. Similarly when looking for a holiday the prospective consumer might want to choose from a whole range of destinations and types of holiday. The retailer can offer this choice, which the manufacturer or producer cannot, and so can match customer needs to product benefits.

Physical distribution. Large retail chains offer the producer centralized warehousing where bulk pantechnicon deliveries can be made. The retailer will then break down the bulk, store and deliver individually to its many outlets. A wholesaler will offer a delivery service, perhaps on a regular daily basis, delivering small amounts to small individual retailers.

Financing. The intermediary will often take title to the goods which means they will purchase and pay for the goods (usually within 30 days but it can be as long as 90 days) and carry the cost of channel management. This acts as a form of finance for the manufacturer as they will receive payment for the products, often before those products reach the end-customer.

Risk taking. There is always some risk involved in channel management including the non-payment by the end-customer, lack of sales, product damage and theft. The intermediary will take on a certain amount of responsibility for these areas.

DISADVANTAGES OF INDIRECT DISTRIBUTION. The biggest disadvantage with indirect distribution is the loss of control over the marketing mix, for example how the brand is presented, the price charged and the channel through which it reaches the end-consumer. This loss of control, and the importance involved, will vary from method to method and product to product but in allowing others to undertake the marketing there will always be some danger that it will not happen in the integrated way necessary for long-term success. The end consumer will also have a greater allegiance to the retailer rather than the producer.

Methods of indirect distribution

Methods of indirect distribution will include the following:

1. retailing;
2. wholesaling;
3. use of a Distributor;
4. the jobber;
5. broker;
6. vending machines.

We can now look at some of these in much more detail beginning with the most widespread method, retailing.

RETAILING. The retailer will operate from a multitude of different outlets and offer a vast and contrasting range of products directly to the end-customer. The retailer will sell products and services as diverse as financial and leisure services, households goods, food, drink, electrical goods, sports goods, furniture, shoes, clothing, holidays, videos, books, confectionery and jewellery – in fact anything. This is the most widespread form of distribution and the health of the retail trade is seen as a crucial economic indicator for the economy as a whole.

There are many different forms of retail outlet and the process is always in a state of change. The following are the areas that we will briefly consider:

1. the independent retailer;
2. the chain store;
3. catalogue selling;
4. department stores;

5. the convenience store;
6. supermarkets and hypermarkets;
7. retail parks and superstores;
8. retailing 'sheds';
9. the shopping mall;
10. the retailing discounter.

The independent retailer. The small independent retailer is on the decline but are still seen as a major participant in most industries. Any company owning from one to ten outlets could be classified as a small independent. The problem they have is competing on equal buying terms with the major national retail chains. The local corner store will stay in business by charging more but offering convenience in terms of time and location. Others come together in *voluntary buying groups*.

The small independents in most trades have tended to come together to buy products in bulk and so gain larger discounts. To do this they form voluntary buying groups either by developing their own distribution set-up or working with an existing wholesaler. If the former method is used all members will pay a joining fee and then a percentage of their turnover on a monthly basis. This money is used to set up and run a central office and warehouse where orders can be centralized and bulk discounts negotiated with the various producers. If the latter method is used the wholesaler will undertake all the organization in return for the joining fee and running costs.

A voluntary buying group may exist simply to obtain favourable group buying terms from the manufacturer or they may adopt a much wider role performing the whole marketing process for group members including the development of an umbrella corporate image, range planning, merchandising and training. The Spar and Londis grocery organizations are examples of voluntary buying groups that have taken on this greater involvement, although voluntary buying groups exist for every possible type of business.

The chain store. Any company owning more than ten outlets could be classified as a chain store organization. Most tend to be publicly quoted companies but the independent chain store still exists. Examples of chain store companies owning hundreds of stores in most big towns across the country include Dixons, Comet, Mothercare, Pricerite, Superdrug, Boots, Halfords, W.H. Smith, and Bairstow Eves Estate Agency.

Catalogue selling. Catalogue selling can take place in any one of the following three ways:

1. *In a retail outlet.* Argos was the company that innovated the first method of catalogue selling in the UK through the use of retail outlets and they now have a national chain of outlets (developed from the original Green Shield Stamp shops). Catalogues are on display in each shop and the customer looks through them, chooses the desired product and fills in the catalogue number on a form. This they take to an assistant, pay for the product and the goods are handed over. It is possible to charge competitive prices because cost savings are made on specialized sales staff and limited display needs. Argos are the major players in this market.

2. *In the customer's home.* Catalogue selling in the home has been with us for decades. It used to be a way that the housewife could earn extra money as she would get a percentage of the cost of all the products ordered by her friends and relatives as well as money off the products she bought for her own use. However, all manner of people, both men and women, young and old now buy from a multitude of catalogues that have become increasingly more sophisticated in their targeting with the development of IT. Companies that use a catalogue to sell a whole range of products, from dresses and underwear to washing machines and TVs, include: Littlewoods; Kaleidoscope; Next Directory; Cotton Traders; Innovations.

3 *In a factory outlet.* It is possible for the customer to go to a factory and order from a catalogue showing all the company's products.

Department stores. A department store will offer a range of different types of products from FMCG, through to shopping and speciality goods, all under the same roof but probably on different floors. The range might include food, electrical goods, light fittings, furniture, haberdashery, carpets, jewellery, toys, china and financial services. There are privately owned local independent department stores (as with independent retailers they also come together to form voluntary buying groups) and national department chain stores such as Debenhams, BHS, John Lewis, The House of Fraser and the Co-op.

Originally department stores ran all the departments themselves, training their staff to sell everything from scarves, video recorders, hats and leather products to corsetry, fine china, perfume and cutlery. However, because of the specialist nature of many of the products sold by the departmental store it was realized that to maintain competitive advantage expert companies should be invited in from outside to manage the marketing process.

Consequently, in many cases the parent company now acts only as the front organization, offering an overall corporate image whilst renting off space within the store (known as *concessions*) to other expert companies to market and sell products.

Debenhams allocate sales space in this way to companies such as Waterford crystal, Wedgwood china, Hat Box, The Sweet Factory, J. Taylor accessories (bags, etc.) Traders (Jeans) and Calvin Klein (perfumes, etc.).

The convenience store. The last decade has seen the emergence and spectacular growth of the so-called 'convenience store'. These are retail outlets that are open when other shops are closed (often 24 hours a day) offering a whole range of products including newspapers, magazines, bread, milk, snack foods, soft drinks, confectionery, batteries, etc.

They are called 'convenience stores' because they offer products when and where the customer has a need, be it at 3.00 pm or 3.00 am. In return for this 'convenience' the customer will be charged a higher price (which they seem happy to pay) for their purchase than they would normally pay in their edge-of-town supermarket.

The last decade has seen tremendous growth in convenience stores on garage forecourts. Companies like BP, Esso, Q8 and Shell realized the potential for selling products other than petrol and car-associated goods. There are now thousands of outlets across the country, selling everything from milk and bread to sweets and newspapers, taking advantage of garage customer flow, location and long opening hours. Many are joint ventures with the large supermarket groups.

Supermarkets and hypermarkets. The self-service supermarket (a sales area of 25,000–50,000 sq ft) emerged from the smaller high street grocery store (Liptons and Home and Colonial) and continually grew in size until lack of parking and customer dissatisfaction with the inconvenience of moving the purchased goods from shop to car demanded the construction of more purpose built customer friendly outlets.

A few of these centre of town supermarkets still exist, but customer demand has lead to the larger out-of-town, or edge-of-town hypermarket (over 50,000 sq ft) where all the week's/month's groceries can be bought in a 'one-stop' shopping expedition. A large car parking area, easy access and room to display a whole range of products (over 25,000 product lines) has ensured success for leading retail grocery chains such as Sainsbury, Tesco, Asda, Somerfield and Safeway who now dominate the market.

Retail parks and superstores. This movement of retailing from the high street to the edge of town, pioneered by the large retail food companies, was quickly followed by other retail organizations recognizing the huge potential created by the hypermarket. They were able to close down expensive centre of town shops and open much bigger outlets – superstores – on these sites. Examples of the superstore include Office World, Toys R Us, Comet, Queensway, Peter Dominic, and Currys. These out of town areas became known as retail parks.

Retailing 'sheds'. Another type of superstore is the inelegantly named retailing 'shed'. These are large edge-of-town outlets selling all types of products including paint, wallpaper, tiles, garden ware, wood, plumbing equipment, fitted kitchens and bathrooms, bedroom and household furniture, clothes and electrical goods. Homebase, B&Q, Do It All and Savacentre are examples of this type of company.

Retail villages. Concomitant with the growth of large retail parks has been the development of purpose built shopping malls within retail villages. These tend to be on the edge of town and cover many acres. The shopping mall will have shops and stores representing most of the national retailers.

Within a dedicated area there are marble, undercover walkways (some moving), garden rest areas, restaurants, children's play area, cinemas and theatres. There are large parking facilities and access is made as easy as possible. The whole family is invited to spend the day, walking, sightseeing, eating, resting, trying and buying products and enjoying what has come to be known as 'a shopping experience'. Examples can be seen at Brent Cross in London, Lakeside in Essex, Blue Waters in Kent and the Metro Centre in Gateshead.

The Town Centre. Most towns and cities have built types of shopping malls around the high street to combat competition (if possible).

WHOLESALING. A wholesaler will purchase products to sell on, not to the end-customer, but to other intermediaries, usually the smaller retailer or trade user (although there are some products that the large retailer might still find convenient to buy from the wholesaler). This can be over the counter or by some form of regular delivery. The wholesaler will usually purchase large amounts from different producers, break this down into smaller amounts and sell on to others in the distribution chain.

A producer might want to use the services of the wholesaler for the following reasons:

- the company produces a limited range of products, e.g. chewing gum;
- the product is of small value, e.g. crisps;
- the product is sold in small amounts to many different dealers and needs extensive coverage, e.g. radio batteries;
- the product is demanded regularly on a daily or weekly basis, e.g. meat, bread, batteries;
- the market for the product is split into many small retailers, e.g. confectionery, cigarettes;
- the wholesaler offers widespread coverage and a comprehensive, regular delivery service to the producer's customers.

Almost any type of product might be sold by the wholesaler. Examples include: small and large electrical appliances; building products; confectionery; snack foods; cigarettes; motor spares; bread; meats; chilled restaurant meals. Figure 8.4 shows the role that the wholesaler plays in the distribution chain.

The club warehouse. Another recent phenomena is the rise of the 'club warehouse'. Members are offered a whole range of products at supposedly low prices in return for bulk purchase. In theory membership is selective and a small joining fee is charged. The customer base is the small independent retailer and the small businessman. It is also open to other groups such as trade union members, employees of contracting companies and other special interest bodies.

Products range from food, drink and household goods to stationery, electrical goods and furniture and these are all sold in bulk at low prices. This channel is basically a cross between the old type wholesaler and the consumer discount

| **Figure 8.4** | *The role of the wholesaler* |

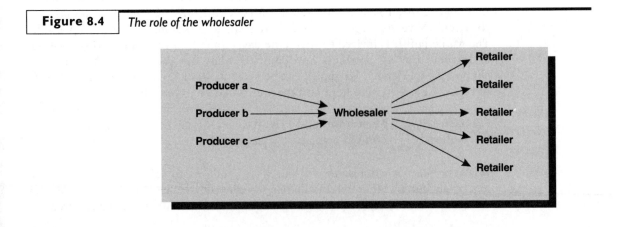

operations like Kwik Save, Aldi and Penny Market. Examples include Costco, and Nurdin and Peacock.

USE OF A DISTRIBUTOR.   A distributor really sits between the producer and the wholesaler or retailer in the distribution chain. A producer will sell to selected distributors who will promote, sell and deliver the goods on their own account, dealing with wholesalers, retailers or directly with the end-customer. The distributor will be allocated a dedicated area within which it can act. This might be regional, national or international. When Italian washing machine manufacturer Zanussi first came into the UK it did so through a distributor.

THE JOBBER.   A jobber (or dealer) is somebody who buys and sells products or services, earning a living on the difference between the buying and selling price. One jobber may sell to another jobber or on to an agent, wholesaler or retailer. The product may not even be seen, all transactions taking place at a distance. They will often deal in commodity products such as tea, flour, metals and simple basic manufactured goods such as clips, fasteners and nuts and bolts.

BROKER.   A broker is similar to a jobber except that they will tend to buy and sell on behalf of other people, never actually taking title to the product.

VENDING MACHINES.   Many products end up in some form of vending machine. The vending machines may be owned direct (Automatic Teller Machines, for dispensing money outside Barclays bank) but are more likely to be owned by a specialized company. They can be seen in public areas such as railway and coach stations, airports, theatres and cinemas, schools, college and work canteens, public toilets – in fact any form of public place. Almost any product can be sold in this way including, drinks, food, reading material, toiletries, confectionery, condoms, sanpro products, cigarettes, videos.

COMBINATION OF DIRECT AND INDIRECT DISTRIBUTION

There are some forms of distribution that might be seen as a combination of both direct and indirect methods of distribution. These will include the following:

1. agents;
2. franchising;
3. licensing.

AGENTS.   An agent is somebody who has been authorized to act for a company. Agents will not take title to the goods and will probably sell on commission. This channel form could also be seen as a direct form of distribution. It is a good form of distribution when the producer has little or no knowledge of the market and the agent does. However the agent may also work for more than one organization and so he or she will not necessarily be pushing for one producer rather than another unless there is some form of exclusivity written into the contract.

FRANCHISING. One way that the producer can maintain control over the marketing mix, yet still get many of the advantages gained by using an intermediary is to use some form of franchising.

There are many different forms of franchising but the basic concepts are the same. In return for an agreed sum of money (e.g. £5000 to £5,000,000) and a percentage of the sales taken, the franchisor (the producer) will set up the franchisee (the intermediary) in business, give help and support, and allow them to sell the franchisor's branded products.

Advantages for the franchisee. The benefits for the franchisee will vary from business to business but might include the following:

- the ability to own their own business;
- the opportunity to keep all the profits above an agreed figure;
- a purpose built or renovated retail outlet to rent;
- the outlet designed and decorated to a corporate standard;
- an established branded product, e.g. McDonald's, Body Shop;
- management training in all corporate systems;
- all staff trained;
- corporate advertising and promotion;
- corporate distribution system;
- access to all other corporate resources.

In return the franchisee is expected to sign a contract promising to operate to exact corporate standards, purchase raw material and other products used for running the outlet only from the franchisor, and to pay the agreed charges on time.

Franchising can operate in many different types of businesses including fast food outlets (McDonald's, KFC, Wimpy); pubs (Allied Breweries); car rental (Hertz), office equipment (Ryman); toiletries (the Body Shop); holidays (travel agencies).

A company will sometimes operate both franchised and directly managed outlets.

Advantages for the franchisor. There are advantages for the franchisor in franchising out their business instead of running it directly themselves. These will include the following:

- Easy access to start-up and expansion capital. This is supplied by the franchisee rather than a bank or financial institution. For the same reason expansion can be fast.
- For a company owning 100 franchised outlets it is like owning 100 individual businesses. If one fails there is no reason why this should affect the others. The same could not be said if they were directly owned and managed.
- More commitment and enthusiasm from the franchisee than from a wage earning manager. From the point of view of the franchisee it is the same as running his or her own business – the harder they work the more profit they

will make. This commitment is especially important in a service industry where the hours are long, competition is fierce and reputation depends on quality service (research has shown that a franchised business is 5 times more likely to succeed in a business start-up than any other form).

Franchising is proving very popular and there has been very high growth over the last 25 years. During difficult market conditions franchising proved to be extremely resilient, with fewer failures than in other forms of distribution.

LICENSING. Another form of distribution is by one party, the licensor, granting permission to another, the licensee, the right to manufacture or produce or the right to market products or services belonging the licensor.

Licensing can take the following forms:

- A company with a patented (or secret recipe) product allowing another company to manufacture/produce in return for some form of royalty payment on each product.

- A company with a well-known brand allowing another to use the brand name on its product in return for payment (Virgin putting its name to a vodka owned by William Grant).

- Allowing another company to undertake a part of the manufacturing and marketing process, e.g. bottling and distributing soft drinks delivered in bulk by the licensing company, again in return for a contracted amount, e.g. Cadbury/Schweppes and Coca-Cola; Britvic and PepsiCo.

Reasons for licensing. An organization might want to licence its product for many reasons including the following:

- No capital outlay in set-up and running costs.

- In some countries it might be the only satisfactory method of market entry because of entry restriction and the necessity for local knowledge.

- The licensee might have an existing dealer/market network already in existence.

- The competition might monopolize the market in some way leaving little or no room for a new player accept by some form of joint partnership.

THE PRODUCER–INTERMEDIARY RELATIONSHIP

The advantage of selling direct is that the producer will retain complete control over how, when, and where the product is sold and and at what price.

The disadvantage is that the producer has to have the skills and the resources to undertake the whole exercise themselves. In working with an intermediary the marketing will be undertaken by others with, arguably, more specialized, relevant skills. If this latter option is chosen it is crucial that the right relationship is developed between producer and intermediary so that the best possible benefit package is offered to the end consumer.

ADVERSARIAL OR COOPERATIVE RELATIONSHIP. This relationship between producer and intermediary could be:

- *Adversarial* – the seller may try to get the highest possible price for his or her products and the buyer may try to negotiate the lowest possible price;
- *Cooperative*, based on the understanding that all parties in the distribution chain ultimately have the same end objectives, customer satisfaction, and through this joint satisfactory profits. This should lead them to work together rather than in competition.

The best method will of course vary according to market conditions but current thinking is that an adversarial relationship along the distribution chain can end in a situation where one channel member wins and the other loses (win/lose scenario) causing the loser to have to compromise in some way on price and product quality, ending eventually in a less than satisfactory customer offering.

On the other hand, it is argued that a relationship based on the understanding that both members have the same objectives (customer satisfaction) and stand to gain more if they work together in harmony (win/win scenario), should develop into a strong partnership, with the parties helping one another with advice and mutual assistance.

Developing a harmonious relationship. To achieve a harmonious working relationship the following conditions should be sought.

- The development of a trusting, sharing, and informative relationship, which recognizes mutual needs and both parties' commitment to the highest quality offering to the customer.
- Product knowledge, training and development offered by the producer to the intermediary in the marketing of its products.
- Quality level and cost reduction training offered by the intermediary to the producer or the producer to the intermediary dependent on the power and knowledge in the relationship.
- A reasonable, agreed return (profit) for all channel members.

CHANNEL MEMBER CONFLICT. Channel member conflict can arise when a producer chooses to use more than one channel to make his or her product available to the customer and the different methods used overlap and interfere with one another. An organization might decide that it will sell predominantly through retailers but occasionally use wholesalers (to cover the smaller retailer); or it might sell most of its products through intermediaries and few direct. This will not be a problem as long as there is a clear understanding about the distribution policy distinction between one method and another.

However problems can arise and channel member conflict can be created when the policy is unclear and one method impinges on the other.

CHANGES IN CHANNEL RELATIONSHIPS

As with all areas of marketing, channel relationships are continuously changing. Below are some of the ways that this is occurring.

GROWTH IN LARGE ORGANIZATIONS. There has been a steady growth in the size of large powerful retail organizations at the expense of the small independent retailer. This has led to centralized buying points and less contact selling points. This is an advantage to the producer because fewer salespeople need be employed – there might be only one buyer to see rather than 20 as in the past. However, in another way it is less advantageous because if the one buyer refuses to purchase there is nowhere else for the salesperson to go.

SHIFT IN THE POWER RELATIONSHIPS. There has been a change in the relationship between retailers and manufacturers over the last 20 years. With the growth in large organizations, centralized buying and the advent of own label products the power has shifted away from the manufacturer – Kelloggs, Heinz, Bird's Eye – to the large retailing chains such as Asda, Sainsbury, Tesco and Dixons.

Many years ago, when retail outlets consisted of small and diverse companies, it was the large manufacturers who would decide which organization would, and which organizations would not, be allowed to stock and sell their products. Now, with this shift in power, it is the large retail chains that could, in theory, shut the door on the major manufacturers (unlikely to happen in practice because of the reasons discussed earlier in the section on branding) and refuse to stock their products.

MOVEMENT FROM THE HIGH STREET TO OUT-OF-TOWN SITES. As discussed earlier, over the last two decades we have seen the movement of many retail outlets from the centre of town to purpose built out-of-town sites and retail villages more easily accessible for the car owning customer. Despite the obvious success of this development (shown by the number of customers who use them) it has caused belated concern amongst environmentalists, town planners and government ministers about the possible debilitating effect on the traditional inner city shopping centre. Many planning applications for out-of-town retail constructions are now being refused in the hope that the trend can be partly reversed.

DIMINISHING ROLE OF THE WHOLESALER. Although there still is a role for the wholesaler in some industries, overall their contribution is diminishing. As retail companies become larger and develop more sophisticated inventory management systems they are able to cut out the wholesaler and deal with the producer direct.

STRUCTURAL CHANNEL RELATIONSHIPS

There are various forms of channel structures and channel relationships which, for different reasons, participating organizations adopt. The prevalance of one structure rather than another will change to accommodate changing environmental circumstances. The following examples of structural types are examined below:

1. vertical integration;
2. horizontal integration;
3. conglomerate integration;
4. contractual integration systems;
5. voluntary integration systems;
6. the Co-operative movement.

VERTICAL INTEGRATION. This will take two different forms, backward integration and forward integration.

Backward integration. Backward integration is where an organization looks back down the distribution chain and seeks, in some way, to control its supplier. This is usually by acquisition or merger but it can be by some form of coercion. In our example see Figure 8.5 a shoe manufacturer acquires its main supplier of leather raw materials.

The major advantages of backward integration include:

- guaranteed supply, important in times of shortage or limited supply;
- control of quality;
- opportunity to make profit that would normally go to the supplier;
- opportunity to diversify, i.e. if there is a downturn in the shoe industry then the company can concentrate on selling leather for the car industry.

However, the major disadvantages include:

- different management skills are needed to run one type of company rather than another – manufacturing is very different from raw material development and to be successful at one will not guarantee success in the other;
- lack of knowledge of the market;
- dilution of company resources.

Forward integration. Forward integration is where an organization looks forward in the distribution chain and acquires the purchaser of its products. In the case of our example the shoe manufacturer acquires a chain of shoe shops.

| **Figure 8.5** | *Backward and forward integration* |

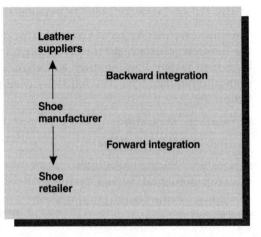

The advantages are similar to those for backward integration:

- guaranteed outlet for products;
- control of the selling process;
- opportunity for diversification and profit.

The disadvantages tend also to be the same as with backward integration.

Some companies will seek both backward and forward integration and so control the whole distribution channel from raw material supplier through to manufacturing and retail. The opportunities and problems are effectively the same as we have outlined for backward and forward integration undertaken individually.

HORIZONTAL INTEGRATION.   Horizontal integration is where a company will buy another company on the same channel level. In our example (see Figure 8.6.) one rubber supplier will take over another rubber supplier or one furniture manufacturer will takeover another furniture manufacturer or one jewellery retailer will takeover another jewellery retailer.

The major advantages of horizontal integration are:

- an improved market share, perhaps even market leadership thus allowing economies of scale;
- eliminating the competition;
- gaining access to customer segments not available prior to integration.

The disadvantages, however, include:

- overstretching of resources;
- loss of management control;
- increased bureaucracy.

CONGLOMERATE INTEGRATION.   With conglomerate integration one company will buy other companies in areas that can often seem to be totally unrelated. A clothing

| **Figure 8.6** | *Horizontal integration* |

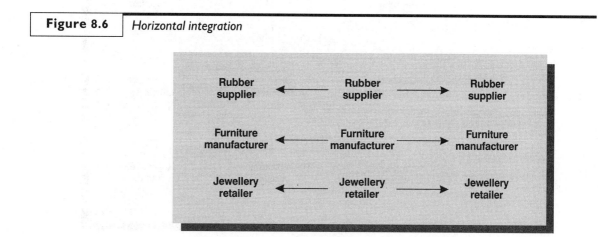

manufacturer may acquire a cigarette manufacture, a wood supplier, a chain of betting shops, a sportswear retailer and a precious metal supplier (see Figure 8.7).

There are many possible corporate strategic reasons (e.g. asset stripping) for conglomerate integration which are beyond the scope of this book. However, the possible marketing advantages might include the following:

■ diversification to gain a balanced portfolio of products;

■ access to transferable resources such as technology, information, quality systems, management skills;

■ access to new markets.

The disadvantages will be similar to those identified with the other forms of integration.

CONTRACTUAL INTEGRATION SYSTEM. This is similar to backward and forward integration except the relationship between channel members is not that of ownership but of contract. A retailer will not takeover manufacturer and/or a supplier but will negotiate working contracts. The contract will probably be written but, in some cases, is only verbal.

The form of contract (the terms and conditions, time period, quality demanded, delivery schedule, etc.) will depend on the power relationship between the participating members. Marks and Spencer, McDonald's, BHS tend to have this type of relationship with channel members which, because of their market size, they dominate.

| **Figure 8.7** | *Conglomerate integration* |

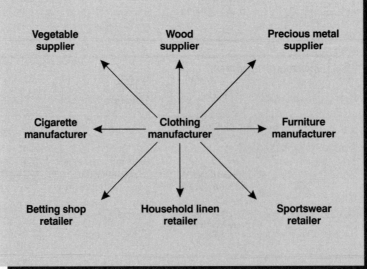

The advantages of contractual relationships are that they allow the most powerful member to demand sole agency, and to dictate quality levels, price, delivery times, etc. to participating channel members without all the disadvantages of ownership identified above. The disadvantages are often only felt by the weaker partner who may deal only with the one buyer and is therefore totally dependent on the relationship.

VOLUNTARY INTEGRATION SYSTEM. A voluntary integration system can be vertical or horizontal and is a voluntary coming together of channel members agreeing to work for a mutual common interest, usually to gain economies of scale and compete against larger competitors. This form of channel structure was identified earlier when we looked at small independent retailers forming voluntary buying groups.

THE CO-OPERATIVE MOVEMENT. It is difficult to know which heading to put the Co-operative movement under. From very small beginnings the Co-op now encompasses a whole range of activities in both the UK and across the rest of the world.

The Co-op operates farms and factories, hypermarkets and convenience stores, banks and travel agencies and is the UK's largest funeral business. Over the last 25 years the movement has suffered from falling sales across many of its businesses because of increased competition, inefficiency, the stretching of resources, and lack of productivity.

The Co-op has no shareholders in the conventional sense (owning equity) but people become shareholders by the fact that they are customers of the organization. The board of directors are voted for by customers who can apply for a vote and profits are paid back to 'shareholders' in the form of lower prices, bonuses on money spent or stamps that can be collected and redeemed.

The CWS (Co-operative Wholesale Society) and the CRS (Co-operative Retail Society) cover the whole of the UK and are the two biggest Co-op organizations. There are many smaller regional Co-ops including Norwich Co-op and Chelmsford Co-op.

The co-operative structure. A co-operative structure exists when groups of workers get together and form some form co-operative way of working. This can be a structure where all the employees of a company own shares, vote on the board of directors for set periods of time, and share any profits that are made (John Lewis or Fagor, the domestic appliance manufacturer in northern Spain, are two examples) or it can be a structure where separate workers come together in a co-operative at some time in the distribution chain to perhaps produce and market a group product (this is common practice amongst the small wine producers in France).

The mutual societies. Mutual societies are financial institutions such as building societies, insurance and pension companies where policy holders are also the shareholders. It is similar to the Co-operative society in that the organization is 'owned' by all the members using the service or product sold.

Examples of these sorts of companies include: Nationwide, Clerical Medical, The Prudential and Friends Provident. Some of the mutual societies e.g. Abbey National, TSB and Halifax have now become publicly quoted companies with shareholders in the conventional sense and many more are following as this book is being written.

DISTRIBUTION COVERAGE OPTIONS

The number of intermediaries needed in a particular chain and the form that the chain will take will depend on the distribution objectives and the coverage needed. Below are three strategic distribution options.

1. mass distribution;
2. selective distribution;
3. exclusive distribution.

MASS DISTRIBUTION. Many products and services are intended to reach a mass market at national or international level and in many cases this will necessitate mass coverage distributing the product through every possible outlet across the country (Figure 8.8).

The type of product able to take advantage of mass distribution will have a wide appeal and will tend to be used by all segments of society. Products that fall into this category will be mostly FMCG goods used by the majority of customers at one time or another. With many different brands on the market the product manager will look for his or her brand to be the nationally accepted product rather than the competitor's brand.

Snack food and drinks like crisps, chocolate bars, peanuts, cola, orangeade, etc. will therefore be found on sale in every type of retail and wholesale outlet including: hypermarkets, supermarkets, convenience stores; confectionery, newsagents, and tobacconists (CNTs); pubs, clubs, off-licences, wine bars; cafes, restaurants, snack bars; DIY sheds; vending machines; the list is almost endless.

Snack foods that have succeeded in reaching a mass market through mass distribution include: Coca-Cola, Pepsi Cola, Walker's crisps, Kit-Kat, Snickers and Golden Wonder peanuts.

| **Figure 8.8** | *Mass distribution* |

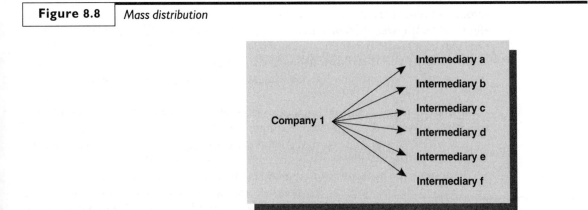

SELECTIVE DISTRIBUTION. A company may chose to limit the number of intermediaries who might want to sell the product and distribute only though selective outlets. The strategy could be to sell the products only through wholesalers, department stores, the large supermarkets or the independent retail sector. In this way the producer can maintain a level of control on how and where the product is marketed.

The Meile dishwasher is marketed as a premium product and the owning company operates a selective distribution policy to maintain a high value brand image, for example by selling to independent dealers, department store groups such as Allders and the House of Fraser, and not into national chain stores such as Currys, Comet and the Co-ops.

EXCLUSIVE DISTRIBUTION. Alternatively the producer might choose to distribute exclusively through one, two or a small number of dealers (e.g. only through Harrods or Debenhams). In return for the exclusive right to sell the product in a designated area the dealer would be expected to work closely with the producer in marketing the product (Figure 8.10).

This method will give the producer much more control than selective distribution. The strategy works well where the product is exclusive, high priced and the target market is narrow, for example a range of men's fragrances or Armani clothes.

Before leaving this section on the channel of distribution it is worth considering the concept of the 'value chain' and how it interrelates with the distribution chain. First articulated by the USA management guru Michael Porter, the value chain model is useful in helping the marketing manager crystallize the need to maintain the highest productivity and quality in all operations along the distribution chain in order to retain customer loyalty and maintain competitive advantage.

| **Figure 8.9** | *Selective distribution* |

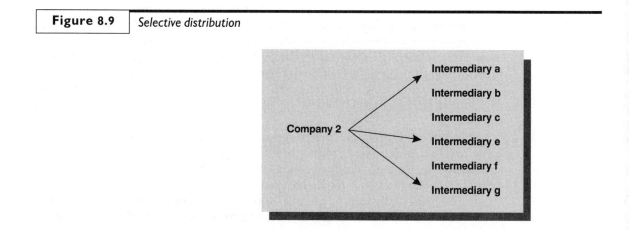

| Figure 8.10 | Exclusive distribution |

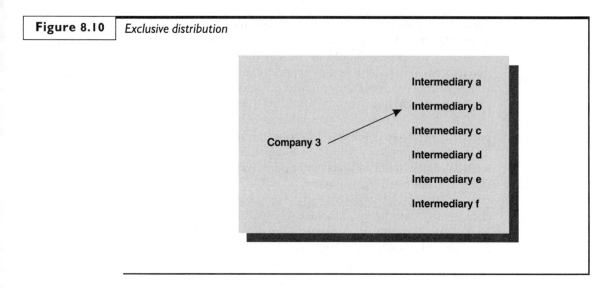

The value chain

The value chain is a model that highlights the importance to an organization of effectively and efficiently managing the whole internal and external distribution chain. Internal control ranges from raw material input through to end-user consumption, and externally the chain from supplier input and output to intermediary input and output.

INTERNAL VALUE CHAIN

The internal value chain considers the entire movement of a product through an organization from raw material input to finished product delivery and after sales service to the customer.

As markets become more competitive customers are offered ever better value for money in terms of product quality levels and the price charged. If an organization is not able to continually upgrade its overall productivity it must eventually become uncompetitive, resulting in loss of sales or the shrinking of profits.

Therefore every stage in the production, development and movement of a product or service through an organization must be thoroughly examined to ensure that it is being carried out in the most cost effective way possible. This task is performed through the use of the internal 'value chain' model (Figure 8.11).

The results must be compared, wherever possible, with the competition, as competitive advantage will be lost if any part of the process is inferior to others in the industry.

The marketing effort will only be successful if all the resources of the company come together in the most productive way. This process of examination must be continuous, as existing and new competitors will always be looking for ways to upgrade their systems and so gain an advantage.

The concept of the value chain is a simple one. Raw inputs come in at one end of the organization and move through the organization until the finished product

| **Figure 8.11** | *The organization value chain* |

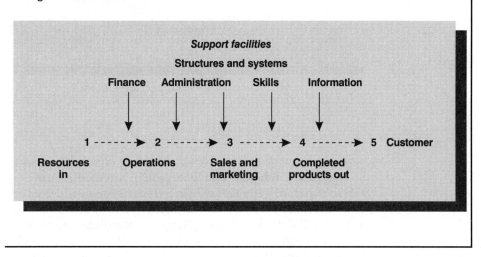

reaches the customer. This is shown in Fig. 8.11 as stages 1 to 5. At each stage of the process some form of value is added until it comes out at the other end with all the benefits demanded by the target customer.

This throughput process is supported by organizational structures and systems involving (amongst other things) finance, administration, people skills and information technology all of which will be in use at every stage of the process.

 The important point to remember is that each and every stage of the process must be undertaken in the most effective, efficient and economical way possible, otherwise competitive advantage will be lost.

THE EXTERNAL VALUE CHAIN

We have discussed above the value chain as it relates internally to the individual producer. However all producers will be involved with other organizations in getting the desired product to the end-customer. If this relationship is to be long term and productive then there must be concern about the value chain along the whole of the distribution chain including both the supplier and the intermediary.

Competitive advantage will be lost if an efficient producer has either an inefficient supplier or an inefficient retailer. So this means that the concept of total value must relate to the whole of the distribution chain – from supplier to producer to retailer to customer.

If we take as an example a simple distribution chain shown in Figure 8.12, it can be seen that there are three organizations involved in the process – the resource supplier, the producer and the retailer. Each of these organizations will have their own value chain.

The dominant partner in our example is the producer who is highly efficient and, being very aware of competitive pressures to stay ahead, continually

Figure 8.12 | *The external value chain*

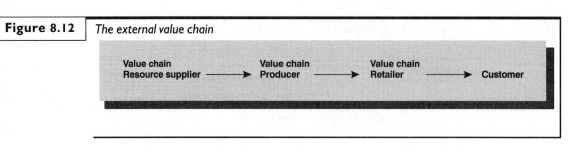

examines its performance along the value chain, benchmarking itself against the best in the industry. Benchmarking is a technique used where management tries to compare and match their own performance in every part of the running of the business with the best in their own and other industries all around the world (see Efficient Consumer Response www.ecr-europe.com).

Value chain analysis uses every possible relevant tool and technique to improve the way that the business is run including: internal marketing, 'just in time' inventory control; activity based costing; total quality management; delayering (getting rid of middle management); modern methods of employee empowerment; and the latest information technology, Internet (the Intranet, Extranet) and marketing research methods.

But an organization will not maintain competitive advantage if the supplier and the retailer are not up to the same level of business effectiveness and efficiency as it is itself. This requires that the dominant partner, that is the producer, helps the other two members examine and improve their own organizational value chains and bring them all to the same level of optimum productivity.

Having examined the role of the channel of distribution in the marketing mix we can now go on to the second aspect of the P for place – physical distribution.

Physical distribution

Physical distribution involves the physical movement of goods and services from the producer to the customer once the desired channel of distribution has been chosen. It involves planning, implementing, and controlling the physical flow of goods and services from the organization to the customer efficiently, effectively and at the lowest possible cost. Physical distribution can be a very costly process, in some cases it can be as much as 25 per cent of total costs, and it is an area where many companies have managed to make huge savings and gain competitive advantage by lowering costs and making savings in the methods used.

 Physical distribution is not only a cost it is also a way in which a company can gain competitive advantage by offering the customer added benefits, better services or lower prices through continuous improvements in the methods used.

Physical distribution and the other elements of the marketing mix

As with all elements of the marketing mix, physical distribution cannot be seen in isolation and must interact and coordinate with all other elements so as to produce the best possible customer offering. There is little point in undertaking marketing research, developing, branding and pricing a new product, selecting a favourable retail outlet, undertaking an expensive advertising and sales promotion campaign and then failing to physically deliver enough stock to satisfy customer demand. This will not only result in lost sales and profits but also customer disappointment and possible long-term resentment.

DEFINITION.   This brings us to a working definition of physical distribution:

Physical distribution is making sure that the requisite goods are available when and where the customer demands at the most optimum cost.

Areas involved in physical distribution will include the following:

1. distribution objectives;
2. order processing;
3. warehousing;
4. inventory levels;
5. delivery methods;

These can now be examined in more detail.

DISTRIBUTION OBJECTIVES

Distribution objectives will be set in terms of the task that needs to be performed and will relate to the overall sales objectives for the product and the channel outlets chosen. If, as an example, we imagine that the sales forecast for the year are 1,000,000 units then the distribution manager must decide how, when and at what cost these will be delivered to the necessary outlets.

If, as an example, selective distribution is the strategy to be adopted then objectives must be set that clearly identify and breakdown the amounts that will need to be delivered to each outlet or delivery point to meet the agreed sales objectives. It is important that these objectives, as with all business objectives, should be Specific, Measurable, Achievable, Realistic and Time based (SMART).

COST AND AVAILABILITY TRADE-OFF.   In most businesses there is an inevitable trade-off between stock availability, stock holdings and costs. In theory, to give the best possible customer service all products and product derivatives should be available at all times. However, in many cases, to achieve this would incur such crippling delivery and stockholding costs as to make the whole exercise unfeasible.

ORDER PROCESSING

The salesperson may feel that his or her task is over once the order has been taken and sent off to head office for delivery. This, however, is far from the case, as there is much more that the organization needs to do before the product is delivered and the cash received. The written or verbal order must be processed, that is to say taken into an organizational system which should check the following:

■ that the prospective buyer is legitimate, does not have a record of bad debt, and has adequate funds for payment;

■ that the needed products – sizes, colours, etc. – are in stock;

■ that the correct products are allocated and a delivery time confirmed;

■ that the products are dispatched and received by the customer, shown by a signed delivery note;

■ a correctly priced invoice is sent on time and a check carried out that payment has been made (reminders to be sent out if necessary).

Despite the development of computerized order processing systems, many organizations still have inadequate order processing systems that can cause several problems, some of which have been identified below.

TIME AND SPEED.   Delays in processing orders and invoices can be costly in terms of the time it takes to get the order from the salesperson, into the system and the products delivered. The speed of order delivery is a major way of gaining competitive advantage. Issuing payment invoices late can mean payment delays and cash flow problems. The use of sophisticated complimentary IT applications have allowed organizations to become more professional in this area.

ACCURACY.   Dispatching the wrong stock because of unsound processing systems can cause both customer irritation and excess company costs. Invoices wrongly assessed can also cost money in terms of underpricing when inadequate payment will be received. If overpriced then extra costs are incurred in rectifying the mistakes.

INFORMATION.   A good order processing system can be linked into the Marketing Information System (MkIS) and so contribute to the databased marketing system.

WAREHOUSING

All companies must at some time or another store products whilst waiting to deliver to the customer. This storage function becomes more important in some industries where factors such as product size, value, vulnerability to decay and theft, amount needed to be retained for seasonal demand, and so on might play a part. The larger the amount and the longer the product is held in the company warehouse the more expensive it will be. As was discussed under distribution objectives the cost of holding stock must be weighed against the level of customer service demanded by the market.

With some products it is necessary to be near the customer, with others this might be less significant. When holding stock the following choices must be made.

CENTRALIZED WAREHOUSE.   Using a centralized system large amounts of stock can be transported in one delivery to a warehouse situated somewhere in the middle of the organization's market and then re-delivered in smaller loads and by smaller lorries to the various customers. Economies of scale advantages would make this distribution method attractive. However, if distance, speed, time, and quantity and size of delivery are factors, a decentralized form might be more applicable.

DECENTRALIZED WAREHOUSE.   A series of decentralized satellite warehouses all serving a viable group of customers is the other major option if the delivery factors identified above are relevant. So an organization might have ten decentralized warehouses strategically sited across the UK each serving 100 customers, rather than two centralized warehouses, one serving 500 customers in the north and the other serving 500 customers in the south.

Many organizations have experimented with variations of the above, especially the grocery giants (who have made enormous strides in terms of cost savings and increased customer service). Whether to use one method rather than another will depend on the type of product and the number and location of the outlets/customers.

INVENTORY

Stock holding is another important area where decisions need to made with regard to customer satisfaction. As discussed above, there will always be a trade-off between stock levels, stock choice, customer demands and the costs involved. The salesperson will always want every item held in stock for immediate delivery whilst the company accountant, ever cost conscious, will want the minimum levels possible. Taking both needs into account will inevitably involve some form of compromise and company policy (hopefully based on the needs of customers) will ultimately decide. IT developments (e.g. EPOs) have dramatically improved all options.

Other factors concerning stock that will often have to be considered will include the following:

- the problem of having to make frequent deliveries to one area, outlet or customer with small and often unprofitable quantities of stock;
- the cost to working capital in holding large amounts of goods in stock (this can often be in the form of a bank overdraft);
- methods used for payment of stock, i.e. COD or credit – if credit what period of time is given to pay, e.g. 30, 60 or 90 days;
- insurance and security costs payable on large stock holdings;
- how to manage problems of stock depreciation and spoilage.

Overall the company will need to balance the loss of sales and possible customer dissatisfaction that might come about because of unfilled orders due to insufficient stock levels with the costs involved in holding too much stock.

DELIVERY METHODS

The other major area where substantial savings can be made is in the choice of delivery method used to move goods from one area to another and eventually to the customer. The options open to organizations will include the following:

1. road;
2. rail;
3. water;
4. air;
5. pipeline;
6. telecommunications.

ROAD.   The most widely used form of transport is road. A company, when deciding where to put factories, storage and delivery warehouses, should look toward the most favourable location to reach its customers quickly, efficiently and at the lowest cost. If road transport were to be the method used then it would make sense to be located near to a suitable motorway system, for example the area bordering the M25 (the so-called M25 corridor).

Road transport.   There will also be decisions to be made about the method and form of transport to be used. Some of the alternative options available are:

■ instruct the suppliers to deliver direct to the company's individual retail outlets/customers rather than to a centralized warehouse for on-delivery by the said company;

■ company ownership of the whole transport setup;

■ lease lorries with drivers or lease lorries only and use own drivers;

■ contract with an outside company to run the whole of the transport delivery service (out-sourcing).

RAIL.   Rail is a cost option if the product to be delivered is of a large quantity, the distance to be travelled is reasonably lengthy, and the railway loading and unloading points are near to the factory and the customer. The closure of much of the rail track and the increase in costs compared with road transport has seen this option used less and less over the last decade in the UK, but it is more of a viable option in some of the European countries.

AIR.   Air transport has the advantage of speed and so saves time. It could be cost-effective on small, high value, urgent items that need to be delivered to customers within reach of an airport. At the moment bulky, low value products would cost too much to deliver in this way although with the development of larger aircraft and price reductions due to de-regulation and competition, this could be a more viable option for some types of producers in the future.

WATER.   There are three possible options that could be considered if using water as a transport method – sea, river and canal. If the organization sells its products abroad then the sea might be the only realistic choice especially if the products are too bulky to send by air. However, for companies selling to Europe, the opening of the channel tunnel now offers a rail/road alternative.

Rivers and canals in the UK, although very busy in the past, are now used by only a few specialized companies although some environmentalists would like their use to be encouraged once more. Again there are many waterways across Europe that are still used a great deal, for example the Rhine and the Danube.

PIPELINE.   Oil, water, gas, sewage (it is a 'product' for the sewage companies) are the only sorts of products that can take advantage of a pipeline as a form of transport although in theory any form of liquid, such as beer or soft drinks could be transported in this way. Although there are high capital costs in building and setting up the network, once it is in place vast amounts of the 'product' can be transported over thousands of miles, overground, underground, under the sea, 24 hours a day, at a relatively low cost.

THE DEVELOPMENT OF TELECOMMUNICATION CHANNELS.   The rapid development and spread of technology has seen an enormous growth in the ability of organizations to send telecommunication products directly into the factory, office or customer's home. There are three basic methods competing with one another and these are briefly outlined below:

1.   cable;
2.   land-based receivers and transmitters;
3.   satellite receivers and transmitters.

Cable.   Some organizations distribute their product to the customer by the use of some form of cable, either above or below ground, and technical progress has seen this method growing in use.

Products that can be transported in this way include: electricity; telephony, fax, video, computer services, shopping services, games, videos; education, CD ROM information discs.

Research undertaken also shows that there will be a big increase in 'tele-working', individuals working on-screen at home, and this is bound to spawn the need for many more new products.

Land-based receivers and transmitters.   Offering many of the products in competition with the above are organizations that use a land-based receiver and transmitter. The main ones are the conventional TV companies such as the BBC and ITV but new technology and government deregulation is allowing many more products and organizations into this market, for example portable telephones and video screens in cars identifying traffic jams and scenic routes.

Satellite receivers and transmitters.   Also in competition with the above models, offering the same or similar products, are organizations using satellites in space to bounce the product from the producer to the receiver (B Sky B). This is another area with enormous (if not awesome) potential growth.

The Internet 'information super highway'.   All of the above three methods are in deadly competition with one another, fighting for superiority in a battle to bring a whole panoply of existing and burgeoning products and services to the customer. The battle involves not only some of the largest telecommunication organizations in the world but also the governments of the USA, Japan and

Europe. At stake is the control of a world distribution system, the Internet 'information super highway' and unimaginable amounts of revenue. Areas involved will include the following.

- *Entertainment products and services*: TV, video, films, games, in many cases in an interactive way.
- *Informational/educational:* the ability to call up almost unlimited information on any subject from anywhere in the world.
- *Home shopping*: simulate a visit to a shopping mall on screen and walk into individual shops looking at specific products, and order for delivery the next day by pressing the screen anywhere in the world.
- *Communications*: talk to and see others any time of the day, anywhere in the world.
- *Business products*: a whole range of business products including: global, multi-person, interactive work stations, product innovation, design simulation opportunities, etc.
- *Promotion*: companies are increasingly aware of the potential for all forms of promotion including: advertising, sales promotions and selling opportunities. At the moment the audience is specialized but this is changing month by month.

In many organizations there is a growing recognition of the part that physical distribution can play in the customer satisfaction process. It is an area of potentially high cost savings, leading to a better service, lower prices and higher profits. Failure in any one area can lead to inefficiencies and loss of competitive advantage.

Factors that determine the distribution strategy and channel choice

We can now pull together some of the areas discussed throughout this chapter into a checklist of factors that might determine the distribution strategy and channel choice of an organization.

DISTRIBUTION OBJECTIVES

Distribution objectives should be set in terms of the amount of products to be delivered, coverage spread required, and types and number of outlets to be used. As with all business objectives these should be SMART, set in conjunction with the other marketing mix objectives and under the umbrella of both marketing and corporate objectives.

TARGET MARKET

The size, profile and spread of the customer will determine which type of approach to use as will preferences and expectations. If the customers are many and are scattered across the whole of the UK then one method might be appropriate, for example through retail outlets, and if they are few and narrowly concentrated then another method might suffice, for example direct mail, the Internet, the QVC shopping channel. Similarly if research has shown a customer preference for home shopping then a house party or home visit by a representative might be the chosen method, whilst in other circumstances the customer may indicate that they obtain enjoyment by visiting a department store and therefore this will be the method to select.

Some organizations operate different methods for different types of customers, for example Peter Dominic, the off-licence chain, has developed the 'superstore' for the urban, choice conscious, sophisticate and the husband-and-wife-run 'neighbourhood' small convenience store for the provincial, home-drinking, family member.

SPEED

Speed is always a consideration when considering methods of distribution. In some cases an organization might want to obtain a wide distribution very quickly and franchising might be the method of choice, for example the Body Shop. In other cases ownership might be the major consideration and so time will be allowed whilst a direct sales team is set up.

COSTS AND BUDGET

Cost will always be a consideration and obviously some methods will be more expensive than others. To set up some form of direct distribution might in many cases be more costly in terms of capital outlay than making the product available through outlets already in existence and owned by others. Whichever method is chosen a budget would be allocated as part of the overall planning process and the wealth or otherwise of the organization will play no small part in this process.

THE MARKETING MIX

As discussed throughout the book, all the elements of the marketing mix must sit comfortably with each other. So the chosen distribution method must compliment and enhance the type of product – FMCG, shopping good, speciality good, taking into account its perishability and so on; its position in the market – up-market or down-market image; the pricing policy – premium pricing, penetration pricing, etc.; and the method to be used for promotion – advertising, direct mail, etc.

INTERMEDIARIES AND SUPPLIERS

If distributing indirectly then the needs of the intermediary will have to be considered. This will include any equipment and training that might be needed, for example system support to develop mutual compatibility, product knowledge, and delivery and installation instructions (if relevant) as well as other forms of resource back-up such as display and point-of-sale material.

As part of the value chain the suppliers' needs will also be a consideration in much the same way as the above.

THE COMPETITION AND EXISTING CHANNEL STRUCTURES

The present channel structure of the industry will determine to a great extent the methods the organization is able to use. The competition will be using particular channel methods and this could block or influence the choices available especially if the distribution channels are in short supply, under contract or restricted because of legislation, loyalty arrangements (the 'old pal act') or some other form of barrier.

It appears that Wall's ice-cream own many of the cabinets in the small grocery and CNT outlets, so preventing their use by any other ice-cream manufacturer. The Monopolies and Mergers Commission found that Wall's were not contravening any restrictive practices legislation.

PHYSICAL DISTRIBUTION

The method of physical distribution to be used will impact directly on the channel that has been chosen. It would seem to be at best careless and at worse total mismanagement to choose a method of physical distribution that detracted rather than added to customer satisfaction.

Both the chosen channel and the physical distribution method should match so that maximum efficiency, effectiveness and economy is achieved.

Summary

In this chapter we looked at the the third 'P' in the marketing mix: the 'P' for place. We began by clearly identifying the difference between the *channel of distribution* and *physical distribution.*

It was stated that the channel of distribution means the different ways that can be used to move (or 'channel') the product or service from the producer to the end-consumer. This was broken down further under the headings of direct and indirect distribution.

Looking first at direct distribution, we identified and discussed different methods including the use of a direct salesforce, telesales, customer collection, producer own retail outlets, mail order, TV and the Internet.

We then went on to compare this with indirect distribution and the advantages and disadvantages associated with the use of intermediaries. Many forms of intermediary were identified, including a detailed look at different forms of retailing and wholesaling. We also considered franchising, licensing, network marketing and direct marketing.

The producer/intermediary relationship was examined and recommendations made about the most productive form.

Under the heading structural development in the market various marketing systems were compared including vertical integration, horizontal integration and conglomerate integration. We also touched on contractual, voluntary and co-operative type structures.

Strategic channel options were considered under three headings: mass distribution, selective distribution and exclusive distribution, and the factors that will determine choice were examined.

The concept of the value chain was introduced and it was shown that all organizations and distribution channels can be seen in terms of a value adding process.

Areas related to physical distribution including distribution objectives, order processing, warehousing, inventory control, and delivery methods where identified and discussed.

Finally the factors to be consider when choosing a distribution method were considered.

Questions for discussion

1. What are the considerations to be taken into account when deciding on a distribution channel?

2. What are the major changes that have happened in retailing over the last ten years? What do you think will happen over the next ten years?

3. Do you think that direct or indirect is the best method for distributing the following products? Give examples and reasons.

   ■ television sets;
   ■ combine harvester;
   ■ financial services;
   ■ snack foods;
   ■ leisure activities;
   ■ household cleaning goods.

4. What are the advantages and disadvantages for an organization in both backward and forward integration; horizontal integration and conglomerate integration? Identify and compare actual examples.

5. How are channel decisions dependent on the other elements of the marketing mix? Give examples from three different industries.

6. Some companies decide to use both direct and indirect methods of distribution. Why might they do this? What are the strengths and weaknesses in following this strategy?

7. Discuss the power relationships between channel members. What form do you think that this relationship should take?

8. Discuss the the relevance or otherwise of the value chain and develop a value chain for the following areas:

   ■ a retail organization;
   ■ a manufacturer;
   ■ a hospital.

9. Discuss potential new methods for distributing products and services with particular emphasis on both the grocery trade and financial services. How has information technology and the Internet been involved in the process?

10. Discuss the development of the following:
   - direct marketing;
   - relationship marketing;
   - direct selling;
   - home shopping.

Case study

It was the first day at work for Otto Becker and he had the same sort of feelings of expectation that most of us experience when first starting a new job. He was 40 and had only worked in three companies since leaving a German University, 18 years ago, with a degree in business and marketing management, so this really was an unusual experience for him and not one that he particularly enjoyed.

A married man with two children, Nikolaus, six, and Helena, three, he had known his wife, Barbara, since their university days and they had been living in a newish house in the suburbs of Frankfurt, a large town in the centre of what used to be Western Germany, for the last two years after moving back to head office from the UK. He had worked at AIK industries in Frankfurt for just over fourteen years but had spent a great deal of this time living and working in the UK initially on his own, but then Barbara and the children had moved out to join him.

AIK industries has many interests and owns many organizations in Germany and around the world predominantly in many different forms of manufacturing including lighting for both industrial and domestic markets; custom built large industrial power presses; and electrical equipment for use in the defence industry.

However the area where it has the highest profile is in the manufacture of domestic electronic products and almost everyone in Western Europe has come into contact with an AIK product whether it be a transistor radio, a video recorder, a compact disc player, a microwave oven, washing machine, tumble dryer, fridge or freezer.

It was in this area that Otto had first started when joining AIK, at the age of 23, working in the marketing department as a product marketing assistant and then rising through the ranks fairly rapidly until he had become the marketing manager for the UK working under the international marketing director Fritz Speilberg.

However, ten years ago the company decided to move into the manufacture and marketing of home computers and since then the company has developed a healthy market and this side of the business now operates under the name of AIK Computers. Initially the company had decided to offer three models, one at a price just above the lowest on the market and the other two progressively more expensive but offering high value for the money. It was argued that the AIK name and brand image would allow a premium price to be charged.

Otto, well respected for the marketing contribution he had made to the electrical goods area, was offered the position of UK marketing manager in this new area, which he willingly accepted, and so for five years he was involved with the marketing of this product and could claim some credit for the not inconsiderable growth in sales in the UK.

At the outset the products were to be assembled in Germany from both own manufactured parts and parts manufactured in the Far East and then shipped to the UK and distributed from existing warehouses utilizing the structure and transport system set up for the distribution of AIK electrical goods. Fortunately this side of the business had some excess capacity and this, combined with a medium expansion programme, proved, initially, to be adequate for the purpose.

The marketing research department had undertaken some research in the UK and had identified a small but growing target segment consisting mainly of men, although some women, between the ages of 18 and 35, social class ABC1 who might be prepared to buy the product.

A marketing department was set up in Croydon, Surrey alongside the distribution depot and it was here that Otto came for five years of his working life, living in a rented house in New Addington on the outskirts of the town with his wife and children. Croydon was seen as an ideal situation for warehousing and delivery because of its proximity to the M25 motorway on one side and the closeness of London and the home counties on the other.

The marketing team consisted of Otto and two marketing assistants, Helen Dobbs and Jill Gibbons, both recruited in the UK at the very beginning before the operation had actually started. Both these women were involved in the early policy discussions along with the international marketing director, Fritz Speilberg.

Initially sales objectives where set on the low side as it was considered more important to both establish and position the product correctly and to chose the most advantageous form of distribution channel method.

At the beginning of the whole operation there were many problems for the marketing team to solve and many decisions to be made (as of course there are with any undertaking of this magnitude). One of the biggest problems – and it was the one that caused the most controversy – was the choice of channel method to be used to make the product available to the customer.

Research, although limited, had also shown that the initial target market for the more expensive products would be relatively specialized consisting mostly of ABC1 men, but some ABC1 women between the ages of 18 and 35, with an income above £20,000 having some knowledge of personal computers and who would want to use it for information storage, analysis and exploration as well as for its word processing, design and printing facilities. It was especially felt that the women's market had potential for growth and could be specifically targeted.

Research had also identified a market for the younger male who might want to use the lower priced model for playing computer games but most of the team felt that this market was too fragile, short lived and too uncertain to deserve long-term commitment.

The channel options discussed ranged across all of the possible options covering both direct and indirect alternatives. Helen favoured direct marketing, probably using some form of direct mail and off-the-page advertising as a viable method, because of the specialized nature of the customer and the availability of detailed mailing lists. She did recognize, however, the problems involved with delivery, installation and after sales service.

Otto favoured using selected dealers who could be trained and who would specialize in the AIK product, selling on added value rather than on price. In this way prices could be held at the higher level and company margins could be maintained. The selected dealers, perhaps the small and medium-sized independent specialists and department stores would impart product knowledge to the customer as well as delivering, installing and offering after sales service.

The marketing director felt that the large multiples such as Dixons, Comet, Bennetts and the Co-ops should be considered because of the coverage these organizations could give and the sales potential they could offer. Perhaps an exclusive contract with Dixons might be negotiated, guaranteeing a minimum level of stock through-put.

Jill wondered whether this type of complex product, demanding detailed and specialist salesperson knowledge, could really be marketed through mass retail outlets where the staff sell, and are expected to have knowledge of, every sort of product from TVs and radios to cameras and videos.

The possibility of setting up own retail outlets was briefly discussed but quickly dismissed because of the capital cost involved and the time that this operation would take. Franchising was considered as a real possibility but rejected because it was felt that the whole organization had little or no experience of this method of distribution (although it was appreciated that they could employ franchise consultants to help in the process) and it did not 'fit' the corporate image.

After much discussion over many weeks involving the marketing team, the finance department, those responsible for physical distribution, outside marketing consultants and after more marketing research with the intermediaries, it was decided that the best strategic method was through selective channels of distribution. The chosen outlets were to be the small and medium-sized independents, as it was felt that by using this method optimum product market effectiveness would be achieved.

This took place seven years ago and sales are ahead of forecast and research shows the product to have been well received. Now Otto is with the new organization, this time as marketing director with a remit to undertake the whole process all over again but with both a new company and a new range of products.

Again a German company, but much smaller than AIK, Dortmunds is a young company started ten years ago by a young, ambitious, well respected entrepreneur Hans Dortmund, manufacturing small electrical appliances such as electrical fans, kettles, irons, toasters and a superb range of versatile food mixers. Otto is moving back to the UK, his wife and children will follow later, to set up marketing operations in the UK for Dortmunds.

Case study questions

1. Discuss the choice of channel method adopted by AIK to distribute its products. Re-assess all the factors that were considered in coming to the final decision. Do you agree with the final choice? What might have been a reasonable alternative?

2. Otto Becker now has to consider the problem all over again, this time working for Dortmunds. What channel options are open to him this time around and

what are the major factors that need to be considered? What information is needed before he can come to any decision?

3. What are the strategic and tactical physical distribution factors that have to be taken into account before a final decision is made?

4. Who are the marketing consultants who could help Otto with his task and what type of help could they offer him?

Further reading

Baily, P. and Farmer, D. (1990) *Purchasing, Principles and Management*, Pitman, London.

Christopher, P. (1990) *The Strategy of Distribution Management*, Heinemann, London.

Christopher, M. (1993) *Logistics and Supply Chain Management*, Pitman, London.

Dunne, P., Lusch, R. and Gable, M. (1995) *Retailing*, 2nd edn; International Thomson Publishing Co., London.

McGoldrick, P. (1994) *Cases in Retail Management*, Pitman, London.

References

Tesco, efficient consumer response: www.tesco.co.uk

Efficient Consumer Response (ECR): www.ecr-europe.com

The Direct Marketing Association: www.dma.org.uk

Be the Boss Franchising: www.betheboss.com

The Direct Selling Association: www.dsa.org.uk

Ray Wright website: www.raynetmarketing.com

Royal Economic Society: www.res.org.uk

Department of Trade and Industry: www.dti.gov.uk

Office of Fair Trading: www.oft.gov.uk

Organization for Economic Cooperation and Development: www.oecd.org

Confederation of British Industry: www.cbi.org.uk

QVC, TV home shopping: www.qvc.com

GUS, Internet home shopping: www.gus.co.uk

9

Promotion

AIMS AND OBJECTIVES

By the end of the chapter the student should:

1. be able to identify the elements involved in the communication process and appreciate the role that it has to play in the marketing effort;

2. be able to identify all the tools and techniques that go to make up the promotional mix, appreciate the strengths and weaknesses of each, and be aware of the interaction that needs to take place so as to achieve optimum performance;

3. be aware of the need to set promotional performance indicators so that effectiveness can be monitored, controlled and measured.

Introduction

Promotion

In this chapter the last part of the marketing mix, the P for promotion is discussed and evaluated. Promotion is the communicative element in the marketing mix and it comes into use only when the other three Ps, product, price and place, have been developed and coordinated and are ready to meet the needs of the identified target market. A company should not promote if the product, price or the place are in some way inadequately prepared to meet customer expectations.

The tasks that the elements of promotion will perform are manifold and these will be discussed as we move through the chapter but the basic objectives of promotion are to educate, inform, reinforce and hopefully eventually persuade the customer to purchase (and in many cases re-purchase) the company's products. This needs to be undertaken in a planned and deliberate manner that can be measured, evaluated and controlled.

THE PROMOTION MIX

Because products, customers and markets are complex and different the promotional tasks that need to be undertaken will also be complex and different necessitating the use of many different types of communication techniques. These will include activities such as TV and press advertising, sales promotions (e.g. competitions and 'free give-aways'), maintaining good relations with the press to obtain free publicity, and employing sales people to talk, discuss product benefits with the customer and hopefully form long-term mutually beneficial relationships. These different techniques are called the *promotional mix* (also called the communication mix and the two terms will be used interchangeably). For reinforcement the completed marketing model is reproduced in Figure 9.1 emphasizing the position of promotion.

Figure 9.1	*The marketing model*

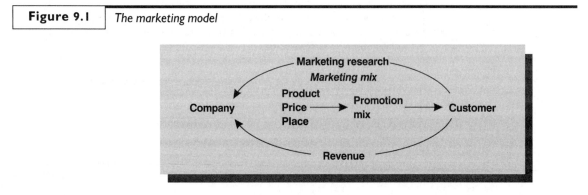

THE ROLE THAT PRODUCT, PRICE AND PLACE PLAY IN PROMOTION

As well as deliberate messages emanating from the company through the use of planned promotional techniques, other messages, not so easy to plan, will also be transmitted to the customer. These other messages with be sent, more haphazardly, via all the other elements of the marketing mix – the product, the price and the place.

PRODUCT AND PROMOTION. For example, if the product, service or brand promises more customer benefits than actually exist (or are perceived to exist), then the customer will be disappointed after trial and no matter how aggressive and intensive the advertising, the customer will feel aggrieved and even cheated and so will not purchase again.

PRICE, PLACE AND PROMOTION. Similarly if the price is too high (or too low) in relation to the product value, or if the chosen channel of distribution is not at the level expected by the consumer (e.g. in a department store or on a market stall), then advertising or selling, while initially creating interest or even purchase, will find that customer disappointment will militate against repeat purchase and might also cause long-term corporate damage.

 The product, price and place will also communicate a good or bad message to the customer.

The role of communications

Before going on to look in detail at the many elements of the promotional mix it will be worthwhile spending some time examining the basic concept of communications. For communication is at the very heart of all the many different forms of promotion used by thousands of organizations 24 hours a day, seven days a week, 52 weeks a year through media as diverse as TV, billboards, packaging, radio, newspapers, magazines, shop windows, the Internet and so on.

THE CHANGING ROLE OF COMMUNICATIONS

In the past this task would not have been so daunting as it is now. The seller and the purchaser of the product would probably have lived in the same hamlet, village or town and so information about product or service availability or development could have been communicated by the town crier, the sandwich-boardman or by word of mouth. Feedback on acceptability and price would have been obtained immediately.

In most cases this directness in the communication process is no longer possible in the modern complex and widespread global marketplace. The seller and the buyer will probably live hundreds, if not thousands of miles apart, never actually see one another, and so be reliant on some form of communications other than those described in the preceding paragraph.

However, these problems are not the only major factors to be considered when attempting to communicate messages to the selected customer. Thousands of other organizations, including competitors and non-competitors, will also be attempting to talk to the customer at the same time and the successful organization must ensure that it is *its* message that is heard rather than the message of another.

THE DEVELOPMENT OF DIFFERENT METHODS OF COMMUNICATIONS

To help overcome all these problems, ease the communication process and ensure effectiveness, ever more intricate and sophisticated methods of communication have, and are, being developed. It is these many different methods that will be identified, discussed, and evaluated in detail throughout this chapter using the concept of the promotion mix discussed above.

It is important to understand that the category is called the promotional 'mix' because it consists of a 'mix' of various promotional methods available to the marketing manager to communicate and persuade the customers to purchase products. A selection of different promotional 'tools' are needed because there are different communication and promotional objectives that the marketing manager must achieve, from creating product awareness through to persuading consumers to try the product.

Different methods are needed because the tasks involved demand a tailored approach and any one method on its own would probably not suffice. The promotional 'mix' consists of a 'tool bag' of assorted techniques that are more effective at achieving one type of objective rather than another. It is highly probable that in any one promotional campaign a complimentary selection of promotional mix techniques will be used. Hopefully this will become more obvious as we move through the chapter.

Understanding basic communications

It is worth repeating, that good promotion is all about *communications*, that is sending specific benefit messages (information obtained through marketing research) to clearly targeted audiences, listening to the feedback, readjusting the message if confusion or ambiguity are apparent and finally being certain that the truth and core of the message are fully understood (and hopefully acted upon) by the customer.

So before looking at the various promotional tools and techniques available to the professional marketing manager to help achieve promotional objectives it will be worthwhile clearly identifying and establishing in detail the role that communications play in the process. This we can do by using and evaluating a basic *communications model* (Figure 9.2). In our simple model five elements – the sender, the message, the medium (the message carrier), the receiver and feedback – are first identified. Each of these elements will now be considered in detail.

THE SENDER

Factors to be considered here will include the following items.

Figure 9.2 | *The communications model stage 1*

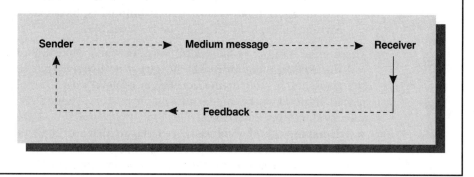

- Clear identification, by the sender, of the target audience and benefits demanded.
- The distance between the sender and the receiver. This might be face to face or on different sides of the world. The use of more sophisticated forms of information technology now make this much less of a problem than in the past.
- The level of understanding by the sender of the receiver's receptive condition.
- Feedback from the receiver may be instant or only achievable through the use of sophisticated marketing research.

THE MESSAGE

Factors to consider here about the message itself include the following:

- The message may be in a simple or much more complex form.
- It must be in a form that will be understood by the receiver.
- It may be in some form of written, visual, auditory, olfactory or tactile form. It might be implicit, explicit or a combination of both.
- The message may demand instant feedback.
- It may only have to travel a few feet or thousands of miles.
- The message might need to be sent, not to one, but millions of receivers at the same time.

MEDIUM

The way the message is sent is identified under the concept of the 'medium'.
The two main media are person to person and non-human.

- *Person to person media*: This will include spoken, written, telephone, body language, facial expression including the use of sound, vision, taste, touch and smell.

■ *Non-human media*: This will include TV, radio, cinema, theatre, all forms of print such as newspapers, magazines, leaflets, point of purchase material, packaging, outdoor forms such as billboards, buses and taxis, shop windows, barrage ballons, sky-writing, the Internet etc.

There are a number of factors to consider when choosing a medium. First of all, will the chosen medium reach the target audience? That this is vital should be self-evident but past media activity is replete with examples of adverts being placed in newspapers, magazines or on posters where they were unlikely to be seen by the target audience.

Secondly, the characteristics of the media are important. Communication media themselves have characteristics that make them more appropriate for one form of message carrying rather than another. For example while the TV might be good at introducing simple visual products, a magazine will be better at introducing products that need a more complex description. Radio is good for products that can be described in story form, whilst the cinema can be used for longer dramatic, mini 'film type' descriptions. Personal selling has advantages for products that need detailed question and answer explanations while packaging is ideal for content description on the supermarket shelf.

Choosing an inappropriate medium may send the wrong messages to the customer and mean that effort and money have been wasted.

THE RECEIVER

In Chapter 3 on behaviour we looked at the factors that influence customer behaviour (i.e. social, cultural, psychological, and personal factors). The same influences also need to be considered when sending messages and identifying receiver states, as they will influence the way that the message is understood (or not understood). The situation and geographical location, for example the time of day, month and season of the year and the location can also influence the message outcome.

FEEDBACK

Good communications includes both talking and *listening*. Feedback is crucial in the communication process as the sender needs to find out whether the message has been received and understood. Lack of feedback can mean money wasted on promotional campaigns that fail to live up to expectations. Only in personal interaction is feedback instant, all other communication forms are more difficult, and so increasingly sophisticated methods of gaining feedback must be developed to try to discover customer response.

COMPETITION

The potential customer is continuously bombarded with product messages everyday, emanating from thousands of companies, all in competition with one another, attempting to influence the consumer and sell their products. We only have to walk down the local high street to hear and see the cacophony of noise, the multitude of colour, and the myriad signs and smells. The enormous task for the promotional manager is to break through this mass of stimuli and get his or her message heard by the customer above, and in spite of, all the others.

ENCODING AND DECODING.

Once the target audience (the receiver) has been identified the sender must put the message into a form that will be both conducive to the medium used and be in a language that will be understood by the receiver; this is known as *message encoding*. The message can then be transmitted and hopefully seen and translated by the receiver in the manner desired; this is *message decoding*.

Problems can arise if the encoding and the decoding processes are out of alignment and the message is either not received by the customer or received in some distorted way. Feedback plays a crucial part in the process of encoding and decoding the message in identifying whether there are any problems with distortion. If problems are identified these can then, hopefully, be rectified.

BARRIERS AND INTERFERENCE TO COMMUNICATION

There will always be many problems with trying to achieve good communications, some of which have been identified above. For an organization to minimize the level of interference and develop effective communications the following factors need to considered:

- Whether the target audience (the DMU) has been correctly identified, e.g. if the decision maker is the wife but has been identified as the husband the message may be placed in the wrong medium.

- That there is an understanding by the sender of the needs of the receiver e.g. if the receiver's needs are for safety and security a message should not be couched in terms of risk and adventure.

- That the appropriate medium is used, e.g. if the audience is social class C1, D and E, the message (advert?) should not be in the *Financial Times*.

- That there is feedback built in to ensure that the message has been decoded and then understood in the desired way, e.g. this could be through the use of some form of market research.

- That there is a recognition and understanding of all other barriers and inter-ference to good communications identified above and effective action is taken to eliminate or minimize them.

The communications model can now be completed (Figure 9.3).

INTERNAL MARKETING COMMUNICATIONS

Internal marketing communications involve imparting information that will have an affect on the development and coordination of the marketing mix within the organization. This will include such activity as management education programmes on the importance of marketing (involving managers from all departments), customer care programmes for the staff (including everybody from the car park attendant and van driver through to the telephonist and accountant),

| **Figure 9.3** | *The communications model stage 2* |

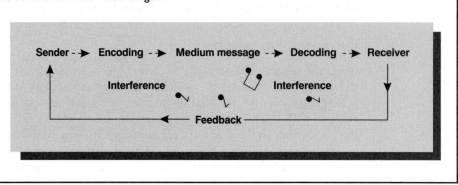

and training courses for salesmen and saleswomen. In many organizations, especially those with a heavy service content, each employee could be considered a brand ambassador representing the company image and building long-term meaningful relationships with every member of the public they come into contact with.

CORPORATE COMMUNICATIONS

Similarly any organization will have many other stakeholders, for example shareholders, governments, governers, local communities, financial practitioners as well as customers. There will be times when benefit messages will need to be sent to any one these groups in response to an identified need. Many organizations now have a dedicated corporate communication role although marketing will often be involved (see *Principles of Corporate Communication* by Cees B.M. Van Reil).

The promotion mix

We can now return to the concept of the promotion mix and the part that it plays in the marketing mix in communicating benefit messages to the customer, informing them about the product in the eventual hope of persuading them to purchase the product.

The organization has many tools and techniques available to achieve promotional objectives and collectively these are known as the *promotional mix*. They are known collectively as a 'mix' because, in any one promotional campaign, many different communication tasks will need to be undertaken, demanding many different methods. It is these different methods that are known as the promotional mix. The methods can be categorized under four simple headings:

1. advertising;
2. sales promotion;
3. publicity (PR);
4. personal selling.

DIFFERENT TECHNIQUES TO ACHIEVE DIFFERENT OBJECTIVES. Before moving on to look at the elements of the promotional mix in more detail it should be explained why there is the need for the four different promotional categories identified above.

It is important to realize that there are many different types of communication objectives and these all demand a different approach. If one promotion technique were good at solving all communication problems there would be no need for a mix of techniques. But in practice this is not usually the case and one promotional technique tends to be good at solving one type of communication problem while another technique good at solving another problem.

In this respect, TV advertising is good at creating mass brand awareness and not so good at actually getting people to try the product, whilst a sales promotion (e.g. a free trial offer) is good at getting the customer to actually try the product but not so good at creating mass brand awareness. A newspaper advert can give a large amount of product detail to the customer whilst the radio cannot. A sales person can explain product benefits in detail but this method would be impracticable and expensive to use across a large target market. TV can offer little product detail but can be used to reach a large number of consumers quickly and relatively cheaply.

THE AIDA HIERARCHY OF EFFECTS MODEL

The AIDA (awareness, interest, desire and action) hierarchy of effects (Figure 9.4) is one of many models developed to aid the understanding of the problem of different techniques being needed to achieve different communication objectives. This model will be used throughout this chapter purely as a vehicle to aid understanding of the complexities inherent in the communication process. It is not necessarily a reflection of reality and, as with all models, its limitations must be continually appreciated.

There are many variations of this model but the concept is simple. The customer is unaware of a particular company product. The promotional manager must then use the promotional mix to take the customer from this state of unawareness through the various stages of AIDA so that they will eventually buy the product.

A promotional mix (different techniques) is necessary because moving the customer through the AIDA process involves different promotional tasks (with different objectives) at different stages of the process.

DIFFERENT PROMOTIONAL TOOLS, TO ACHIEVE DIFFERENT OBJECTIVES

To build on a concept touched on earlier, each of the promotional tools have characteristics that are more suited to one sort of task and objective rather than another. For example, *TV advertising* is good at creating mass awareness and

| Figure 9.4 | *The AIDA model* |

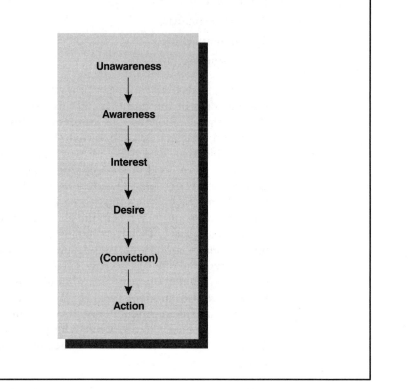

interest but not at encouraging the customer to rush out and purchase. *Sales promotions*, on the other hand (free samples, two for the price of one, extra discounts, etc.), are not particularly good at creating awareness but they are good at encouraging product trial and product purchase (desire and action on AIDA). *TV* is good at promoting one sort of product and the press another. *Publicity* might be used in one set of circumstances while *personal selling* or *sponsorship* would be appropriate in another.

All the different promotional tools have characteristics that make them more conducive to one part of AIDA than another and these will be discussed further as we move through the chapter.

MORE THAN ONE TECHNIQUE USED.   Very rarely will one promotional mix technique be able to move the customer through the whole AIDA process (i.e. from a state of unawareness through to product purchase) and the use of two or more is usual. How the different media may be introduced to different stages of the AIDA process is illustrated in Figure 9.5.

DIFFERENT CUSTOMER LEVELS ON THE HIERARCHY.   In any one market, target customer groups may be at different levels on the AIDA hierarchy. So some customers may be completely unaware of your organization, product or brand whilst others might be at the interested or desire stage. Customers can move backwards or forward

| **Figure 9.5** | *AIDA model in action* |

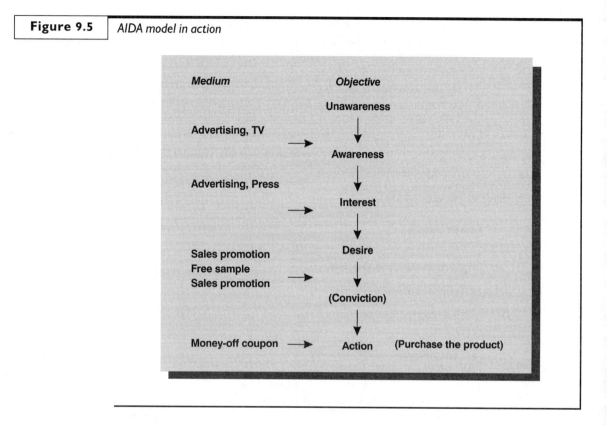

along the AIDA so that they could be interested now but because of inertia might move back to some form of low level awareness tomorrow. The level the customer has reached should be identified by research and then the relevant and most effective promotional technique used to move the customer down through the stages toward purchase of the product.

THE CONCEPT OF DAGMAR.   It is worth mentioning here the concept of DAGMAR, the original title of a book by Russell Colley advocating the evaluation of advertising effectiveness by communicating goals rather than sales. DAGMAR is an acronym for Defining Advertising Goals for Measured Advertising Response and it is the basis of the approach used below with the AIDA model.

SETTING 'SMART' OBJECTIVES AT EACH LEVEL.   Understanding that different, SMART, objectives (Specific, Measurable, Accurate (and agreed), Realistic and Time based) must be set for every promotional task undertaken as the company moves through the AIDA process is one of the most difficult concepts for marketing students to understand and we will return to the subject time and again throughout this chapter. These objectives must then be monitored and controlled all the way through AIDA.

 Only if each promotional technique objective is achieved can the whole promotional campaign be said to be successful.

The model of AIDA is again used to emphasize this point in Figure 9.6. On the left hand side of the model is the medium to be used; in the middle is the objective to be achieved; and on the right is the objective set down in a clear business manner (SMART).

As you can see in Fig. 9.6 for each technique used, SMART objectives are set at the beginning of the campaign (i.e. quantifiable objectives, a time period and an imaginary budget figure have been added). These objectives can then be monitored and controlled as the organization moves through the campaign. To re-emphasize only if *each* objective is met can the campaign be said to be successful.

The different elements of the promotional mix can now be examined in more detail.

Advertising

The first of the promotional tools to be examined is advertising. The following might be used as a definition.

Figure 9.6	*AIDA model with SMART objectives*

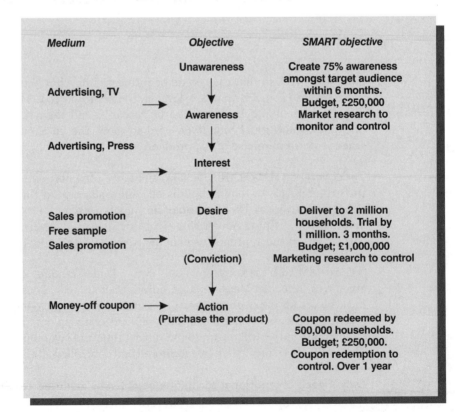

Advertising is some form of paid-for method of communicating with a target audience to inform, educate, reinforce or persuade, leading to a mutually satisfactory exchange (usually the eventual purchase of the product in return for money).

Advertising can be used to:

- *inform*: e.g. about the opening of a new store or the availability of a new product;
- *educate*: e.g. about the need for road safety training or the use of seat belts;
- *reinforce*: e.g. give reasons why the customer should remain with the brand;
- *persuade*: e.g. the purchase of domestic appliance products during the period of a sale.

Advertising can be used between the following parties:

- *consumer to consumer*: e.g. selling one's car through classified ads in the local paper;
- *business to consumer*: e.g. marketing Persil, Gold Blend, Kodak to the consumer;
- *governments to consumers*: e.g an AIDS campaign; or speed restriction aimed at drivers;
- *business to business*: e.g. one company marketing capital equipment or raw material to another;
- *business to stakeholders*: e.g. financial company reports aimed at shareholders, financial journalists or city financiers;
- *One business in cooperation with another*: e.g. Hotpoint and Currys sharing the costs for advertising Hotpoint fridges on sale in Currys.

THE MEDIA MIX ('ABOVE THE LINE' PROMOTION)

The media mix, known as 'above the line' promotion, consists of the major methods of advertising products and services identified under the following headings: TV, print, radio, cinema, theatres, outdoor. This form of promotion is usually undertaken by outside, specialist advertising and media buying agencies. We will look, in detail, at each of these in turn beginning with television.

TELEVISION. Probably the most recognizable form of advertising is through the use of television. There have been enormous advances in the development of this medium including global availability and digitalization and the growth in the number of different channels, from the traditional land-based (ITV, Ch 4, and 5,) through to cable and satellite (BSkyB). Marketing opportunities will increase as TV and computers combine in Internet and multi-media offerings.

The advantages of television advertising are as follows:

- *Mass reach*: a product can be advertised across the whole of the country with the potential to reach 95 per cent of the population. No other medium has the same capability.
- *Speed*: this mass audience can be reached very quickly, e.g. one advert in Coronation Street can reach 19 million people, in one night.

■ *Dramatic appeal*: through the use of sound, vision and colour the product can be seen and demonstrated in the best possible manner.

■ *Objectives*: TV is good at commanding attention and creating awareness (remember AIDA) although it is argued that an advert must be shown at least three times to be certain of audience penetration.

There are, obviously, some possible disadvantages of television advertising.

■ *Costs*: it is an expensive medium, although cost must always be related to outcome, e.g. 19 million viewers reached at a cost of £60,000 equals roughly 3p per viewer. This can mean that it is available only to the larger, wealthier, company. Advertising costs can be acquired by looking at the British Rate and Data, the BRAD directory, published monthly and available in most business libraries (www.brad.co.uk).

■ *Use with small markets*: the ability of TV to reach smaller niche markets, cost effectively, is questionable and often parts of the message are wasted covering areas not within the target market (sometimes identified as the 'shotgun' rather than the 'rifle' effect). However with the growth of hundreds of more and more specialized channels this will be less of a problem in the future.

■ *Instant medium*: unlike the written word, which can be read over and over until inculcated, TV is an 'instant' medium, here one second, gone the next, so only very simple messages (usually one benefit only) can be put over, and must be repeated so as to gain recognition, e.g. 'Beanz Meanz Heinz', 'It's good to talk' (BT), Top dog breeders recommend Pedigree Chum'.

■ *Fragmentation*: as more TV channels appear the market is becoming more and more fragmented and large audiences for any one programme are starting to diminish. Without this mass appeal the medium will become less attractive to the mass advertiser.

■ *Difficulty with measurement*: there is often difficulty in measuring the effectiveness of TV advertising, especially in terms of sales. To spend a large amount of money on a series of adverts and yet be uncertain about the results is a weakness that has caused some organizations to use other promotional techniques (e.g. sales promotions) where effectiveness is more easily measured. BARB is responsible for all TV audience measurement.

Other factors to consider. Information technology advancement and change is having an enormous effect on the use of TV as an advertising medium. Liberalization of the markets has led to greater competition and ever more channels. Greater choice for the consumer – 40, 50, 100, 1000 or more different channels – will mean the possibility of tighter segmentation but, as stated above, fewer opportunities for mass promotion. More competition should also drive the price down, making it attractive to more organizations. Inter-active multimedia TV will also be used to get instant feedback, allow the purchase of products in response to an advert, or enable home shopping, and make TV advertising's productivity more readily testable.

PRINT MEDIA. Like TV, modern technology has brought about tremendous progress in this medium. Information technology now allows newspapers, books and magazines to be produced and launched much quicker than ever before with more pages, better quality and lower prices.

The print media consists of:

- *Newspapers*: quality, tabloid, broadsheet, national, local, freesheets, etc.
- *Magazines*: women's, men's, children's, speciality, trade, commercial, etc.
- *Journals and directories*: trade, commercial, yellow pages, etc.

The possible advantages of using the print media are:

- *Costs*: it is probably less expensive to advertise in the national newspapers than on TV. However, as with TV, cost must always be considered along with effectiveness (again, consult BRAD for cost levels).
- *Mass reach*: national newspapers, e.g. *Daily Telegraph*, *The Times*, the *Sun* and the *Mirror* are read daily by most of the population.
- *Accurate targeting*: unlike TV, the print media can be used to target the desired customer very accurately. There exists some form of publication for almost any given market segment, be it goldfish lovers or train spotters. Through market research surveys readership can be clearly identified and so messages can be aimed directly at the required audience, e.g. ABs through the *Daily Telegraph*, C1, C2s through the *Sun*, women through *Women's Own*, computer buffs through *Computer Weekly* and so on.
- *Longevity and 'opportunity to see'*: unlike TV, the printed word has a certain permanency and so can be read and re-read. Some magazines might lie around for a week, a month or even longer, e.g. the *Radio Times*, *Reader's Digest*, *House and Garden*, etc. allowing many so-called 'opportunities to see' (OTS).
- *More detail*: as opposed to the instant nature of TV, more detail can be given about the product on the printed page as the reader can take his or her time and this allows more complex benefits to be advertised, e.g. detailed information about pension plans or a long explanation about a hair-restoring product.
- *Coupon response*: as well as more detail, an advert can also include some form of coupon encouraging the customer to send away either for more information or to purchase the product (called 'off-the-page advertising'). This is also a great help in measuring the response rate, i.e. by counting the number of coupons received.
- *Objectives*: like TV, the press is good at creating awareness and interest (AIDA) and it is often used as a support medium for TV reinforcing the message, e.g. the TV advert may be used to introduce the product followed by an advert in the newspaper with more detailed information. Audit Bureau of Circulation (ABC) and the Joint Industry Committee for Readership Research (JICREG) are responsible for measurement.

There are two main disadvantages of using the print media.

- *Demands active participation*: printed matter does not have the same dramatic, active impact on the reader that TV has on the viewer as it has to be picked up and deliberately read. It also lacks movement and sound and is not so instantly appealing as TV.

◼ *Adverts are easily missed*: adverts can also be easily skipped or inadvertently missed, especially if the advert is too small or one of many, or has been placed in the wrong position in the newspaper or magazine.

Other factors to consider. The bulk of all advertising (over 90 per cent) takes place through TV and the print media and there is almost double the amount of advertising money spent on the print media as on TV. The two media will often be used together although competition between the two is intense. Which medium to use, if a choice needs to be made, is open to debate and the factors to consider would include the type of product, the target market, the objectives of the promotional campaign and the budget set.

RADIO. Following deregulation, the growth in radio as an advertising medium is one of the success stories of the last decade. There are now many more commercial channels both at the national and local level and advertising revenue is expected to continue to grow in the next decade.

The possible advantages or radio advertising are as follows:

◼ *Targeting*: the appearance of programmes such as Classical FM and Capital Gold has lead to well-defined niche markets with clear customer profile audiences. This makes it a very attractive option for organizations trying to match customer profiles.

◼ *Coverage*: there are now over 120 different commercial radio stations nationwide, three broadcasting at the national level and the rest locally. This makes it an ideal medium for the small, local organization.

◼ *Cost*: it is a relatively inexpensive medium and segmented programming and local stations allows the smaller company to make very cost effective use of this medium.

◼ *Pervasive*: some consumer groups have the radio on all day (e.g. a mother working at home) and this presents the opportunity for an in-depth audience reach.

There are two main disadvantages connected with radio advertising.

◼ *Background*: although often left on all day, radio is frequently used as a background 'wallpaper' medium, with listeners inattentively just conscious of the music and so adverts can very easily pass by unnoticed.

◼ *Lacks impact*: it is a good medium for some types of products, e.g. CDs, financial services, but like the print medium it lacks the visual impact of TV.

Other factors to consider. The development of digital broadcasting will allow for many more radio stations over the next decade and so this form of advertising can only grow. However it is also bound to become much more competitive, which will drive down profits and may cause some radio companies to go out of business.

CINEMA. There was a big drop in cinema audiences in the 1970s and early 1980s but since then the industry has adopted more of a marketing approach and now offers a product more in tune with customers' demands. Attendances have subsequently increased.

There are a number of possible advantages of cinema advertising which might include the following.

▪ *Targeting*: research has shown that there is a clear customer segment that regularly goes to the cinema (people between the ages of 18 and 35, no children, outgoing lifestyle) and it is a good medium for certain products aimed at this age group with this lifestyle, e.g. alcoholic drinks, night clubs and fashion wear.

▪ *Compliant audience*: the audience is there to be entertained and is prepared to sit through and watch entertaining adverts. They will not be distracted, as when watching TV, by needing to zap to another channel, or go to make a cup of tea when the adverts come on.

▪ *Less restrained adverts*: cinema adverts can be longer, tell a story, and contain more explicit images not allowed on the TV (e.g. some adverts for alcohol and holidays). The Cinema Advertising Association is responsible for CAVIAR which measures audience numbers.

▪ *Flexible*: flexible promotional packages can be made available to use in one or more cinemas. This is an ideal medium for the organization with customers in selective areas as a promotional programme can be devised that shows the advert only in the cinemas where potential customers exist. This then creates a 'rifle effect' (rather than a 'shotgun' affect) with very little 'wastage'.

The main disadvantage of targeting a tight and limited customer profile is that this medium is only profitable for a limited range of products.

THEATRES, OPERA, CLUBS AND OTHER FORMS OF ENTERTAINMENT. It is not intended to go into detail here except to say the advantages and disadvantages are similar to those applicable to the cinema. Some organizations will be more attracted to this form of advertising than others depending on specific circumstances, for example a financial service organization might like to be associated with an opera or theatre company because of the reflected sense of social class, respectability and culture.

OUTDOOR. The last, but not least, component in the media mix, is the use of outdoor poster sites for advertising. It used to be seen as a secondary media (to be used as a reinforcement to the primary or main medium such as TV or the press) but outdoor advertising is now beginning to be seen as a primary medium in its own right.

Posters can be almost any size from the smallest that might be seen in the underground train (46mm × 30mm) to the very largest giant posters (3m × 12m) seen on the sides of railway tracks and motorways. Sites can be seen at railway and underground stations, airports and other possible waiting areas, by the side of the railway track and roads, on bus shelters (Adshel) and on the sides of buses (or even over the whole of the bus), taxis and in trains. There are also purpose built vehicles, with nothing on the back except a double sided, 3m × 9m advert, which travel about and park where these adverts can be seen by the target market.

The possible advantages of outdoor marketing include:

▪ Targeting: poster sites can be purchased singly or across the whole of the country. They can also be purchased according to the passing customer profile.

- *Impact*: the biggest advantage with poster sites is the immediate impact they might have. Most tend not to have much writing on them, relying on visual image and colour to project the message. Observation by the reader might lead them to agree with the writer that this is often achieved in a highly imaginative and creative way.

- *Longevity*: sites tend to be bought for a minimum of one month and more often three. This means that there are many opportunities for the consumer to see the advert.

- *Costs*: the cost can be relatively inexpensive but this must be weighed against impact.

The possible disadvantages are:

- *Targeting*: poster sites are sold at varying price levels with regard to the target audience. They are classified according to the quality of the site in terms of numbers of passing consumers, the probability of being seen/read and the different customer profiles. Poster Advertising Research (POSTAR) is responsible for measurement.

- *Restricted information*: most sites cannot have any detailed information on them as they tend to be seen only in passing. The exception might be where the consumer has to hang around and so has time to read, e.g. sitting on the tube or waiting at the airport.

Other factors to be considered. The use of outdoor poster sites used to be considered as the least attractive advertising option by many companies as the industry organization was considered by some to be haphazard and less than should be expected, making its effectiveness, at times, problematic. However, an increase in professionalism and tighter controls now makes this a very viable alternative for many organizations.

OVERALL STRENGTHS OF 'ABOVE THE LINE' ADVERTISING

Pervasiveness. Through the use of the 'media mix' an organization can now select a combination of the right communication techniques so that everybody in the UK will be aware both of the organization and its products, no matter where they live. Customers can be reached whether in the car, on a train or plane, on foot, in the home or at work. The ability to do this is rapidly extending to the whole of the industrialized world.

Immediacy. An organization can now talk to the whole of its target audiences almost immediately. Through the use of modern technology many adverts can be changed at any distance and at a moment's notice. This allows messages to be sent that are flexible, fresh and relevant. A news story today can be taken up and used, in an advert, the following day (e.g. when a walker was found alive on a mountain, after disappearing for three days, he said he survived by eating a Mars bar. This appeared in a Mars newspaper advert the next day).

Legitamacy. The very fact of advertising in the press or on national TV can give the participating organization an image of respectability and steadfastness. It engenders a feeling that 'the company appears on TV, or is in the national press so it must be a respectable and reliable organization'.

Dramatic.   Creative thinking and modern technology have allowed advertisers to use movement, colour, shapes and sizes, sounds and even smells in ever more exciting and dramatic ways across the whole of the media mix.

OVERALL WEAKNESSES
One-way.   The real problem with above-the-line communication is that it tends to be a one-way process from the advertiser to the consumer. An advert goes out on TV or in the newspaper, which it is hoped will be seen by the desired audience, however, the advertiser cannot always be certain that this is the case and the advert may remain unseen. The organization will attempt to obtain feedback (by the many different forms of market research) but not only is there a limit on the amount and quality of the feedback that can be received, there will be also a time delay. Without reliable and adequate information about the customers' reactions to the communication messages there will always be the possibility that value for money needs have been compromised. Industry bodies exist for all the media discussed above with the explicit task of monitoring and measuring results (BARB, ABC, NRS, JICREG, POSTAR, RAJAR, CAVIAR).

Competition.   When undertaking any form of advertising the competitors' reactions must always be a consideration as there are many organizations all wanting to get at the same target audience. As one company develops a new exciting communication method others will immediately follow suit. With all this stimuli the eventual result can often be consumer boredom, apathy or indifference brought about by information overload and the organization's adverts remain unseen, unnoticed or undigested.

OVERALL MEDIA MIX OBJECTIVES.   The advertising manager must be clear about what he or she wants the media mix advertising to achieve.

This means setting clear objective (SMART) performance indicators that can be measured, monitored and controlled and this must be done for every different technique that is used.

Seldom will this be in terms of sales – more likely in terms of awareness (of company, product or brand), level of interest, intention to purchase, etc. The measurement, monitoring and control process will take place through the use of some form of marketing research.

Media mix objectives in terms of sales.   Of course an organization would like to use sales as a direct measure of the success or otherwise of its TV, newspaper, radio or poster campaign but this is difficult to do because there is often a *time delay* between the advert and the purchase or there might be reasons, *other than the advert*, why the customer might purchase, or not purchase, the product, for example the packaging, a special offer, the price, peer group pressure, the product being out of stock, a competitor's product being better value, etc.

MEASURING THE SUCCESS OF THE CAMPAIGN. To measure the success of the campaign the end results have to measured. If the objectives set at the beginning have been achieved then success can be claimed. If the objectives have not been achieved then the campaign must be deemed a failure. If sales cannot safely be used as a measure then objectives will need to be set in surrogate behavioural terms such as awareness or level of interest generated and then market research will have to be used to discover whether the desired increased levels of awareness or interest have been reached. This market research should be carried out:

1. *before the media campaign*: to ascertain current awareness levels (e.g. 20%);
2. *during the campaign*: to monitor progress;
3. *after the campaign*: to see whether desired awareness levels have been reached (e.g. 75%).

Whatever objectives are set they must be in some form or other that can be measured, monitored and controlled. Only if this is done can the success or otherwise of the campaign be judged.

CHOOSING THE RIGHT MEDIA MIX

As we can see all the above media have their own strengths and weaknesses. Choosing the right combination to advertise the product will depend on:

- the nature of the target audience;
- the needed benefits demanded;
- the type of message to be sent;
- the size of the budget;
- the campaign objectives;
- the type of product or service;
- the characteristics of the selected media;
- circulation/readership/viewers/listeners numbers;
- the ability to measure and control value for money.

Sales promotion ('below the line' promotion)

The second major promotional mix method to be examined is the use of sales promotions (known as 'below the line' promotions in contrast to 'above the line' promotions). Sales promotions are short-term incentives used to encourage the trial or purchase of a product or service. It takes the form of some kind of extra value that is added to the product for the period of the promotional campaign. This can be done in three basic ways:

1. consumer sales promotions;
2. trade sales promotions;
3. staff sales promotions.

CONSUMER SALES PROMOTIONS

Consumer sales promotions tend to be used in conjunction with 'above the line' media advertising. Advertising is used to create awareness and interest followed by some form of sales promotion that will build on the advertising to encourage trial or purchase (this was discussed above using the AIDA model).

A working definition of a consumer sales promotion is:

A sales promotion is adding some form of short-term incentive or value to the product in order to persuade the consumer to try/purchase the product.

DIFFERENT TYPES OF SALES PROMOTIONS.   Sales promotions are widely used by every conceivable type of organization and the reader need only walk down the high street or visit the local supermarket to see many, many examples. These will include such things as competitions, money off, extra value, free trial, free tastings, etc., offered for a limited period. They can be categorized under the following headings:

1. short-term extra content;
2. price discount;
3. competitions;
4. vouchers, points or stamps;
5. free gifts;
6. displays and demonstrations.

Short-term extra content/value.   A whole range of ways exist to offer extra value:

- 10% extra content for the same price, e.g. coffee;
- two for the price of one, e.g. chocolate bars;
- banded packs, e.g. buy toothpaste with a free toothbrush;
- pay for the adult and the child goes free, e.g. the zoo;
- money off next purchase, e.g. cans of beer;
- free trial sample size, e.g. liquid detergent;
- self-liquidating offer, e.g. buy teabags and then send off for a unique branded mug at cost price.

There are many more and the list of options is only restricted by the limits of human ingenuity.

Price discounts.   This is probably the easiest of the sales promotions both for the customer to understand and for the organization to operate. Money off is offered on certain products over a given period. However care should be taken when using this form of sales promotion as it can be considered a double-edged sword. By concentrating the mind of the customer on the price rather than other forms of added value it can devalue the image of the company, store or the product, and it comes to be seen as a cut-price operation rather than one of quality.

Competitions, sweepstakes and games. These can take many forms but the general idea is that prizes can be won in return for buying the product one or more times and then entering a simple competition, sweepstake or game.

Vouchers, points or stamp collection. The voucher, points or stamp collection method of sales promotion is particularly favoured because it is used to develop loyalty and so keeps the customer 'hooked in' to buying the product throughout the period of the promotion.

Point-of-sale material, free gifts. Promotion material available at, or near, the point of purchase might include banners, show cards, free leaflets, magazines, videos, CDs, cassettes, items carrying the company name or logo such as ballons, T-shirts, pens, diaries, etc. as well as newspaper and magazine fillers (the loose-leaf adverts placed inside the newspaper, usually by the newsagent).

Decorated product packaging (seen as the 'silent salesman') including pictures, cartoons, competitions, free 'give aways' writing on the product box, package, bottle, label might also be categorized under this heading.

Displays and demonstrations. Product displays and demonstrations can be seen at exhibitions, museums, galleries, school fetes, etc. as well as at many types of retail outlets. An example might be a cheese tasting at Sainsbury or wine tasting at Bottoms-Up which might also include a free sample or money off offer.

DIRECT RESPONSE ADVERTISING. Direct response advertising can also be categorized under the heading of 'below the line' promotion. An advert is placed offering a product for sale or a letter, card or booklet is sent through the post and the customer is asked to respond directly and purchase the product (as stated earlier, sometimes known as 'off-the-page' advertising). TV, radio and the Internet can also be used in the same way. The advantage of this form of advertising is that its effectiveness can be measured directly by the customer response either in terms of sales requests or coupons sent in.

CONSUMER SALES PROMOTION OBJECTIVES. As with all other business and promotional objectives these should be SMART and will include the following objectives: customer trial; purchase and re-purchase of the product; brand loyalty reinforcement; brand switch (from a competitor); cash flow generation; and to sell slow moving or discontinued products.

Measurement and control. Unlike advertising, sales promotional success (or otherwise) can be measured in terms of actual sales made, as well as the take-up of special offers, coupon redemption, and competition entry numbers (commercial agencies exist that will undertake the coupon redemption scheme, monitoring, measuring and controlling the process).

TRADE PROMOTIONS

Trade, or dealer, promotions are the same as consumer promotions except that they are for the trade. The 'trade' is the name given to the intermediary (middleman) between the producer and the end-customer. This will probably be the wholesaler, the retailer, or both. Trade promotions will include many of the promotions itemized under sales promotions but tailored to meet the specific needs of the particular dealer.

For example there might be competitions and point collection schemes for the dealer's staff as well as special discounts (e.g. buy 20 cartons and get one free) and short-term extended credit for the company itself. These offers will often be run in conjunction with advertising and consumer sales promotions.

Merchandising.   Merchandising is the term used for caring for the product whilst it is on display, usually in the retail outlet, and so can be seen as a sales promotion activity. It is often undertaken by manufacturers' representatives (although sometimes retailers will perform the task themselves), who travel around from store to store making certain that their product is prominently and attractively displayed, kept in pristine condition and that there is adequate point-of-sale material. The representative will also undertake dealer staff product knowledge training and generally be expected to work with the retailer, helping to form long-term mutually beneficial relationships aimed at consumer satisfaction.

TRADE PROMOTION OBJECTIVES.   Trade promotion objectives might include the following:

- the opening of new accounts;
- to encourage the intermediary to shift slow moving stock more quickly so that new stock can be sold in;
- to encourage the stocking of seasonal lines;
- to repel the competition and create organizational brand loyalty;
- to create, develop and reinforce long-term relationships.

Measurement and control.   Objectives can be set and measured either by the amount of products sold into the dealer or/and by the amount sold out from the dealer to the end-consumer (measuring the quantity of products sold out from the dealer can be undertaken by one of the many market research agencies).

SALES STAFF PROMOTION

Sales staff promotions are used to encourage and motivate the organization's salesmen and women. These can take many different forms but are basically some sort of incentive or reward given to the sales staff for extra effort in increasing their sales turnover or for selling certain products. The incentive can consist of points awarded that can subsequently be converted into prizes, as well as a straightforward cash or benefit-in-kind incentive.

SALES STAFF PROMOTION OBJECTIVES.   Sales staff promotion objectives can be set to encourage overall sales or sales of particular products (high profit margin products, moving old stock) into, or out of, dealers if selling indirect and to consumers if selling direct. They can also be used to encourage the sales staff to sell into new intermediaries.

Measurement and control. The sales manager should monitor, measure and control the staff sales promotions with the same rigour as any other sales promotion.

OVERALL SALES PROMOTION STRENGTHS. The overall strength of the sales promotion can be identified under the six headings, briefly discussed below.

Communication. A sales promotion can be seen as a means of attracting attention and providing information, especially where there is no salesperson and a myriad of competing products (such as on a supermarket shelf).

Incentive. Promotion is used as an incentive, adding some form of value to encourage the purchase of one product rather than another.

Invitation to buy 'NOW'. This form of promotion is usually a short-term incentive that urgently trumpets the message to the consumer 'buy now rather than later otherwise it will be too late and the opportunity will be lost'.

Develop long-term relationships. Increasingly organizations are recognizing the value of sales promotion in rewarding consumer loyalty and hopefully creating lasting friendships.

However it could be argued that once a promotion becomes almost continuous it is then seen as an added value benefit, that is as part of the product rather than a conventional sales promotion, for example money off in the form of points earned when money is spent at Sainsbury (on its loyalty card) or when using a Barclaycard.

Support advertising. Although sometimes used as the main medium, promotion is more likely to be used as a 'support' or secondary medium working in conjunction with advertising, picking up on the awareness and interest (A and I of AIDA) created and moving the customer towards desire and action (D and A of AIDA) (i.e. purchase of the product). When used in this way it is imperative that there is a complimentary 'fit' between the methods used.

Easily measured. Sales promotions tend to be favoured by marketing managers, especially during times of recession, because the end results can be more easily measured, as they can be linked directly to an increase in sales (unlike advertising).

OVERALL WEAKNESS. Sales promotions could be said to suffer from the following two weaknesses.

Short-termism. Sales promotions tend to encourage purchase whilst the promotion is on, but which stops when the promotion finishes. The hope is that not all customers will do this and some will continue to purchase.

Image damage. The company may gain a reputation for continuous sales promotions and customers will only purchase when there is a special offer in operation (known as 'cherry picking').

A 'PUSH' AND 'PULL' PROMOTIONAL STRATEGY

'Push' and 'pull' models are illustrated in Figures 9.7 and 9.8 to show how both advertising and sales promotions can be used to mount a promotional campaign along the distribution channel aimed at the wholesaler, the retailer and the end-consumer. The 'push' promotion will be described first of all.

A PUSH PROMOTION. Through the use of sales promotions, products are sold ('pushed') to the wholesaler who in turn 'pushes' them to the retailer who in turn 'pushes' them out to the customer (Figure 9.7). The process works in the following way:

1. The wholesaler is offered extra discounts (or some other form of trade promotion) to take larger quantities of products. Any advertising will also be aimed at the wholesaler and will probably be in some sort of trade magazine.
2. The wholesaler now needs to sell ('push') this extra stock on down the distribution chain so will offer some form of similar trade promotion incentive to the retailer to take more stock.
3. The retailer will now create some form of sales promotion, e.g. commission payments on selected products for its sales staff, to motivate the sales effort and/or a consumer promotion, e.g. some form of competition, to encourage the end-consumer to purchase.
4. Alternatively the producer could organize the whole sales promotion campaign at the wholesale, retail, sales staff and consumer level.

It is important to set clear (SMART) objectives for *every separate part* of the sales promotion (advertising) campaign.

A PULL PROMOTION. A pull promotion, on the other hand, works in the opposite way (Figure 9.8).

1. The producer will advertise (using the media mix, TV, newspaper, radio) directly to the end-customer.
2. This will (hopefully) excite the customer enough to go along to the retailer to demand the product.
3. The retailer, appreciating the opportunity for increased profit and sales will then approach the wholesaler for stock.

Figure 9.7	Push promotion

| Figure 9.8 | *Pull promotion* |

4. The wholesaler will in turn approach the producer for the demanded products so 'pulling' the products through the distribution chain.

A COMBINATION OF BOTH. It is more than likely that a producer will use both push and pull techniques at the same time so as to develop an overall effective promotional campaign.

This process is now seen increasingly in terms of a joint exercise between both producer and intermediary (rather than one persuading or bullying the other) as both appreciate that end-consumer satisfaction profits all members of the value chain.

ADVERTISING, SALES PROMOTION, PUSH, PULL AND AIDA

We can now take the two promotional mix techniques so far identified, advertising and sales promotions, and by the use of the push and pull strategy relate them both to the AIDA model to show how they can all be used together to move both the intermediary and the consumer from a state of unawareness through to action and purchase (Figure 9.9).

Publicity

The next major promotional mix technique to be examined is the use of publicity. This consists of items of news or stories that appear in newspapers, magazines and on the television about organizations, their products, the directors, the employees, etc.

Unlike advertising, the news items will not have been paid for and some of these items will be favourable, for example 'man survives on mountain top for three days by eating a Mars Bar' and some will be unfavourable, for example 'head of public utility has 70% pay rise whilst the staff have to settle for 2%'. Some of the items will be planned, for example Richard Branson announcing the launch of Virgin Cola on 'News at Ten', and some unplanned, for example Persil Power, a controversial new washing powder allegedly found to damage clothes.

| Figure 9.9 | *Push and pull promotion* |

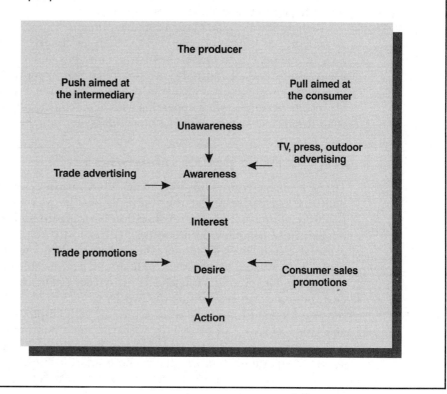

However for publicity to be seen as a marketing promotional tool it must have the following characteristics:

1. be planned;
2. be free at the point of communication;
3. project favourable images about the organization and its products.

So a definition of publicity might be:

Any form of planned, unpaid for media exposure that promotes the company or its products in a favourable light.

GREATER USE OF PUBLICITY.   The more progressive companies now understand the value of good publicity. The most commonly used way of obtaining publicity is through the use of the print media. A magazine or newspaper needs to unremittingly fill its pages with news stories and so a publicity campaign planned and well run will be welcomed by the media and will reap valuable publicity for the company at very little cost.

It should be remembered that a newspaper will have many thousands of press releases sent to it for publication. The item that will be printed will be the one that is newsworthy and helps to sell the paper. So when writing, a press release it should be considered more from the point of view of the newspaper – what benefits do they want (in marketing terms the newspaper is the customer) – than from the point of view of the marketing department.

Richard Branson, head of Virgin, has come to be seen as an expert on the use of publicity as a promotional tool. As well as cleverly using the 'News at Ten' programme on ITV to launch his new cola he has generated news stories in the press, radio and TV on balloon and speed boat record attempts across the Atlantic; he was pictured with royalty at the launch of a new aircraft; he has had front page headlines when appearing with a famous racehorse to launch his bid to run the national lottery (which, unfortunately for him, he did not get).

PUBLICITY, PUBLIC RELATIONS AND MARKETING

There is often confusion about the relationship between public relations, publicity and the role that they both play in the promotional mix. The role of public relations (PR) in an organization is to create and maintain a favourable image of the company on a continuous basis with regard to both internal and external stakeholders. To support the process the larger organization will probably have a dedicated PR department. To maintain a favourable image of both the organization and its products will also be the concern of marketing, so there will obviously be some overlap between the two areas.

The PR department will work internally with employees, employees' families and trade unions and externally with the local community, pressure groups, government, city financiers, shareholders, journalists – and of course customers – seeking to maintain good and harmonious relationships.

Some activities the PR department will want to have publicized, for example charity involvement or environmental care campaigns. However, other activities, for example a new car which continually breaks down or using animals for product experiments the PR department will not want to have publicized.

Other PR activity will be directed at ameliorating or minimizing situations that could be seen as damaging to the company some way, for example a plane crash, a ferry capsizing, or somebody putting poison in the company's fruit drink on the retail shelf. The marketing department may well be involved in many elements of the PR role described here, and in some companies the functions are combined.

Whatever messages need to be communicated, in defence of something detrimental or to promote good news, the PR department can use free publicity, for example a press release and a story in the national press, or it can use paid for advertising, for example an advert in a national newspaper. Again in many cases the marketing department may be involved in both cases.

However, marketing is concerned in using public relations and publicity as a *planned element* of the promotion mix specifically to communicate favourable messages to its customers about the organization's products and services.

THE TOOLS OF PUBLICITY.   There are various ways that planned publicity can be gained and we briefly consider four.

The press or news release.   The press release is probably the most widely used method of gaining free coverage in the national or local press. Information is sent to the newspaper in the hope that it will be printed. A newspaper will receive many more thousands of press releases than it will ever print so a company must develop the necessary press release skills to be successful. It is often worth cultivating relationships with particular journalists to facilitate this process.

Press and news conferences. The news conference is another method of building relationships and gaining publicity. Journalists from both TV and the press are invited to a hear some form of news story. There will be time allowed for a question and answer session. The hope is that favourable company or product stories will then be printed or broadcast.

Events. This is the planned staging of an activity knowing that it will be reported in the media. The Richard Branson record attempts outlined earlier are prime examples.

Public service activities. This includes any activity that may benefit the community in some way or another. This could be at both the local and national level. Examples of this include: working with a particular charity such as the National Society for the Prevention off Cruelty to Children; Tesco building new roads in return for planning permission; McDonald's running a street clean-up service within the environs of its fast food outlets. Such programmes need to be carefully managed so that favourable publicity results.

THE ADVANTAGES OF PUBLICITY

High credibility. Publicity, in the form of a news item about the company or its products, will usually be more readily believed by customers because it is seen as a company/product endorsement by a neutral and often well-respected observer (the journalist), unlike an advertisment which, no matter how well it is presented, is always seen by the customer as a paid for message that is biased toward the organization.

For example a favourable story about a company's new product on the TV programme 'Tomorrow's World', or a newspaper story about the success of a university, will always carry much more credibility than a paid for advertisment that proclaims the same message.

Dramatic presentation. Boosting the idea of high credibility is the fact that a news item can be presented in a dramatic fashion. A new product launch or brand name change written or broadcast as a news story will have much more dramatic impact than if it were announced by the company through the use of advertisments, for example the launch of Virgin cola discussed on 'News at Ten' as a news story or Anita Roddick of Body Shop shown visiting primitive tribes to purchase products and help protect their environment.

Presented in this way it is more likely to be seen, read and often discussed as it can be regarded, not as an advertisement to be avoided, but as a legitimate news story that is of public interest.

Free or low cost. The eventual publicity that an organization might get is free and this is often its attraction, especially to the smaller company with limited promotional funds. However, it should be understood that with some forms of publicity there is often a cost involved in setting up the event or entertaining journalists and feature writers.

DISADVANTAGES OF PUBLICITY

Difficulty in setting clear objectives.   The definition of publicity used earlier included the word 'planned' this means that SMART objectives must, wherever possible, be set. Unfortunately publicity is probably the most difficult of the promotional mix techniques for which to set clear, quantifiable objectives.

As with all other elements of the promotional mix, the promotions manager would usually like to set objectives in terms of sales achieved but, as with advertising, this is not possible because it is so difficult to link the news item directly to an increase in sales. This, however, should not be used as an excuse not to set objectives and these should be in whatever form is most manageable. For example SMART objectives may be set in terms of column centimetres obtained over a six month period or in terms of the number of favourable mentions in all forms of media over a year.

Control.   The big problem with much publicity is the difficulty in controlling what is eventually said about the organization even when it is carefully planned. A press release carefully written by the company promotion person may be doctored by the newspaper editor, published in an adulterated form and major areas missed out. Similarly a newsworthy event may be pushed off the agenda, often at the last minute, by the advent of another story considered more important. The skill is to minimize the above wherever possible.

Measurement.   Control is made more problematic because the measurement of results can be so difficult. If unrealistic objectives are set then the measurement of results will be impossible. Depending on the objectives set it is highly likely that some form of before and after marketing research may be used.

Uncontrolled publicity.   Much publicity is uncontrollable and so cannot be used in the formation of planned promotional campaigns. Unexpected events can cause stories and news items to appear that are beyond the influence of the organization. This is not usually a problem if the items are favourable but it can be disastrous if the opposite is the case. Unplanned unfavourable publicity probably falls under the remit of the PR department who should develop some form of *crisis management plan* to deal with the problem.

Publicity through word of mouth.   There is no doubt that the image of an organization and its products are often disseminated by one consumer passing on their experiences and talking to another. This is wonderful for sales if the experience is rewarding but potentially threatening if it is not. However the difficulty for promotions manager is the inability to control the process. If it is to be built into the promotion plan then clear objectives must be set and the results monitored and controlled. The problem is that this cannot realistically be done when talking about 'word of mouth' and so its inclusion in the campaign, often crucial, can only be at the level of subjective comment.

Personal selling

Personal selling is the last major element of the promotional mix to be examined. Any form of communication or promotion that involves direct interaction between a company salesperson and a customer can be seen as personal selling. The customer might be an intermediary – the retailer or wholesaler – the end-consumer, or a combination of both, depending on the channel relationships.

It is a truism that no profit can be made until the products are sold, so the importance that personal selling plays in the promotion process cannot be over-estimated.

Only when the product is sold can marketing be said to have performed its major function (of course it must still look towards long-term continuous customer care).

The salesperson is usually the last link in the promotional chain, and his or her task is to persuade the customer to actually buy the product. In performing this role the salesperson will hopefully capitalize on the vast amount of work put in by others in developing a customer-centred marketing mix offering. If the organization gets this part wrong then all the effort that has been expended on shaping the product, the price, the channel of distribution and the other elements of the promotional mix, to meet the needs of the customer, will have been fruitless and wasted.

PERSONAL SELLING AND AIDA.   It is possible for the salesperson to work in isolation in selling the organization's products, unaided by any other elements of the promotional mix, taking the customer all the way through the AIDA process from customer unawareness through to desire and the purchase of the product.

However this would tend to be an exception rather than the rule, as customers will tend to be wary about buying from a salesperson when they are unaware of either the company or the product. Advertising, sales promotion and publicity would all generally be used in some form or another to create this initial awareness and so support the selling process.

THE ROLE OF SELLING

Along with advertising, sales promotion and publicity, personal selling has its strengths and its weaknesses in its use as a marketing tool. However, it is probably more flexible and more wide-ranging in the activities and tasks it is able to perform and the roles it can play within both the promotional and marketing mix, than any of the other three elements. We can now examine some of these roles beginning with the role of the salesperson.

THE ROLE OF THE SALESPERSON.   The possible roles the salesperson might perform for the organization are many and will include the following:

- providing information educating, helping the customer make decisions;
- collecting information about markets and customers;
- prospecting, or cold canvassing, for new customers;

- problem solving, including dealing with customer complaints;
- working with other elements of the promotion mix;
- acting in a PR capacity, generally promoting the good name of the company, ameliorating problems and building long-term relationships;
- most important of all, selling the company's products.

DIFFERENT TYPES OF PERSONAL SELLING.   Personal selling can cover a whole range of different activities and have varying degrees of importance within the organization. These differences can be seen in the many different names by which salespeople are known, for example sales director, sales manager, sales supervisor, sales executive, account executive, sales representative, salesperson, etc., and the amount of money they might be paid – from £5000 to over £1,000,000 a year (in some organizations the top salesperson earns more than the Chief Executive Officer).

Some of the different roles that the salesperson might perform in any one organization are outlined below.

Order-taker.   The order-taker is often described as a salesperson when little actual selling is taking place. Many shop sales staff would fall into this category as they stand behind a counter handing over products on request. Other order-takers might include individuals working with FMCG products such as confectionery, bread or batteries in a situation where the contract has been signed at head office and the salesperson travels around from shop to shop, on a weekly or monthly basis, just 'topping up' requested orders.

Merchandiser.   The merchandiser has the responsibility of looking after the product once it is sold into the retail outlet. The tasks required from this type of salesperson will include: undertaking dealer staff product knowledge sessions; making certain that the product is on display in the best possible way; distributing and setting up point-of-sale material and generally acting in any way that will enhance short- and long-term dealer/producer relationships.

Educationalist/specialist.   The educationalist or specialist travels around offering information and advice on company products. This could include advice on products as diverse as washing powder, computer systems, financial services, cookers, fitted kitchens and the correct usage of building materials. Because of escalating costs many companies have tried to encourage the educationalist to take on the job of selling the product as well as giving advice. However this can be quite a problem as the two roles demand different skills not always to be found in one person.

Creative selling.   Creative selling could be considered the only 'true' form of personal selling as it involves persuading customers to purchase the organization's products and actually taking the order. Activities involved in creative selling will include: talking and selling to new customers who might never have bought the product before; persuading customers to switch over from a competing brand; negotiating on price and other product/service variables. As organizations have grown, and the buying departments have become more centralized, the opportunity for this form of 'creative' selling has decreased.

SELLING TO DIFFERENT CUSTOMER CATEGORIES. The salesperson will often sell to different types of customer depending on the product or service being offered. These customers will have many varying needs and so will demand a slightly different approach. The customer category types are identified as business to business, intermediary and domestic consumer.

Business to business. In business to business selling the number of customers will be less than when selling to the domestic consumer and so the opportunity to make a sale will be less. The reason for purchase will usually be rational rather than emotional as the purchase will be for company and not individual use. The amount and volume of each order will tend to be high as the product is for organizational rather than individual use and the time the salesperson will need to spend with each customer before, during and after the sale will often be longer, especially if the product or service is expensive and complex (sometimes months, or years, if the contract is large, for example a multi-million pound computer system for a hospital trust). The knowledge needed by the salesperson will often include detailed and specialized business and industry knowledge.

Intermediaries. A salesperson may sell to intermediaries. The majority of customers here will be wholesalers and retailers and the product sold will be for resale on to an end-consumer. Most of the factors relating to business to business selling will also be a consideration here. Additional areas to take into account will include:

- product training for the intermediary sales staff;
- merchandising the product in the retail showroom;
- undertaking some form of joint 'above' or 'below the line' promotion;
- dealing with the retailer's customer e.g. servicing the product, giving advice, dealing with complaints, etc.

The domestic consumer. Many salespeople are involved directly with the domestic consumer. This could be because the organization uses a direct channel of distribution to bring its products to market rather than indirectly through an intermediary, for example Avon cosmetics, Amway household products, Prudential financial services, or it could be because the salesperson works for some kind of retailer, for example John Lewis or Dixons. The approach needed here will differ from the previous two categories because of the following factors:

- There will be large numbers of individual customers all able to make a purchase.
- The reason for purchase is more likely to be for emotional rather than rational reasons.
- Purchases are more likely to be for the consumer's own use (or family) rather than for company use.

A combination of all three. Some organizations sell to all three types of customer at the same time, sometimes using the same salesperson. However it is more likely that different salespeople will be used because different selling methods are needed for the three different categories. It may not be easy to find any one individual with all the requisite skills. Problems can arise for an organization that attempts to sell to the three different types of customer. Channel conflict can arise when an organization uses more than one channel in distributing its products to its customers.

THE ADVANTAGES OF PERSONAL SELLING.   The major advantages that personal selling has over all other elements of the promotional mix include the two reasons discussed below.

Two way, interactive.   Personal selling takes place face-to-face with the customer. This allows for instant feedback and message flexibility. The salesperson is able to adjust, and re-adjust, the benefit messages in response to the customer's verbal and bodily language reaction as the conversation proceeds. Requests for more information can be dealt with, misunderstanding and confusion can be rectified, objections overcome and, finally, techniques used that will enable the sale to be made. The organization is unable to achieve this amount of subtlety with any other one of the promotional techniques we have discussed.

Relationship marketing and building long-term relationships.   The unique role the salesperson is able to perform has taken on added importance with increased understanding on the importance of relationship marketing and the need to maintain close mutual beneficial relationships. Close interaction allows for long-term, confidence building, relationships to be developed between seller and buyer. This is especially important where the meetings take place on a regular basis and trust is an important part of the process, for example in selling financial or computer services (the relationships can last a lifetime). The loyalty and friendship engendered can sometimes make it difficult for the buyer to go elsewhere to purchase the products.

THE DISADVANTAGES OF PERSONAL SELLING
High costs.   It is often argued that the biggest disadvantage with personal selling is the heavy fixed cost involved, as building and maintaining a sales team is an expensive process (the last figure seen by the writer quoted an average industry cost of £50,000 per sales representative). This cost includes factors such as wages and national insurance, administration costs, running a company car, hospitality allowances, and so on.

It must be remembered however that cost should always be related to effectiveness. So having said it is costly, if the salesperson is bringing in a million pounds worth of sales and making a reasonable profit the overall effect would be positive and therefore worthwhile.

Over-aggressive sales people.   In some industries, for example fitted kitchens, double glazing, classified advertisements, financial services, the salesperson has gained a reputation for an aggressive, and at times offensive, approach to the selling process by over-pressurizing the customer in an attempt to sell the product. In some cases this reputation may be justifiable (especially if the salesperson is paid on commission only, i.e. paid only if they make a sale) but in other cases it is often the result of a lack of sales training.

THE PERSONAL CHARACTERISTICS OF THE SALESPERSON

Whenever personal selling is discussed, arguments about the characteristics and skills needed by the best type of salesperson inevitably come to the fore. Which characteristics and skills are considered the most important will vary from commentator to commentator but the factors identified below would certainly be included. The sales person should be:

- knowledgable;
- a good communicator;
- able to get on with other people;
- persistent (without being offensive) i.e. have the ability to keep going when others have given up and gone home;
- strongly self-motivated, especially if working from home, alone all week in the marketplace, travelling from buyer to buyer.

Other attributes sought might include qualities such as: sincerity, helpfulness, enthusiasm, attentiveness and friendliness.

GOOD SALESPEOPLE: BORN OR TRAINED?   The discussion about what makes good salespeople often ends up questioning whether they are born or whether they can be trained. Although there are certain personality types that make good sales-people (gregarious, extrovert, outward-going and so on) general informed opinion seems to agree the right kind of training and development can help to create good salespeople.

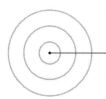

Exhibitions and sponsorship

Some forms of promotion tend to combine some or all of the promotional techniques we have already identified, including advertising, sales promotion, publicity and personal selling. The use of exhibitions and sponsorship fall into this category and we will look at each of these in turn, beginning with exhibitions.

Exhibitions

An exhibition will take many forms and can be seen as a marketplace for both displaying products and services and as a way of getting producers and customers together. The mounting of an exhibition may well include all the elements of the promotional mix.

- 'Above the line' advertising to announce the forthcoming event.
- 'Below the line' activity such as window posters, point-of-sale material.

- Some form of sales promotion to encourage visitors to the stand, e.g. the visitor may leave their visiting card and at the end of each day a draw is made with a magnum of champagne as the prize.

- Publicity to obtain a story about the exhibition on TV or in a newspaper or magazine.

- Personal selling with a salesperson on the stand disseminating product knowledge or persuading the customer either to purchase the product now or to accept an appointment for a later visit.

Participating organizations at an exhibition rent show areas within a complex and erect some form of stand to display their products or services. This can take place indoors or outdoors, in a purpose built exhibition centre (National Exhibition Centre in Birmingham), in a stadium complex (Wembley Conference and Exhibition Centre), a town or village hall, a hotel or any other convenient forum.

Some exhibitions are permanent (Business Design Centre) and some temporary. For the producer it is an opportunity to show off products and for the buyer an opportunity to meet new companies and see a whole range of products.

DIFFERENT TYPES OF EXHIBITIONS.   There are many different types of exhibitions and some of these are identified below.

Consumer exhibitions.   This type of exhibition will probably be the most familiar to the reader. An example of a consumer exhibition is the Ideal Home Exhibition held every year at Olympia in London. Others examples include a 'gay' exhibition held for the first time at Earls Court in 1993 (a good example of niche marketing) and Crufts Dog Show where many canine products are on show.

Trade/business exhibitions.   These are exhibitions held every year for businesses to make contact with one another. Examples in this category include the Toy Fair held at Harrogate, the Direct Marketing Exhibition in London and the Electrical Appliance Exhibition at the National Exhibition Centre at Birmingham.

Trade/business and consumer exhibitions.   Some exhibitions combine both trade/business and consumers in one exhibition. The Motor Show, the Boat Show and the Caravan Show are examples.

International trade fairs.   International trade exhibitions and fairs are organized where businessmen and women from all around the world can come and see what opportunities are available in the host country. This is especially important in developing economies such as Poland, Hungary, China and Vietnam because of difficulties with other forms of promotion.

Outdoor exhibitions.   Some exhibitions are held outside and these tend to be for products that need to be demonstrated, for some reason, in the open and include agricultural, building and heavy machinery products.

Seminars and conferences.   Companies will also organize seminars and conferences usually to entertain and inform their business intermediaries. These can be staged in hotels, specially designed conference centres in the home country or in some exotic location abroad. They can take place on board a train, a ship or even a plane.

EXHIBITION OBJECTIVES

The following reasons have been given for why companies rent space at exhibitions:

- to build goodwill, inform and educate, and pave the way for future sales;
- to make appointments and take sales leads;
- to communicate corporate image, meet existing and new customers;
- to sell products;
- because the competition is there.

As with all other forms of promotion it is important that exhibition and trade fair objectives are set in quantifiable terms. Only then can they be monitored and controlled so the real value is realized. Ideally this should be terms of sales but many trade fairs are more about meeting new customers or introducing new products.

In this case objectives should be set in terms of leads taken or appointments made.

Advantages of using an exhibition

Buyers and sellers come together. In many cases an exhibition is the quickest, easiest and most cost effective way for a company to demonstrate all of its products and to meet a whole cross-section of the market in friendly and un-intimidating circumstances.

Disadvantages

Uncertain objectives. In many cases companies are uncertain why they continue to go to a particular trade exhibition. Reasons such as 'customers expect to see the company there' or 'because the competition is there' are not adequate, because they cannot really be quantified and results measured.

High costs. Exhibitions can be very expensive in terms of rental charge, cost of building the stand, and transporting the products back and forth. Also to be considered is the opportunity cost of taking the sales staff away from the sales territory, with the lost sales this might incur.

Sponsorship

The last promotional technique we will examine is sponsorship. Like exhibitions this can also be a combination of all the promotional tools and techniques available in the promotional mix. A definition of sponsorship can be given as:

the giving of some form of support, usually money, in return for an advertising, sales promotion, publicity or sales opportunity.

There has been enormous growth in this media form over the last decade and this looks to continue into the future.

FORMS OF SPONSORSHIP. Sponsorship opportunities can now be found in all the following areas.

Sports. Probably the method of sponsorship with the highest profile. Almost every type of sport now attempts to attract some form of sponsorship (money, equipment, expertise). This includes: football (Littlewoods sponsoring the FA cup for £12 million); motor racing (Labatts larger, Camel cigarettes, amongst many others); cricket (Nat West trophy); tennis (Dunlop); the list is almost endless.

Pop concerts, pop stars, personalities. PepsiCola sponsorship of Michael Jackson and his pop concerts came about because he was seen as an opinion leader/role model with a worldwide following of young people. Unfortunately for Pepsi (but fortunately for Coca-Cola?) this might be seen as a sponsorship that went wrong, as unfavourable publicity became associated with the Michael Jackson lifestyle.

Theatre, opera, ballet, films, the arts. Many companies decide that their corporate/ product image is best served by being seen to support the theatre, opera, ballet or the arts. Examples are companies such as National Westminster Bank (classical piano concerts); Woolwich Building Society (opera); and Mercury Communications (theatre).

Charities. Many companies see a corporate benefit in being seen to sponsor various charities and good causes.

Other areas. Other possible areas for sponsorship include:

- special events, e.g. St John Ambulance centenary celebrations;
- education and research;
- books and exhibitions;
- TV programmes, Internet websites;
- individual endeavour, e.g. climbing a mountain, walking across Antartica, etc.

In fact almost anything can be sponsored as long as the sponsoring company sees some form of accruing benefit.

BENEFITS FROM SPONSORSHIP

In return for the sponsorship money, the company may obtain the following advantages.

- *Advertising*: This might appear on such things as: outdoor billboards, e.g. football hoardings; cricket grounds; racing cars; football shirts (hopefully with exposure on TV).
- *Merchandising*: The company name on clothing, programmes, CD covers, balloons, pens, plastic bags, etc.

- *Sales promotion opportunities*: These might include; competitions, free give-aways, free tickets, etc., run in conjunction with other elements of the promotional mix developed by the sponsoring company.
- *Publicity*: This might include coverage of the event or news items on TV or stories in the press about the sponsor/sponsored relationship.
- *Hospitality*: The sponsor has the opportunity to take clients/customers along to an event (football, tennis, golf, opera, theatre, etc.). The clients will get a privileged view and a dinner in sumptuous fashion, again cementing long-term relationships.
- *Personal selling*: The opportunity to sell products at the event, e.g. Coca-Cola, Snickers, Nike, at the World Cup.

SPONSORSHIP OBJECTIVES

As with publicity, sponsorship objectives can be very difficult to define in business terms. Nevertheless the effort must be made and performance indicators set for wherever the emphasis is to be put. This might be on advertising, sales promotion, publicity or personal selling.

If it is intended to use all four areas, then objectives should be set for each technique.

ADVANTAGES OF SPONSORSHIP

Extra publicity. Hopefully the sponsorship will result in favourable publicity, but this is not always manageable.

Image enhancement. Many organizations will sponsor particular activities because they want the associated image enhancement.

Increased corporate awareness. Sponsorship can be a most cost effective way of achieving corporate awareness, especially when entering a new market. The Japanese company Cannon sponsored the football league for five years and during this time took corporate awareness (knowledge of the company) from 10 per cent of the population to over 75 per cent.

Reaching areas where other media forms are banned. Sponsorship can be used when other forms of media are banned. This is put to good use by the tobacco companies who sponsor golf (Dunhill Masters); snooker (Embassy World); and cricket (Benson and Hedges). At the time of writing the UK government and the EU has announced that they intend to ban all forms of cigarette advertising, which would affect sponsorship of this nature.

Entertainment. The hospitality opportunities offered by sponsorship can be used to reward both customers and staff for their loyalty and commitment. It can also be used as an incentive to increase performance and develop motivation.

Increased sales. There are opportunities to actually sell the product (depending what it is) as part of the sponsorship contract. However an increase in sales due to the overall effect of the sponsorship can be very difficult to measure and tends not to be used as a sponsorship performance indicator.

Cost effectiveness. Depending on the price negotiated, sponsorship can be a very lucrative form of promotion. As we have seen there are very many spin-off opportunities that can be profitably exploited if managed professionally.

DISADVANTAGES OF SPONSORSHIP

Uncertainty. It can be very difficult to clearly forecast what the full opportunities of sponsorship might be. A high price paid to sponsor Manchester United Football Club could look very bad indeed if they where knocked out of all competitions at an early stage, causing TV coverage to be curtailed.

Association. The customer might view some types of sponsorship in a poor light by the dint of association. Sponsorship of boxing, motor racing or fishing might well be considered unethical by the more morally concerned. Similarly, association by Pepsi-Cola with Michael Jackson was considered to be well worth the millions of dollars paid until the unfortunate alleged child abuse accusations.

Using the promotional mix

We have now identified all the major tools and techniques that go to make up the promotional mix. The tools and techniques identified were:

- advertising;
- sales promotions;
- publicity;
- personal selling;
- exhibitions and sponsorship.

It is called a 'mix' because one technique is better than another at achieving one particular objective. To take the customer from a state of unawareness to purchasing the product will demand a varying use of one or more of these techniques.

The promotional campaign

Finally when planning a promotional campaign the following factors will need to be considered:

PROMOTION OBJECTIVES. What does the company want to achieve through the use of communication techniques, for example to create awareness, to reinforce existing beliefs, to get the customer to try the product, etc. (in terms of AIDA). These are business objectives and should be SMART.

PROMOTION STRATEGIES. What major methods will be used and why, to achieve these objectives. This stage will consist of choosing one or more of the promotional mix techniques identified in detail in this chapter, for example advertising, sales promotions, publicity, personal selling.

TARGET AUDIENCE.   The organization needs to be clear about the audience at which it is going to aim its messages. This will involve constructing detailed customer profiles for the targeted segment, including such factors as size, age, income, social class, behaviour, reading or viewing habits, etc.

MESSAGE.   The message content and the method of presentation will need to be in line with the product positioning statement.

PROMOTIONAL TACTICS.   The promotional strategy will need to be broken down into its constituent parts. For example if above the line advertising is the chosen strategy, then the elements of the media mix (i.e. TV, radio, press, cinema, outdoor) must be chosen. If below the line sales promotion is the strategy then again the method (i.e competitions, give-aways, coupons, etc.) must be chosen and detailed.

BUDGET.   An amount of money must be allocated and a promotional budget set. The amount given to the budget will depend on the budget method used.

TIMINGS AND ALLOCATION OF RESPONSIBILITY.   The exact timings of the campaign must be spelt out, for example over six months with objectives set for each week/month of the campaign. Clear responsibilities must be identified and agreed with all relevant marketing staff.

FEEDBACK, MONITORING AND CONTROL MECHANISMS.   Feedback, monitoring and control mechanisms must be implemented to make certain that agreed promotional objectives and performance indicators (e.g. to create a certain level of awareness or sell a particular number of products) are achieved. This process can be operated through the use of some form of market research.

INTEGRATION.   Finally it is crucial that all methods used are integrated in a cohesive, consistent, logical manner to clearly meet the (researched) needs of the target audience.

Summary

In this chapter we have examined and discussed the last of the 4 Ps – that of promotion. This has included advertising, sales promotions, publicity and personal selling.

To emphasize the importance of good communications it was considered vital to first go back to basics and look at the communication process through the use of a simple model.

The promotional mix was examined in detail beginning with advertising through the main media: TV (recognizing the Internet and multi-media opportunities), print, radio, cinema and outdoor. This form of promotion was identified as 'above the line'.

'Below the line' promotion was identified as all other forms of promotion. This includes sales promotions, which were described as incentives offered to the customer so as to persuade product trial and product purchase. Different techniques were evaluated and the relative merits of each briefly discussed. The differences between consumer promotions, trade promotions and staff promotions were also considered.

Using the AIDA hierarchy of effects model, and the 'push' and 'pull' models, the way that advertising and sales promotions might work together in a promotional campaign was examined. The need to set specific, measurable, achievable, realistic and time-based (SMART) objectives for each part of the campaign was stressed.

The use of publicity as a planned promotional tool was considered. It was seen as an under-used method of obtaining free (or low cost) favourable promotional benefits. The relationship between public relations and publicity was recognized and the differences highlighted.

Personal selling was discussed, looking at the role of the salesperson, the essential personal qualities needed as well as the selling process itself.

Finally exhibitions and sponsorship were examined, showing the part that all the elements of the promotional mix might play in utilizing these events.

Questions for discussion

1. Can you identify the many barriers to communication? How might some of these barriers be overcome?

2. Marketing is all about advertising and sales promotion. Discuss.

3. Identify the elements of the media mix looked at in this chapter and discuss the relative merits of each. What part might the Internet play in the future?

4. 'Advertising cannot be measured in terms of sales'; would you agree or disagree? Give reasons and examples. Identify the role of advertising in the promotion process.

5. What role might marketing research play in advertising?

6. Identify different forms of sales promotions and highlight their strengths and weaknesses. Give real examples of how organizations have used sales promotions. What are the kinds of problems that can arise? Give actual examples.

7. Using a snack food as an example how might advertising, sales promotion and personal selling come together to form a promotional campaign (use the AIDA and the push and pull models to help in the explanation).

8. It has been argued that the planned use of publicity is the most under-used promotional form. Why might this be? What forms of publicity can be used and how might objectives be set? What is the difference between public relations and publicity? How might an organization use both? Give actual examples.

9. Identify the factors involved in the sales process. How might this be used in the selling of the following products: financial services; business to business products and computer systems? How is the sales role changing?

10. Outline and discuss the benefits that might accrue to an organization in the brewery industry through the use of both sponsorship and exhibitions.

Case study

A few years ago Walt Disney opened a new theme park, south of Paris in France. In a joint venture with European investors, the Walt Disney Corporation invested billions of francs into developing a holiday theme park for children and adults in the hope that it would rival other similar enterprises elsewhere in the world. It was argued that, within a few years, total customer numbers from all over Europe visiting the French theme park would equal the amount that went to the other Walt Disney theme parks in the USA.

During the long financial and planning negotiations European and UK interest was intense and this continued during the long months as construction took place. Stories abounded in the press about the ups and downs and the trials and tribulations of the whole project. At the onset all types of investors, from large institutions to the small individual shareholder, were invited to own a part of this exciting new enterprise by buying shares in the company.

This invitation was communicated in many different ways from paid for advertising in both the press and on TV to a series of press releases issued to the media all over Europe. The press and TV adverts used well-known and well-loved Disney cartoons to put over messages about the longevity, stability and attractiveness of the Walt Disney organization as an investment, while the press stories majored on the optimism of the parent partner and the success of Walt Disney theme parks in other parts of the world. The communication messages all contained phone numbers for prospective buyers to ring for a share application form and information about the company and its new enterprise.

During the building many different stories found their way to both the press and TV; some arrived by accident and were uncontrolled, while others were the result of deliberately planned publicity campaigns and were in the most part controlled. At one time there seemed to be a spate of unfavourable stories about the different demands that the organization was making on the people working on the site. This involved the level of the wages being paid, the poor working conditions and the excess demands placed upon the staff. This was contrary to the official press releases that communicated messages about a happy, contented, working environment full of youthfulness and fun.

The opening was promoted by a massive campaign across Europe utilizing all the elements of the promotional mix. In the UK, TV adverts used Disney classic cartoons to inform, excite and persuade potential customers to come and enjoy the trip of a lifetime. Tickets could be purchased by telephone, through intermediaries or at the park entrance.

Sales promotions involved added value attractions such as introductory price reductions, competitions, product packages that offered hotel accommodation combined with the entrance fee as well as the chance to purchase other Walt Disney products at special prices.

Publicity was generated through the many TV programmes and TV current affairs stories that featured episodes about life and the theme park. These varied from exposure on holiday magazine programmes to human interest stories about disabled children transported free of charge to enjoy the holiday of a lifetime.

From the start of the project through to opening day an immense amount of interest was generated so that there could have been very few people who were unaware of the new Walt Disney theme park and the magical experience it offered to both children and adults. Unfortunately the number of people who were expected to use the theme park never reached the levels forecast and in the first years of operation the project had lost its shareholders large amounts of money. Whether this was because the original forecasts were over optimistic or because the overall attraction of a Walt Disney theme park in the middle of France, with the associated changeable weather pattern, would never match the appeal of the sun-drenched Florida alternative, only time and market research will reveal. At the time of writing, publicity about the park is still being generated and the injection of more capital and an increase in sales turnover may augur well for its long-term future.

However corporate life has not all been doom and gloom for Walt Disney, and in 1994/95 it achieved one of its biggest worldwide successes ever with the launch of a new full-length cartoon film *Aladdin*. This was promoted all over the world using every relevant promotional technique including advertising, sales promotions, publicity, exhibitions and sponsorship.

In the UK, a major publicity campaign was developed as part of a larger overall promotional campaign for the launch of the *Aladdin* video. One item in the publicity campaign, was a record breaking attempt, the most balloons to be released into the atmosphere at any one time, set up and sponsored in conjunction with the Guinness Book of Records. Most importantly for the Walt Disney marketing department, they had arranged for this record attempt to be broadcast as a news story on the children's TV programme 'Record Breakers'.

The target was the release of over two and half million balloons into the atmosphere at the same time. Gigantic marquees where erected in the grounds of a stately home and thousands of children invited along. The children then spent sometime blowing up the balloons, the adults put in the gas and the balloons were allowed to float to the roof of the huge tents. Soon the whole of the interior roof areas were smothered by hundreds of thousands of red, blue and yellow balloons. When the requisite amount had been blown up and were ready, the count down began.

At the end of thirty seconds the marquees where dismantled and the massed ballons allowed to gradually billow into the sky. A shortened version of the whole process was filmed and the publicity event took up half the 'Record Breakers' programme. The *Aladdin* video was discussed at length, a small part was shown and free copies of the video where given away to all of the children taking part.

Apart from the cost of staging the event the resultant exposure on children's TV cost nothing.

Case study questions

1. Identify the stakeholders involved in the Walt Disney theme park project. What different messages would need to be sent to all the various stakeholders? What media might be used to do this?

2. What factors would the Walt Disney promotions department need to have considered when:
   - it was developing a communications plan for the sale of shares in the French theme park?
   - it was developing a promotional plan for the launch and the subsequent continuous sale of tickets for the park?

3. What objectives could be set for all the different forms of promotion? How could they be measured, monitored and controlled?

4. The launch of the Disney *Aladdin* video included an attempt on a world record balloon releasing event. What factors must be considered when setting up this type of publicity event? How could the success or otherwise be measured?

5. How might the other elements of the promotional mix – advertising sales promotion and personal selling – be incorporated with the publicity generated with this record attempt to make a more comprehensive promotional campaign?

Further reading

Cees B.M. Van Reil and Blackburn, C. (1995) *Principles of Corporate Communications*, Prentice Hall, London.

Colley, R. (1961) *Defining Advertising Goals for Measured Advertising Response*, DAGMAR, Association of National Advertisers, New York.

Cummins, J. (1993) *Sales Promotions*, Kogan Page, London.

Govoni, N. and Galper, M. (1986) *Promotional Management*, Prentice Hall, London.

Hart, N. (1995) *The Practice of Advertising*, Butterworth-Heinemann, Oxford.

Howard, W. (1992) The Practice of Public Relations, Butterworth-Heinemann, Oxford.

Jefkins, F. (1988) *Secrets of Successful Direct Response Marketing*, Butterworth-Heinemann, Oxford.

Jefkins, F. (1989) *Advertising*, M&E Handbooks, London.

Kent, R. (1994) *Measuring Media Audiences*, Routledge, London.

Lancaster, G. and Jobber, D. (1990) *Sales Technique and Management*, Pitman, London.

Roberts, M.L. and Berger, P.D. (1989) *Direct Marketing Management*, Prentice Hall, London.

Thomas, J. and Lane, R. (1996) *Kleppner's Advertising Procedure*, (Prentice Hall, London.

Wilmshurst, J. (1995) *The Fundamentals of Advertising*, Butterworth-Heinemann, Oxford.

References

Ray Wright: www.raynetmarketing.com

Electronic Telegraph: www.telegraph.co.uk

The Newspaper Society: www.newspapersoc.org.uk

The Economist: www.economist.com

Financial Times: www.ft.com

The Association of Publishing Agencies: www.apa.co.uk

Periodical Publishers Association: www.ppa.co.uk

Audit Bureau of Circulation: www.abc.org.uk

Joint Industry Committee for Readership Research (JICREG) local newspapers: www.adweb.co.uk

National Readership Survey: www.nrs.co.uk

Nielsen Media Research: www.nielsenmedia.com

AGB N. Taylor Nelson glossary: www.agb.mediatel.co.uk/tutrack/glossary

Zenith Media: www.zenithmedia.com

Institute of British Advertisers: www.isba.org.uk

Institute of Practitioners in Advertising: www.ipa.co.uk

International Advertising Association: www.iaaglobal.org

The Advertising Association: www.adassoc.org.uk

Cable TV: www.cable.co.uk

The Salesdoctor Magazine: www.salesdoctor.com

Radio Advertising Bureau: www.rab.co.uk

Radio Advertising Bureau: www.rab.com(USA)

Media Outdoor Advertising: www.maiden.co.uk

Institute of Public Relations: www.ipr.press.net

Institute of Sales Promotions: www.isp.org.uk

Advertising Standards Authority: www.asa.org.uk

Independent Television Commission: www.itc.co.uk

Campaign Magazine: www.campaignlive.co.uk

Broadcaster's Audience Research Board, TV (BARB): www.barb.co.uk

Poster Audience Research (POSTAR): www.postar.co.uk

Radio Joint Audience Research (RAJAR): www.rajar.co.uk

Cinema Advertising Association, 12 Golden Square, London W1R 3AF

Cinema and Video Industry Audience Research (CAVIAR)

ACNielsen Worldwide, responsible for MEAL: Monitors media adspend:www.acnielsen.com

10

Marketing planning and control

AIMS AND OBJECTIVES

By the end of the chapter the student should:

1. identify the types of information that go to make up the marketing audit;

2. be able to undertake a simple marketing audit;

3. be aware of all the factors that are involved in marketing planning including, objective setting, strategic choice analysis and selection and tactical and operational implementation;

4. be able to put together a simple marketing plan.

Introduction

Marketing planning

At the beginning of the book we looked at different definitions of marketing before deciding to use the one that defines marketing as 'the management process that anticipates, identifies and satisfies customers' needs and wants at a profit'.

Another definition that was touched on (and more or less says the same thing but in a different way) was that marketing could be seen as 'a matching process developing the resources of the organization to exactly meet the needs and demands of the target market, effectively, efficiently and economically' and it is this definition that lends itself more readily to the idea of marketing planning and control.

So marketing planning is about taking all the areas of marketing discussed throughout the book (marketing research, understanding consumer behaviour, product development, packaging, branding, pricing, distribution, promotion and so on) within the organization and combining these resources in such a way that products and services are offered that meet the current and future needs and demands of the marketplace better than those of the competition.

To be able to do this successfully the whole marketing process must be thought through and planned, taking into account the state of current organizational resources and the present and future market direction.

This is why any marketing planning must begin with an investigation into prevailing company and market circumstances before any decision can be made about long-term, strategic direction. This investigation is about the collection, classification and analysis of all information that would be relevant to the company's market position. It would be impossible, for arguments sake, to make decisions about selling existing products into new markets without knowledge of the company's product portfolio mix and present financial situation or the level of competition and potential sales volume in the selected new market.

Therefore, stage 1 of the planning process consists of asking questions and collecting and analysing as much information about the current situation as is considered both manageable and relevant. This we call the *marketing audit*.

Once the audit has been conducted we can move on to stages 2 and 3 in which the analysed information is used to decide both the marketing objectives and the strategic methods that must be employed to achieve these objectives.

Finally, we look at stage 4 of the process, the factors to be considered in the implementation of the plan. The process can now be laid out as follows:

Stage 1   The marketing audit: a situational analysis
          (Where are we now?)
Stage 2   Objective setting
          (Where do we want to go?)
Stage 3   Choice of strategy
          (How are we going to get there?)
Stage 4   Planning, implementation and operations
          (How will the process be implemented?)

We will now look at each of these areas in more detail beginning with the marketing audit.

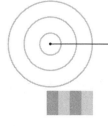

Stage I   The marketing audit

Situational analysis: Where are we now?

The meaning of the word 'audit' is an 'examination' and a marketing audit is an examination of an organization's current marketing activity. Only if there is a thorough understanding of the present state of the company's resources in relation to the demands of the market environment can realistic decisions be made about its future direction.

The job of the audit is to collect, classify and analyse information so that understanding can take place and realistic decisions made about future organizational direction.

To facilitate understanding the intention here is to look at the marketing audit process in two parts:

Part 1   The collection and classification of information from:
    1   the external environment,
    2   the internal environment;
Part 2   The analysis of the information collected.

Part I   Information collection and classification

There exists an infinite amount of information both within an organization and in the outside world where it operates. The difficulty that faces the marketing manager, the consultant, or the marketing student is where, and how, to start this information gathering process. How to decide what information is relevant and so should be collected and considered; which information is irrelevant and should be discarded; whether to start the process from outside the company looking in, or from the inside looking out and so on.

To help in this first part of the audit process, information collection and classification, we will return to the simple models developed and discussed at the beginning of the book.

FACTORS IN THE EXTERNAL ENVIRONMENT

Under the heading of the external environment we identified two areas for consideration. The wider or macro-environment and the immediate or micro-environment. Within these two areas acronyms were developed to guide us.

THE WIDER OR MACRO-ENVIRONMENT.   The information to be collected here was identified under the acronym **PEST** which stands for:

Political/legal;
Economic/demographic;
Social/cultural;
Technical/physical.

THE IMMEDIATE OR MICRO-ENVIRONMENT.   Areas where information needs to be collected from the micro-environment were identified under the acronym **SPICC** which stands for:

Suppliers;
Publics;
Intermediaries;
Competition;
Customers/Markets.

('Publics' includes those stakeholders who have an immediate interest in the company, including pressure groups, the media, local government, local communities, etc.)

FACTORS IN THE INTERNAL ENVIRONMENT

We can now introduce the concept of the '7 Ss' recognizing that marketing mix success must be dependent on a coordinated approach from the whole organization.

The relevant factors in the internal environment can be broken down in the following way:

The 7 Ss: the organizational Structures, Systems and Strategies (the 'hard' side of management), plus Skills, Staffing, Shared values and Style (the 'soft' side of management).

The 6 Ps: (the wider definition will now be used) or the marketing mix: Product, Price, Place, Promotion, People and Profits (financial concerns).

This can be illustrated (Figure 10.1) in the marketing model first shown in Chapter 1.

THE USE OF ACRONYMS AS INVESTIGATORY TOOLS

We now have a series of acronyms, PEST and SPICC, applied to the external environment, and the 7 Ss and the 6 Ps applied to the internal environment and these are the tools of marketing auditing (Figure 10.2.)

These acronyms are at the very heart of the auditing process because they give a formula to both ease the marketing auditor into the initial process and then to undertake the auditing process itself.

It should be remembered that PEST, SPICC, the 7 Ss and the 6 Ps are arbitrary ways of classifying information to facilitate information collection and to make sure nothing important is missed. These tools can be used in their entirety, in part, or dispensed with as the marketing auditor sees fit.

| **Figure 10.1** | *The internal and external organizational environment* |

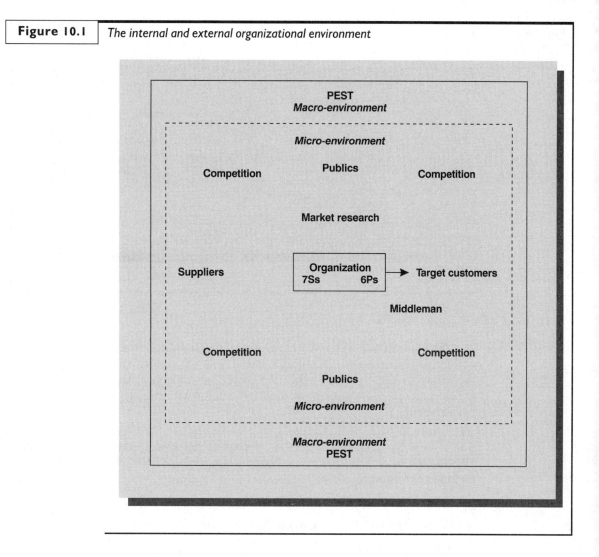

Other marketing auditors may choose to use different methods with full legitimacy as the end demand is an understanding of the present situation as it relates to both the marketing resources of an organization and the needs of its markets. Now with the aid of the marketing auditing acronyms we can move on to look at the sorts of information that need to be collected for analysis from both the external and internal environments.

INFORMATION NEEDED FROM THE EXTERNAL ENVIRONMENT

Starting with the external environment some of information to be collected will be very broad and will have only a marginal effect (PEST factors), whilst other information will have much more of an immediate and important influence (SPICC factors such as competition, customers, etc.).

Figure 10.2 | *Tools of the marketing audit*

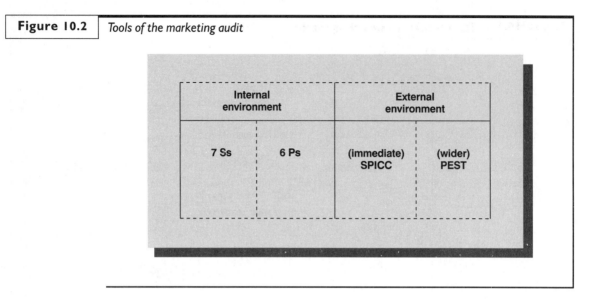

The following are examples of the questions that might need to be asked when collecting information, although these will of course vary in importance according to the type and condition of the organization, the structure of the industry and the environmental climate. We begin with the macro/wider or 'PEST' environment.

THE MACRO- OR WIDER ENVIRONMENT – POLITICAL, ECONOMIC, SOCIAL, TECHNOLOGICAL (PEST) FACTORS.   Information needed about the PEST environment might include the following:

- What laws are relevant or could be relevant in the future?
- What is the political climate, will it change?
- How stable is the region?
- What is the economic level and trend of activity – GDP/per capita income/income spread/disposable income?
- What are/will be the interest/exchange/inflation/employment rates?
- What are the demographic movements?
- How important is social class/marriage/the family?
- What are the major cultural norms? Are customs and practices changing?
- What are the education/literacy levels?
- How important is technology? Is new technology being developed?
- What infrastructure is in place?
- How important is the climate?

Of course these are just a few areas that might be relevant and many other questions should be asked according to the needs of each particular case.

THE MICRO- OR IMMEDIATE ENVIRONMENT — SUPPLIERS, PUBLICS, INTERMEDIARIES, COMPETITION, CUSTOMERS/MARKETS (SPICC) FACTORS.   We offer here just a small selection of the sorts of questions that need to be asked about the immediate or SPICC environment:

- Who has the power in the marketplace along the distribution chain? Is it the suppliers, the producer, the intermediary or the consumer?
- How many suppliers are there? How efficient are they? How much are they charging? Do they deliver on time?
- Are there any pressure groups, local community interests/concerns?
- Do the intermediaries offer added value? Are they well trained?
- Who is the competition? Who are the major players/market leaders/market shareholders in the relevant market? What are their product portfolios, product advantages? Are there substitute products?
- How easy is it for competition to enter (and leave) the market?
- Who are the target markets – customer profiles/size? Are they growing/declining? Are new markets opening up?
- Are customer tastes, preferences, customs and practices changing?
- Is spending power increasing?

This is just an indication of the type of information needed. In undertaking an external audit the practitioner must tailor the approach and the questions to be asked to meet the needs of the organization and the industry being studied.

INFORMATION NEEDED FROM THE INTERNAL ENVIRONMENT

We can now look at the internal environment – the information needed from the internal audit will cover the 7 Ss and the 6 Ps.

THE 7 Ss.   This is background information that is needed about the organization's structures, systems and strategies as they might *affect the marketing effort*. Information required here will include the following:

- What sort of structure does the company have? Is it bureaucratic? Is it 'tall' and hierarchical or 'flat' and flexible? Which structure will be more conducive to the company's marketing effort?
- What systems and processes (communication, finance, MkIS, training, etc.) are in place? Are they adequate and sufficiently customer orientated? What controls are in place?
- Is there evidence of long-term strategic marketing thinking across all marketing areas?
- Are staffing levels adequate? Can they meet customer service requirements?
- What skills, or lack of skills, exist? What training and development might be needed?
- What is the culture (shared values) of the company? Is is customer orientated? Are people well motivated?
- What is the style adopted by the company? Is it democratic, autocratic, patriarchal? How does it affect the corporate image?

These are just a few of the questions that need to be answered about the supporting framework within which marketing must take place. If there are deficiencies here the marketing effort will be disjointed, diluted and ineffectual.

THE MARKETING MIX (6 Ps). At the heart of the marketing audit is the marketing mix. This will cover the use of marketing research, the company's product portfolio (including people if there is a service input), its channels of distribution, the pricing policies and the amount and type of promotion carried out. The marketing mix will also be concerned with costs, profit levels and cash flow ratios. We will look a little more closely at the information needed in these areas, beginning with a brief look at marketing research, before moving on to each of the 6 Ps.

Marketing research. The evidence of an MkIS will give some indication of how important the company considers the need for a marketing database. Questions can also be asked about the level/type of marketing research undertaken (if any), how it is used and to what degree is involves the use of IT.

Product/service. Information needed on the organization's products or services will include the following:

- What are the product/service sales and sales trends?
- What is the company product/brand portfolio? How do all the products interrelate? Where are they on the PLC and BCG matrix? Is there synergy across the product range?
- What are the cost/profit structures?
- What are the brand strategies? Do they still work?
- What is the level of new product development/innovation/market research? How important are these in the industry?
- What do customers/suppliers/intermediaries think about the products/service offered?

Place (channels of distribution and physical distribution). Information needed here will cover the various channels used and the method of physical distribution and will include:

- Is the company getting the coverage it wants both in quantity and quality? Are the existing methods it uses still relevant? Is there conflict between channels?
- What physical distribution techniques are in use? Is centralized or decentralized warehousing employed? How is information technology being used? What costs are being incurred?

Price. Information needed on price will include the following:

- What pricing methods are used? Are they sufficiently customer oriented?
- Is there an adequate return on the prices charged? What is the relationship between fixed and variable costs across the product portfolio?
- How does the pricing relate to the other elements of the marketing mix?

Promotion. Examples of the type of information needed here will include the following:

- What is the level of promotion spend in relation to sales and to others in the industry? How is it measured? How successful or otherwise has it been?
- What promotional mix methods are used? How long has the existing advertising agency been used?
- What is the image of the company/brands?

People. Information will be required which covers all the areas that relate to the people within the organization, at all levels, and will include the following.

- What are the skills of the management/workforce/marketing/salesforce? Are they adequate and is there training and development available to supplement their skills?
- Is there a shared company culture/values? It it positive and motivating? Is it geared toward customer satisfaction and is everybody marketing orientated?

Profit. Examples of the questions relating to profit will include the following:

- What are the fixed and variable costs across the product portfolio?
- Is the company making a profit? What are the different product profit levels? Are they rising or falling?
- Is there synergy between costs, volumes and profits?
- How do the company's financial ratios compare with the industry ratios? Is there heavy company debt level? Does it have any cash flow problems?

As you can see there are many questions that need to be asked about the marketing mix and only a few examples have been given. As with the 7 Ss, the importance that the company will attach to the different elements of information will vary according to products, markets and the industry. We can now move to the second part of the audit: the analysis.

Part 2   The analysis of the information collected

Once all the relevant information has been collected and classified it can be analysed (of course in practice a certain amount of analysis tends to go on at the same time as the information is being collected but judgement should be postponed until an overall picture is obtained). There are many different models available to simplify and so aid the process of analysis. The model used here is the SWOT model.

SWOT ANALYSIS

SWOT stands for strengths, weaknesses, opportunities and threats.

- *Opportunities and threats* are used to analyse the external factors (PEST and SPICC factors), which can be seen as uncontrollable.

■ *Strengths and weaknesses* are used to analyse and categorize the internal factors (the 7 Ss and the 6 Ps), which can be seen as controllable.

It is important not to confuse internal and external factors because if this happens it might also confuse both the management approach and the decisions that are eventually taken (see Figure 10.3).

Probably the best way to undertake the SWOT analysis is to use separate sheets of A4 paper for the four areas. It is better to start the process by taking all the information collected on the external environment (i.e. under PEST and SPICC) first and, after discussion, identify and write down under the relevant heading, what might be the opportunities and threats to the organization posed by the external environment.

The same process can then be applied to the internal environment analysing the internal information (i.e. 7 Ss and 6 Ps) and categorizing these date under the headings of strengths and weaknesses.

REPEAT AND REFINE THE SWOT.   The process can continue for as long as the participants feel it is productive, the SWOT information being bought forward and refined and developed through argument and discussion. Eventually there should be some form of agreement on which information to reject and which information to retain so that the final SWOT will contain only the *major* strategic marketing

| **Figure 10.3** | *The SWOT* |

external opportunities and threats and the *major* strategic organizational internal strengths and weaknesses.

The value of the SWOT exercise is as much in the 'doing' as in the final document and practitioners should not be afraid to argue, discuss, adjust and re-adjust before coming up with the end product. The important thing is that debate takes place involving all interested parties.

THE SWOT AS A MATCHING PROCESS.   It should be noted that the internal factors are defined strengths and weaknesses relative to the external marketing opportunities and threats.

Ideally an organization would like to match the strengths of the organization to the opportunities in the market (you may remember that this matching process, i.e. matching the resources of the organization to the needs of the market, was used as one of our definitions of marketing in Chapter 1).

However this is not always possible because of the circumstances pertaining to the organization and the state of the environment. Therefore it can be the case that the weaknesses of the company are such that the organization cannot take advantage of the external opportunities. In this case it might have to seek some form of outside resource investment (e.g. financial capital or even a merger or acquisition) so that it can take advantage of these opportunities.

The SWOT analysis might show the company to be in the unfortunate position where the threats from the environment are so large and the weaknesses internally so dire that the only organizational strategy possible might be to divest or liquidate, depending on the seriousness of the situation. Figure 10.4 lists a number of SWOT scenarios accompanied by possible strategic options on how to rectify the position.

| **Figure 10.4** | *The SWOT strategic options* |

SWOT position	Possible strategies
Strengths > weaknesses Opportunities > threats	Match strengths to opportunities for success
Weakneses > strengths Opportunities > threats	Seek help to eliminate weaknesses and take advantage of opportunities
Strengths > weaknesses Threats > opportunities	Move to new markets; strengths can be optimized and threats eliminated
Weaknesses > strengths Threats > opportunities	No hope, divest or liquidate

Figure 10.5 is an example of a finished SWOT using *imaginary* internal and external information. A real SWOT would be much more specific and relate directly to the organization under investigation.

SWOT ANALYSIS AS A DECISION MAKING AID. SWOT analysis can now be used as a decision-making aid in objective setting and in looking at the strategic marketing options open to the company in deciding long-term direction. Ideally the marketing manager would now like to use the marketing planning process to take advantage of the market opportunities, defend against the market threats, build on the company strengths and minimize or eliminate the company weaknesses.

As an example it is possible to take the small amount of information in the imaginary SWOT in Figure 10.5 and come up with outline, simple, imaginary solutions. Working on the SWOT in Figure 10.5. we might come up with the following solutions:

- Marketing opportunities could point to a rationalization of the product portfolio.

- Move out of markets with foreign competition that are price driven.

- Concentrate on those markets that are growing by offering added value products based on quality and service using production skills and excess capacity.

- Move from a bureaucratic to a more flexible, customer reactive structure.

- Develop management in the art of marketing planning and strategic thinking and retrain other employees where necessary.

| **Figure 10.5** | *The SWOT in action* |

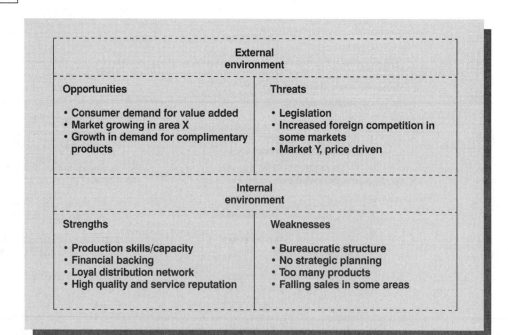

Before moving on to stage 2 of the planning process, objective setting, it will be useful to briefly outline the position of the marketing audit with regard to the overall company audit.

WHERE THE MARKETING AUDIT SITS WITHIN THE OVERALL COMPANY AUDIT

The marketing audit is part of the much wider company or business audit and will only be undertaken in isolation if management decides there is a special need in this area. Even if this were the case it would still demand cross-company consultation. An organizational audit should be undertaken by the whole organization, division by division, function by function, department by department. So personnel, finance, production, administration, marketing, etc. will all collect and analyse information within their departments (in joint consultation with all the other departments). When completed all the information will be pulled together to form the company audit (Figure 10.6).

It is also possible to undertake much smaller audits within the marketing mix such as a product, promotion or sales audit, as and when necessity demands.

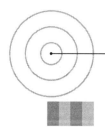

Stage 2   Objective setting

Where do we want to go?

At some point in the planning process, the company mission statement should be clearly defined and overall corporate objectives set.

Figure 10.6 | *The organizational audit*

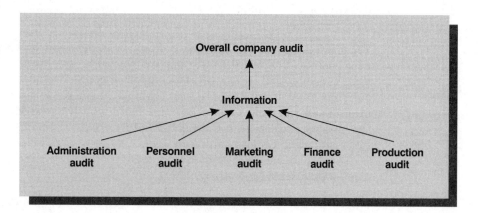

The mission statement and corporate objectives

The importance of the organization's mission statement and its corporate objectives must not be forgotten as marketing planning will need to take place *within the framework* set by both the mission statement and the corporate objectives.

The need for common objectives at every level cannot be over-emphasized, because experience has shown that a disaster can occur when all, or some departments within the same company ignore, confuse, or seem to be unaware of overall company direction and behavioural policy, preferring instead to implement their own aims and objectives. The end result of this could be each department/area going its own way, causing the company to perform its corporate function in an inefficient and un-coordinated fashion, promising eventual bankruptcy.

THE COMPANY MISSION STATEMENT

The mission statement should lay down the long-term corporate aims and values and answer the following questions (suggested possible answers to these questions are given in brackets using a retail supermarket chain as an example):

1. What business is the company in?
    (Retailing grocery and allied household products.)
2. What constitutes value for the shareholders?
    (Adequate return on the capital employed, attractive dividend payout and long-term growth.)
3. Who are the customers?
    (The relevant target market and customer profiles.)
4. How should the company conduct its business with regard to:
    - its customers?
      (Offering high quality innovative products and services at affordable prices.)
    - its employees?
      (Treat employees as we would like to be treated ourselves.)
    - all other stakeholders?
      (Seek mutually beneficial relationships with suppliers and intermediaries.)
    - the environment?
      (Act as responsible and caring corporate citizens.)

The answers to the questions above should be understood, and hopefully believed, by all members of the organization and should be the overall guiding principle that gives direction and moves the company forward.

For a mission statement to work it should be offered in a simplified form, have meaning for all employees and be in use continuously in the day-to-day running of the business, otherwise it will remain nothing other than a list of esoteric intentions gathering dust at boardroom level.

THE CORPORATE OBJECTIVES

The corporate objectives are the business objectives for the whole of the organization (including production, human resources, administration, finance, marketing, etc.) and they should spell out for all stakeholders the exact purpose of the organization. As with all business objectives, corporate objectives should be quantified over time (SMART) so that the results can be monitored and controlled.

If the organisation is a public limited company then the corporate objectives will be set in financial terms this being the return (profit on their investment) to the owners of the company, the shareholders, for the use of their capital. The measures (sometimes known as corporate performance indicators (CPI)) that tend to be used are the return on capital employed (ROCE), the return on investment (ROI) or the return on shareholders' funds (ROSF). All these forms of corporate objectives are very similar and basically measure the effectiveness (or otherwise) of the board of directors in the running of the business. Shareholders put money into a company and they want to know how this is being used and how much profit it will earn.

The Corporate Performance Indicator we will explore in a little more detail is the return on capital employed (the ROCE). The ROCE is the amount of money invested in the business (this includes, shareholders' funds, long-term loans and retained profits) divided by the amount of profit earned each year. This should be multiplied by 100 to give a percentage amount. For example:

$$\frac{\text{Net profit (the return) for the year}}{\text{Amount of money invested in the business}} \times 100\% = \text{ROCE}$$

$$\frac{\pounds100{,}000}{\pounds1{,}000{,}000} \times 100\% = 10\% \text{ ROCE}$$

An average return of 10 per cent ROCE employed would be quite acceptable if this were the corporate objective set at the beginning of the time period (say 5 years), but would be considered a failure if the corporate objective had been set as an average of 15 per cent ROCE over this five year period.

Marketing objectives

The planning process discussed up to now would apply to all the different functions within the organization. The marketing role in the planning process really begins with the marketing objectives. The marketing objectives are the overall performance target for the whole of the marketing function and will tend to be set in terms of sales and profit levels over a set time period and should be SMART. The time period is usually 3–5 years and whatever length is chosen should be broken down to cover short, medium and longer periods.

An example of one organization's *marketing objectives* might be as follows: 'To achieve overall company sales of £5,000,000 over the next three/five years at an average profit rate of 15%.' This can then be broken down to give sales and profit performance indicators (PI) for the short, medium and long term. This can then be further broken down across divisions if it is a multi-divisional organization.

As you can see the marketing objectives in our example have been set in terms of sales. Non-profit organizations (NPO) objectives can still be SMART, but can be couched in terms of revenue generated (charities); efficient use of capital (hospitals); speed and coverage given (fire brigade).

CLOSED AND OPEN OBJECTIVES. It is worth mentioning at this stage that there are closed and open objectives. All business, or primary objectives should be closed, that is they should be objectives which can be quantified over time (SMART). This is so that progress can be clearly monitored and controlled and success or otherwise can be measured. The corporate and marketing objectives identified above are closed objectives.

However an organization will sometimes use open, or secondary objectives. These are objectives that are less defined than the closed-end type and are not usually capable of clear measurement. Examples of this type of marketing objective will include:

- To create greater customer satisfaction.
- To strive to develop innovative products.
- To contribute to a safer market environment.

The difficulty with the open type of objective lies in the subjective nature of describing exactly what is meant by 'greater customer satisfaction' or 'to develop innovative products'. Measurement will be difficult as one person's definition will probably be different to another's, leading to uncertainty and confusion as to whether the objective has been achieved or not.

Methods of forecasting

An important function of the marketing manager is to forecast future sales and of course marketing objectives cannot be undertaken without some form of sales forecasting taking place. The importance of reliable predicted levels of sales cannot be over-estimated as it is on this figure that all other budgets are based. If the predicted sales figure for next year is £10,000,000 then other budgets, capital expenditure, cost of labour, production, raw materials, advertising, etc. will all be set with this figure in mind. Imagine the problems if sales of only £5,000,000 were achieved when sales of £10,000,000 were predicted.

The need to forecast future demand will apply to overall industry markets as well as individual company and brand markets. The task can be undertaken both in-house by marketing staff and out-of-house by professional agencies.

Forecasting methods can be divided into two simple categories:

1. qualitative forecasting techniques;
2. quantitative forecasting techniques.

QUALITATIVE TECHNIQUES

Qualitative forecasting techniques are those based on the opinion, judgement, and experience of those groups involved in the marketing process. Several such groups can be identified.

PANEL OF EXPERTS. This is where top managers, from all functions across the company, come together and use their knowledge and expertise to predict future sales. It is probably the most inexpensive method but is possibly limited by the parochial nature of the experts.

DELPHI TECHNIQUE. Similar to the above but here panels of experts from outside the company are also used. Possible candidates are university lecturers, scientists and consultants or any other individual or group with market knowledge. This method can be expensive and time-consuming, although a wider sphere of experience and expertise is canvassed.

TRADE AND COMMERCIAL SOURCES. Many trade associations and private companies offer a sales forecasting service. There is usually a charge and the information, more often than not, will tend to be industry wide rather than company specific (this information could also be quantitative).

THE SALESFORCE. Many argue that this is an under-utilized sales forecasting resource. The salesforce are the 'ears and eyes' of the company out in the marketplace and many have years of experience to call on in predicting future sales. However care should be taken with salespeople either over-estimating future sales to curry favour with management, or under-estimating so as to gain a lower and more achievable sales target (sometimes called 'bottom-up' forecasting as opposed to 'top down' when it is undertaken by senior management).

THE CUSTOMER. A survey of buyer intentions can be undertaken using some of the techniques discussed in Chapter 2 on market research, although customers will not always be able to predict their own future needs. It is a more practicable source for companies with small markets than for those with national and international markets. It can also be time consuming and expensive.

THE INTERMEDIARY/SUPPLIER. This source involves asking members in the value chain – the suppliers and retailers/wholesalers – what they think future demand might be. This is an inexpensive method that can be undertaken by the salesforce in the normal course of their work.

QUANTITATIVE TECHNIQUES

Quantitative forecasting techniques use a more scientific approach to forecasting sales. They attempt to minimize the element of guesswork inherent in qualitative techniques. A number of methods are available.

TEST MARKETING. With test marketing the product is offered for sale in a smaller, representative version of the larger market. In this way the whole marketing mix can be tested and the sales achieved can be extrapolated to predict future potential sales in the wider market. This method can throw up very positive results although it can be expensive. Intermediaries, if involved, are not always willing to cooperate.

TIME SERIES ANALYSIS. Time series analysis is used to predict future sales based on statistical analysis of past data over a period of time. This process can be undertaken at different levels from the simplistic through to the complex. Methods of time series analysis include the following:

Extending a trend. This method can get quite sophisticated, but simply put it involves looking at past sales over a number of years, plotting them on a graph, and using the same rate of growth to extend sales into the future.

Cyclical influences. There tend to be identifiable cyclical troughs and peaks in business activity, over both the medium and long term, resulting from general economic activity. As with extending a trend, past cyclical activity can be used to predict future market movements.

Seasonal movements. With many products the demand will change at different times of the year. There are many possible examples including: holidays (mainly spring and summer); liqueur drinks (Christmas); speciality chocolate products (Christmas, Easter); motor cars (August and December); etc. Once these seasonal demands are identified for a product or service they can be used to forecast future sales, for example liqueur sales at Christmas.

LEADING INDICATORS. Many companies try to forecast their sales by finding one or more leading indicators that change in the same direction, but in advance of company sales. Movements in these indicators will then be a guide to changes in the demand for their own products. This method works well where the company is associated with and heavily dependent on specific markets. A good example might be the building trade. A pick up in building planning applications and commencement of building will signal the future need for plumbing and electrical equipment.

On a wider macro-environmental scale, indicators such as a reduction in personal tax, or the lowering of interest rates, may well be seen as leading indicators for a future increase in retail demand.

Relevant leading indicators should be continuously monitored by interested organizations and the information then used in helping to forecast future demand.

STATISTICAL DEMAND ANALYSIS. There are many statistical procedures and models available that can be used to look at the interplay of the variables that will affect demand. The variables most commonly analysed include demographic movement, income, price levels, competitor activity, promotional spend and government fiscal and monetary policy. The variables are given mathematical representation and values assigned. Using proven statistical formulae, the interaction is examined and future market activity predicted.

Techniques available include correlation and multiple regression analysis. It is not intended to explore these techniques in this book and interested readers should consult a specialist publication.

THE USE OF INFORMATION TECHNOLOGY. The ability to store, analyse and manipulate more and more information allows extremely sophisticated models to be developed incorporating all the methods identified above. Unpredictable events, such as a really bad winter one year or high sales of a fad product in another, can all be programmed in (or programmed out) so as to obtain a more realistic picture.

SCENARIO PLANNING. This method can use both qualitative and quantitative techniques. Scenario planning attempts to take a very wide view looking at the whole industry/market of an organization, if necessary on a global scale.

Scenario planning is operated by bringing together groups of senior managers and setting up a projected series of alternative events affecting the whole market. Many people might contribute to the exercise from both within and without the organization. The models used should be based on realistic possibilities and will probably be something like best, middle and worse case market scenarios.

A word of warning: as with marketing research, market and sales forecasting methods are all about predicting the future which, despite the sophisticated methods available, is still more of an art than a science and should be used as an aid to decision making, not as a substitute.

Gap analysis

Once the sales forecasting has taken place and marketing objectives have been set, strategies must be developed to show how these objectives are going to be achieved. This introduces us to the model and concept of 'gap analysis'.

Gap analysis is a model that can be used for looking at the difference (the 'gap') between where the company sales will be in x years time if present strategies are followed (sales A in Figure 10.7) and where shareholder pressure, research and forecasting demand it should be (sales B in Figure 10.7).

Objective A shows the sales the company would achieve in three years time if existing strategies remain unaltered. Objective B (the marketing objective) shows where the company *would like to be* in three years (dictated by sales forecasting).

| **Figure 10.7** | *Gap analysis* |

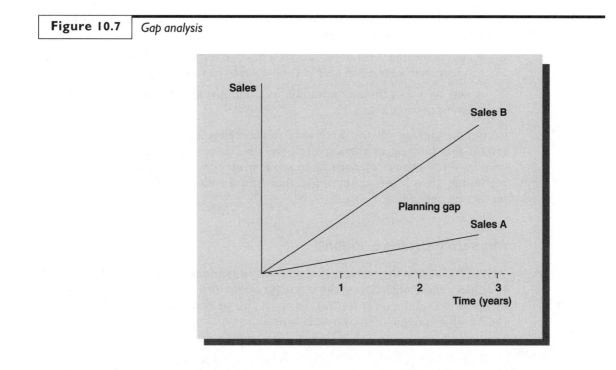

The 'gap' (sometimes known as the planning gap) between sales of A and the increased sales indicated by B must now be filled by both analysing existing strategies and developing and choosing new ones and we will return to this later in the chapter.

SALES FORECASTING, GAP ANALYSIS AND MARKETING OBJECTIVES

Using both qualitative and quantitative forecasting techniques, future sales potential can be predicted and marketing objectives set. A 'gap' will now exist between the point that the company has decided is 'where it wants to go', that is its marketing (sales) objectives and where it will end up if it does nothing.

This gap must be filled by identifying the ways the company can obtain the desired level of sales over the time period stipulated. This 'how are we going to get there' is known as the marketing strategy. The marketing audit, 'where are we now' with the completed SWOT, will be the company's guiding reference.

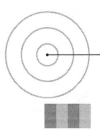

Stage 3   Marketing strategy

How are we going to get there?

Strategy is the combination of methods used by the company to obtain its objectives. The important thing to remember about strategy is:

1. it should clearly describe the major way (or ways) that the organization intends to achieve its objectives;
2. it should be long term (long term is a relative term and will vary according to product/market but 3–5 year periods tend to be used);
3. it acts as a coordinating umbrella function giving the same direction to all relevant departments.

Corporate strategy will give direction to all company functions – human resource, production, finance, marketing, etc. – so that they work in harmony to achieve corporate objectives. Likewise, marketing strategy will give direction to all the marketing areas bringing them together into a cohesive effort so as to achieve marketing objectives.

Marketing strategic options

Having decided on the marketing objectives, the various methods that can be used to achieve these objectives – the strategic marketing alternatives – must now be analysed to find the most fruitful. To assist this process another model known as the Ansoff (strategic option) matrix is used.

THE ANSOFF MATRIX

Like all models, the Ansoff 4 x 4 matrix is a method used to simplify a very complex situation and should not be judged as an ultimate reflection of reality. Having said this it is still a very useful tool for trying to identify and analyse the many strategic alternatives available to the organization when looking for ways to achieve its marketing direction, as long as its limitations are recognized.

In very simple terms, through the use of the Ansoff matrix, it can be argued that there are four major alternatives a marketer could use when looking for ways to fill the planning gap and achieve its marketing objectives. These four methods are:

1. existing products in existing markets: *market penetration*;
2. new products in existing markets: *new product development*;
3. existing products in new markets: *market development*;
4. new products in new markets: *market diversification*.

This is shown in diagrammatic form in Figure 10.8.

In order to look at strategic choice, we can now consider these four strategic options in turn.

Figure 10.8 | *The Ansoff strategic option matrix*

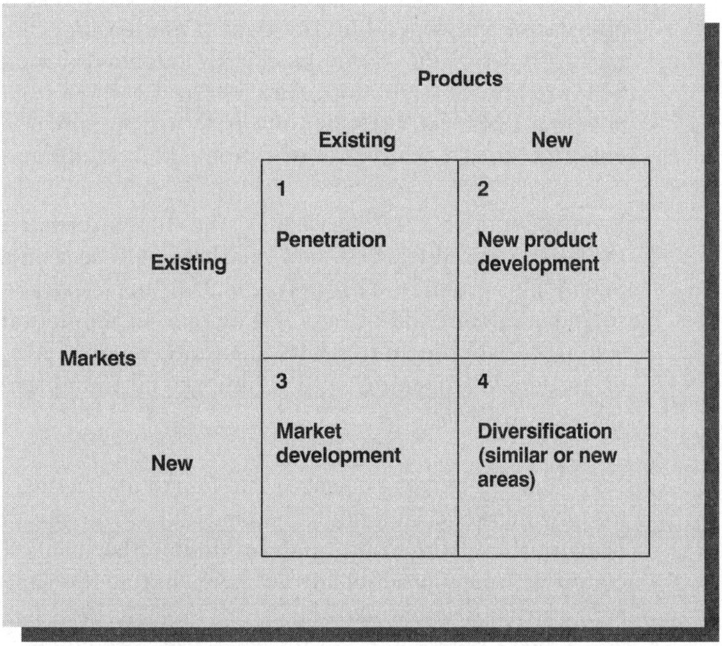

EXISTING PRODUCTS IN EXISTING MARKETS.   The first option to examine is the potential, or otherwise, of the existing market. This is the only one of the four options identified that all organizations have to consider and it will probably be the first that is undertaken. This is sometimes identified in gap analysis as the 'operations gap' as it relates to current activities (operations). Within this option the following alternative strategies exist:

- *consolidation*: strengthen present position;
- *divestment*: sell off unwanted products/brands/divisions;
- *liquidation*: close down unprofitable products/brands/divisions;
- *increase sales*: market penetration.

One or more of the above could be chosen depending on the results of the marketing audit. The first three strategies will strengthen cost and profit position while the last will increase sales. In times of market optimism companies tend to expand and when the market contracts so-called non-core areas tend to be closed down or sold off.

Whether more of the same product can be sold in the existing market (market penetration) will depend on PLCs and market growth, competitor activity and the level of resources that can be committed to the task.

It should be clearly noted that if the existing market is in the mature stage – that is it is no longer growing – any further sales increase can only happen at the expense of the competition who will retaliate to prevent any attempt at incursion into their markets. This must be taken into account in strategic planning.

NEW PRODUCTS IN EXISTING MARKETS.   The second alternative is to develop new products for the existing markets. Here readers should refer back to Chapter 6 on the product and new product development (NPD). Whether this option is a viable alternative will depend on the type of market and the level of resources that are committed to NPD. Some marketing commentators argue that innovation and NPD are crucial to the long-term survival of most organizations. Mars ice-cream, portable pensions, high definition TV or Bernard Matthews' 'dinosaur roll' for children are all examples of new products in existing markets.

EXISTING PRODUCTS IN NEW MARKETS.   The third alternative is to find new markets for the existing product. The 'new' market could be seen as any group not at present buying the product. This concept of a 'new' market could include any of the segments identified in Chapter 4 on market segmentation. Johnson and Johnson selling its baby cream to adults, Lucozade repositioning its drink for sports people or McDonald's opening up in China are all examples of existing products being taken to new markets.

NEW PRODUCTS IN NEW MARKETS.   The fourth alternative is to develop new products for new markets. This might be considered the most risky of the four strategies because there is the potential for 'double risk'. This double risk is the risk associated with new product involvement and at the same time the risk associated with entry into a new market.

A 'new product in a new market' strategy could take many forms including the following.

■ *Backward and forward integration*: e.g. a manufacturer moving forward into retail or backward into raw material supply.

■ *Conglomerate integration*: moving into product areas not connected with present activity, e.g. a shoe manufacturer buying a chain of betting shops.

■ *Totally new product*: through internal research and development launching a totally new product into a new market, e.g. the discovery and launch of 'Post-it' removable self-stick notes by 3M or alcoholic lemonade launched by the Two Dogs organization.

'New and existing': definitions explained.   Confusion is sometimes caused by the terms 'new' and 'existing'. Arguments can develop about whether a product or market is new or just some form of development of the existing product or market. There is no clear cut explanation here. Some products might well be totally new to both company and market. Other products might be new to the company but not to the customer and vice versa. The same might be said about markets.

What is important to understand is that, if the product/market is considered to be new by either the customer or the company management, then it will have to be marketed in a specific way that takes this newness into account.

Strategic choice

Having identified the four alternative strategic options the company must now decide on the marketing strategies it will use to fill the 'gap' between the sales and profit it will achieve if nothing is changed and the sales and profit objectives analysis and forecasting have shown could be achieved.

EVALUATION IN STRATEGY CHOICE

A thorough evaluation needs to take place before strategies are chosen, linked very closely to the results of the SWOT analysis developed through the use of the marketing audit. For example, investigation into the market may have indicated the need for some form of new product. Whether or not the company will be able to take advantage of this opportunity will depend on the internal resources it has available – a strength. Similarly, if research has shown that the market has potential for growth then market penetration may be possible if the company has, or can obtain, the necessary resources.

CRITERIA FOR STRATEGY CHOICE

We can now identify the criteria that will be considered when choosing which of the strategies, identified above, to use and which to reject.

1. *The company mission/corporate objectives*. The chosen strategies must be within the scope of the company mission statement, corporate objectives and corporate image, otherwise senior management will reject them.

2. *The results of the audit/SWOT*. The SWOT, if used properly, should have identified the more obvious strategic options.

3. *The competitive structure of the industry*. High competitive rivalry and low profits in some markets may preclude some strategic options. Similarly the presence of a market leader with high market share and high economies of scale will severely limit what can and cannot be done.

4. *The target markets*. Some markets may be growing whilst others are falling, some are more profitable, some are more approachable and some may match more closely than others the skills developed within the organization.

5. *The level of risk involved with each strategy*. Some strategic options may be much riskier than others in terms of the certainty of reward. A high risk strategy usually means a greater reward, but with more danger of failure. Whether or not to undertake this form of strategy will depend on the size of the project compared with the overall strategy and the wealth of the organization.

6. *Financial implications*. It should be remembered by readers that all strategic options will have financial implications that must be considered. Usually this means using discounted cash flow and/or payback techniques to compare one suggested project with another.

7. *Opportunity cost*. There will always be alternative strategies competing for the use of company resources. The opportunity cost is the cost of giving up strategy *x* for strategy *y*.

8. *Time/speed*. In some cases speed may be of the essence. This could be to block others, build market share before the competition can enter the market, or it could be that the PLC is very short and the market transient.

9. *Existing marketing mix*. All marketing mix factors need to be considered here including the need to maintain and develop product portfolio synergy, brand integrity, profit margins, cost advantages, value chain loyalty and promotional expertise.

10. *Overall company resources*. Ultimately the balance and capacity of all company resources – physical, financial, human and informational – must be considered.

When planning, clear succinct reasons should always be given why one particular strategy has been selected and another, seemingly good, candidate has been rejected.

ASSUMPTIONS

Planning and forecasting looks into the future and so certain assumptions must be made and articulated by the marketing planners otherwise the whole exercise could be called into account by senior management questioning the relative wisdom of particular strategies.

CONSTRAINTS

Similarly, there will always be certain constraints on an organization preventing a particular strategic direction being taken. These constraints maybe internal or external. As with assumptions, these should be made known within the marketing plan.

The strategic planning process

It is possible to distinguish between strategic planning and the tactical implementation of that plan. Strategic planning is concerned with broad long-term marketing mix decisions and the implications of these decisions, whilst tactical planning is concerned more with the short-term resource gathering and implementation of the strategic plan.

In this chapter we have been discussing the many factors that need to be considered as part of strategic planning and, for ease of understanding, we can now begin to pull these factors together into a diagrammatic presentation of the strategic planning process. This can be seen in Figure 10.9.

THE STRATEGIC POSITIONING OF THE MARKETING MIX

Under each selected strategy – market penetration, new product development, etc. (shown in Figure 10.9) – a little more information is required about the long-term direction that needs to be taken with regard to the marketing mix elements. This concerns the coordinated *strategy* that will be adopted for the product, price, the place and promotion.

| **Figure 10.9** | *The strategic planning process* |

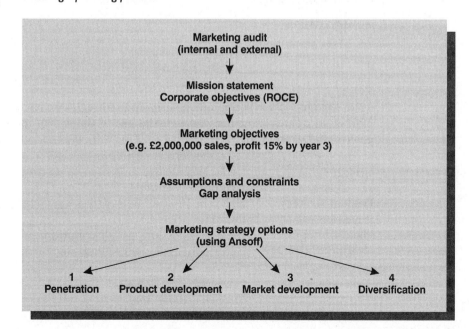

This is known as the marketing mix *strategic positioning* and will be spelt out in a *strategic positioning statement*. The strategic positioning statement will be in *simple terms*, not in detail (the detail will come later in the tactical plan) and will be the approach that is to be adopted in the long term.

THE MARKETING MIX STRATEGIC PLANNING OPTIONS.   The simple strategic approach options for the product, price, place and promotion can now be identified.

Product strategy options

- Make the product/service *better* (than the competition)
- Make the product /service *different* (from the competition)
- Make the product/service *cheaper* (than the competition)

Price strategies options

- Pricing for sales volume; for profit; market share.
- Premium pricing; charging more because of extra value.
- Market/product discriminatory pricing.

Place strategies options

- Indirect or direct distribution.
- Extensive distribution.
- Selective distribution.
- Concentrated distribution.

Promotion strategic options

- Advertising.
- Sales promotions.
- Publicity.
- Personal selling.

As an example of marketing mix positioning strategies we can now take two of the market strategies identified through the use of the Ansoff matrix and identify a positioning strategy for each of the 4 Ps. This will take the following form:

Strategy 1:	*Market penetration*
	Strategic positioning
Product strategy:	Make the product better than the competition.
Price strategy:	Premium pricing.
Place strategy:	Indirect; concentrated distribution.
Promotion strategy:	Advertising; personal selling.

Strategy 2:	*New product development*
	Strategic positioning
Product strategy:	Make the product different.

Price strategy: Price for market share.
Place strategy: Indirect, mass distribution.
Promotion strategy: Advertising; sales promotions.

MARKETING STRATEGY OBJECTIVE.   Each identified strategy will now need a SMART objective. This is known as the marketing strategy objective (or the strategic marketing objective). Taking our examples above, marketing strategy objectives can be invented to aid understanding.

Strategy 1: Market penetration.   Marketing strategy objective: Sales of £1,500,000 over 3 years

Strategy 2: New product development.   Marketing strategy objective: Sales of £500,000 over 3 years

All marketing strategy objectives added together will constitute the overall marketing objectives e.g. £2,000,000.

A word of warning: marketing strategy objectives are sometimes shown as marketing objectives. The is no problem as long as the subtle differences are understood.

TARGET MARKET AND COMPETITION.   Each strategy adopted will have a clear target market/customer profile description written into the strategic plan so that every participant in the planning process will be in no doubt about the make-up of the target market. Similarly there will be some form of competition in the markets identified through the use of Ansoff and a description spelling out their names, size and market approach must also be given.

MONITORING, FEEDBACK AND CONTROL MECHANISMS.   Monitoring, feedback and control mechanisms must be added to any form of planning whether at the strategic or tactical level. This is to make certain that the plan follows the course set down and that the desired objectives are achieved.

We can now return to the marketing plan developed above in Figure 10.9 and add the marketing mix positioning strategies, target market and competition, and monitoring, feedback and control mechanisms to the diagram (Figure 10.10.) for the two strategies selected, strategy 1 and strategy 2.

The process illustrated in Figure 10.10 would need to be undertaken for every strategy that was to be used to achieve the marketing objectives set down in the marketing plan.

OTHER MARKETING STRATEGIES.   As well as the Ansoff matrix there may be other marketing strategies that will contribute to the marketing department achieving its marketing objectives. This might include such things as:

■ setting up an MkIS (a Marketing Information System);
■ employing a new marketing manager;
■ implementing a sales training programme, etc.

Marketing strategy objectives (MSO (SMART)) must be set for all these areas and they will sit alongside the Ansoff marketing strategy objectives.

| **Figure 10.10** | *The strategic planning process* |

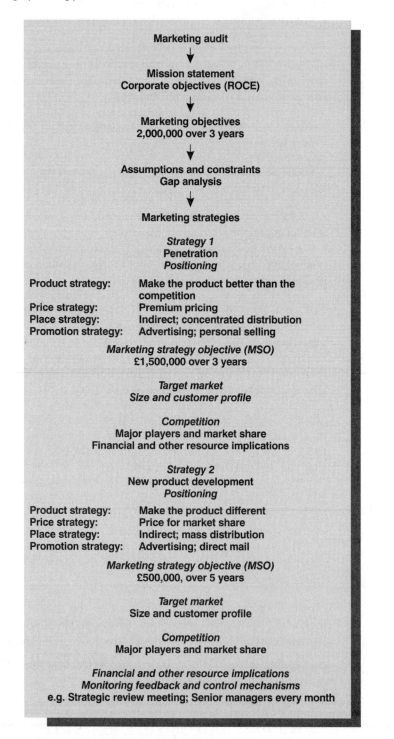

Marketing audit
↓
Mission statement
Corporate objectives (ROCE)
↓
Marketing objectives
2,000,000 over 3 years
↓
Assumptions and constraints
Gap analysis
↓
Marketing strategies

Strategy 1
Penetration
Positioning

Product strategy: Make the product better than the competition
Price strategy: Premium pricing
Place strategy: Indirect; concentrated distribution
Promotion strategy: Advertising; personal selling

Marketing strategy objective (MSO)
£1,500,000 over 3 years

Target market
Size and customer profile

Competition
Major players and market share
Financial and other resource implications

Strategy 2
New product development
Positioning

Product strategy: Make the product different
Price strategy: Price for market share
Place strategy: Indirect; mass distribution
Promotion strategy: Advertising; direct mail

Marketing strategy objective (MSO)
£500,000, over 5 years

Target market
Size and customer profile

Competition
Major players and market share

Financial and other resource implications
Monitoring feedback and control mechanisms
e.g. Strategic review meeting; Senior managers every month

Stage 4   Planning implementation and operations

How will the process be implemented?

We can now move on to examine the last stage in our planning process – the implementation of the strategic plan. All stages of the planning process are important, but making certain that the strategic plan is implemented and actually works is probably the most difficult and the most important part.

There is little point in the marketing management team spending hours, weeks and months on the planning process if the strategic plan ends up gathering dust in a boardroom cupboard and no action is taken.

The beginning of the implementation process

The implementation process begins with taking the 3–5 year strategic marketing plan and then developing every strategy adopted in detail over a shorter period, usually the first year. This must be done in detail because this is the working document that everybody within the organization is going to work with on a day-to-day basis.

This can be called the marketing tactical or action plan.

Marketing tactics and marketing strategy

There is often confusion in the use of the terms 'strategy' and 'tactics'. This is not surprising as the meaning shifts as we move down the organizational hierarchy. What is seen as strategic at the corporate board level can be viewed as tactical when given to the level below for further development.

Similarly what is seen as strategic by the level below can be viewed as tactical when passed on for development to the level below them and so on down through the organization. To add to the confusion, whether a factor is strategic or tactical will depend to a certain extent on management opinion. Basically the differences between tactics and strategy are:

- marketing strategy is long term; marketing tactics are short term;
- marketing strategy is a broad description of what needs to be done to achieve marketing objectives; marketing tactics is how the resources are to be garnered and tailored so as to implement strategy;
- marketing strategy plays a coordinating role giving the same direction to all functions;
- marketing strategy is broad; marketing tactics are narrow and detailed.

Stories are told of management being so wrapped up in the day-to-day running of the organization (tactical) that they forget to develop future business for next month or next year (strategic). Ultimately whether a factor is strategic or tactical will depend on management opinion.

Marketing tactics and the marketing mix

Each identified strategic marketing objective adopted (i.e. strategy 1 and strategy 2 identified earlier) will now need a separate *detailed* marketing mix description of intentions over the coming year.

It is here that all the many different elements of the marketing mix which have been identified, discussed and evaluated throughout the book will be analysed and used wherever relevant.

MARKET PENETRATION AS AN EXAMPLE OF TACTICAL PLANNING

We can take, as an example, Strategy 1, market penetration, identified earlier. What needs to be done, to the product, price, place and promotion should be described in detail so as to achieve the strategic marketing objectives. This is known as marketing tactics. Also needed, again, is a description of the target market and competition for each strategy area identified but in much more detail than is given in the strategic plan.

MARKETING TACTICS: STRATEGY 1, PENETRATION
Product (strategy: make the product better).   Product tactics will be concerned with all the factors discussed in Chapter 5 on the product. It is here that the detail concerning how it is intended to make the product better will be worked out and discussed. Areas covered will include decisions on branding, quality, packaging, size, speed of delivery, added features, warranties, after sales service, etc.

Price (strategy: premium pricing).   Pricing strategy will be broken down into greater detail and more information given on the form that the premium pricing might take over the first year. This might be to remain 15 per cent on average above the competition in the north of England where competition is light but only 10 per cent in the south where competition is heavy. It will also include pricing policy with regard to promotions, for example will the discounted price be used as a sales promotion and will quantity discounts be given to intermediaries.

Place (strategy: indirect, concentrated distribution).   Which outlets are to be chosen and why will be spelt out in detail here. This will include the type of outlets to be used, for example department stores and high class retail chains, as well as the amount of stock to have in which individual outlet and by when.

Promotion (strategy: advertising, personal selling).   The promotional tactical plan will go into intricate descriptive detail on every promotional technique to be used and examples are given below.

- *Primary media*: TV; channel 4, 10 slots, 19.00–20.00; which programmes and why.
- *Secondary media*: *Reader's Digest*, 6 insertions; *Radio Times*, 10 insertions.
- *Detail of the personal selling programme*: Sales targets for sales areas, sales teams, and individual salespeople will need to be worked out and allocated, staff sales promotions detailed and sales training needs allocated.

BUDGETS.   An overall amount of money will be allocated (the budget) to cover the costs involved in meeting the 4 Ps tactical objectives set. The amount should be agreed by all participants. This will then be broken down into smaller budget amounts to meet the demands of the very many different tactical tasks that must be achieved, for example quality development, packaging, POS, advertising, etc.

DELEGATED RESPONSIBILITY.   The clear allocation of responsibility is part of the monitoring, feedback and control mechanism. Only if staff and management are clear about who is responsible for what can realistic control checks be undertaken.

OBJECTIVES, DATES AND TIMINGS.   There must be a clear indication of what tasks need to be finished by when. SMART objectives must be set for *every part of the process*. This will consist of breaking the overall objectives down into interim performance indicators so that the process can be monitored and controlled, and adjustments made if necessary, at set times and dates in the year, as the programme moves forward.

MONITORING, FEEDBACK AND CONTROL MECHANISM.   Discussed and agreed by all participants, feedback, monitoring and control mechanisms must be built in to see that what is supposed to happen, does happen.

TARGET MARKET.   The target market will also appear on the tactical plan as well as on the strategic plan. But here the information needed will be greater and in much more detail. In will include everything about the customer that will be of interest to the company including; size of overall market; expected market share; whether it is growing, static or declining. The customer profile must also be detailed, for example single woman aged 40–50, social class ABC1; geographic – lives in the city; lifestyle – conservative and refined; psychographic – introvert.

COMPETITION.   Here details of the major players in the market and their respective market share must be supplied, giving as much relevant information as possible. This will include information on their product portfolios, positioning statements, financial ratios and future plans.

CONTINGENCY PLANNING.   It must be accepted that planning into the future can never be an exact science and that it will always be vulnerable to the vagaries of change. Wherever possible alternative plans should be developed to take account of these changing circumstances. This is called *contingency planning*.

MARKETING PROGRAMMES. Detailed tactical planning must be undertaken for every part of each strategy used and these are known as marketing programmes. These marketing programmes will be an exposition of every part of the marketing mix over a short time period such as 6 months to one year.

DIFFICULTIES WITH IMPLEMENTATION. The difficulties involved with the implementation of a marketing plan cannot be over-emphasized and it has to be the most difficult and problematic part of the whole planning process. It is almost certain that problems will arise because:

1. planning is about looking at and predicting the future;
2. it is virtually impossible to take account of every single difficulty that might arise especially when dealing with people and events.

Internal marketing. Internal marketing can help in the process. If all employees understand why certain policies have been adopted and are able to contribute to the marketing planning process then motivation, commitment and enthusiasm should be more forthcoming.

At its minimum, planning must be justified because it attempts to put some form of order, logic and consistency to marketplace activities that would otherwise seem to be chaos and confusion.

We can now return for reinforcement to the simple description of the whole process delineated at the beginning of the chapter.

Stage 1   The marketing audit: a situational analysis
             (Where are we now?)
Stage 2   Objective setting
             (Where do we want to go?)
Stage 3   Choice of strategy
             (How are we going to get there?)
Stage 4   Planning implementation and operations
             (How will the process be implemented?)

RATIONAL PLANNING. The process followed here is known as *rational planning*. Every part of the process is examined, evaluated and decisions made into the future which are then written down, distributed and used as a guide for future action. The system works on the premise that companies and markets can be described and acted on in this way. The reality is much more complex than this and so is the planning process. It is true that some companies seem to undertake very little long-term planning whilst other are more dedicated. Some long-term planning might be discussed by top management on a regular basis, and given a high profile whilst in other organizations the short term seems to have priority and strategic thinking might take place only in the mind of the company owner, is rarely discussed and just seems to emerge.

If the truth be known all planning is probably a combination of the rational and the emergent. It can also be argued that the real benefits of planning are in the 'doing' and the 'taking part' by all.

However this does not alter the value in learning a measured and accountable approach to the whole process of marketing planning as long as its limitations and restrictions are understood and appreciated.

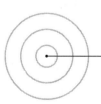

Summary

In this last chapter we have taken all the elements of marketing and attempted to pull them together to show how they might be used in the planning process. Marketing planning is about taking a systematic, disciplined approach in deciding the future direction of an organization. It involves an analysis of the company's present situation, the setting of short-, medium, and long-term objectives, strategic choice and the implementation of the plan.

We began the process by looking at the marketing audit. This was identified as a process that involves an examination of an organization's current situation and it was argued that only if this is thoroughly understood can realistic decisions be made about future directions.

Under the heading of the external environmental audit, the need to look at the wider or macro-environment was discussed. This type of information was identified under the acronym PEST (political, economic, social, technical). The more immediate or micro-environment was treated separately and identified under the acronym SPICC (suppliers, publics, intermediaries, customers/markets and the competition).

The internal organizational environment was identified through the use of the 7 Ss, (systems, strategies, structures, staffing, skills, shared values, style) and the 6 Ps (products, price, place, promotion, people and profit).

The SWOT (strengths, weaknesses, opportunities and threats) model was used in the second part of the process as a way to analyse the collected information ready for future decision making.

The role of the corporate mission statement and corporate objectives in marketing planning was briefly outlined before moving on to examine the role of gap analysis and the setting of marketing objectives.

The Ansoff matrix model was used to assist the process of strategic direction analysis and strategic choice. The need to produce clear positioning statements, identify the target market and the relevant competition, and to set SMART marketing strategy objectives for each selected strategy was discussed.

The factors to be considered when implementing the tactical marketing plan over the first year were examined. This included a detailed description of the work to be carried out on the marketing mix; a detailed description of the target market and the competition; performance indicators being set at every level; timings and budgets; the allocation of responsibilities and the building in of feedback, monitoring and control mechanisms.

Questions for discussion

1. What external information might be needed, both at the macro- and micro-environmental level, by a tinned dog food company wanting to market its products in Germany?

2. Discuss the sorts of questions that should be asked about:
   - the competitive environment;
   - the customer/market environment.

   Relate your answers to the following industries:
   - pharmaceuticals;
   - holidays;
   - financial services.

3. The organization mission statement is meaningless as all organizations make the same bland statements about quality and value and it never permeates down through the whole company. Discuss. Identify and comment on the mission statement issued from three major organizations (one from the not-for profit sector).

4. What are the differences between qualitative and quantitative forms of forecasting? How reliable are the many different methods?

5. Discuss the meaning and the value of the following terms:
   - gap analysis;
   - assumptions and constraints;
   - feedback monitoring and control.

   Relate your answer to an industry of your choice.

6. Identify the criteria necessary for strategic option analysis.

7. How valuable is the use of the Ansoff matrix when looking at strategic option alternatives? Give examples of how it might be used by an FMCG company marketing grocery products.

8. Outline, and put into order, all the factors that need to be identified when undertaking marketing planning.

9. Develop an imaginary promotional plan for the launch of a new product of your choice. What factors must be considered.

10 What marketing mix factors must be considered at:
   - the strategic level?
   - the tactical level?

   What are the differences between the two?

Case study

Johnson and Little have been manufacturing a range of fitted kitchen furniture for the last 35 years. They started in a small warehouse in Hackney, north London, working under contract to one large national intermediary. They supplied a range of economy kitchen furniture in five basic colours and delivered in a flat pack version to a central warehouse. The intermediary then delivered on direct to the customer with their own name on the product. As the intermediary grew in size more work was offered and Johnson and Little expanded until the company had over 50 employees.

However, 10 years ago the demand for their product slowly began to decline as UK retail sales began to dip and the competition became ever more fierce. Fewer orders were received and the profit mark-up was continually under attack. The managing director, Paul Johnson, said that at times they were manufacturing and supplying at very little over cost price. Joan Little, his partner and finance director agreed, showing that in some periods they were actually losing money and if the process continued they would soon be out of business. Something had to be done and so it was decided seven years ago to invite a third partner, Andrew Little, Joan's son, to join the company as sales and marketing director. Andrew was 30, had a business degree and was seen as somebody who could add business and marketing acumen (as well as knowledge on IT methods) to the company. Paul Johnson was not particularly happy with this choice as he was used to being in control (especially with Andrew being Joan's son) but agreed after some discussion.

Over the next seven years Andrew managed to stop the rot and turn the company around. Sales increased five-fold until they were running at close to £1,000,000 a year. He achieved this increase by persuading Paul to borrow from the bank, buy more up-to-date machinery, expand the range (although still all own label and flat-pack) and sell to more intermediaries.

Johnson and Little now have a staff of 100. Many employees are skilled craftsmen taken on in the recession from different areas of the furniture industry which had had to shed labour or close because of falling sales. Some of the employees have been with the company from the early days in Hackney and are due to retire. The production manger, Bert Summers, is now in his late 50s and has been with the company since it started. He is fastidious in the way he works and knows the 'flat-pack' business like the back of his hand. His early years as a sergeant in the army were put to good use in helping him organize and manage the running of the factory.

The company now specializes in an economy range of furniture offering many different models in many different colours at the request of the purchasing organization. Despite selling at the lower end of the market, Johnson and Little have built themselves a good reputation for quality, responsiveness and quick delivery, and overall the company is well respected in the trade.

Unfortunately, over the last three years, although turnover has increased, profits are down. This is because the bottom end of the market has been increasingly attacked by cheap self-assembly packs from abroad where labour costs tend to be much lower. Another problem is that having to react to the vagaries and demands of the intermediaries rather than stimulating the market themselves tends to work against any long-term planning.

Andrew, aware of the problem with falling profits, persuaded the partners a year ago to take on a sales manager, Beth Baily a young marketing graduate. Beth had spent three years selling financial services for a large multinational finance company and Andrew felt that her experience and enthusiasm would be an enormous asset in helping him look for ways of developing the marketing mix in new and more profitable areas.

Beth is full of new ideas and in a series of protracted discussions argued that the company should move up-market and manufacture their own quality branded products which they could then sell to more fashionable retail outlets as well as directly to end-customers. This added value would then enable them to charge a higher price and make a larger profit. She also mooted the idea of diversifying into fitted bedroom furniture arguing that, as it was a similar type of product to fitted kitchen furniture, economies of scale could be achieved and synergy developed.

However Paul Johnson was not happy moving away from own label. He argued that they would have to borrow more money from the bank to buy the up-to-date machinery and electronic equipment as well funding the cost of taking on a predicted sales force of ten people. He argued that the company had always sold own label and had not got the necessary production, marketing and selling skills needed to market their own products. If they sold to up-market retailers they would need to advertise and promote and if they sold direct they would need to consult with and advise the customer on everything from building alterations and furniture installation to measurement, colour and design. He also felt that this new market was too uncertain and competitive and that they would be at a tremendous disadvantage knowing nothing about the prospective customer base.

Paul, Beth – and too a lesser extent Joan – disagreed. They felt that there were many opportunities in this area, the markets were expanding, retail sales were up, interest rates were down and the economy was showing steady improvement. Beth had evidence to show that it must be possible to compete with the main competitors for these types of products because they were based outside the UK in Germany and France, and they delivered, not in flat-pack form, but in expensive pre-built units which incurred extra transport costs not applicable to a home-based manufacturer. They also usually took eight weeks to supply.

There were other problems that would need to be addressed if the management decided to adopt some of these new ideas. Despite the expansion over the last decade Johnson and Little still operated from the original site in

Hackney although they had been able to purchase adjoining sites and now owned quite a large freehold. Increased traffic leading to almost continuous congestion had been making life increasingly difficult and they now had an opportunity to lease and expand into a larger manufacturing unit just off the M25 motorway at Grays.

Finance

Sales	1994	1995	1996	1997	1998
	£650,000	£750,000	£900,150	£901,500	£1,000,035
Cost of sales	£600,000	£725,000	£900,000	£903,000	£989,000
Current ratio	.95	1	.75	.79	.85
Gearing	.60	.59	.58	.57	.60

Case study questions

1. What factors need to be considered if Johnson and Little are to adopt some or all of the suggestions discussed in the case study?

2. Using the tools and techniques shown throughout the book, and particularly in this chapter, undertake a marketing audit for Johnson and Little. The audit should be both internal and external and will include the use of SWOT analysis.

3. Put together a simple marketing plan for Johnson and Little to cover the next three years. This should be at both the strategic and tactical level. Give reasons for all directions suggested.

Further reading

Ansoff, H.I. (1979) *Strategic Management*, Macmillan, London.

Ansoff, H.I. (1979) *Corporate Strategy*, Penguin, London.

Argenti, J. (1992) *Practical Corporate Planning*, Routledge, London.

Clifton, P. et al. (1986) *Marketing, Analysis and Forecasting, Made Simple*, Heinemann, London.

Kotler, P. (1991) *Marketing Management: Analysis, Planning and Control*, Prentice Hall International, London.

McDonald, M. (1986) *Marketing Plans*, Heinemann, London.

Porter, M.E. (1980) *Competitive Strategy: Techniques for Analysing Industries and Competitors*, Free Press, New York.

Peters, Thomas J. and Waterman, Robert H. (1988) *In Search of Excellence*, Harper and Row London.

Sloma, Richard (1984) *No-Nonsense Planning*, Collier Macmillan, London.

Wilson, R., Gilligan, C. and Pearson, D. (1992) *Strategic Marketing Management*, Butterworth-Heinemann, London.

Index